Multiculturalism, Liberalism and Democracy

The selections in this volume focus on major issues of community rights, individualism/communitarian dialectic, the conditions for a peaceful, symbiotic relationship between diverse cultural groups, the justification or otherwise of affirmative action. The essays challenge the desirability of a unicultural polity, but do not accept multiculturalism uncritically.

Philosophers, historians, anthropologists, and political scientists from India, Canada, Europe, and Africa wrestle with the dilemmas within multiculturalism and explore the resources within liberalism, republicanism and democratic theory to resolve them.

Multiculturalism, Liberalism and Democracy

edited by

RAJEEV BHARGAVA
AMIYA KUMAR BAGCHI
R. SUDARSHAN

OXFORD
UNIVERSITY PRESS

OXFORD
UNIVERSITY PRESS

Oxford University Press is a department of the University of Oxford. It furthers the University's objective of excellence in research, scholarship, and education by publishing worldwide. Oxford is a registered trademark of Oxford University Press in the UK and in certain other countries

Published in India by
Oxford University Press
YMCA Library Building, 1 Jai Singh Road, New Delhi 110001, India

First published 1999
Oxford India Paperbacks 2007
Fifth impression 2011

ISBN-13: 978-0-19-569298-3
ISBN-10: 0-19-569298-5

Typeset in Garamond TTF
by Excellent Laser Typesetters, Pitampura, Delhi 110 034
Printed in India by Rakmo Press, New Delhi 110 020

Acknowledgements

India can claim to be the largest multicultural society in the world where people speak a variety of languages. The range of scripts used is probably the most varied in the world. All the major religions—Buddhism, Christianity, Hinduism, Islam, Sikhism, Zoroastrianism—have large numbers of followers in India. Virtually all these religions are divided into a number of sects and all these sects have hundreds, thousands or millions of adherents, in the country. If human beings can be categorized into so-called racial types by anthropometric criteria, practically all the racial types and their rich admixtures will be found to have their representatives in India. This society of multiple cultures, in every sense of the world 'culture' we can think of, also practises a thriving, sometimes rumbustious, democracy. But the plurality of cultures also has to fight enemies who try to enforce homogenization of one kind or another.

The UNDP has been greatly involved in tracking and advancing human development in all its aspects. It was, therefore, natural that its assistance should be forthcoming when the Centre for Studies in Social Sciences, Calcutta, proposed an international conference to take stock of and analyse the experience of living in a matrix of multiple cultures in India and other countries. It was felt that philosophers, political scientists, economists, students of local cultures and historians of social and economic change should be invited to contribute their expertise to the analysis and evaluation of multicultural societies. With such eminent professionals gathered under one roof, we did not presume to tell them exactly how to address questions of plurality of cultures in a working democracy. As it happens, major issues of community rights, rights of individuals against intrusion by the state or a coercive collectivity, the conditions for peaceful symbiosis of different culture groups, the justification or otherwise of affirmative action, were thrown up during the discussion, and many of them were incorporated by participants when they revised their papers. The present volume is the outcome of the deliberations as embodied in the revised papers.

The introduction by Rajeev Bhargava summarizes the major theme of the seminar and the arguments that it generated. No added comments on the contexts of this volume are needed. One observation, however, should be made. At the outset, itself, the conference was planned along lines that would enable the participants to interact extensively with one another without the external distraction that a metropolis could pose. Thus, Kasauli in Himachal Pradesh was chosen as the location, amply fulfilling our needs. A house which had once belonged to the great Indian artist, Amrita Sher-Gil, and which now belongs to her nephew Vivan Sundaram, himself a leading artist, provided the ideal setting. An added luxury was a view of the immense Himalayan mountainscape. We must express our heartfelt thanks to Shri Sundaram for allowing us to use his house and providing facilities for its smooth running.

We owe our thanks to many persons belonging to the UNDP, the Government of India and the Centre for Studies in Social Sciences, Calcutta (CSSSC) for the help they provided in making the conference a success. Mr Hans Von Sponeck, the Resident Representative of the UNDP in New Delhi was at all times supportive of this venture, as was Mr S. Varadachari, then Joint Secretary, in the Department of Economic Affairs of the Government of India. Sri V. Sukanta also rendered help in smoothing over organizational hurdles. Shri Susanta Ghosh, the then Registrar of the CSSSC, ably assisted by Shri Sisir Ghoshal of the same Centre, provided all the arrangements for transporting the participants from various points of the compass and back, for housing them comfortably and supplying them with the needed creature comforts, and helping to make the occasion one of enjoyment as well as enlightenment. We express our gratitude to the persons mentioned, and many others who worked behind the scenes, typing out papers and memoranda, taking telephone messages and relaying them, and chasing much of the paperwork. Finally, we must thank all the participants and paper-writers whose contributions, after all, provide the substance of this volume.

RAJEEV BHARGAVA
A. K. BAGCHI
R. SUDARSHAN

Contents

List of Contributors

JAVEED ALAM is retired Professor, Centre for European Studies, Central Institute of English and Foreign Languages (CIEFL), Hyderabad. He is the author of *Domination and Dissent: Peasants and Politics* (1985) and *India: Divine with Modernity* (1999).

CATHERINE AUDARD is Chair and co-founder, Forum for European Philosophy, European Institute, London School of Economics, London. Her most recent book is *Anthologie historique et critique de l'utilitarisme* (1999) in three volumes. She has translated in French, John Rawls' *Theory of Justice* (1987), *Political Liberalism* (1995), and J. S. Mill's *Utilitarianism* (1998).

AMIYA KUMAR BAGCHI is Professor and Director, Institute of Development Studies, Kolkata. His publications include *The Political Economy of Underdevelopment* (1982) and *Private Investment in India 1900–1939* (1972).

TISTA BAGCHI is with the Department of Linguistics, University of Delhi, Delhi. Her research interests include linguistic theory, cognitive science, and languages of northern and north-eastern hills of India.

RAJEEV BHARGAVA is Senior Fellow and Director, Centre for the Study of Developing Societies, Delhi. His publications include *Individualism in Social Science* (1992), *Secularism and Its Critics* (edited) (1998), and *Politics and Ethics of the Indian Constitution* (edited) (2008).

AKEEL BILGRAMI is Johnsonian Professor of Philosophy, Columbia University. His publications include *Belief and Meaning* (1992).

G. A. COHEN is Chichele Professor of Social and Political Theory and Fellow, All Souls College, Oxford University. His publications include *Karl Marx's Theory of History* (1978), *History Labour and Freedom* (1988) and *From Each According to His Ability, To Each According to His Needs* (1997).

VIVEK DHARESHWAR is Senior Fellow, Centre for the Study of Culture and Society, Bangalore. He has co-edited *Interrogating Modernity: Culture and Culturalism in India* (1993).

P. K. DATTA is with the Department of English, University of Delhi, Delhi. He is the author of *Carving Blocs: Communal Ideology* in *Early Twentieth-century Bengal* (1999).

PREBEN KAARSHOLM is Associate Professor in International Development Studies at Roskilde University Denmark. Trained in comparative literature and cultural studies, he has published books and articles on European literature as well as on colonial and anti-colonial culture, African studies and development studies.

MAHMOOD MAMDANI is Herbert Lehman Professor of Government and Professor of Anthropology, Columbia University. His publications include *Citizen and Subject: Decentralized Despotism and the Legacy of Late Colonialism* (1996).

SHAIL MAYARAM is Senior Fellow, Centre for the Study of Developing Studies, Delhi. Her publications include *Resisting Regimes: Myth, Memory and the Shaping of a Muslim Identity* (1997) and *Creating a Nationality: The Ramjanamabhumi Movement and The Fear of the Self* (co-author, 1995).

ALAN MONTEFIORE is Visiting Professor at the Centre for Research in Modern European Philosophy, Middlesex University. He has published books, either as author or editor or both, on moral philosophy, the university and political commitment, contemporary French philosophy, and the political responsibility of intellectuals. His publications include *Neutrality and Impartiality* (1975) and *A Modern Introduction to Moral Philosophy* (1958).

M. S. S. PANDIAN is Visiting Fellow, Sarai Programme, Centre for the Study of Developing Societies, Delhi; and is the author of *The Image Trap* (1972).

ALOK RAI is Professor, Department of English, University of Delhi, Delhi. His publications include *Orwell: The Politics of Despair* (1988) and an English translation of Premchand's *Nirmala* (1999).

R. SUDARSHAN is Governance Adviser, Regional Centre, United Nations Development Programme (UNDP), Bangkok. He has published articles on politics and the judiciary in India in learned journals, on liberalization and economic reforms in newspapers, and has co-edited three books, *Human Development and Structural Adjustment* (1993) and *Sites of Change: The Structural Context for Empowering Women in India* (1996), *Beyond Income Poverty: Human Development in India* (with Raja J. Chelliah) (1998).

CHARLES TAYLOR is Professor Emeritus, McGill University, and winner of the Tempelton Prize. From 1976–81 he was the Chichele Professor of Social and Political Theory at Oxford. His books include, *Hegel* (1975) and *Sources of the Self: The Making of Modern Identity* (1989).

1

Introducing Multiculturalism

Rajeev Bhargava

I.

The term 'multiculturalism' gathers a number of interrelated themes; it underscores the need to have a stable identity, emphasizes the contribution of cultural communities to the fulfilment of this need and brings out the link between identity and recognition. It stresses the importance of cultural belonging and legitimizes the desire to maintain difference.

Current interest in such issues must be understood as part of a larger intellectual move away from the mainstream tradition of Enlightenment political philosophy. For much of this century, Anglo-Saxon political theory not only foregrounded a particular set of ethical values but also interpreted them in a specific way. It concerned itself with *freedom* understood as a condition without constraints on meaningful choices and—what is widely believed to be a necessary condition of free life—with *equality* or *justice* in the distribution of material resources. These values were then given a pronounced individualist colouring: the primary unit of analysis of theories of distributive justice is the individual conceived as independent of the community to which he belongs; equality of material resources is to enhance the well-being of people, where well-being too is understood within an individualist framework. Finally, the unit of decision making is believed to be not the group but the individual.

All this appears to have changed. First, the communitarian challenge showed that the formation of beliefs and desires is a function of loose or closely knit communities. Second, the relevance of culture to identity formation was more explicitly registered. Finally, the belated recognition came that culture-relative self-esteem matters to people as much as the fulfilment of material needs. Equally significant was the recognition that the sense of identity and self-worth of persons derives from cultures that they not only know well but can and may call their own. Therefore, not culture in general but a *particular* culture matters to people. This foregrounds issues of cultural belonging as also that people have an interest in ensuring the survival of particular cultures, even when other cultures can perform the same job as their own.

If the communitarian standpoint questioned a political order constructed purely from the vantage point of individual well-being, the importance of cultural particularity raised doubts about the desirability of a unicultural polity. Instead, it enjoined us to design a community with a multicultural ethos. It still remains to be asked, however, what precisely is asserted by this claim. Does it mean that groups are to be not only socially acknowledged but publicly recognized? No matter what its content, should every culture be publicly recognized? If not, which cultures deserve recognition? Should cultures that deem themselves intrinsically superior to others or that sanction oppressive practices be publicly recognized too? And, what does it mean to publicly recognize cultures, anyway? Does recognition imply group-specific citizenship rights? And do such rights require the endorsement by the state of the customary practices of each cultural group? Does it mean that each cultural group has some laws that apply uniquely to it? Does public recognition require that the language of every cultural group be used in parliament, by the bureaucracy and the courts? Should every cultural group have publicly funded education in its mother tongue? Should internal boundaries within the nation-state be drawn to enable cultural minorities to form a majority within a local region? And, should political office be allocated in accordance with the principle of national proportionality? Is the presence of different cultures within one political order likely to be trouble-free or always conflict ridden? When conflict bubbles over, how can it be resolved or managed?

The recognition of cultural plurality within an enduring, democratic framework of moral equality is one thing but a destructive, vengeful politics of difference is altogether another matter. Note the scale of civil strife in Sri Lanka, ethnic-cleansing in Bosnia, the excesses of nationalism after the disintegration of the Soviet Union and the enduring conflicts in Rwanda, Afghanistan, Macedonia, Greece, Turkey and closer home, in Kashmir. How can difference be expressed without the destruction of painstakingly built political structures? Can we limit the damage to political structures wrought by movements that generate wild dreams and acute collective frenzy? What forms does self-assertion take and does it always require aggressive mass mobilization? Can institutions that reflect difference be created with a greater economy of violence than is usually witnessed? How is the expression of cultural difference to be made compatible with the rule of law and with conditions of equality and freedom? It may well be that a unicultural state aggravates and not contains cultural conflicts but can cultural difference really be accommodated by simply fine-tuning existing constitutional democracies? Besides, some homogenization is required by stable democracies and by the ideal of citizenship implicit in it. If so, to what extent does this reduce the possibility of genuinely meeting the fullest requirements of cultural autonomy?

Issues such as these at times provide the background and other times become the very focus of several papers in this volume that puts together the proceedings of the conference organized in Kasauli by the Centre for Studies in Social Sciences, Calcutta. The extremely interesting papers found in this volume nevertheless form a rather disparate lot. Knitting together an introduction that tries at once to clarify the main concerns of multiculturalism, offer a reasonably distinctive viewpoint on such issues and weave into it the theme and principal argument of every single paper has been difficult but challenging. Perhaps an overview of my attempt to do so will make what follows somewhat easier for the reader. In the next, section II, I establish the link between identity and cultural communities. Section III draws out some implications of the previous section. First, the importance of a politics of collective goals and recognition, and conversely the suffering caused by misrecognition and the devaluation of collective goals. Second, the different forms assumed by multiculturalism: hierarchical and egalitarian, liberal, authoritarian and democratic.[1] Third, the role of the state in preventing the marginalization of cultures and the precise justification by which this role is legitimized. Section IV briefly mentions different levels at which multicultural issues emerge. Section V discusses liberal individualism, republicanism and Rawlsian political liberalism as possible solutions to problems also addressed by multiculturalism and notes their limitations. Section VI tries to deal with skepticism over multiculturalism. In section VII, I take up the problems of existing formulations of multiculturalism, particularly their tendency to gloss over the exclusion of marginalized groups and to tolerate oppressive communities. Finally, section VIII focuses on especially bitter or intractable cultural conflicts.

II. Identity and Community

What is it to have an identity? What is the link between community and identity? What is a community and how is it different from other social relations? A brief answer to these questions may help provide the necessary background to several issues raised in this volume.

It is a commonplace in logic that the concept of identity has to do with sameness. Equally trivial is the observation that anything whatsoever is the same with itself at any given time. At the very next instant, however, it may already be different from what it was

[1] I have frequently encountered opposition to the term 'multiculturalism' simply because of its Western, American-Canadian origin. Though I sometimes understand the spirit underlying such attacks, I remain uncomfortable with such blanket condemnation. There is no need to invent another term if the one in use is able to perform the required function or if, on suitable interpretation, it can be made to do that job. For me, 'multicultural', by virtue of being an abstract enumerative term, simply registers the presence of many cultures. When loaded with value, it celebrates their presence. Thus, it challenges either the fact or the value of a single culture. Its evaluative content also suggests the unlikelihood of a single culture realizing every conceivable good. This much baggage the term carries, but no more. Indeed, its indefinite quality makes the term flexible and open to a number of ideological incarnations (liberal, democratic, etc.). It also enables its easy applicability across space and time. (Hence, not only American or Canadian but also an Indian multiculturalism.) Before appraising it therefore, one has to be extremely attentive in any given context to its precise use.

a moment ago. If an object is to retain its identity, it must remain same with itself overtime. A thing with a plausible sense of identity must endure.

However, it is impossible for anything to remain same with itself in all respects all the time. The demand that it do so imposes such a stringent requirement that no object can meet it. It renders any object incapable of ever retaining its identity over time. A thing can remain identical with itself in *some*, not in all, respects. Equally, if sameness over time of any odd set of features was sufficient for the identity of an object, then everything would forever remain identical with itself. If nothing ever lost its identity, then the problem of identity does not even arise in the first place. As a matter of fact, to say that a thing has remained the same with itself over time is almost always elliptical for the statement: A thing has remained the same with itself over time in some *relevant* respects. A criterion of relevance is built into a statement of identity.

To repeat, sameness of relevant features over time is integral to any notion of identity. To have an identity, a thing must have features that are both relevant and enduring. Likewise, for two discernible things to be identical, the enduring features of one must be identical in relevant respects with the enduring features of the other. If this is true of the identity of all objects, it must equally be true for the identity of human persons. To remain constant over time with herself or himself or with others, to possess or share an identity, a person must be identical with some of her/his enduring and relevant attributes.[2]

[2] This conforms to the minimal sense of identity with which we are all acquainted, with a simple phenomenology of identity. To have an identity is to recognize the presence of something stable in the midst of change and diversity. It is to be located somewhere, to possess a tangible sense of being at home in the world. More importantly, this sense of being anchored obtains from identifying with something that, on the face of it, appears different, but is the same as me. I must be able to call it by the name with which I call myself or at least call it my own. Assertions of unity assimilate, synthesize, and establish connections among diverse elements that go so deep that little point remains in calling them different. My features can be mapped so smoothly on to something else that it is no longer possible for me to call them by anything else. Conversely, to lose one's identity is to be dispossessed of one's bearings and the ability to see where one stands, to be unhinged, detached and to feel insecure. It is to fail to choose or discover something that is one's own, to be unable to find the relevant sameness with anything.

Which entities or features can provide a proper anchorage for us with which we can identify? A person's physical or bodily features must be one such set. Some relevant bodily features of a person must endure for a person to have an identity. At the same time, bodily features can hardly be a sufficient condition for the identity of a *person*. Persons cannot be exhaustively identified only with their bodies. The complete identity of a person is at best supervenient on bodily features. This is so because a person is a person only in so far as he/she has mental attributes. Strawson is surely correct in viewing a person as an entity to which both corporeal characteristics and states of consciousness can be ascribed.[3] The identity of persons must minimally but crucially depend on the identity of states of their consciousness.

But what can the identity of states of consciousness mean? States of consciousness are of two kinds. To begin with, bodily sensations exist like pains and tickles that cannot occur without a minimal awareness of them by the subject. Roughly the same reasons that disqualify the body as the sole criterion of personal identity apply to sensations. However, there also exist beliefs and desires, states characterized by what Brentano called intentionality, and the ascription of which always involves the use of a 'that'-clause as in 'The Indian electorate believes that democracy alone can help solve its problems.' Beliefs and desires are endowed with intentional content. Unlike sensations, beliefs and desires do not require that we be conscious of them. At the same time, persons cannot have their beliefs and desires without some minimal awareness. It is necessary, therefore, that to have an identity a person must consciously be able to identify with some of his/her beliefs, desires and acts.

Beliefs and desires can, however, be viewed in two fundamentally different ways. The intentionality of beliefs and desires ensures that they necessarily possess a content. But the individuation of this content may be seen as wholly independent of anything external to the individual mind or to crucially depend on the natural environment and social context, in particular the linguistic practices of the community. The first atomistic and psychologistic view of intentional content I find unconvincing for reasons I cannot go into here. If indeed my view is correct, then, on the assumption of the

[3] P. Strawson, *Individuals*, Methuen, London and New York, 1964, p. 104.

centrality of beliefs, desires, and acts to the whole issue of personal identity, the identity of persons is constituted in large measure by the language and vocabulary used by them. The identity of persons, one can legitimately say, is defined by the language they happen to use. Identification with beliefs and desires is impossible without language because a person would not know what these beliefs and desires mean and therefore what they are, unless he/she possesses one. Since entry into a world of meaning is crucial for the formation of beliefs and desires, the identity of humans is related to a world of meanings. Briefly put, persons identify with their particular languages and with members of their linguistic communities. That is why, one identifies oneself, as one is identified by others, by being located in a common world of meanings, a culture.

This is not to say that *any* set of beliefs and desires can constitute the identity of a person, for this is misleading if not altogether false. A person has many beliefs and desires. The criterion of permanence and relevance must enter our discussion of identity in order not only to pick out beliefs, desires and acts but also to specify which of these are critically defining. Obviously, not all but only enduring beliefs and desires which people persistently hold and strive to realize are crucial for identity. More importantly, of the ones that endure, only relevant ones count; if they are to enter the definition of their identities, beliefs and desires must matter to them, be viewed by them as relevant.

A person cannot have an identity in the absence of qualitative distinctions between the worth of different desires and beliefs because only such distinctions furnish the criterion of relevance constitutive of identity.[4] I call these *identity-constituting* beliefs and desires. Since such beliefs and desires are formed within an enduring framework, not to posses such a framework is to fail to have an identity. What is relevant to a person's identity is what he values strongly. The identity of a person is defined not by any odd set of beliefs but only those held firmly, with good reason, and by values that cannot be reduced to mere desires, are judged by him or her to be more important than unevaluated desires. Only those beliefs and desires that a person strongly values, finds worthy, are crucial to his or her identity.

[4] See Charles Taylor, *Sources of the Self*, Cambridge University Press, Cambridge, 1989.

A framework provides a person with a springboard from which to aspire to do or be something. This aspiration to be moved by something regarded as valuable is central to the notion of commitment. To strive for some value, no matter how unattainable, is to be deeply engaged with it, to have entrusted oneself to it. It is to constantly judge our desires and hope to guide our actions by standards set by these values. It is to want our lives to be directed by them. Hence the tie between commitment and identity. Indeed the identity of a person is defined by the commitments and identifications which provide the frame within which he or she tries to determine from case to case what is good or valuable, what ought to be done, what he or she endorses or opposes. In other words, it is the horizon within which a person is capable of taking a stand.[5]

In his contribution to this volume, Alan Montefiore argues for roughly the same thesis. Montefiore begins by problematizing the simple gesture of 'pointing to oneself' in response to the complex question, 'Who am I?' In answering this, any characterization always involves subsumption under a particular classification. It is impossible to offer a self-characterization without deploying sortal terms that pick out the kind of individual one is. Such terms, he argues, necessarily belong to the particular language of one or another speech community and the meanings they bear are an integral part of a particular network of meanings. It follows that language plays an important role in the formation and the ongoing definition of identities. Furthermore, if language is understood in its widest possible sense and therefore as coincident with culture, then the link between identity and culture is also obvious. So, Montefiore argues, is the relation between identity and integrity. A person with integrity is one 'who does not cheat with or over what he or she fundamentally stands for', and therefore is one who consistently holds on to his or her fundamental commitments, precisely the outstanding feature entering into that person's identity.

Two more points are worth noting. First, a world of meanings can only be held in common with others. Therefore, to identify with beliefs and desires is to identify with something which is ineluctably social, necessarily shared with others. A human indi-

[5] Ibid., p. 27.

vidual recognizes his identity in socially defined terms. Indeed, since these desires and beliefs emerge through interaction with others, it might be legitimate to assert that the identity of a person is largely a matter of social construction. This is true as much for a manufactured identity as for an identity engendered by the more gentle, almost invisible process of social interaction.

Second, beliefs and desires have two modes of existence; they exist as mental representations of which individuals are conscious but also exist directly in action.[6] Much of our knowledge of such wants, and of beliefs about how to fulfill them is neither theoretical, nor stored in a prepositional form. Indeed, it is frequently not even represented in our consciousness. All we possess is a practical sense of these beliefs and desires and this sense is enough to guide our behaviour. Furthermore, some beliefs and desires are embedded not exclusively in the behaviour of one individual but rather in an interlocking behavioural system of several individuals at once. When this happens we obtain what can be called a social practice.[7] A social practice consists of actions of several individuals whose individuating descriptions are social and precisely because they do not exist as internal mental states, are never immediately available to agents. Many of our identity-constituting beliefs and desires exist directly embedded in such social practices, and therefore are irreducibly collective. I propose to define community as a network of such practices in which identity-constituting beliefs and purposes are embedded. It follows that the identity of a person is directly embedded in particular communities and its knowledge is not fully present in the person's consciousness. The link between the identity of a person and his or her community lies deep and is not entirely explicit. I suspect this explains why issues of identity sometimes appear not to matter at all, and at other times, nothing matters more than them; the very survival of a person hinges on such issues.

III. Politics of Different Collective Goals

Several implications emerge from the brief discussion of identity, culture and community. One implication is the importance of

[6] On this see Rajeev Bhargava, *Individualism in Social Science*, Clarendon Press, Oxford, 1992, p. 209.

[7] Ibid., pp. 205–12.

irreducibly collective goals. The objective of a more equitable distribution of some collective goods such as security, prosperity and justice can be met by policies grounded in individualist political theory. However, claims to the equal right for the expression of cultural particularity or to national independence or even to equal treatment in the international arena cannot be easily accommodated by them.[8] From different perspectives, both Will Kymlicka and Charles Taylor make this point. Kymlicka argues that minority rights cannot be subsumed under the category of human rights. 'The theory of rights present in modern constitutionalism is individualistically construed in that the rights protect the vulnerable integrity of legal subjects who are in every case individuals.'[9] Their 'only focus remains the individual legal person.' Taylor takes the example from the Canadian province of Quebec.[10] To safeguard its form of life from threat by Anglo-Saxon majority culture, the Francophone group has regulations forbidding the French speaking population and immigrants to send their children to English language schools. This, for Taylor, shows how the promotion of the collective goal conflicts with the theory of individual rights. Taylor then provides an alternative that, under certain conditions, may permit the restriction of some non-basic rights solely in order to maintain the integrity of endangered forms of cultural life. It is because of its inability to take into account such matters that liberal individualism simply evades issues of culture and community.

Another implication of the important point about the social construction of identity is also effectively drawn by Charles Taylor in a characteristically Hegelian manner.[11] He argues that identities are formed in a continuing dialogue and struggle with significant others. People know who they really are only through contact with and by confirmation and endorsement by others. Self-knowledge

[8] For an illuminating discussion of some of these issues, see Jurgen Habermas, 'Struggles for Recognition in the Democratic Constitutional State', in Amy Gutmann (ed.) *Multiculturalism*, Princeton University Press, New Jersey, 1994, pp. 107–48.

[9] See Will Kymlicka, *Liberalism, Community and Culture*, Clarendon Press, Oxford, 1989.

[10] Charles Taylor, 'The Politics of Recognition', in Gutman (ed.) *Multiculturalism*.

[11] Ibid., pp. 32–3.

is mediated by others and therefore involves not just cognition but *re*cognition. To have an identity, to stabilize a sense of who one is, requires that significant others also properly see what we see in ourselves. This dialogical model of the formation and continual reinforcement of identity holds true for the wider social universe as well as for the narrower public sphere within it. It is in this second domain that a more clearly defined politics of recognition is found. People want their identities and significant attributes of their community to be not merely socially acknowledged but publicly endorsed and respected. Such recognition in the public arena may take various forms. For example, groups may be accorded special rights to express their cultural particularity, be given a voice in the political process by special representation rights, may procure special subsidies from the state or, if concentrated within a particular territory, may even earn self-government rights, and therefore considerable political autonomy.

Keeping this in mind, multiculturalism embodies the politics of collective goals as well as a politics of difference. This is sometimes believed to necessitate the politicization of group identities and the abandonment or at least a modification of the ideal of equal treatment under common laws. Every law of the land need not be followed by all cultural groups. The demand for a strictly uniform set of laws may unfairly impose great burdens on some groups. It may for example be unfair to expect Sikhs to abandon their turbans in order to meet the requirements of a uniform dress code, say in the army. Fair treatment entails that a slightly different dress code be acceptable if their religion so requires. Once again, it hasn't exactly helped Western political theory to have operated with an idealized model of the polis in which fellow citizens share a common descent, language and culture.[12] This has only resulted in a silence on minority rights, cultural difference and recognition.

Forms of Multiculturalism

It is important to understand the current context within which such demands for political recognition are made. To emphasize this context, it helps to situate this issue in what I call the

[12] Will Kymlicka, *Multicultural Citizenship*, Clarendon Press, Oxford, 1995, p. 2.

broader dialectic of multiculturalism. The first moment in this dialectic is the moment of *particularized hierarchy*. Here we have two or more communities in a hierarchical relation, a dominant community to which other communities are subordinate. Differences between cultural communities are maintained but only within this relation of subordination. In short, the only way in which difference is sustained is by treating communities unequally. The second moment may be called the moment of *universalistic equality*. The only way to sustain equality here is to deny the significance of cultural difference. People are equal because their membership in a cultural community is deemed inconsequential. Rather, what matters is their status as individuals and their membership in an abstracted political community. The third moment may be called the moment of *particularized equality*. Here people are different but equal. Membership in a particular cultural group is important but so is the relationship of equality among different cultural communities.

With the context unravelled, it is easy to situate current demands for political recognition as belonging clearly to the moment of particularized equality rather than particularized hierarchy. This means that recognition must be made available to everyone within society. No community and therefore no member of it can be subordinate to other communities or its members. Recent demands for a multicultural society constitute a plea for *egalitarian multiculturalism*. Second, neither class nor level of achievement is the basis of recognition but rather one's overall way of life, a culture. Any politics that requires the exclusion of cultural identity as a condition for membership or recognition is ruled out. A demand to renounce cultural identity as a condition for free and equal citizenship no longer appears to be viable.

Within egalitarian multiculturalism, it is useful to distinguish between liberal and authoritarian forms of it. *Liberal multiculturalism* is liberal because equal recognition of cultural groups must be compatible with requirements of basic individual liberties and perhaps even with individual autonomy. *Authoritarian multiculturalism* affirms equal recognition of all cultural groups including ones that violate freedom of individuals. A good example of authoritarian multiculturalism comes from many successor states of old empires. On examining the history of empires, it is found that different cultural groups were brought together by imperial powers and divided for more effective political domination.[13] Each group was granted considerable autonomy in exchange for their acceptance of imperial hegemony. Such was the case in the Ottoman empire that developed the millet system. Groups within the system were given *equal* legal standing, every individual was required to identify himself with one of these and *submit* to its laws pertaining to marriage, divorce, inheritance and so on. Roughly the same is true of the British empire in India where Hindus, Muslims, Parsis and Christians were given equal legal status and every individual gradually felt compelled to identify with one of these communities and to comply with their separate laws. (However, this process was only partially successful. It is widely known that many individuals in India are still able to retain membership of more than one cultural group, a point made with telling effect by Shail Mayaram in her article.) Both Mamdani and Kaarsholm in their papers discuss how the generation of such illiberal cultural communities was part of the system of apartheid in South Africa. Both make the extremely relevant point that prolonged colonial rule has set up an opposition between liberal individualism and some version of republicanism on the one hand and an authoritarian, illiberal multiculturalism on the other, neither of which yields social justice. The modernist language of rights has come to be associated with dominant groups and the language of communitarianism with internal authoritarianism that valorizes customary force. Thus there is a breach between rights and community on the one hand and social justice on the other. Mamdani argues, therefore, for the sublation of both modernist rights discourse and communitarian perspectives.

Egalitarian multiculturalism requires recognition or respect for culture which in turn is possible only after a degree of interaction, familiarity and mutual understanding. This clearly brings up a crucial epistemological issue central to the current debate on multiculturalism but perhaps insufficiently examined in this volume. It is interesting to note that moral and cultural diversity has not always appeared puzzling to us.[14] Without the dissolution of

[13] On this see Michael Walzer, 'Education, Democratic Citizenship and Multiculturalism', in Yael Tamir (ed.) *Democratic Education in a Multicultural State*, Blackwell, Oxford, 1995, pp. 23–31.

[14] Steven Lukes, 'Moral Diversity and Relativism', in Tamir (ed.) *Democratic Education*, pp. 15–22.

religious and rationalist certainties, issues such as the possibility of genuine multicultural understanding or sound intercultural judgments would have never been foregrounded. Within academic circles this change could not have been possible without a revival of interest in hermeneutics and a vigorous impetus from anthropological studies which challenged the view that knowledge of cultures can be obtained by observing them from the outside. Understanding between cultures is impossible without a grasp of distinct conceptual universes and this is unavailable unless one gets under the skin of agents, and obtains a view from the inside. Without this change, the project of dismantling false cultural stereotypes or of debunking the smug superiority of any one culture could hardly have taken off.

Misrecognition and Stereotypes

If recognition is based on a fair degree of understanding and getting at least something right about other cultures, then it follows that persistent or wilful misunderstanding must lead to misrecognition. The failure to respect difference and a pronounced tendency to misrecognize is often underpinned by the process known as stereotyping.[15] A stereotype is a one-sided description generated when complex differences are reduced to a simple cardboard cut-out. Different attributes are condensed into one, crudely exaggerated and then suffixed to an individual, group or culture. At the end of this process the subject is viewed exclusively through this cut-out and any evidence challenging it is brushed aside. The theme of misrecognition is indirectly examined by many papers in this volume. Tista Bagchi addresses it head-on by carefully looking into an important feature of the process of stereotyping.

It is a common place that communal politics thrives on false stereotypes which constrain rather than help intercultural understanding. By virtue of what features of the natural language is this possible? Bagchi claims that this is due to the attribute of vagueness that is found in non-accidental, nomic generic sentences which typically have the form: All Xs are Ys. (For example, Women are biologically constrained.) These sentences are such that they are

[15] On stereotyping see, for example, P. Hulme, *Colonial Encounters: Europe and the Native Caribbean*, 1492–1797, Methuen, London, 1986.

never invalidated by existing states of affairs. Counter examples to them can easily be pigeonholed as exceptions. Only by exploiting this feature of natural language can the subtler rhetoric of communalism be developed. Of course, nothing can be done about this vagueness in the sense that it cannot be eliminated from language. However, by paying attention to this feature, and by questioning the assumptions underlying the process of stereotyping, Bagchi claims that false stereotypes can be challenged and communication between communities opened up in order to make proper recognition possible.

State Support for Cultures

How else can misrecognition be prevented? To begin with, the right kind of educational curricula must be introduced. If dominant forces in any society discourage this curricula, then fairness requires that there be state support and subsidy for cultures that fail to find their deserving place in the media or in educational institutions. It follows that a policy of strict government neutrality, say a line of abstinence towards the education of children in an overall environment where the dominant culture controls the media and the educational curricula, only ends up permitting disrespect for marginal cultures.

The issue of state support for embattled cultures is a subject of much discussion in contemporary Western political theory. A large part of this debate centres not only around whether support is justified but over grounds for why this should be done. An influential justification offered by Will Kymlicka draws upon Dworkin's egalitarian liberalism to argue the case for state support for minority cultures.[16] On Dworkin's view, a distinction exists between unchosen circumstance for which compensation is appropriate and preference for which it is not. A handicap such as physical paralysis is an unchosen circumstance and therefore redistributive compensation is appropriate for persons affected by it. Expensive tastes on the other hand are a matter of preference and compensation is obviously due to persons who have them. Kymlicka accepts the distinction between unchosen circumstance where compensation is appropriate and mere preference for which it is not, and argues in favour of compensation for minority

[16] Kymlicka, *Liberalism.*

cultures on the assumption that culture is unchosen circumstance, not a matter of taste or preference.

Precisely this view is challenged by Jerry Cohen in his contribution to this volume. He too supports subsidies for minority cultures but not on grounds adduced by Kymlicka. Cohen disagrees with Kymlicka's views on expensive taste.[17] Moreover, Cohen argues, culture is akin to expensive taste. Since expensive tastes, on Dworkin's account, are voluntary preferences for which compensation is inappropriate, Dworkin's view militates against rather than supports special state subsidy for culture. Cohen further argues that Kymlicka has two options if he is to be consistent. The first is to abandon support for minority cultures. Alternatively, to repudiate the Dworkinian view on expensive taste. For Cohen, Dworkin's treatment of expensive taste is fundamentally mistaken, and so Kymlicka should really go along with Cohen in rejecting Dworkin's understanding of expensive taste and see it more like he himself does, as a preference shaped by unchosen circumstance. On Cohen's view, culture is much too much like involuntary tastes, part of a person's constitution in that she can be properly satisfied only by her own particular culture. The same resources do not yield the same amount of satisfaction for everybody because by virtue of their respective cultures, people differ in capacity to obtain fulfilment from identical quantity of resources. Therefore, if people happen to have, by birth or history, physical handicaps or expensive tastes, and if redistributive compensation is justified for physical handicap, then it must be similarly justified for expensive tastes. So, justice requires, Cohen argues, that Dworkin's

[17] What is the so-called problem of expensive tastes? Some people argue that in principle people with expensive tastes can make a legitimate demand for an additional income. The reason being that the satisfaction they obtain from a set of goods is different from what it yields to others. The amount of satisfaction yielded by an expensive claret may be just about the same to a group of people as the satisfaction achieved by others from inexpensive beer. People are treated fairly if they have access to goods which yield the same level of satisfaction but if the same satisfaction is secured by different goods then they must get different goods, even if these goods are more expensive relative to other goods. In short, the idea is that fair treatment requires compensation to those with expensive tastes. The rejoinder to this claim is that people cannot complain about burdens placed on them by their own beliefs or tastes.

equality of resources yield to what Cohen calls equality of access to advantage. This defence of state subsidy for minority cultures comes from within a broader claim that egalitarian liberals ought to be somewhat kinder to expensive tastes as conceived by Cohen. By failing to do so, liberals often misunderstand what is required by their own principles of neutrality and equality.

It is also worthwhile to note that interventionist policies by the state may be (a) undertaken to take account of the *fact* of multiple cultures or (b) endorsed on the ground that some otherwise unrealizable *value* inheres in every cultural group, so that the well-being of the whole society is dependent on the health of stable cultural groups within it and the stability of such groups dependent in turn on some commitment on the part of the state to encourage or support them.[18] (b) assumes a link between multiculturalism and value-pluralism, an ethical standpoint for which, because of practical and conceptual limits, all values required for an exhaustive idea of human flourishing, cannot be realized in any single culture, by any one group. Such value-pluralism admits of incompatible values that may also generate practical conflicts. A multicultural society cannot meet, therefore, the highest standards of stability. For it, only a good-enough stability is possible, that too by a constant renewal of its inventive resources and by the capacity of its people for a sustained but 'inspired adhoccery' to manage more or less persistent conflict.[19]

Reflection on some of the points made above compels me to come to the following conclusion: Both sameness and difference can be a source of inequality and injustice. We must neither be discriminated on account of particular features of religion and culture nor, as a condition of citizenship, be compelled to set aside our cultural particularity. Somehow a space has to be found to accommodate cultural particularity within the political sphere shaped already by liberal individualism and republicanism, for neither on its own is able to deal with extremely important issues raised by multiculturalism. I return to this point in section V.

[18] See J. Raz, 'Multiculturalism: A Liberal Perspective', in *Ethics in the Public Domain*, Clarendon, Oxford, 1994, pp. 158–9.

[19] The phrase is Taylor's, quoted in Stanley Fish, 'Boutique Multiculturalism, or Why Liberals are Incapable of Thinking about Hate Speech', *Critical Inquiry*, vol. 23, no. 2, p. 386.

IV. Levels of Multiculturalism

In the preceding sections, I claimed that multiculturalism brings together a set of issues that relate to the need for community, a sense of belonging to it, the importance of a secure sense of identity, of status and recognition, of particularity and the need to recognize and maintain difference with others. The concerns of this framework, the framework of identity and cultural particularity, smell different from issues raised within another framework that dominated mainstream political theory since the second World War—the framework of material welfare and a cultural-neutral universalism that underscores the importance of individual choice in one's profession, relationships, life-style and basic moral convictions, the compulsion of a more equitable distribution of material resources and the need to belong to a wider social and political universe where neither one's class or status nor cultural inheritance was a source of advantage or disadvantage. Proponents of these broad frameworks (let me call them the ICP-framework and the MU-framework, for short) are suspicious of one another and frequently vie for the same space. My own view is that the two frameworks are not irretrievably opposed. Both are concerned with questions of power and hegemony as well as with questions of dignity. Whereas one concentrates on direct political domination and economic exploitation, the other focuses on the more subtle ways in which disabilities and inadequacies, loss of self-esteem and self-confidence develop within individuals and groups. In real-life situations both are frequently intertwined. Consider a system in which non-market private power has been abolished. Even in such societies the initial conditions of inequality of wealth and access to education can permanently deny large groups of people their right to dignity as human beings, and the right to their own culture as a sign of that dignity.[20] It remains true however

[20] Thus the USA had to enact the Homestead Act in order to see that land belonged to cultivating farmers rather than rentier landlords, and make primary education compulsory in order to ensure that people had a certain minimum command over information regarding their rights in a republic. Even then, the USA has not been able to accord equality of opportunity to the Afro-Americans who are discriminated on the basis of non-market stigmata, stigmata which are ineradicably associated with the accident of birth. I am grateful to Professor Amiya Bagchi for drawing my attention to this point.

that the two frameworks cannot easily be reconciled by a subsumption of one by the other. Issues grouped under multiculturalism cannot be incorporated without remainder into the domain of social justice as conceived by the first framework. The two can be reconciled but only after they have evolved in a direction away from how they are currently conceived and formulated. I shall return to this point in section VII.

For the moment, I wish to emphasize that both frameworks operate at three distinct levels. There is *first* the international level, either outside national boundaries or across them. Questions of economic justice, political domination and sovereignty can arise within the global order, between nation-states. Territories that have turned into colonies of an empire are denuded of wealth and resources and the collective sovereignty of distinct peoples is severely curtailed. This results in forms of injustice and severe deprivation of material well-being. Likewise, dominant cultures generate stereotypes of the dominated which they get their victims to accept and that results in the loss of confidence and pervasive self-images of inferiority. People then lose respect for their own cultures and hasten the progress of homogenization induced by dominant cultures. Here multiculturalism opposes cultural imperialism and homogenization. The *second* level operates at the site of the nation-state and is concerned vitally with its basic structure. At this level the MU-framework allows for questions such as: what is the class character of the nation-state? The ICP-framework enables us to ask: How relevant is religion, language or culture to the imagination of the nation and to the determination of the criterion of citizenship? The principal issue here is whether the nation is legitimated by the ideology of an exclusionary ethno-nationalism or else by an inclusive nationalism. At this level, multiculturalism is the view which directly challenges ethno-nationalism by conceiving the nation-state as formed out of and giving ample space to diverse cultural groups. Perhaps it also challenges weaker versions of ethno-nationalism that enjoin the state to uphold the culture of the majority, by making its language the language of public affairs, celebrating its holidays, and teaching only the history of the majority. Multiculturalism opposes states whose only objective is the survival and well-being of the dominant cultural group. Finally, there remains a *third* level operating at sites within the nation-state. At this level, the MU-framework addresses interclass issues. Within the ICP-framework, we ask, for example, how minority groups are to be treated. Must they be given special privilege and immunity and on what grounds? Should they be given special representation rights in the political arena? Should state subsidy be given for small but embattled cultures and if yes, what is the best justification for it? Strong multiculturalism gives an affirmative answer to these questions. Weak multiculturalism reflects the institutional history of immigrant societies. Here all groups, including the first that displaces or subordinates the indigenous population, has an immigrant status. Over time the state is forced into a kind of neutrality, which is first expressed in religious toleration and secularism and then in a slow disengagement from the national history and cultural style of the first immigrants. Such disengagement is no doubt partial and incomplete but in principle each immigrant culture must sustain itself without mandatory support from the state which celebrates its own history and teaches values of toleration, neutrality and mutual respect but not the particular values of any one group.[21]

V. Rule of Law, Republicanism and Rawlsian Liberalism

At the heart of multiculturalism is cultural difference and the political conflict it may generate. Can such conflicts be prevented? One answer is that such conflicts can be managed and contained by the effective rule of law. In this volume, R. Sudarshan focuses on the capacity of a political system to deal with cultural conflicts. In particular, he asks if, by providing a shared framework of basic values and common interests, constitutionalism and rule of law can foster or maintain diversity. He argues that they cannot on their own do so. Of course, it is well known that at least two conceptions of the rule of law exist. One embodies features of an eminently desirable system of government in which liberties and rights of individuals are protected. For example, Dworkin's conception of a rights-based rule of law has a rich substantive content along roughly these lines. The other narrower conception incorporates values that inhere in the notion of law and rejects dependence on a comprehensive political theory of good government. The narrow

[21] On the discussion of this issue, see Walzer, 'Education, Democratic Citizenship and Multiculturalism' p. 24.

conception argues for an internal morality of law with important principles such as the generality of law, its publicizability, consistency, clarity, feasibility, stability and its prospectivity. It does not rely on substantive values promoted by particular legal rules and is compatible with injustice, with even undemocratic politics.[22] Which of these can prevent cultural conflicts? Sudarshan appears to argue that neither the narrow nor the broad conception is able on its own to properly handle cultural conflicts. In any case, rule of law in India has its own pathologies; there is great dissonance between the legal regime and requirements of local traditions.[23] He appears to endorse the view that I myself hold that to view rule of law as the panacea for cultural conflicts evades rather than effectively faces issues raised by multiculturalism.

A second response derives from the French republican tradition that emphasizes a thick unity of purpose to be realized in the political sphere. This view exhorts us to build an alternative, purely political identity as an analogue of narrower, conflicting cultural identities. A republican political identity besides being warm is also meant to be more inclusive. The relationship between fellow citizens should be as thick as between members of a cultural community. At the heart of republicanism is the idea of democratic participation available to everyone irrespective of religious or ethnic affiliation. Everyone is required to leave behind one's ethnic identity in order to enter a domain of political equals. The republican version of liberty, equality and fraternity combines political freedom with a thick unity of purpose that excludes any differentiation.[24] Some residue of this, as Catherine Audard in her paper confirms, still remains in the model of nation-state in France

[22] However, the content of pure law may be richer and may provide a basis for establishing a necessary connection between law and substantive morality. Some values may indeed be promoted by even this narrow notion of the rule of law. For example, L. L. Fuller believes that the internal morality of law though neutral over a wide range of substantive moral aims rules out pursuit of some evil aims. For a discussion of these issues see C. L. Ten, 'Constitutionalism and the Rule of Law', in Robert Goodin and Philip Pettit (eds) *A Companion to Contemporary Political Philosophy*, Blackwell, Oxford, 1995, pp. 394–403.

[23] Sudarshan considers and rejects the view that the problems of a formalistic system of law can be overcome by an ideology of nationalism.

[24] See Taylor, *The Politics of Recognition*, p. 51.

which at least in part is a political project of a strong community of citizens. She also points out that this demand is made equally on everyone, in roughly the same manner and is strongly assimilationist. From the vantage point of this model, the division of people along ethnic or cultural lines must be seen as destructive of solidarity among citizens. To people who take cultural identity seriously, this must be unduly harsh and over demanding—a point emphasized in papers by Dhareshwar and Kaarsholm. The constitution of the citizen-subject of the Indian nation-state has had to devalue, what Dhareshwar calls, the communitarian subject tainted always with either religion or caste. To be sure, the attraction of a strong republican identity, Audard tells us, must not be underestimated, particularly when the very same cultural identity is a ground for discrimination, or in circumstances where people are struggling to emancipate themselves from the crushing burden of second-rate identities in authoritarian empires. Under conditions where the returns from citizenship are unable to offset the loss suffered by the forsaking of one's culture, assimilation is likely to be resisted but a richer content of citizenship brings substantial gains which override the loss resulting from the marginalization of one's culture. The point, however, is that an assimilationist republican identity is meant to entirely replace a person's cultural identity and therefore is insensitive to the loss entailed by this substitution. This insensitivity, Audard rightly reminds us, is due largely to simple-minded ideas of dignity and self-respect and an equally simplistic view of their implications for moral identity. The French variant of repulicanism in particular never fully comprehended that cultural rights can be an essential part of the moral identity of citizens. For Audard, the French republican model has frequently equated democracy with majority rule. Only greater judicial review of political decisions and an even greater sensitivity to cultural difference, she argues, will secure a proper model of citizenship.

Audard's views may be contrasted with the position of Michael Walzer who defends a more austere republicanism and argues that in deeply divided societies, the bond of citizenship encouraged by democratic participation may be the only glue that holds people together.[25] In Israel, the country discussed by Walzer, as well in

25 Walzer, 'Education, Democratic Citizenship and Multiculturalism', p. 26.

India, discussed by several papers in this volume, many religions, nationalities, and ethnicities exist that lead to a phenomenal intensity of ineradicable differences. These can probably be accommodated only within a framework of common citizenship. After all, people vote in the same elections, obey the same laws, pay the same taxes and participate in the same argument about the objectives of the state. The democratic arena, Walzer tells us, is very different from civil society with its multiple divisions. True, political parties reflect differences but it is equally true that they are willing to look for votes wherever they can find them, and, in order to form a government, negotiate deals with other political parties. The logic of the democratic system forces them not to focus on only a single group of voters. A narrowly ideological party therefore cannot form a government. If it does not compromise its ideology in order to win voters, it must do so in the search for coalition partners. No matter how different political groups may be in civil society, the democratic arena per force bridges the difference. It follows that if co-existence is a real objective, then it must be found in the political rather than in the arena of civil society. People must learn to think of one another as fellow citizens. Walzer makes clear that this fellowship need not be particularly warm. It provides an alternative to communal solidarity and is not an expression of it.

Whatever other weaknesses it might have, the republican model with its emphasis on democratic participation and common identity is not usually found wanting in its attempt to bring together people with profound cultural differences. But does democracy *really* include everyone? A note of caution comes from a sympathetic critic. In his contribution in this volume, Charles Taylor draws attention to the potential of exclusion hidden, ironically, within democracy. For Taylor, democracy embodies a vision of inclusion no doubt, but something in its dynamic pushes towards exclusion too. Taylor draws attention to the temptation to exclude over and above what people may feel out of historical prejudice or narrowness of vision. His paper explores this dynamic and offers ways of compensating for this exclusionary ingredient within the democratic process. Taylor argues that democracy cannot function without a degree of cohesion among individuals. Democracy needs a common identity; for people to be sovereign, a new self-understanding among individuals as collective agents who are more than a mere disparate set of individuals must come into existence.

Unless this happens little reason exists for people to accept the decisions of the majority. A people must believe that by virtue of ruling in common they are free or else those excluded by majority decision remain alienated. But precisely at this point it is easy to succumb to the idea that the unity required for collective agency is antecedently achieved by culture or ethnicity. The very requirements of collective agency central to the democratic vision simultaneously generate the temptation to nurture a strongly exclusionary ethnic or cultural nationalism. The democratic age itself poses new obstacles to co-existence which was possible to achieve within an undemocratic political structure.

Do other philosophical strategies to cope with cultural difference fare better? A related response to deep cultural difference comes from Rawlsian political liberalism which differs from republicanism in the central importance it gives to civil rights but shares with it an enthusiasm for a common political project centred on the value of citizenship. Rawls' primary question is: how is it possible for there to exist over time a just and stable society of free and equal citizens who still remain profoundly divided by culture understood in the broadest sense to include reasonable religious, philosophical and moral doctrines?[26] The core of Rawls' answer to this question is that the basic structure of society must embody a political conception of justice that 'may be shared by citizens as a basis of reasoned, informed and willing political agreement', which 'expresses their shared and public political reason'[27] and that can 'gain the support of an overlapping consensus of reasonable religious, philosophical and moral doctrines in a society regulated by it'.[28] Both republicanism and political liberalism have the same enemy, the ethnic nation in which political membership is based on cultural and emotional links and where cultural difference and the corresponding lack of warmth it induces become a reason for excluding people from membership in a political community. Is political liberalism suited somewhat better than republicanism to deal with cultural difference?

Two fairly widespread interpretations of Rawls' work exist. For the first, political liberalism is an austere doctrine of excessive

[26] John Rawls, *Political Liberalism*, Columbia University Press, New York, 1993, p. 47.

[27] Ibid., p. 9.

[28] Ibid., p. 10.

self-restraint for which principles concerning the basic structure must be justified in terms wholly independent of particular conceptions of the good (particular reasonable and comprehensive doctrines).[29] On this view, the Rawlsian ideal of public reason is so stringent in the justification of the two principles of justice, that it leaves no place at all for reasonable, comprehensive doctrines (hereafter, RCDs).[30] This, critics argue, carries a wholly unrealistic conception of human motivation. The second view claims that, having abandoned an earlier advocacy of a strategy of avoidance, Rawls now recommends a straight-forward priority of the good over the right, seeking justification for principles of justice by invoking all RCDs. Even though different conceptions of the good form the starting point of the argument about a doctrine of justice, they arrive at the same conclusion, namely, the soundness of a political conception of justice. On this interpretation, the idea of overlapping consensus intends to capture unanimity in conclusion despite its lack of unanimity in the route to it. Critics argue that in a different way this too is unrealistic because it underestimates the diversity of modern societies which is 'just too great'. (The phrase is Raz's but the argument belongs, I think, to Michael Perry). This is an empirical argument against the possibility of overlapping consensus.

In his contribution to this volume, Bilgrami interprets Rawls' Political Liberalism in the first of the two ways and finds it implausible. Having done so, he himself takes a position roughly identical to the one attributed to Rawls by the second interpretation. Bilgrami's own objective in the paper is not merely to offer an interpretation of Rawls but to find a way out of an intolerable impasse that results from the binary opposition between statist and internal communitarian reform of Muslim personal law. He does so by a detour into moral psychology. For him, an uneasy choice is forced upon us between a state oriented, coercive liberalism and a supposedly uncoercive communitarianism wholly outside the arena of the state largely because of an inadequate understanding of the moral psychology of the agents that undergirds both. As an instance of a version of liberalism with an impoverished moral psychology, Bilgrami takes up the philosophy of Rawls. A rights

[29] See M. Sandel, 'Review of Rawls' Political Liberalism', *Harvard Law Review*, vol. 107, no. 7, May 1994, pp. 1765–94.

[30] M. Perry, *Love and Power*, OUP, New York and Oxford, 1991, p. 23.

based liberalism, for Rawls, can be derived in abstraction from substantive commitments. The real question which Bilgrami compels us to address is whether or not such abstraction is possible for religious communitarians. Rawls' answer in the affirmative asserts that every person, were he even to discover himself as a staunch communitarian, accepts and therefore chooses the policy of non-interference embodied in institutional rights because of the higher order desire to revise and at the very extreme to reject one's own conception of the good. Bilgrami finds this utterly unbelievable. In order to show its implausibility, Bilgrami proposes a fine-tuned moral psychology of identity. To have an identity is to have fundamental commitments and to be fundamentally committed, Bilgrami claims, is to have a higher order desire to live by those commitments in the future even if currently one lacks the desire to do so. In other words, to have an identity is to live one's life in the future by a conception of the good that one has right now. If this is what identity entails, then the Rawlsian person lacks identity altogether. A moral psychology without a proper place for identity, Bilgrami argues, is considerably impoverished. A central weakness of Rawlsian liberalism, therefore, is that it does not hold true for normal persons, that is, people with identity. Bilgrami also claims that on the Rawlsian account, no person has rational reason to uphold liberal ideals. For Bilgrami, given that the rationality of desires is a function of how they are reinforced by one another, the Rawlsian person, who abstains from reinforcing her commitment to secular ideals with the help of a conception of the good, is being akratic at best, but definitely irrational. The Rawlsian view is untenable because of an implausible psychology not only of identity but also of rational behaviour.

Bilgrami reaches his conclusions irrespective of the truth of the communitarianism argument and depends solely on considerations of moral psychology. Against communitarians who dismiss the discourse of rights, Bilgrami defends it although not on usual grounds. For Bilgrami, the justification of rights must appeal to the very substantive values with which rights themselves are quite properly contrasted. Bilgrami reinforces his point by taking recourse to the distinction between internal and external reasons. For Rawls, a commitment to liberalism can flow from external reasons. This is unacceptable to Bilgrami. This, he himself agrees, joins him with Foucauldian critics of liberalism who claim that a policy justified by external reasons, that is, with no place in the motivational set of the agent, is necessarily coercive. No person has a reason from within to comply with it, so that any compliance must be out of coercion. Therefore, a Rawlsian defence of liberalism is open to communitarian objections. Against both, Bilgrami proposes a third option in which people find reason to accept liberal ideals as well as reforms within their community. Since these reforms get going only by virtue of reason from within, they are internal to the community and non-coercive. Moreover, this feature is not changed simply because reforms take place on statist sites. They remain internal and non-coercive even when initiated by the state. If the state can give reasons that are understood and accepted by people from within their internal motivation set, then it can turn into a site for internal reform. Liberal ideals such as secularism may be accepted when negotiated from within different communitarian perspectives. Bilgrami believes that this can happen provided one empirical premise is true, that is, a large majority of people are not fundamentalist. To help locate precisely such people is the most important task before a democratic state. It must identify voices to whom internal reasons can be given. The democratization of the state is essential because without it even non-fundamentalist persons find it difficult to oppose absolutism. The state must actively support and encourage people to bypass the reactionary elite which persistently holds them back.

I have substantial agreement with Bilgrami's views. However, I also detect some disagreement over the precise interpretation of Political Liberalism. I believe both interpretations mentioned above are equally mistaken because of a failure to see the Rawlsian answer as a two-tiered doctrine with distinct justifications appropriate to each level.[31] Let me elaborate. The exposition of Rawls' answer involves four distinct moves, each successive one marked by greater analytical focus and precision. Rawls' first move is to claim that an institutional design that makes living together possible must embody some general abstract, moral principles endorsed by all relevant persons. The second move specifies principles that are

[31] I have discussed this at length in an unpublished paper entitled 'Between Abstinence and Indulgence: Rawls' Politics of Restrained Engagement', delivered at the APSA Conference, San Francisco, 1996.

acceptable to persons motivated by diverse conceptions of the good but a shared desire to cooperate and to justify their actions in terms that no one can reasonably reject. Rawls claims that these principles must embody a political conception of justice and include guidelines provided by public political reason with which this conception is defended, discussed, justified, criticized and opposed. His third move straightforwardly follows from the second. Here, Rawls' prescription is not to rely on RCDs in public or official fora the justification of public policies connected with the basic structure. Rawls argues that we must rely on public reason, that is, justify only in terms of plain truths, general beliefs, uncontroversial conclusions of science because only these formulations are acceptable to all. To accept a political conception entails, for Rawls, a commitment to particular ways of reasoning and certain types of considerations. It follows that at least some reasons must be jettisoned because they are inappropriate and some evidence and information eschewed on grounds of relevance. Here, Rawls appears to advocate epistemological restraint, the harsh imperative for which the belief in truth of the doctrine is not by itself a reason for it to become ground for a public policy. All this is pretty familiar, I am afraid. It is his fourth move that is unexpectedly novel. A place is found once again for RCDs. Removed from first order justification in public fora, RCDs are brought back in as second order justification to support a commitment to public reason. Given their desire to cooperate and to justify actions to others, people choose to remove RCDs from first order justifications. This may be viewed as a form of pre-commitment. This deliberate reshaping of the feasible set—certain choices that flow from directly relying on RCDs are excluded—is nevertheless endorsed from within RCDs. What could explain this move? I believe that in doing so Rawls acknowledges that hitherto he had insufficiently emphasized the motivational power of RCDs. People can act or justify independently of conceptions of the good only when a second order justification for these actions and justifications exist from within such conceptions. Rawls acknowledges the insufficiency of the agreement motive to get us to principles governing our basic structure. But he insists that a conception of the good, provided it is reasonable, can be self-limiting. When all reasonable doctrines limit themselves, they open up a space for the acceptance of a non-RCD principle that can be rejected by none. Principles of justice occupy precisely this space and depend ultimately on the self-limiting capacity of all relevant reasonable doctrines. This is Rawls' primary motivation for this move. A secondary reason is the idea that no single route to standards of public reason is necessary, and that forms of reasons and evidence on which we converge need not be identical with the entire set of reasons and evidence available from within each RCD.

A liberal, democratic, multicultural state depends for its survival on people with real flesh and blood, who actively support or at least do not actively oppose it. If this is to happen, they must have the right kind of motivation. What is the nature of these motivations? How deep must they go? How do they relate to other elements of a person's culture? Such questions are addressed by Bilgrami. However, another set of questions exists. It is difficult to believe that everyone and every group in society will have these motivations. We must therefore ask which of the many groups in society possesses or is likely to have them? In his contribution, Amiya Bagchi tries to answer this question. In particular, he asks if the Indian bourgeoisie can support a secular, democratic, multicultural state. Of course, it is true that in the past the bourgeoisie has lent support to a secular state. But, for Bagchi, support in the past does not ensure its continuation in the future, if grounds for that support have been purely instrumentalist. After all, the bourgeoisie used religion to beat down the rebellious artisan as well as to defy the superiority of the modern British. It frequently goes along with those who play the game of mobilizing people along communal lines and has no qualms about fomenting communal trouble. For Bagchi, the bourgeoisie is unlikely to break down barriers; rather more likely to build walls around cultural communities. To be sure, the existence of deep religious beliefs, Bagchi claims, is compatible with democracy. Both Gandhi and Tagore show how this can be possible. However, the Indian bourgeoisie is unlikely to have the same openness. Unlike Europe where the bourgeoisie played an important role in supporting the separation of religion and politics, in India, Bagchi concludes, the struggle for a multicultural democracy and for values underlying it is likely to be fought in opposition to rather than with the support of the Indian bourgeoisie.

VI. Scepticism about Multiculturalism

The multicultural approach delineated so far postulates a rather straightforward link between issues of identity and the domain of particular cultures. It also assumes that the identity of a person corresponds to a particular culture and that such cultures are wholes with easily discernible boundaries. Differences in identity therefore correspond to differences in clearly identifiable and mutually distinct cultures. It further assumes that cultural communities are homogeneous and cultural identities distinct and extremely well demarcated. Each of these assumptions can be questioned. For example, it is doubtful if cultures are neatly separated, internally coherent wholes. Cultures may in fact be more like clusters of heterogeneous elements with varying origins.[32] A similar point is made in her article by Shail Mayaram who argues that existing models of multiculturalism are not only insensitive to internal differentiation within groups but also to the fluid, criss-crossing and overlapping nature of identities, at least in many non-Western societies. Western models of multiculturalism are anti-syncretic, she claims, because they are unable to grasp the simultaneity of or mobility within different identities, the fact that people can be simultaneously X and Y or move easily from X to Y.

If the above is true, then it must surely alter our understanding of multicultural polities. However, suppose that this assumption is dropped or at least modified to mean only that people act frequently on the belief that cultures are separate wholes and that their identity and self-esteem is linked to culture so conceived, then it might be said that multiculturalism registers this fact about a generally held belief among a very significant number of people. Similarly, the first assumption that social identity is linked in an uncomplicated way with affiliation to a particular culture is questioned in the American context by Anthony Appiah, a

[32] It does not follow that cultural differences do not exist but they are more like 'differences within climatic regions or ecosystems than like the frontiers drawn with a pen between nation-states'. See Steven Lukes, in Tamir (ed.) *Democratic Education*. Nonetheless, such holistic perceptions of culture are fairly widespread and sustained in different degrees, at different times and places, by imperialist powers, nationalist movements, populist leaders and social anthropologists.

significant intervention given that the term multiculturalism is very much an American original.[33] Appiah notes that in the United States of America cultural diversity has disappeared over the years. Much greater cultural homogeneity exists there than people generally like to believe. Most Americans share a common language, enjoy the same sport, watch the same films and television programmes. Indeed Judaism and Islam too are extraordinarily Americanized. Much of American Islam is as comfortable as Protestantism is with the separation between church and the state. So, if America is not culturally diverse and if in the last instance multiculturalism is about cultural diversity, then multiculturalism is irrelevant to the United States. If anything, the term tries to capture an altogether different phenomenon, namely the presence in the US of diverse social identities. A large number of people in America, Appiah tells us, insist that they are profoundly shaped by groups to which they belong, that their social identity and membership to these groups is central to who they are. They also demand that these social identities be acknowledged publicly as their authentic identities. It follows that America is marked by the presence of a variety of social identities without an accompanying cultural diversity. Each distinct identity is not necessarily co-related with a distinct culture. A uniform culture generates different identities and anxiety about maintaining such difference.

If this is so, Appiah concludes, an appeal to cultural difference obscures rather than illuminates the situation of offence and disrespect shown, say, to the blacks because it is not black culture that the racist disdains but blacks. 'Culture is not the problem, and it is not the solution.' Appiah therefore pleads that 'we should conduct our discussion of education and citizenship, toleration and social peace, without the talk of culture'.

Have the multiculturalists then been barking up the wrong tree? I believe all that Appiah's argument shows is that a politics of cultural difference presupposes a significant degree of cultural homogenization and assimilation but not that the recognition of cultures is 'not part of the solution to the problem'. For a start, Appiah selectively draws evidence of cultural sameness in order to downgrade the possible significance of the fact and value of cultural

[33] Anthony Appiah, 'The Multicultural Misunderstanding', *The New York Review of Books*, vol. XLIV, no. 15, 9 October 1997, pp. 30–5.

difference. But even if his factual claims are entirely true they leave unanswered the question of how and why the belief in cultural difference is so easily accepted among people who apparently are culturally very similar. Appiah is correct in rejecting the view that sees cultural difference as primordial or essential but not in jettisoning the idea that some difference, no matter what its origin, matters to a significant number of people. It is of course true that cultural difference is not natural and transparent but is variously constructed. No doubt it is important to recognize that cultural difference is recovered and invented half way up a path of cultural interaction among unequals but it doesn't follow that the politics of cultural difference rests on total hoax, that difference is entirely invented and that the real issues lie elsewhere. The plain fact is that at one level French and English speaking Canadians are culturally different and *this* is not altered by showing that *objectively speaking* there exists a larger quantum of cultural sameness. Appiah is right that respect for people's food and music does not guarantee that they be treated with equal dignity. They can still be looked down upon on the ground that in countless relevant respects that matter hugely in society, they are less able or inferior. Such an attitude towards blacks may well exist among say the middle class white professional and even among intellectuals. However, Appiah underestimates the reach of the belief that, despite evidence of cultural sameness and even appreciation of some aspects of the culture of blacks, for example a respect for their sport and music, current disabilities of blacks are linked in the minds of people to inferior cultural backgrounds. In such an environment, a proper education in cultural matters is crucial.

Appiah suggests an additional argument against multiculturalism in which fierce inter-group conflict appears not to be due to cultural difference. Plenty of social friction exists in America among people who by objective standards are culturally quite similar. The various peoples of Bosnia—Serb, Croat or Muslim—are fairly homogeneous in critical terms as are Hutus and Tutsis in Rwanda. There is something to chew on in Appiah's claim. The saliency of cultural difference can be created by manufacturing cultural conflict. Indeed, cultural difference is brewed by cultural conflict.

It is of course true that motivations for the creation of cultural difference have diverse origins. Culture alone cannot generate unbridgeable social distance or prolonged hostility between groups. But whatever its origin and motivation, and, compared to cultural sameness, no matter how small objectively speaking it is, cultural difference is significant in the minds of the relevant agents whose motivations may differ vastly from its direct beneficiaries. It is true that when looked from the outside, Serbs and Croats look strikingly similar; they speak roughly the same language and have shared the same village life for centuries. Urbanization and industrialization have further slimmed down even their religious differences. But we will do well to remember Freud's perceptive comment that the smaller the real difference between two peoples, the larger it looms in their imagination. This 'narcissism of minor difference' implies that it is precisely when external markers point towards the absence of any major differences that people act as if they are deeply divided.[34] The objective fact of a common past should no doubt result in harmonious co-existence and subjective states of fraternity and mutual respect. What is frequently produced instead is a painful narrative of how two peoples have been at the throat of each other ever since the clock began to tick. Thus, history and collective memory frequently stand irretrievably opposed to each other. Careful sociological examination shows that cultural homogenization tends to implode, to collapse into a black hole before it comes to fruition; just when complete cultural sameness comes to be reasonably expected, tiny, seemingly insignificant differences are first foregrounded and then consolidated as a conglomerate of major cultural divisions. By a curious dialectic, what comes to be widely accepted and legitimized, that is, cultural differentiation and division, is the result of a process of cultural homogenization. The conclusion to be drawn is this: Appiah correctly points to the absence of significant cultural difference in the initial stages of this process—that no primordial cultural differences exist—but he mistakenly concludes that it is not present at the end. The difference created *on the way* is real and cultural, a point brought out clearly in Alok Rai's contribution. Rai claims that language was not a conventional, usual site of communal differentiation in northern India. Only from 1880 through to 1930 'a tragic wedge was inserted into the common language of north

[34] See M. Ignatieff, *Blood and Belonging*, Farrar, Straus and Giroux, New York, 1993, pp. 21–8.

India and a great lingua franca was mutilated into two half languages, modern Hindi that belongs to Hindus and Urdu that belongs to the Muslims'. Rai does not say that a period of supreme harmony existed prior to this differentiation. Rather, he claims 'to finesse something between subverted harmony and primordial difference'. My own view is that once such differentiation and division is created, there is a foreclosing of any reversal. No simple way of undoing it is available anymore—henceforth, culture will remain both a problem and must be at least a part of the solution. Perhaps a failure to recognize this resulted in the demand for Pakistan. A failure to shift focus away from the relative absence of cultural difference at the very beginning of anti-colonial struggle and register its robust presence at the end of it led the leaders of the Indian National Congress into insisting, Appiah-like, that 'culture is not the problem and it is not the solution'. Perhaps it is the denial not the affirmation of multiculturalism that results in prolonged, bitter, inter-group conflicts and mutual separation.

Much the same lesson can be drawn from evidence provided by Pradeep Dutta in his compelling account of a minor episode in Calcutta of 1926 where the burial of a local fakir became the site of struggle and contestation of a much larger nationalist movement. Dutta traces the transition from one phase of the nationalist movement in which Hindus and Muslims were mobilized for a common cause to the other, marked by fractured consensus and prolonged outbreak of intermittent riots. Precisely this transition is reflected in local events such as the burial of a fakir. What began as a symbol of Hindu–Muslim unity turned over time into a site of intense internecine conflict between the two. European refusal to bury the fakir in the public space near the market initially provoked stiff opposition from both Hindus and Muslims. However, a change in background conditions, such as the death of C. R. Das, the breakdown of the Bengal Pact, and the murder of Shradhanand, generated among Muslims and Hindus differences over attitude to the site of the burial. Like Rai, Dutta shows how a process that could bring people together ultimately led to the creation of difference. Perhaps it also shows that people united by a common grouse against a third party can divide when the likelihood increases of alleviating the grievance. Dutta's paper has other objectives too. He shows how and why the common public sphere, dependent as it is on the contingencies of the political process and the play of social interests, could not acquire a self-sustaining autonomy. He weaves the story of this local event into a larger narrative of the development of public sphere in India and also tries to show why a politics of collective identity is insufficient.

VII. Problems of Multiculturalism

I have claimed above that multiculturalism comes in different guises. It is egalitarian but it can also be hierarchical, is liberal but also authoritarian. So an advocacy of multiculturalism is not exactly free of problems. Some of these are easily explicated. First, it tends to essentialize and harden identities that generate radical exclusions of people. Second, by its encouragement of cultural particularity, it appears to deepen divisions and to undermine the common foundation necessary for a viable society. Third, multiculturalism supports aggregative community power over individual freedom and by according equal right to oppressive cultures it corrodes values of liberal democracy.

The first problem of the hardening of identities, the closure of communities and the exclusion generated by processes of congealment and closure is the topic of several papers in this collection. For example, Dhareshwar claims that the history of the Indian nation-state, 'in fashioning itself as a history of sovereignty, has had to exclude and delegitimize other idioms and agencies'. Attention is invariably drawn by others to the notorious issue of communal exclusion—communalism in India usually brings to mind the spectre of the exclusion of cultural communities defined predominantly by religious markers. But Pandian carefully registers the threat of other forms of exclusions, for instance of smaller regions and lower castes. He does this by taking up the question of citizenship and claims that the model of citizenship implicit in the official discourse of Indian nationalism appears to embody freedom and equality but in fact and spirit remains upper caste, male and Hindu—imposed almost always from above, nearly never negotiated from below. Fortunately, it was contested, Pandian argues, even as it was being formulated. Pandian explores the ambivalent margins of the nation-state where such contestation is enacted. He examines in particular the ideas of E. V. Ramaswamy who used nation as 'a metaphor for the ever fluid, free and equal citizenship for the oppressed locating it in the anticipatory mode'.

With the help of this, Ramaswamy was able to challenge official nationalism, a result of an attempt to hegemonize subordinate social groups. Accepting this nationalism, he claimed, would have been equivalent to suicide on part of the common people. For Ramaswamy, therefore, as important as the fight against British imperialism was the need to free oneself from the binary of nationalism–colonialism. Did Ramaswamy uncritically favour Tamil nationalism, pitching it against a pan-Indian nationalism? Pandian argues that the conception of the Tamil nation, being somewhat more egalitarian in its content, was marginally better. This does not mean that Ramaswamy uncritically privileges a Tamil past. Rather, he used it to deny legitimacy to Hindu north India and to struggle against its hegemony over other regions. For Pandian, Ramaswamy's main attempt shows that the past does not resonate with a monological voice but rather contains a range of other voices. A proper conception of the nation, for Ramaswamy, could be built only by a complete recovery of self-worth of the entire people.

The problem of oppressive communities is addressed by several contributors in the volume, notably by Javeed Alam and Shail Mayaram in the case of India and Mahmood Mamdani and Kaarsholm for South Africa. Alam contrasts modern communities in the West with premodern communities in India. Communities in the West, he claims, leave private space for individuals as well as a place for their autonomy. Communities in India, on the other hand, act as collective personalities, allowing no autonomy or private space for individuals and forcing into silence any dissent from a community's way of thinking and acting. Indeed, Alam argues such communities do not even allow individuals the right to exit. Mayaram too draws our attention to communities in India that are particularly oppressive to women. In the South African context both Mamdani and Kaarsholm point to the 'unusually coercive' customary practices of 'natives', particularly when seen in contrast to the seemingly free and rational spirit of the colonial settlers.

Why are communities within successor states of old empires and imperial powers so closed and oppressive? Mamdani argues—and Kaarsholm confirms this—that the consolidation, if not the birth of oppressive communities can be explained by the dual system of power evolved by colonial regimes all over Africa. The settlers developed one system for themselves and quite another for indigenous populations. This had to involve segregation of 'natives'. Of their many practices some were identified as customary and it is these practices which are particularly detrimental to individual freedom. Mayaram takes a different track on this issue, arguing that the formation of oppressive communities is a result precisely of Western models of multiculturalism that first unleash a process of homogenization and then constitute communities operating with rigid distinctions and binary oppositions. These models, she claims, are also unable to see how individuals and groups can choose ambiguity and doublespeak. She substantiates her claims by rich data from her field-work on the Mer community in Rajasthan which offers 'multiple choices with respect to sectarian affiliations as also the possibility of switching affiliation'.

How can egalitarian multiculturalism be prevented from be-coming hierarchical? How must it be prevented from turning authoritarian? How may its liberal content be retained? How can a multicultural society formulate laws that recognize cultures but prohibit the moral devaluation of individuals and restriction of their autonomy? How can it do so when multiculturalism also requires that proper respect be accorded those social practices that combine traditional wisdom with oppression of individuals? Can we reconcile the conflict between future generations and the autonomy of individuals living now? It is true that individuals need larger narratives within which to fit their own life plans, with the help of which to tell their life stories. It is equally true that such narratives are provided by collective identities.[35] Given this, do individuals still have the option of choosing which features are part of the collective dimension of their identities? In other words, is there a scope for looser scripts? These are some of the dilemmas that must be faced by a defensible theory of multiculturalism.

Many of these dilemmas have already been noted within political theory, especially in the debate between liberals and communitarians. Attempts have also been made to develop fresh perspectives that resolve them. Let me go over some of that ground and link some issues of that debate with the points raised

[35] This way of framing this issue is found in K. Anthony Appiah, 'Identity, Authenticity, Survival', in Gutmann, *Multiculturalism*, pp. 149–63.

above.[36] To begin with, liberals and communitarians are divided over the core values of a comprehensive public morality. Liberals appear to hold on to freedom and equality as central values. Reasonable communitarians do not deny their importance but believe that individuals cannot pursue their goods independent of cultural traditions and social roles. So, one difference is this: liberals value the ability of individuals to take a critical distance from social and cultural practices and if need be to change them by generating forces within civil society, outside the arena of the state and without the help of state power. Critical distance enables individuals to see possible oppression within cultural practices when it exists and to ensure that existing social practices are not used to license any abuse, injustice and cruelty that may be present within the culture of a community. Communitarians on the other hand believe that critical distance is at best one value among several others and cultural belonging matters even when it undermines critical reasoning. When taken to extremes this leads communitarianism, at least so the liberal fears, to turn a blind eye to oppressive cultural practices, and to ignore injustice, even cruelty within cultures. There is an obvious tension here between liberalism and communitarianism so conceived, a conflict between autonomy and cultural belonging, one of the many contentious issues subsumed under the individual versus groups debate.

I wish to dwell on the conflict between cultural belonging and individual autonomy as part of more general conflict between proponents of the irreducible value of groups and the thesis of value-individualism.[37] Value-individualism is the view that (a) only lives of individuals understood aggregately have ultimate value *and* (b) collective entities derive their value from their contribution to each of these lives.[38] Liberal multiculturalism *qua* liberal is

[36] A number of good discussions of these issues exist including Charles Taylor, 'Cross-purposes: The Liberal-Communitarian debate', in N. Rosenblum, *Liberalism and the Moral Life*, Harvard University Press, Cambridge, Mass., 1989, pp. 159–82. For a good overview see J. Hampton, *Political Philosophy*, OUP, Delhi, 1998, ch. 5.

[37] For a detailed discussion see Rajeev Bhargava, 'Should We Abandon the Majority–Minority Framework?' in D. L. Sheth and Gurpreet Mahajan (eds) *Minority Identity and the Nation State*, OUP, Delhi (forthcoming).

[38] M. Hartney, 'Some Confusion Concerning Collective Rights', *Canadian Journal of Law and Jurisprudence*, vol. IV, no. 2, July 1991, p. 297.

committed wholeheartedly to value-individualism. Other versions of multiculturalism do not accept it. Some deny it explicitly; others are not fully committed to it. I believe the wholehearted commitment of liberals to value-individualism is mistaken. To briefly support my claim, let me first introduce a distinction between the purely material lives of individuals, possessed by them no matter which group they belong to (for example, the pleasures of drink, sleep, sex, warmth, ease and the pain of injury, sickness, thirst, excessive heat, cold or exhaustion) and lives of individuals with an ineliminable collective dimension and value (for example, food, language, art, emotional states such as indignation, and some kinds of solidarities). I believe (b) in value-individualism is true only if (a) is modified to exclude the term 'only' from it, and 'lives of individuals' refers exclusively to their material lives. As it stands, as an exhaustive claim about every single dimension of human living, value-individualism seems to me blatantly false. I take it that since some aspects of human living are impossible without particular communities, the value that inheres in these communities is not reducible to the values of individuals understood purely materially and aggregatively.

Now, I believe, group-values are threatened in at least three ways that lead to a demand for their protection: (a) When values of one group are imposed on another. Here a real, external threat obtains. (b) When members of the group, out of akrasia, wilful or unwitting neglect (self-interest or laziness), ignorance, confusion or delusion cease to care for group-values. This might be called an internal threat.[39] (c) When members deliberating over these values realize their inadequacy or limitation and find better formulations thereof or discover still better values.

Notice that (c) threatens existing formulation of values but rarely the values themselves. Even when values are genuinely threatened, the purported threat comes from new values that sublate (cancel and preserve) older ones. (c) never entails insensitive rejection. Therefore, I do not count (c) as a real threat. This is not to say that it not *perceived* as one. However, perceived threats cannot legitimate the policy of special protection to groups. Some

[39] Tocqueville comes immediately to mind as one who warned us of internal threats. A retreat from the public good consequent upon over-privatization was viewed by him as a serious threat to liberty, see C. Taylor, *Philosophical Papers*, vol. 2, p. 310.

collectivists mistakenly or deliberately subsume (c) under (a) or (b). Individualists rightly emphasize the importance of (c), but generally tend to think of all changes in value as exemplifying only (c). And, although the less optimistic among them have begun to see the danger of external threats, they hardly ever recognize internal threats. Anyone pointing to these dangers is instantly suspected as a closet authoritarian, willing to sacrifice the individual for the group, an enemy of (c), in short, as an advocate of the subsumption thesis.[40]

So, one contentious issue on which individualists and non-individualists stand divided is internal threats to group values. Whereas individualists gloss over these dangers, non-individualists see them as worth combating. Now I am not unaware of why individualists find such threats difficult to handle. Indeed, they see the problem all right. But they locate it exclusively within the individual. Let me explain. Consider an individual, X who desires Y and who also values Z and suppose that Z contradicts Y (she wants to eat meat, but has the second order desire not to have this desire; she values vegetarianism). The individualist happily endorses that X can exercise power over herself, literally force herself into doing Z rather than Y. Surely this is an exercise of autonomy. But now change the agent, X, from an individual to a group: Suppose again that X desires Y but values Z. Can X be autonomous and force or discipline itself into doing Z? The problem, when we transfer the issue to groups, is that the X that coerces and the X that is coerced need not exactly coincide: Under group-description, X retains its identity in both acts, but on another equally valuable individualist description, it does not: the coercing subject and the coerced subjects are not identical. In response to this, call it the problem of an ethically grounded legitimation, individualists disband the idea of group morality converting the issue into an inter-individual conflict.

There is something to worry about here, I agree, but the correct conclusion to be drawn is not that groups have no independent value but that we, humans, are far from solving the problem of ethically grounded legitimation of group-values. As yet, we have no fair,

[40] By the subsumption thesis I mean the view for which the description of the well-being of an individual is exhausted by the description of his well-being as a member of any group to which he belongs. The overall well-being of the individual is just his well-being in the group of which he is a member.

non-coercive way of protecting group-values. Generally, four possibilities exist in face of internal threats. The first is to let group values die. Second, to coerce or manipulate some individuals into protecting them. Third, to rely on the heroism of individuals. Finally, to ensure that no one free-rides, that each sacrifices some of his desires and does his fair bit in sustaining group values. Individualists rightly oppose the exercise of the second option. They grudgingly accept the third option but, because they do not see the full force of group values, are unable to grant validity to the fourth.

I believe societies rarely commit suicide, but also that they hardly ever deploy the fourth option and that therefore, grave moral inequalities abide. Societies perpetually face internal threats and in response plunge into what can be called an unfair division of moral labour.[41] Group values are preserved by the moral hard work of those who sacrifice their desires for the sake of that group, while others free-ride. The ideology par excellence of free riders is a moral individualism that denies group value.

So, groups need protection from internal threats which may require an individual to overlook current self-interest. Does this imply a commitment to the subsumption thesis? I do not think so. How and why so? Well, simply because no group requires that an individual work for it all of the time-enjoined precisely by the subsumption thesis. Two reasons suffice to show why not. First, individuals must be exempt from moral work and attend to their own material well-being, and to sometimes pursue their desires. Second, they must be permitted to work for other groups. But attention must also be drawn to a difficulty that arises because individuals shirk moral work when tempted by free rides. In fact, a basic character of groups permits liberty to individuals on all three counts.

A group survives without all its members working for it all the time. This, first of all, enables its members to lead their material

[41] The division of moral labour means different things to different people. For example, Nagel uses it to refer to the division within us between the personal and the impersonal standpoints. For others, it is linked to role-morality and to how society divides moral labour into different institutions and roles. I mean something related but the core idea is dependent upon how the protection of group-values requires that the members set aside self-interest or claims of autonomy and how the costs of setting them aside are distributed amongst its members.

lives. Second, to be members of other groups, both overtime and at any given time. Third, to leave one group and join another. Groups can bear the cost of the departure of some of its members. But the same feature of groups that gives positive benefits secretes a disadvantage too by encouraging moral inequality. Groups build into themselves asymmetries so that some persons or types of persons bear disproportionately unfair costs for nurturing goods that benefit all. An obvious example comes to mind. Most of us value family life for the enduring relations that it makes possible. Both men and women equally share the joys of family life but its burdens are unfairly distributed. Women selflessly and routinely suppress their desires by an indirect strategy that internalizes their role as glorified mothers or wives. That such asymmetries exist within the family makes it a repressive group. This is the truth in the individualist claim. But from this it does not follow that the institution of family has no independent value.

What does an internal threat to groups and the unfair division of moral labour imply? Does it mean that rights of groups override the rights of its individual members? After all, rights are granted against protection from threats. If internal threats exist, then groups may as well be immunized against those acts of individuals that create such threats. Does this amount to an advocacy that groups have rights against other groups as well as against its own members? My answer is no, but for reasons other than ones generally given. I shall be very brief in my response here. Much literature on the subject assumes that the very possibility of the right of a group over its own members, inherent within the idea of collective goals, is decisive argument against the normative claim that groups ought to have independent value. I think the reason for not granting legally enforceable rights to groups against its own members stems from the great practical difficulty of first, distinguishing (b) from (c) and then, of separating cases of genuine free riding from those in which individuals work to take care of themselves or other groups. Moral complexity makes it prudent that groups are at best granted moral but not legal rights over their members.[42]

[42] It must be emphasized that this moral right may be exercised in the presence not of (c) but (b), and even here it must be grounded in claims of injustice, in the face of an unfair division of moral labour. A group does not have a moral right to prevent me from working for other groups or for the genuine care of my self.

I have argued that part of the value of groups is not reducible to its value for individuals when understood in abstraction from groups, and that this moral worth of groups needs just as much protection as does the moral worth of individuals. This creates potential conflict between group values and individual rights. I have argued that certain individual rights are more basic that any group rights. It follows that groups that violate these individual rights are morally guilty. It is part of my claim that these morally suspect features do not rob them of their entire moral status. It is of course true that if the violation of basic individual rights is the sole raison d'être of the existence of a group, then this group has no moral value at all. Such groups have no rights against other groups. That such morally depraved groups have existed in the past, even acquired power is the principal reason for the liberal distrust of groups. But liberal individualism mistakenly concludes from this that the value of all groups must be their value for individuals.

Allow me to bring out the implication of this abstract philosophical discussion for one issue that is briefly discussed by Bilgrami too, the question of Muslim personal law in India. For my limited purpose I need a brief outline of the content of these laws of which four aspects may be noted. The first is concerned with inheritance: Muslim personal law requires that women share in property of the parents albeit roughly half the amount granted to male descendants. The other three aspects relate to marriage, divorce and maintenance. Of these much has been written on polygamy and I shall not add to it. The position on Talaq is familiar too: if convinced that the marriage has broken down, the man can quietly pronounce divorce which becomes effective only after the period of *iddat* (roughly three months). If the man does not retract during this period, the marriage is dissolved, though this need not be permanent; the man can revive the marriage provided the women consents. This renewal is permitted twice during the lifetime of the couple, however. With the third pronouncement of Talaq, the marriage is irrevocably dissolved. If divorced, the woman must be paid her *mehar* (her share of matrimonial property). She gets alimony but only till she is re-eligible for marriage, which, once again is roughly three months.[43]

[43] Under the old criminal procedure code of 1898, all neglected wives, including Muslim women, were granted rights of maintenance. Confined to

Do Muslims have a right to *these* laws? Opinion on this has been sharply divided for long. Modernists in India, Muslims as well as Hindus, Sikhs and Christians, have firmly demanded the abolition of separate personal laws for religious minorities and the institution of a uniform civil code on liberal grounds of justice for women qua individuals. Let this radical individualist position be called A. Pitted against them is conservative communitarianism, (B), which obdurately seeks the strict maintenance, indeed further extension of existing separate personal laws for each religious group (It cannot stomach diversity in customs that more freely indulges in inter-cultural borrowing). I believe that both positions are unsatisfactory.

If what I have said about the relationship between individuals and groups is reasonable, then position (A), which denies the value of groups or the need for their protection, is indefensible. Value individualism is implausible or false. But (B) is not justifiable either; it misunderstands the nature of groups and their relations to individuals. Groups do not hover over and above individuals and though they have irreducible value, it does not follow that the value of the properties of individuals is any less or can be overridden. In short, (A) does not recognize any group rights. (B) recognizes them but in the wrong way with no place for individual rights. It follows that Muslims as a group have rights and given the importance of law within Islam and the contextual significance of the domain of the private in India, they have a right to their personal laws. It does not follow, however, that Muslims have a right per force to the protection of existing interpretations of laws that are grossly unjust to women. For a start, my account

---

the privacy of her home, with little opportunities for employment, the amount for maintenance was surely her only means of survival. This right, therefore, was grounded in her basic material needs. But frequently, when Muslim women sought the help of the court to secure maintenance, the husband divorced her, thus freeing himself from payment of maintenance beyond the required three months. To check this malpractice, the CPC of 1973 amended the relevant act to include divorced women in this category. Muslim orthodoxy mischievously objected to this amendment, complaining that it violated their religious laws. Viewed thus, the conflict between group and individual rights appears irreconcilable, heading for collision between the rival world-views of modernity and Islam. I deal with this conflict at greater length below.

rules out, in an unabashedly individualist vein, the violation of basic individual rights in the name of group value. Freedom from domestic violence, a right to *some* share in inheritance and the right to maintenance for divorced and destitute women (flowing from the agent and group-neutral reason of fulfilment of basic needs) must be legally enforced, irrespective of the group to which women belong. The state must simply enforce the exercise of such rights, no matter how incompatible this is with the personal laws or customary practices of any group. Any custom or law of Muslim orthodoxy that violates these basic rights must be set aside.[44] Muslims cannot reasonably argue that the abolition of such laws constitutes an internal threat to their culture. But, and this is the crux of the problem, a *prima facie* incompatibility of Muslim personal laws exists with the best available standards of equality and autonomy. Surely, by these standards polygamy should be abolished, women must have an *equal* share in inheritance, and divorce must occur by mutual consent rather than by the punitive exercise of exclusive male prerogative. Does this mean that a uniform civil code is undeniably desirable and must therefore be pushed through? There is need for caution here. It may well be argued that in the absence of a clear perspective on where Islam stands on the values of gender equality and autonomy, without proper discussion at all levels on these issues and under conditions where there anyway exists an external threat, any permission to tamper with personal laws is tantamount to an internal threat to the culture of Muslims. I believe there is something here in favour of this view and therefore a reconciliatory reformist position, (C), may be supported wherein personal laws need internal reform, not outright rejection.

However, this position, morally speaking, is still too simplistic. Sensitivity towards the complex moral dimensions of this issue needs an explication of how this reform must come about. So, (C), the reformist position, bifurcates further. One position, (C1), which I awkwardly call direct paternalist reformism, argues that these reforms can be imposed from above, on the initiative of the state much the same way as reforms were introduced within

[44] My use of the term 'basic' does not imply that, relative to other rights, they matter more to all individuals. It does mean though that other rights supervene on them.

Hinduism.[45] The other view claims that such reforms must come from within the community. The latter view is subject to further division. The first, anti-paternalist reformism, (C2) argues that the argument of reform from within entails that the state adopt a strict policy of non-interference in the personal matters of Muslim community. The second which I call indirect paternalist reformism, (C3), argues for a distinction between paternalistic coercion and parentalistic interference, and claims further that paternalistic coercion must be eschewed but the state is obliged to provide such conditions as will facilitate reform within the community. A combination of (C) with (A) in a contrasting system of priorities completes the picture. Citizens in India have the option to comply with the uniform civil code rather than with the personal laws of the community into which they are born. Before independence, this option was conditional upon the complete renunciation of religion and therefore of even cultural identity. This effectively blocked the right to exit. Since independence, it is possible to keep religious identity and yet opt for the common civil code.. This means (D), a policy of optional civil code: combining (B) or (C) with (A). Finally, (E), an automatic compliance with a common civil code, may exist but citizens may still have the option to be governed by personal laws. (A is more basic but an option exists for (B) or (C).[46]

I prefer the solution that advocates (D), i.e. C3 with A. I believe reforms within Muslim personal law must come from within, but that a liberal-democratic state is committed to creating conditions that make possible full and free deliberation over the issue, a

[45] This statement needs qualification. One misleading aspect of the majoritarian demand for a uniform civil code is the implicit assumption that the Hindus have a uniform civil code. In fact, Hindu inheritance is still governed by different laws embodied in variants of the Mitakshara and the Dayabhaga codes. Under neither code are women treated on the same basis as men. Any return of the inheritance laws, including those relating to Hindus and Christians as well as Muslims, must embody this basic principle of civility and must allow the right of exit to those who want to opt for another code, without injury to their interest. The existing law of contract is insufficient for ensuring this. I am grateful to Amiya Bagchi for reminding me of this point.

[46] The two policies differ in the relative weight they place on secular-individual and religious-group identity. The optional component in the policy is also given less importance.

precondition of any reform. Muslim women must be given the right to exit from the system of personal laws. Since no one advocates the removal of the option to be regulated by a common code (a sign, surely, that the Muslim orthodoxy does not view it as threat and a sign too that Muslim women do not see it as a reasonable option), on the question of the choice between a uniform civil code and separate personal laws, I support personal laws not because they are sacred but on the ground that Muslims have a right, like all other citizens of the Indian republic, to a separate cultural identity. This more general reason grounds the right and entails duties on individuals, groups and the state. It is wholly consistent with my position if, on grounds of justice, personal laws are eventually overhauled and replaced by something that better protects their separate identity. However, my point is that whatever it is that replaces personal law is unlikely to and perhaps should not entail a common civil code. India has and should have a common criminal code. It has a set of fundamental rights which are and should be uniform. Since laws pertaining to contract apply equally to all groups, our civil code is already common enough. Any further uniformity is unnecessary and incompatible with the cultural rights of groups.

The general implication of what I have said bears on a difference between liberals and communitarians over the nature of the state and the role it is expected to play. For the communitarian, the ideal state must use its power and authority to encourage the continuation and health of cultural traditions and roles through which each person must find her good life. On the whole, the liberal believes in keeping the state out of the pursuit of the good life by an individual. Liberals generally distrust state power, are more optimistic about the potential within voluntary associations in civil society to realize freedom and to maintain self-limiting devices to check exploitation and domination. This may have to do with differences over how they conceive the state. Although this is not always the case, the residual Weberianism in liberals can't but help viewing the state as an organized monopoly of power and violence, fundamentally authoritarian and therefore always in need of being checked *from the outside*. Communitarians hold the view that the state is a political community and do not hesitate therefore to bring about self-limiting mechanisms *inside* the state. They hope to bring controls within the state by the democratic organization of the political community. For political communitarians, reins on the authoritarian content of state power are necessary and can be effected by the presence of people within state-structures which enable them to bring virtually everything into the political process. This differentiates them from the liberal who keeps certain issues altogether out of the political agenda because they are too personal or contentious.

Notice immediately the two distinct senses in which the term community is used in the preceding paragraph. For democratically minded political communitarians the central issue is the need to shed the traditional liberal fear of the political domain and to bring into it everything, the most personal, even the most contentious. For cultural communitarians, the crucial issue hinges on the constitutive link between identity and particular cultural communities. A cultural communitarian is not necessarily a political communitarian. Likewise, political communitarianism can exist without a commitment to cultural communitarianism, for instance in Rousseau's republicanism. By itself, multiculturalism has close affinities with cultural communitarianism. This is why it may enlist behind authoritarian, anti-democratic political structures. The distinctiveness of *democratic multiculturalism* is that it combines cultural and political communitarianism. Democratic multiculturalism recognizes the importance of cultural identity, the need to maintain cultural difference *and* is committed to bringing these differences into the political domain. Since these differences frequently turn into conflicts, it is also committed to their resolution through dialogue, discussion and negotiation.

Allow me to briefly recapitulate the perspective discussed above. Multiculturalism emphasizes the importance of particular cultural communities and by implication the need for cultural difference. Both republicanism and liberal individualism are equally blind to the importance of multiculturalism and altogether evade multicultural issues. Authoritarian multiculturalism negates individual liberty and autonomy, is obsessed solely with identity and belonging. Liberal multiculturalism recognizes the value of both but denies the entry of issues of identity or belonging into the political domain and therefore, in the last instance, antecedently tilts in favour of individual autonomy. Democratic multiculturalism is fully prepared to tackle the tension between identity and belonging on the one hand and requirements of individual autonomy on the other, and to bring into the political domain both sets of issues. Upon closer examination, many papers in this volume unknowingly converge upon a commitment to democratic multiculturalism, the perspective to which I am sympathetic. Perhaps in two papers this commitment is most explicit: Taylor's and to a degree, Bilgrami's.

Why is democratic rather than liberal multiculturalism a better perspective? By denying the importance of practices and cultural traditions the liberal individualist is unable to even notice the systemic bias and domination of these practices. Liberal multiculturalism is able to at least see these oppressions but by making large areas of public life immune from political intervention, it simply allows in-built oppression and subordination to persist and by insulating the political domain from different identities it ends up—to use Dhareshwar's evocative phrase—'freezing difference'. The plain truth is that oppressive cultural practices flourish due to the indifference of the state. Unless the state uses non-punitive measures that its considerable authority makes possible, and encourages a variety of non-governmental organizations to move in a certain direction, subordination and oppression are likely to continue. The success and failure of Indian secularism provides ample evidence in favour of the need for democratic multiculturalism. The removal of oppression and subordination has been a function of a successful and effective democratic state. The state has had to democratically intervene in religious and cultural practices to get rid of oppressive practices. Such practices have continued, congealed and become worse whenever the state has refrained from intervention or acted without democratic legitimacy.

Does democratic multiculturalism work in all contexts? Can conflicts always be resolved through discussion and dialogue? Is democratic multiculturalism insufficiently attentive to the depth and extent of conflicts? Is the liberal multiculturalist fear of the political domain simply an effect of its acute sensitivity to deep conflicts hidden within cultural difference? Of course one should not be blind to differences but should we not be wary of exacerbating the morally repugnant forms that cultural conflict assumes? Suppose that the complete set of political strategies is divided broadly into two categories: the politics of involvement and the politics of detachment. The first entails an engagement with disagreement and brings every issue out into the open. The second kind compels an abstraction from the public domain, imposes restraint, and asks us to keep some issues to ourselves rather than force them into the glare of the public eye. Is democratic multiculturalism a politics of involvement and is it wise to implement it no matter what the context? Perhaps the politicization of culture and collective identity is justified, but are there any limits to this? Can an issue be unwittingly over-politicized? Isn't this dangerous? I believe it is. Elementary sociological investigation draws attention to another painful fact, i.e. that involvement requires self-confidence which flows from sustained participation and the habits of winning. Those excluded from participation and those who lose persistently tend to detach themselves from politics. In this context, an assertive politics of involvement cuts both ways. It brings hitherto marginalized groups within the domain of politics. Conversely, it may help those already in politics to take complete control and exclude some groups altogether. To prevent such domination, a better strategy may well be to support mutual detachment. Occasionally, the best available strategy to contain hegemonizing forces is to get everybody to support *a politics of reciprocal detachment*. In short, a space must be found within democratic multiculturalism for liberal politics because at least it ensures that no one loses out completely—a wise choice in certain contexts—and, therefore, it remains a reliable fall-back strategy. Let me reformulate this point by deploying some terms I introduced in section III. When the first moment of particularized hierarchy is safely buried in the past, we can confidently move from the second moment in the dialectic to the third, final moment of particularized equality—to democratic multiculturalism. If on the other hand one step in the direction of the third really takes us two steps back to the first moment, then we must simply hold on to the moment of universalistic equality that constitutes liberal multiculturalism. Under certain conditions, the eminently liberal fear of over-politicization is justified. Since I believe that subordination is never a thing of the past but always an ever present danger in societies everywhere, even within egalitarian social structures, I cannot help but conclude that a version of liberal multiculturalism must have a permanent place in larger democratic politics.

VIII. Multiculturalism and Bitter Conflicts

So far in the discussion on multiculturalism an underlying assumption has been that cultural conflicts are fairly controlled, and occur within the parameters of civic peace. But societies may also undergo civil war or be on the verge of it. Under such volatile conditions what if cultural communities are over-politicized? What if we are dealing with problems not of inferiority, internal oppression or conflicts within acceptable moral limits, the usual kind that liberals take into account, but with acute, intractable, insurmountable difficulties of a multicultural society where bitter relations between groups have soured and turned rancid? Consider for example post-partition societies where members cannot cope with new boundaries and borders. Michael Ignatieff reports a conversation with an East German, inhabitant originally of Upper Silesia, a German province of what is now Poland.[47] When asked if he ever wanted to visit Upper Silesia, he said, 'Not as a tourist, never. Only with a German flag.' Such resentment was not exactly uncommon among Punjabi refugees in India. Consider the bitter legacy of apartheid in South Africa or the emotional environment of hatred and revenge that exists in Palestine or Bosnia. What strategy can be devised to cope with societies with a bitter aftertaste of horrific conflicts?

It is a brute, frequently neglected fact that splenetic memories of the past fester in the mind. David Hume wrote perceptively about animosities bequeathed from one generation to another. 'Nothing is more usual than to see parties, which have begun upon a real difference, continue even after the difference is lost. When men are once enlisted on opposite sides, they contract an affection to the persons with whom they are united, and an animosity against their antagonists; and these passions they often transmit to their posterity.'[48] Only the very dogmatic or blind analyst will fail to see that a great deal of nationalist agenda place after place is merely about settling old scores.[49] People are often divided by the mere fact that at some time in the past one group ruled over the other. It is the memory of domination not difference by itself

[47] Ignatieff, *Blood and Belonging*, p. 83.

[48] David Hume, *Political Writings*, Hackett Publishing Company, Cambridge, 1994, p. 160.

[49] Ignatieff, *Blood and Belonging*, p. 161.

which turns conflict into a downward spiral of political violence. Some societies have the luxury of ignoring the past or looking at only its pleasant dimension. Others must deal head-on with it and face its ghosts, phantoms and demons.

If I were to single out one important issue that has been inadequately discussed in this volume then surely it is collective memory, the problem of confronting the past; a confrontation that goes beyond mere cerebral engagement. How does a divided nation work its way towards this deeper, more meaningful engagement with its past? Remembering the past is always a tricky issue, however. For a start, it may reinforce asymmetries of power. The fear of physical suffering in the future feeds on the remembrance of past acts of violence or repression. It encourages passivity and obedience in victims which feed interests of the powerful. But such remembrances cut both ways. If memory of suffering is kept alive, reprisal may occur at future, opportune moments. Therefore, among former perpetrators, a motivated forgetfulness of their own wrong doings, accompanied with the hope that former victims will quickly forget past suffering is not uncommon when asymmetries of power dissolve. In this context, calls to let bygones be bygones, to wipe the slate clean or to start afresh, work unabashedly in favour of the perpetrators. Forgetting is not a fair compromise and should be unacceptable to victims. At any rate, a state of forgetfulness cannot be brought about intentionally. The demand on the victim to forget past injustice is in reality an injunction to forgive and not to publicly recall past injustice.

Most calls to forget are attempts in disguise to prevent victims from publicly remembering in the fear that 'there is a dragon living on the patio and we had better not provoke it.' But it is doubtful if this is a good strategy for repairing wounds or achieving reconciliation. When a person is wronged, he is made not only to suffer physically but is mentally scarred, the most injurious of which is the damage to his sense of self-respect, if he is left with any residue of it. As Jeffrie Murphy points out, when a person is wronged he receives an unequivocal, clear indication about his irrelevance and marginality.[50] The aggressor communicates that in his scheme of things the victim counts for nothing at all. Since self-esteem hinges upon critical opinion of the other, messages sent

[50] J. G. Murphy, 'Forgiveness and Resentment,' in Murphy and Hampton, *Forgiveness and Mercy*, OUP, 1990, p. 25.

by the wrongdoer significantly lower self-esteem in the wronged. The insult and degradation inflicted is in fact a deeper moral injury. This loss of self-esteem is not addressed by demands to forget past injuries. Indeed, it inflicts further damage. Asking victims to forget past evils is to treat them as if no great wrong to them has been done, as if they have nothing to feel resentful about. This only diminishes them further. Another way in which this happens is to what Jeremy Waldron draws attention:

> When we are told to let bygones be bygones, we need to bear in mind also that the forgetfulness being urged on us is seldom the blank slate of historical oblivion. Thinking quickly fills up the vacuum with plausible tales of self-satisfaction, on the one side, and self-deprecation on the other. Beneficiaries of injustice then come to believe that gains accrue to them due to the virtue of their race or culture and victims too easily accept that their misfortune is caused by inherent inferiority.[51]

Waldron is on to something important here. The call to forget reinforces loss of self-esteem in the victim. Furthermore, neglected moral injuries putrify the demoralization of the victim. Under these conditions, past perpetrators feel that they can get away with murder and they grow in confidence that such injuries can be inflicted without resistance even in future. Therefore, rather than prevent, forgetting ends up facilitating evil. I can't help but conclude that proper remembering alone restores dignity and self-respect to the victim.

A proper remembrance is critical if wounds of the victim are to be healed. It is also necessary to fulfill the collective needs of a badly damaged society. A pervasive social condition bolstered by an argument from Hobbes challenges the pro-remembrance view. It is an ugly, uncomfortable fact that societies remember their heroic deeds but suppress memories of collective injustice. Recall Ernest Renan's remark that nations are constituted by a great deal of forgetting. In a perceptive essay, Sheldon Wolin wonders if collective memory is an accomplice of injustice and whether by its silence on collective wrongs, it does not signify the very limits of justice.[52] He asks if a society can ever afford to remember events in which members feel tainted by a 'kind of corporate complicity

[51] J. Waldron, 'Superseding Historic Injustice', *Ethics*, vol. 103, October 1994, p. 6.

[52] S. Wolin, 'Injustice and Collective Memory', in *The Presence of the Past*, Johns Hopkins University, 1989, pp. 32–46.

in an act of injustice done in their name'. Can France remember the Saint Bartholomew massacre, America, its civil war, India, its partition? Can these be remembered by being represented in civic rituals? One philosopher who endorsed collective forgetting was Thomas Hobbes. Suppression of memories of past wrongs is essential because if society is treated as a building made of stones then some stones that have an 'irregularity of figure take more room from others' and so must be discarded. Hobbes's covenant was a device to incorporate social amnesia into the foundation of society. Commenting on this, Wolin notes that, for Hobbes a necessary condition of social amnesia is the dehistoricization of human beings.

Is dehistoricization possible? I think not. Besides, it is to live in a fool's paradise to imagine that as grievances recede into the past and are half-forgotten, they will somehow cease to be real. As Ignatieff put it, 'Collective myth has no need of personal memory or experience to retain its force.' Muslims invaded India in the twelfth century but for many Hindus, even destitute Muslims continue to be invaders who killed, destroyed and converted. The conquest of Quebec by the English happened more than two centuries ago but the project of Quebec nationalists 'involves a reconquest of the conquest'. In many countries, people remarkably similar in essential respects are ready to kill simply because once upon a time one was ruled by the other. The simple strategy of forgetting has simply not worked. Only an appropriate engagement with the past makes for a livable common future. Of course, one must guard against cosmetic remembrance. An engagement with the past must take place by reason but also at the level of emotions. If grievances are not properly addressed old resentments bubble forth. Oddly, animosity between groups is sustained even when it goes against their current interest. This happens because emotional reactions ingrained in the human mind remain insensitive to altered circumstances and passed on to successive generations. Like property, animosities are inherited too!

Nonetheless, former victims in fragmented societies eventually need to get on with their lives rather than be consumed by their suffering. Perhaps victims need to forget just about as much as they need to remember. People who carry deep resentment and grievance against one another are hardly likely to build a society together. Therefore, an injunction to forget is not *entirely* unreasonable. I believe timing is of the essence here. Forgetting too quickly or without redressal, by failing to heal adequately, inevitably brings with it a society haunted by its past. One can't forget entirely, too soon and without a modicum of justice. Clearly, while some forgetting at an appropriate time is necessary, a complete erasure is neither sufficient nor desirable for healing or for the construction of a minimally decent society. Moreover, while specific acts of wrongdoing need to be forgotten eventually, a general sense of the wrong and of the horror of evil acts must never be allowed to recede from collective memory. Such remembering is crucial to prevent acts of wrongdoing in the future. Without a proper engagement with the past and an institutionalized remembering, societies are condemned to repeat, reenact and relive the horror. Forgetting is not a good strategy for societies transiting from morally obnoxious to morally acceptable situations.

Reflection on some of these uncomfortable issues shows the inadequacy of the philosophical treatment of multiculturalism. The deficiency is due to several sources. Perhaps liberal philosophy screens out the full range of experiential motivation. For instance, it wrongly supposes that grievances cease to be real just because they are in the past.[53] Quite possibly, it is too rationalist and does not give emotion its due. Could it be that a proper multicultural philosophy develops only by accepting that violence is neither feared nor hated by everyone? Could it even be true that 'liberals have not understood the force of male resentment that has accumulated through centuries of pacification of politics'?[54] Perhaps there is need to understand how ethnic revolts tap this male resentment. Alternatively, the very framing of issues may be flawed. To pin the blame for conflict on rival cultures conceptually and ethically segregated from one another may miss the real nature of conflict in which togetherness, sameness and a variety of emotions which these produce play a much greater role than is allowed by rationalist traditions within liberalism.[55] Is it not true that the dialectic between ethnic and civic nationalism is determined 'as much by ethnic groups as by those who wish away problems of unity or who suppose that patriotism is for fools'?[56]

[53] Ignatieff, *Blood and Belonging*, p. 246.
[54] Ibid.
[55] Ibid., p. 244.
[56] Ibid., p. 102.

The hold of face-to-face interactions on nationalist imaginations, in particular the clutch of the family may be a real factor in deep conflicts.

Communitarian advocates of cultural belonging will benefit from recognizing the relationship between violence and an intense sense of belonging. If belonging sanctions self-sacrifice, it also legitimizes killing the other. Proponents of a politics of recognition may not fully see that even when self-affirmation is unavoidable, it takes positive as well as negative forms. People justify all manner of wrong deeds in the name of self-affirmation. Only a proper appreciation of these facts gives an adequate explanation of why people who have lived peacefully with each other for long suddenly turn hostile and also why large, abstract ideologies manage to enthuse ordinary people. Bilgrami rightly points out that ordinary people are not fundamentalist but perhaps like most of us, he insufficiently recognizes just how enmeshed the lives of ordinary people are in little holocausts hidden within each small community. We may never hit upon a stable solution to these problems without grasping all of this.

It is in this spirit that I interpret Stanley Fish's critique of philosophical multiculturalism: that it is superficial and unable to appreciate cultural difference where it ought to matter most.[57] Some forms of multiculturalism respect other cultures up to a point, stopping short just where some value lying deep at the centre of the other culture produces an action that violates norms of 'civilized decency'. Fish aptly calls this boutique multiculturalism that 'opposes the death sentence on Rushdie, is hostile to Afro-centrist curriculum, detests animal sacrifice or use of a control substance, and cannot grant legitimacy to polygamy'. In short, boutique multiculturalism fails at the very point where any kind of multiculturalism must succeed, namely in arenas of deep difference over values; it cannot take seriously the core values of the cultures it ostensibly tolerates. It rejects the idea of deep difference because the core identity of humans is constituted for it by elements shared by all. Fish distinguishes boutique multiculturalism from what he calls strong multiculturalism, the view for which at least a part of our identity is shaped by differing particular cultures. For strong multiculturalism, at some level a

[57] S. Fish, 'Boutique Multiculturalism'.

deep irreconcilable difference exists. But in the last instance even strong multiculturalism bows to some supra-cultural universal and so, like boutique multiculturalism, it misinterprets at least some conflicts between particular cultures as a clash between the particular and the universal. By elevating one particular culture wrongly on a universalist pedestal, it creates new asymmetries of power or suppresses the distinctiveness of separate cultures. The lesson to be drawn, according to Fish, is to refuse to see multiculturalism as a philosophical problem or conceptual puzzle but rather to see it as a demographic fact that generates crises diffused only by what Taylor calls inspired adhoccery. Philosophically, reconciliation may never be possible but a way can be devised of accommodating particular differences within a community without coming to blows with each other. Each situation provides an opportunity for improvization rather than annotation for the application of principles. A solution for it is bound to be temporary, anyhow.

I don't share Fish's skepticism about the possibility of transcultural universals. So I guess for me strong multiculturalism goes roughly along the right path. Without dismissing the possibility of universals, strong multiculturalism allows for deep difference as also for fierce conflicts. It fractures the complacency of liberal individualism, of a simple-minded republicanism and of boutique multiculturalism. It shatters the myth that conflicts are always generated, to borrow a term from the philosophy of science, under conditions of closure. I concede, however, that in more open situations, where conflicts spin out of hand and human behaviour is anything but predictable or systematic, only Stanley Fish's recommendations are likely to work. *A modus vivendi* is the only way out for societies where divisions go very, very deep or where relations are particularly raw.

Two other things are more or less certain. First, no strategy can work in the absence of an effective state. Conditions of peaceful coexistence are not reproduced automatically but require a fairly strong state. Second, a solution is hardly likely to work unless a modicum of democratic politics exists. A minimally democratic state may not be good enough but what it may manage to prevent is much worse.

2

Identity and Integrity

Alan Montefiore

There are all sorts of ways in which the terms 'identity' and 'integrity' may be taken. Equally there are all sorts of ways in which people may express their concerns, in one natural language or another, about what many would very naturally talk about as matters of identity or integrity without making use of either of these terms at all. So much is obvious. There is also, perhaps, some more or less vague general sense that identity and integrity must be in some way intertwined, that to deny or refuse one's identity is to exhibit a certain lack of integrity, that a threat to the one is likely (or bound?) to constitute a threat to the other; but what this vague general sense actually amounts to is rather less obvious.

Let us start with identity. There has, of course, been a great deal of debate among analytic philosophers and their more obvious ancestors about the proper way to understand the (not always distinguished, but not altogether equivalent) notions of personal and self identity. This debate has tended to focus on and at times to become entangled in a number of distinguishably different issues. In the introduction to her collection *The Identities of Persons* Amélie Rorty has the following passage:

Controversies about personal identity have been magnified by the fact that there are a number of different questions at issue... (1) Some have concentrated on analyses of class differentiation: What distinguishes the class of persons from their nearest neighbour...? (2) Others have been primarily interested in individual differentiation: What are the criteria for the numerical distinctness of persons who have the same general description?... (3) Still others have been interested in individual reidentification: What are the criteria for reidentifying the same individual in different contexts, under different descriptions, or at different times?...(4) Yet others have been primarily interested in individual identification: What sorts of characteristics identify a person as *essentially* the person she is, such that if those characteristics were changed, she would be a significantly different person, though she might still be differentiated and reidentified as the same?[1]

Although there are other ways in which this essentially untidy field might be divided up, most philosophers in the so-called Anglo-Saxon tradition have been predominantly interested in one or another interplay of one or another version of Amélie Rorty's first three sets of questions. Conversely, most cultural or political theorists have been predominantly interested in one or another version of her fourth set of questions, whether focused, as she herself focuses, on questions of individual identity or, more typically, on that of the various types of group or society to which individuals might be held or hold themselves to belong. I myself have tried to argue elsewhere that there is, despite initial appearances perhaps, 'a fundamental structural interrelationship between what one might call the outline concepts of individuation and reidentification on the one hand and those of what Amélie Rorty calls essential identification on the other.' All the same, there is a certain rationale to this division of interest in as much as while questions of individual and class individuation and reidentification raise issues of a primarily conceptual order, those of 'essential identification' are bound to depend very largely on essentially contingent considerations of historical and social circumstance and of personal or social evaluation.

As one who was philosophically brought up in post-war Oxford, I have been trained to set out on the basis of essentially conceptual considerations. My starting-point here, however, is to be found within the tradition of European philosophy as a whole, and rests on the consideration that so far as human beings are concerned at least, the (self-)identity of their own self-identifications is indissolubly bound up with difference. Here I am thinking not only of the references implicit in each one's own self-identification to the differences between it and those irreducibly

[1] Amélie Rorty, *The Identities of Persons*, University of California Press, 1976.

'external' identifications that other potential participants in one's own universe of discourse must in principle be able and may in practice be ready to impose upon oneself, important though these differences certainly are. Nor am I thinking only of those differences between self and other which so many contemporary thinkers have seen as somehow jointly, if uncertainly, constitutive of the respective identities of both. I am thinking also of the sense in which one can never identify oneself as the particular participant in the world of human discourse (reflection and communication) that one is, without opening up at least some potential gap, some failure of integral coincidence, between oneself as self-identifier and the self-identification that one may in one way or another have provided. But this calls for some brief explanatory recapitulation of what in their fuller versions are certain long and complex, even if by now very largely familiar, lines of argument.

The first and most crucial point to make is that to identify oneself at all presumes a certain continuity of self-identity, a certain identity of oneself with oneself, through a certain period of time. This dependence of identity on a certain temporal persistence is just about self-evident in the case of anyone's 'essential identity'; there is no normal sense in which I can be, say, an Englishman, a Jew, a white male, a political liberal, a vegetarian, a philosopher or a supporter of Manchester United for just a few hours at a time. It is also true for self-identification as the particular individual that one is, whether as this individual rather than some other or as the same individual as that of some shorter or longer time ago. This is not to say that something may not come into existence in some fleeting instant and be gone the instant after. If modern physics is to be believed, for instance, certain particles behave to all intents and purposes just like that. But such entities do not identify themselves; they just are whatever they are, and are identifiable as such by quite different sorts of entities, in this case by the scientists who have the relevant capacities to do so.

To identify anything, oneself included, as being this one (of a particular kind) and not another one (of the same relevant kind), one has to be able to make some appropriately meaningful gesture. One might put this by saying that one has to be able, in some way or another, to point to oneself. But pointing to oneself, as indeed to anything else, cannot be understood simply in terms of the alignment of a finger along some appropriate axis. Such physical alignments are only to be understood as constituting meaningful pointing in contexts where the putative pointer may reasonably be understood to be capable of picking out that at which he or she is 'pointing' from the overall context or environment as constituting some specific feature or configuration of it—that is, in effect, to be capable of characterizing it, whether explicitly or implicitly, as coming under one sort of classification rather than another. Otherwise there can be no reason to interpret the positioning of the finger as a gesture signifying the pointing out of any one feature of the environment rather than any other. For it to be *meaningful* as appropriate to the identification of *this* rather than of *that*, it must, so to speak, bear as presupposition some classificatory sense.

The appropriateness or inappropriateness of an in effect classificatory gesture, however (and if there is no sense in which it might be or have been inappropriate, there can be no sense in which it could be appropriate either), is wholly bound up with its in principle repeatability by the same agent of signification on some other or further occasion. (Or, in special cases, with the possibility of its being envisaged in *advance* of the occasion of its use as being either appropriate or inappropriate.) There has to exist between the symbol and the symbolized, between the pointing and that which is being pointed at, the logical space for an in principle fallible intention of signification, if we are to have anything more than the simple coexistence of two different features of the physically occurrent environment. Either way, we—we human beings, as Kant might have said—can have no access to the *logical* space necessary to acts of meaningful signification other than through a reference to the time of *real* possible experience, a time through which whoever may seek to identify or to reidentify himself or herself as this person rather than that, must clearly persist, if meaningfulness is to be sustained and the identification or reidentification is to have any sense.

To persist as self-identical with oneself through time, however, is to persist across a space or gap within which differences between oneself and oneself, and not only those differences between oneself and all that is not-self which are necessarily implicit in every self-identification, are bound to emerge. The reason why this is so is that if between times t and $t+1$ nothing *whatsoever* had changed in the nature and configuration of the universe, there would be no basis for saying that there had in fact been any lapse of time between the two, and t would in effect simply equal t+1. But if there *have* been changes, as there necessarily must have been, then even if they are not strictly to be counted as changes in myself, there must be certain changes in my relations to some other features of my universe; and we can have no *a priori* guarantee that changes in my relations to others or in my general situation are not to be counted as relevant to how I am myself most appropriately to be identified from some relevant point of view.

All this, then, is fairly evident in the case of what, following Amélie Rorty, I have been calling essential identity. She may have been thinking primarily of the individually personal characteristics that may be held to 'identify a person as *essentially* the person she is', but for the great majority of people, of course, their relations to certain other people, their job or their role in society, their origins or their status within some broader social group or groups to which they belong—a family, a caste, a tribe, a nation, a religious organization and so on—may also count, be counted by themselves or by others, as among the strands entering into their 'essential identity'; and in such cases changes to others or changes in the nature or status of the relevant group, whether brought about by its own activity or by changes in the attitudes of others towards it, may well constitute changes in the essential identities of whoever is to be counted as remaining among that group's members.

Changes over time in the nature, behaviour, ruling principles or status of a social group may affect those whose membership of it is taken by themselves or by others to constitute part of their essential identity in different ways. It may indeed be that what happens to the group, or what is done in its name, is of such significance that it carries over to affect those whose own essential personal identities are defined by reference to it. I have known people who, while deeply disapproving of certain of their country's policies, have nevertheless felt themselves to so contaminated by them, by virtue of their inescapable involvement through their own personal 'essential identity' in whatever their country did, as to have to accept with shame some share of vicarious responsibility for what had been done. (One may recall Sartre's 'acknowledgment' that World War II was also his war, not because he himself individually had done anything to bring it about, but simply because it was, as he judged it, a bourgeois war and he, Sartre, was inescapably a member of the bourgeoisie.) It is never, of course, easy to decide no longer actually to belong in the relevant essential sense to what had previously counted as one's own nation or family, whatever one may think of the way in which it has evolved. Often, indeed, there may be no serious or honest sense in which any such option is open; in other cases, however, ceasing to be a member may nevertheless be a real possibility. (The plight of the abandoned or ejected Communist, for example, who may need to turn to some other strongly authoritarian group to re-establish a 'sense of identity', is all too familiar in our time.) In yet other cases certain kinds of change in the nature or status of a group may (not always wholly predictably) raise the question of whether it is actually any longer to be identified as 'numerically' one and the same group at all. The criteria for the continuing identity of such groups are, not surprisingly, often a matter of controversy, sometimes extremely bitter, either between their own members or among concerned outsiders. (The Anglican Church, for instance, may be thought to have provided a number of such examples.) Whichever way such controversies may go, someone who has hitherto defined himself in crucial part by reference to his membership of a group that he now deems to have ceased to exist as such, is likely to have to face no little disturbance in the manner of his own self-conception. And there are, of course, many other possible variations on these themes.

In fact, changes in the general environment may lead to changes in what may be counted as constituting numerical identity even in cases of individual identification and reidentification. As we have already noted, it is only possible to identify a given individual by pointing meaningfully at him, her or it against the background of some understanding of what *kind* of individual or item it is that one is pointing at, that is to say against the background of some in principle communicable awareness of the nature of the classificatory or sortal term by which the kind in question may be determined. But, notoriously, different kinds of sortal terms determine (or leave partially indeterminate) different conditions for what may be counted as the continued identity through time and space, through one kind of surface change or another, of *any* given type of individual (and not only of social groups) before that individual is deemed to have undergone transformation into something altogether different. And we know that many different factors may affect the evolution of a speech community's sense of the sortal terms to be adopted in one context or another or of the changes in sortal terms that it may come to seem necessary to accept.

Hence the familiar riddles asking whether the oak is or is not the very same plant as the acorn from which it has grown, the butterfly the same 'what?' as the caterpillar of its beginning, the car the same vehicle, or alternatively the same item of property, as that which I used to possess, but virtually all parts of which have now been replaced. The conditions of human existence being what they are, 'we' do not normally expect the internal or external differences that may have occurred in the state of a man or woman between their identification as a given individual at one moment and their attempted reidentification at another to give rise to any analogous perplexity. However, there are real puzzles about how one should best interpret the phenomena of such known conditions as, for example, commissurotomy; and some have been led to wonder how we might deal with analogous riddles of identity should brain transplants, for example, enter the realm of practical medicine or, a much more fantastic Parfitian hypothesis, should we start to behave like amoebae and simply split from time to time or at other moments fuse together.

But who exactly in this 'we' to whose 'normal expectations' I have just rather lightly referred? Does it include, for instance, believers in the possibility of reincarnation or possession? Or those for whom a ruling principle of individual human identity might be constituted by some ancestral or other relational principle, carrying with it even changes of name as any given individual was transformed by being either received into or expelled from the relationship? 'Something', of course, must be identifiable as the same something even under such major changes of identity as these. We may have no immediately available term for whatever it is that is first caterpillar, then chrysalis and finally butterfly, but we know that such a term must be constructible on the basis of what we understand to be the continuities that underlie these transformations of identity. The question of how far and in what way apparent subjective awareness, or memory, may or may not constitute, or perhaps only contribute to, a criterion of personal identity is puzzling in a not altogether dissimilar way. We shall return to this point in a moment. The immediate point, however, is that we cannot on the basis of formal considerations alone determine which of those differences in the particular individual or group which may intervene between one moment of self-identification and another, may or may not be such as to force us to recognize a break in the continuity of even an otherwise spatio-temporally continuous chain of apparent identity.

Identification and reidentification, identity, difference and time, numerical identity and 'essential identity' are themes which are all intertwined, by one's primary concern with the identities of historically given social groups or with those of the individual human beings who may make up their membership. What exactly may be at stake in the general contemporary preoccupation with such feelings as may find expression as, say, pride in one's own personal, cultural, racial or national identity, or as distress or disorientation in the face of its threatened or perceived loss, may often be far from clear; what is clear is that this is typically a concern with the nature of what we have been calling essential identity rather than with the criteria for individual differentiation or reidentification. People may often, of course, be concerned to determine *whether* the person they have to deal with now is the same person as whoever it may be; whether, for example, the old man before them in the dock is the same person as he who was a prison guard at Treblinka. But they are not, for the most part puzzled as to *what* being the same person would consist in.

This is not to say, however, that uncertainties over the very nature of individual numerical identity may not sometimes involve issues of very real practical importance. We have already noted the rare and very special case of commissurotomy. But there are other examples. In the second half of the century in Germany, for instance (but it might have been almost anywhere), a girl was killed in the course of a ceremony designed to expel Hitler from possession of her body; that at any rate was the description of the affair as presented by the prosecution in the ensuing trial, though not all of those involved might have agreed that it was, strictly speaking, the girl who had been killed. (I presume, though I do not know, that some might have claimed that what, unfortunately, had happened had been the destruction of the body which was normally that of the girl in question, but which had been temporarily in Hitler's possession.) Or again, there was in the late forties the case of Gunther Podola, a professional armed robber, who in the course of business, so to speak, shot and killed a policeman. When he was eventually run to earth and 'jumped' in a hotel bedroom he suffered some degree of concussion in the course of arrest and, so he claimed at least, a degree of retrospective amnesia stretching back sufficiently far to cover the time of his crime. The defence accepted that the bullet which had killed the policeman had come from the gun still in Podola's possession at the time of his arrest and that it had been the hand of his body that had held the gun, and the fingers of that hand that had indeed squeezed the trigger, at the time of the murder. Appealing, however, to a Lockean theory of what constitutes the identity of a person (according to Locke a 'forensic' term as opposed, of course, to that of 'a man', which, he argued, refers simply to the biological individual), they maintained that as the person before the jury had no memory of the crime of which he was accused, he could not properly be held to be identical with the person responsible for it. In the event, the case went right up to the House of Lords, who decided against Podola *on grounds of 'public policy'*, namely that, claims to amnesia being so difficult to determine, if once they were admitted as constituting an acceptable defence, it might prove unacceptably difficult to obtain convictions and most of the deterrent force of the punishment stipulated by law might well be lost. Podola went to the gallows—for at that time the death penalty was still in force—still protesting that he had no memory of the killing for which he was being executed. In such a case it is perhaps not misleading to say that an issue of numerical personal identity, where the stakes were those of life or death, was decided on broadly political grounds.[2]

It is also worth recalling that there is, as I noted earlier on, 'despite initial appearances perhaps, a fundamental structural interrelationship between what one might call the outline concepts of individuation and reidentification on the one hand and those of what Amélie Rorty called essential identification on the other.' On the one hand, there can be no discursive (or descriptive)

[2] Compare, for a very different illustration of the same basic point, the very interesting paper by Len Ang 'To Be or Not to Be Chinese: Diaspora, Culture and Postmodern Ethnicity', *Southeast Asian Journal of Social Science*, vol. 21, no. 1, 1993, which ends up as follows: 'In short, if I am inescapably Chinese by *descent*, I am only sometimes Chinese by *consent*. When and how is a matter of politics.'

identification of anybody or anything at all unless the identifier, or describer, is able to identify himself and other participants in his discourse as the persisting individuals that they must be if any of them are to secure the necessary minimum stability of intelligible meaning across time; on the other hand, there can be no way of identifying a particular individual as such unless the identifier is also able in principle to say, or otherwise to indicate, something about the individual that he seeks to identify in broadly descriptive or classificatory terms. But such terms must always belong to the particular language of some one or another particular speech community. This means that the meanings that they bear will belong to that network of meanings through which the speech community in question articulates its own particular way of discriminating and structuring the world (and, above all, the world of its own social relations). Moreover, since in living language there can be no way of cleanly separating off meaning from force, it means too that the ensemble of terms through which each new entrants on the social scene learn to identify themselves will carry with them, into their very identities as it were, some vestige of those forces which 'belonged' to the first place (or places) of identification in the speech community (or communities) to which they first found themselves belonging. In later life one may, of course, go on to acquire further languages. However, no one can easily shake off or lose touch with the deep formational influence of their own first language or languages; and those who do so risk finding it a less than unqualifiedly happy experience. All this, no doubt, helps to explain why language plays the central role that it nearly always does in the formation and on-going definition of so many different types of cultural identity.

There is one other point to be made concerning the identifications of selves and others, before we return to pick up the threads of integrity. It concerns this time a difference, a tension indeed, to be found lurking within both self and other, as they are identified or identify themselves as participants in the realm of human discourse, that is to say as human subjects. This point remains, certainly, a controversial one; I nevertheless make it with considerable confidence—even though it would need vastly more detailed working out than it can possibly be given here.

To identify oneself (or anyone else) is, whatever else it may be, to situate oneself (or whatever other person) within the world of nature in relation to whatever other items are to be located within the bounds of space and time. This is, on Kant's view of the matter, for example, at once to introduce within oneself a fundamental dichotomy, the dichotomy, as he put it in the Transcendental Deduction in the second edition of the *Critique of Pure Reason*, between 'the I that thinks' and 'the self that is given to myself in intuition'. (B155) The problem, in Kantian terms, arises broadly speaking in the following way. Mere sensory inputs cannot on their own provide their recipient with a reflectively (reflexively) recognizable world of experience. For such a world to be possible, the intuitions (or sense-data) have to be brought under concepts. But, (i) conceptualization, being a matter of classifying experience according to certain rules or norms, is possible only in so far as the conceptualizer can make sense of the distinction between how things may appear to him or her at any given moment and how they might actually be. However, (ii) this distinction only makes sense on the assumption that things are in general determined to be what they are, to appear in the time, place and manner in which they appear, by something other than the way in which they happen to strike the observer at any given moment of perception. Nevertheless, (iii) this 'something other' cannot intelligibly be thought of as some sort of 'object in itself' inaccessible to sensory perception, some sort of substance existing unknowably behind a Lockean veil of perception. It has rather to be understood as rooted in the way in which the world of experience is structured by the conceptual ordering which thinking experiencers are bound to impose on their own 'manifold of intuitions', or sensory field, as they bring it to the intelligibility of concepts by virtue of the way in which all conceptual thinking must be structured at its very highest level of generality. It is this structure that provides the indispensable objective reference of all recognitional judgement; and it is, according to Kant, essentially one of a thoroughgoing causal determinism of all that can appear in space-time. This means that to identify anything or anybody, oneself as much as anyone else, as existing as an individual item within the structure of the spatial-temporal continuum is *ipso facto* to identify it as coming under strict causal laws. At the same time this causally determinate order or ordering derives from the conceptualizing activity of any rational or thinking subject that is itself spatio-temporally embodied. Such a subject—you, me, any and every other thinking human being, according to Kant—can in principle never actually observe itself in the meaning-giving act of imposing this order; in so far as it does meet with itself (as object among other objects) in observational experience, it meets itself as belonging to this causally determinate world. It is, nevertheless, inescapably aware of itself as active, as thinking and as seeking to determine the ordered movements of its thought not according to the laws of causal temporality, but according to its own atemporal order of validity. How can it be both these things at once; how can it lie, as Kant put it, from one point of view under the laws of heteronomy and yet from another point of view be autonomous? Herein lies the fundamental puzzle of Kantian duality.

Kant, of course, thought that he could somehow resolve this tension by distinguishing between the realm of appearances, or phenomena, and that of noumena, or things in themselves. Most of his successors have thought that this distinction provided no resolution, but rather a dead-end of unacceptable paradox. For myself, I should agree that we are faced here with a paradox, but one that seems to me to be not so much a dead-end as a source of constantly renewed stimulus, a reminder of the limits as well as the necessity of rationality. Still, however that may be, the dualities of agent and observer, of subject and object, of reason and cause, of 'pour soi' and 'en soi' recur in one form or another in the thought of many other philosophers, radically opposed although most of them are to any form of Kantian dualism. Thus, while different thinkers may lay very different stress upon, may draw very different morals from, their recognition of some such fundamental duality within men's and women's identifications of themselves and of others, as human beings in this sense at least like unto themselves, and while most perhaps would insist that any such duality must ultimately be resolvable at a level of ontological monism, nearly all would seem to recognize that some version of this difference lies close to the heart of human identity—the difference between the self-directing and (morally) responsible agent and the self that is the object of that agent's observation and attempts at causal understanding.

So much, for the moment, for identity. What of integrity? It is no longer the fashion to go in for what one might call dictionary philosophy. Nevertheless, the Oxford English Dictionary may provide us with a usefully sober starting-point. The root meaning of integrity has, of course, to do with wholeness and that, unsurprisingly, is where the dictionary starts: '1. The condition of having no part or element wanting; unbroken state; material wholeness, completeness, entirety.' It goes on: '2. Unimpaired or uncorrupted state; original perfect condition; soundness. 3. a. Innocence, sinlessness. b. Soundness of moral principle; the character of uncorrupted virtue; uprightness, honesty, sincerity.' (None of the dates attached to these diverse headings, incidentally, is later than 1678.) By way of cross-comparison and confirmation it is also worth noting what Le Grand Robert has to say under the heading of Intégrité: '1. Etat d'une chose qui est dans son entier, complète, intégrale... qui est demeurée intacte, inaltérée... (Intégrité est plus qualitatif qu'intégralité, réservée généralement à ce qui est mesurable.) 2. Etat d'une personne intègre. Voir Honnêteté, incorruptibilité, justice; probité...' It is clear that so far as the two terms 'integrity' and 'intégrité' are concerned the two languages are not very far apart.

It is helpful to hold on to what both dictionaries identify as the first or root meaning of 'integrity', namely, 'wholeness' or 'completeness'. Both connect this notion with that of an original state. A state of integrity is a state of completeness that has not been broken or corrupted, qui est demeuré intacte, inaltéré. This reference to an 'original perfect condition' is preserved in the OED in the transition to an overtly moral sense: 'original perfect condition... the character of uncorrupted virtue; uprightness, honesty, sincerity.' Corruption is like rust, something which, coming later, eats away at that which it attacks, so that that which was once in pristine condition is now corrupted, spoilt, abîmé. The ruling underlying metaphor is that of a fall, of a human nature that is, in terms of its origins, good or 'innocent', but from whose original perfection something has been, perhaps almost from the beginning, lost. If something had not gone wrong, we should all have remained intact, unchanged—still upright, honest and sincere in our original wholeness.

There is, of course, no overall reason, outside a certain theological view of the world, to insist on preserving within our present understanding of the virtues of integrity, uprightness, honesty and sincerity this reference to an original state of perfection and 'sinlessness'. It is equally possible to think of perfection as a state to be achieved, or at any rate aimed at, by individuals, societies or mankind at large. The metaphor of a fall is, nevertheless, an enormously powerful one, and its influence seems somehow to remain even when one has abstracted from its apparent temporal dimension. Corruption remains, if not an actual fall, a falling away from some ideal standard of that which would not be corrupt. It is not hard to follow the line of thought which leads to a view of sin, of evil, of lack (if not loss) of integrity as a deprivation, as an absence of virtue, as a fundamental incompleteness, as a pure negativity.

The reference to completeness is probably more fundamental to the notion of integrity, however, than the reference to origins; one may well feel obliged to struggle towards the 'condition of having no part or element wanting', even without having any clear idea of that in which it might actually consist, rather than to defend or to maintain it as best one may. One may think of a perfect poem, for example, as somehow existing (or subsisting) as some sort of Platonic form, and of poetic creation as some sort of discovery or rediscovery; but one may think of the poet as struggling to create something altogether new. All the same, even though the reference to completeness may be somehow fundamental, we have still to be careful if we are not to allow it to lead us astray.

The OED's third heading for 'Integrity', leads directly from 'Soundness of moral principle [and] the character of uncorrupted virtue' to 'uprightness, honesty, sincerity'. It would be risky, however, to take all these as straightforward synonyms for each other. If to be sincere, for example, is to mean what one says or indicates by one's words or gestures, then sincerity may go along with such inconstancy of belief and attitude as to make for a high degree of unreliability. I may, for example, be each time sincere in my protestations of undying love and commitment to a different person every other week, but my constantly renewed sincerity will hardly make me a reliable partner. Maybe the price of such sincerity has to be a well-developed capacity for self-deception; but may not someone who is self-deceived be as sincere in his self-deception as is he who is deceived by another? Conversely, it is not obvious that everyone of manifestly genuine integrity is *ipso facto* bound to be sincere in all that they say or do. Spies, for example, are committed to having to dissemble a great deal of the time; but is it impossible for a professional spy to be in his own way a man of honour and integrity? (Another case in which these terms may be used differentially is that, made famous once again by Kant, of the grocer who is honest in all his dealings because to be so is good for trade, but who, if dishonesty should finally turn out to be even better, would have no inner qualms about turning to it. One would hardly call such an honest grocer a man of genuine or sincere integrity.)

It would be mistaken, of course, to lean too hard on the variable idiom of so-called ordinary language. One should not be surprised if a set of randomly chosen native English speakers did not see any systematically clear distinctions between the meanings of such words as 'integrity', 'probity', 'sincerity', 'honesty', 'uprightness', 'responsibility', 'trustworthiness' and 'truthfulness', or if in some contexts they used some of them almost interchangeably. In other contexts, no doubt, they may indeed use them to mark particular distinctions of recognizably practical importance—such as that, to which I have just pointed, between the man of integrity and he who is always sincere in his constant and hence radically unreliable changeability. One may perhaps be more confident of the recognizable importance of this distinction than one can be that this way of contrasting the languages of sincerity and integrity will be recognizable by all as a clearly appropriate way of marking it. The reference to wholeness in the OED account of 'integrity' is carried even more explicitly by the closely related terminology of integration; and the great majority of contemporary English speakers would almost certainly still recognize it in the language or discourse of integrity today. If my example really is as plausible as it seems to me to be, it will be because the reference to wholeness is altogether more central to the meaning of 'integrity' than it is to that of 'sincerity'.

'A reference to wholeness'; but what kind of wholeness might that be? It is at this point that we may return to link up with the theme of identity. I started by pointing to some of the ways in which the identities which we accord to ourselves and to others are bound up not with wholeness, but with difference—that difference which is internal to any human being's self-identity. But, as we have seen, there are differences within this difference. There are those differences which are internal to the *numerical* identities of given individuals over time and which, if they cannot be subordinated to or integrated with their identities as particular members of the classes, whether of persons or of motor cars, to which they belong, may end up by terminating, even shattering, their identities altogether. There are those which are internal to anyone's *essential* identity over time, and these in turn may take a number of different forms. To the extent that people's individual essential identities are bound up with their membership of some social group or another, these are going to be affected by whatever differences over time affect the essential or even numerical identity of the relevant group. In other cases it will be some factor wholly internal to a member's individual essential personal identity which changes in ways which, while leaving his numerical identity intact, make it effectively impossible for him or her to remain within the scope of group membership, precisely because the group, *qua* group, has *not* evolved correspondingly. Finally, there is that difference, internal to every self-identifier, which makes it impossible for the self-identifying subject wholly to identify with itself as the object of its own identification in fully perspicuous self-unity. And in so far as the capacity for self-identification depends on possession of the reciprocally necessary capacity for identifying other potential participants in one's own form of 'language game' or discourse as subject-objects of strictly analogous status, a reference to the same fundamental difference must be contained, however obscurely, within all one's identifications of others as well.

Someone of integrity is, one might say, one who is fundamentally all of a piece, who is responsible in the double sense of being someone upon whom one may rely and of being ready to answer for whatever they may do or have done, someone who does not cheat with or over what they fundamentally stand for, someone who is thus true to himself or herself. None of these expressions are quite equivalent; all of them bear some close relation to each other; all of them are significant.

'Someone who is fundamentally all of a piece.' There must be a fundamental inner consistency to such persons' characters, to their dispositions to act or to react in certain ways rather than in others. Their dispositions will not exhibit apparently arbitrary fluctuations and discontinuities (or if they do, the appearances must mask a deeper constancy), and they will support rather than conflict with each other. Such a person must, *ipso facto*, be capable of a high degree of self-integration over time (Kant would have called it 'synthesis', no doubt). Such a capacity is indeed fundamental at once to responsibility, to integrity and to self-identity. In one of the letters which he wrote from prison to his wife, Olga, Vaclav Havel has a passage which makes the point with striking clarity. Only, he says, 'by assuming full responsibility... today for one's own yesterday... does the "I" achieve continuity and thus identity with the self. This is the only possible way it can become something definite, limited and defined, related to its environment in a graspable way, not dissipated in it, not haplessly caught up in random processes.'[3]

Such a degree of self-integration, of self-synthesis, is not only psychologically and morally very demanding; it is also theoretically essentially problematic. In Kantian terms the problem is that of finding a way of rendering intelligible the interaction between the non-temporal but nevertheless actively self-synthesizing and freely self-governing 'I' with the temporally and causally determined 'me'; it is also that of finding a way of rendering intelligible the very notion of non-temporal activity. In Sartrian terms, to take another example, the challenge is that of finding some conceptually common measure between the past and the future. As one looks back on that past to which all our yesterday's selves belong, one sees it as fully determinate, in principle open to no form of change and constituting a retrospectively unbroken network of interlocking causes and effects; as one looks forward to the future, on the contrary, one sees the field of its possibilities as boundlessly open. The present, far from constituting the place of reconciliation between the wholly determinate and the limitlessly open, the principle of commensurability between the now objectively given self of one's past and the self-recreating 'I' of one's self-projection towards the future, is but a 'nothing', a non-place, an emptiness to be constantly refilled by the future as it metamorphoses itself into the past, the site of the paradoxical non-coincidence of the human subject with itself. In Davidsonian terms the problem is that of finding some conceptually neutral way in which one might in principle be able to pick out that individual state or token event in a 'rational being's' life, which under one type of description might be identified as motivating cause and under another type of description as justifying reason, but which *qua* token was still one

[3] Vaclav Havel, *Letters to Olga*, Faber and Faber, London, 1990, p. 350.

and the same item under whichever description. In moral terms the problem is that of finding a perspective within which to hold together an understanding of the causal factors underlying people's behaviour with a moral judgement of those concerned as agents responsible for what they may have done or may do. It seems to me that in none of the versions of the problem can this difference or incommensurability at the heart of human identity between active subject and observed object ever be totally effaced. While there can be no doubt that Havel was right, and that integrity demands that one should take responsibility for one's own identity and continuity with one's self over past, present and future, it seems also that truthfulness to oneself requires one to acknowledge that this continuity can never be given, but only reasserted as the identity of a self that refuses the limitation of a difference that it nevertheless knows can never be fully eliminated.

It might seem that if identity and integrity both depend on a capacity for self-integration across time, they must depend very crucially upon memory. So even if Locke was mistaken in taking continuity of consciousness to be a sufficient criterion for the identity of the person in his sense, would he not have been right to take it to be a necessary condition? The answer, I think, is that although the capacity for memory is indeed a necessary condition—its total disappearance in, for example, the last stages of Alzheimer's disease does seem to signify the concomitant disappearance of *self*-identity, he would still have been wrong to treat memory of particular events as a necessary condition of responsibility for them—though morally wrong rather than demonstrably so.

Many people, I suspect, would feel at least sufficient initial sympathy with Gunther Podola's plea to enable them to see its point. Indeed, while reference to memory alone cannot plausibly be worked up into a definition of the very concept of a person, it might more plausibly be held that no one should properly be held responsible for acts which they truly cannot remember committing or for social commitments of which they are genuinely unaware. Yet a promise which one has totally forgotten is still a promise that one has given; and could one easily endorse the morality of a society in which forgetfulness was always sufficient to release from a promise? We seem to have returned, by a different route, to the distinction between integrity and sincerity. A man may quite sincerely protest that he has no recollection at all of ever having made a promise; but if it can be shown to him that he nevertheless *had* promised, would he not show some lack of integrity if he sought to make of his (still sincere) inability to remember a conclusive ground for release? Persons of integrity are those upon whom one can rely to answer for what they have in fact done, for the commitments that they have in fact undertaken or which are incumbent upon them in virtue of their roles; they may be counted upon to recognize their past and the responsibilities of their positions as belonging to them, whatever their present recall of that past and those responsibilities. Responsibility *is* in this sense a matter of accepting the relevant aspects of one's past as belonging to the past of oneself as agent and as member of society, however problematic such a synthesis (or self-integration) may be from other points of view.

In trying to think through such matters one has to take one's clues from current idiom, while yet recognizing that idiom can never serve as the sole basis of argument. Of course different people will use words such as 'sincerity' and 'integrity' in a number of different ways; of course the meanings to be attributed to them will often be far from determinate on the edges. Nevertheless, the point at issue goes well beyond the niceties of any local idiom. To identify oneself at all as the particular individual that one is presumes a certain identity of oneself with oneself, a certain continuity of self-identity, through a certain period of time. This is true at what one might call the level of the conceptual analysis of self-identity or, if one prefers, at that of its ontology. It is also true at the level of moral identity, which, if not exactly the same as, must certainly be very close to what Locke called personal identity. Fundamentally, the conditions which have to be satisfied for self-identification to be possible are those which make possible the establishment of one's *numerical* identity as a potential participant in discourse, as a being capable of reflection, while those which have to be satisfied for one's moral identity as a person of integrity to be established have to do rather with what we have been calling *essential* identity. So far as our numerical identity is concerned, we have, broadly speaking, very little choice about the matter. We come to discover ourselves, and who we are, as beings who, as they say, are 'always already there'. The criteria by which we learn to individuate and to re-identify ourselves and others are very largely given (as facts) in the world which we willy-nilly inhabit. So far as our essential, and more particularly our moral, identities are concerned, choice and resolution can have some more significant part to play. The degree to which individuals regard themselves as free to determine the values and commitments around which to build their 'essential' personhood varies considerably from one culture or society to another; nevertheless, it is always at least partly up to us to determine the loyalties and responsibilities that we may accept or reject as forming the very basis of what we may stand for or the criterion of where we 'essentially' belong.

Still, though this contrast is real enough, it should not be exaggerated. The interplays between what we have to accept as given and what we may determine through the attitudes that we may choose to adopt towards the given are always delicate, complex and shifting. The relevant shifts will very largely be those of the times in and through which we live; they may, perhaps must, also be thought of as shifts in the relative balance of power between the (autonomous) 'I that thinks' and the (heteronomous) 'self that is given to myself in intuition', that inseparable pair between whom the difference can nevertheless never be wholly elided. Moreover, the nature of such interplays will vary depending on whether the 'we' in question is to be understood as a 'we' of individuals or a 'we' of speech communities—though once again the interplay between them will be delicate, complex and shifting. (To take an example I have discussed elsewhere: there have been times in the history of certain societies when someone of Jewish origin might reasonably have claimed that it depended autonomously on himself whether or not to count himself as a Jew. Even then not everyone, of course, would have agreed. Still, the distance between the 'I' and the 'me' might, at such contingently occurring times, be close enough for it to be for all practical purposes ignorable. At other times, however, the given historical facts may impose tight limits on the freedom of the 'I' honestly to think its relation to the group of its origins in one way rather than another. Anyone born as a Jew, who thought in the Germany of 1939 that he had sovereign freedom to decide whether to maintain that identity or not, would have to have been remarkably naive, if he was not to be guilty of some form of bad faith. There are times when integrity seems to demand that the 'I' should accept its own plural in the nominative 'we' and not strive to keep it remote from its own 'essential' identity by relegating it to the far distance of the accusative 'us'.)

It is, however, out of the question to embark on even a preliminary reconnaissance of all these further complexities here. Suffice it to note that if 'a person of integrity is someone who...does not cheat with or over what they may fundamentally stand for, someone who is in that sense true to himself or herself', we are in effect talking of someone who has a certain 'essential identity', whether thought of in those terms or not—of someone who stands in their present for what they have stood for in the past, or, if they do not, still 'integrate' their present with their past by taking full responsibility for their acknowledged change of position. Moreover, to stand by whatever one may stand for in the present is necessarily to stand in a certain general relationship to one's future. It is not for nothing that Bernard Williams has so insisted on the intimacy of the relation between the integrity of moral agents and their own most cherished projects for the future; nor, indeed, that Heidegger—whatever one may think of his own integrity—has so insisted on the connection between what he calls authenticity and a recognition of one's own finite temporality. One might even say, without stretching too many points, that integrity lies in the commitment to oneself to maintain one's essential identity, over the space-time of one's life and across the infinite/infinitesimal divide of the 'I' and the 'me' in the full recognition that the final achievement of that identity, the final securing of one's own integrity, is something that in principle one can never oneself come to know. Indeed, to allow oneself the conviction that one *has* finally completed the distance is perhaps the ultimate way of falling short.

I have tried in this paper to deal with two vast and entangled subjects and to show some of the ways in which they are themselves deeply entangled with each other. From time to time I have made passing but explicit reference to Kant; as is the case with so many who have struggled to achieve some grip on his texts, one ends up by finding oneself making use of many of his themes and concepts to try and work out one's own thought. As I look back over what I have written, I realize that one may find in it the transposition of yet another Kantian theme. I have tried to deal, as I say, with the two major themes of identity and integrity and to show how they necessarily interconnect with each other. But, as Kant might have said, such interconnection can only be secured through the mediation of some third factor, common (or homogeneous) to them both. Kant's common third factor in his Schematism was furnished, of course, by time. Here, too, time has emerged as the common factor—the (non-totalizable) integration of oneself through and in time that constitutes not only a certain basic fidelity to oneself, but also the very grounds of one's own never wholly completable identity.

3

Expensive Tastes and Multiculturalism*

G. A. Cohen

Will Kymlicka believes that state support for disadvantaged cultures is consonant with the leading theses of Ronald Dworkin's egalitarian liberalism, theses which Kymlicka enthusiastically affirms. Here, I argue otherwise. I show that Kymlicka's case for subsidy to cultures in difficulty rests on principles that defeat Dworkin's position.

Section I expounds and criticizes that position, which Dworkin calls 'equality of resources', a dispensation which, so he maintains, suppresses differences in people's circumstances that are due to brute luck. I argue that equality of resources fails to suppress those differences. That is because equal amounts of resources satisfy different people to different extents, and, in particular, because, under equality of resources, people who are burdened with unchosen expensive tastes fare worse than others do through no fault of their own.

Section II addresses the skepticism of those who think it bizarre to plead *in the name of equality* on behalf of expensive tastes. I put the concept of an expensive taste into sharp focus, in order to recruit the reader's agreement that people should not fare worse than others do because of expensive tastes for which it would be unreasonable to hold them responsible.

* A longer version of this paper appears in my *From Each According to His Ability, To Each According to His Needs*, Cambridge, 1997.

The target of section III is liberal confidence in the justice of market outcomes. I show that its insensitivity to expensive taste undermines the market's claim to be an engine of justice. Section IV measures the policy implications of that critique of the market.

Section V introduces Kymlicka's view that Dworkin's liberalism requires state support for threatened culture. I argue, against Kymlicka, that the terms in which Dworkin contrasts resources and tastes militate against state support for culture. From the liberal point of view which excludes judgments about the quality of different forms of life as a basis for policy formation, being attached to a culture which requires special support is, so I claim, relevantly like having an expensive taste.

Section VI defends that claim in detail, by showing that distinctions that Kymlicka must draw between expensive culture and (other) expensive taste are unsustainable. I conclude, in section VII, not that embattled cultures merit no support, but that the reasons why they indeed merit support are such as to unfound Dworkin's market-endorsing liberalism.

I

Anglophone political philosophers of egalitarian persuasion disagree on the matter of *which* equality is demanded by distributive justice.

According to Ronald Dworkin, *equality of resources* is the correct answer to that contested question, whereas I believe that the correct answer is akin to *equality of opportunity for welfare*.[1] Equality of resources is expounded forthwith. The meaning of equality of opportunity for welfare will emerge below.

Equality of resources is equality *not* in the satisfaction or fulfilment that people have in life, but in the wherewithal that they use to pursue that fulfilment, where 'wherewithal' includes not only external resources but also personal capacities and powers.

[1] I say 'akin to' because, strictly, I endorse not equality of opportunity for welfare but equality of access to advantage. For the former conception, see Richard Arneson, 'Equality and Equality of Opportunity for Welfare', *Philosophical Studies*, vol. 55, 1989. For the latter, see my 'On the Currency of Egalitarian Justice', *Ethics*, vol. 99, 1989, pp. 916–17 in particular for the difference between my view and Arneson's. I rest on his view here, because it is simpler, and because the distinction between mine and his is orthogonal to the present polemic.

This proposal purportedly meets the salient liberal requirement that the state must practise neutrality with respect to people's varying conceptions of what is good in life. For no judgments about what sorts of life are good and bad are made when one estimates how equal people's wherewithal to make their lives good, by their own lights, is.

In his seminal article of 1981 on 'Equality of Resources', Dworkin describes what his ideal implies for a very simple case, the case, that is, of people with identical personal capacities and talents, who vary only in their tastes, preferences, conceptions of what is good in life, and so forth. He imagines a set of shipwrecked egalitarians whose rafts bring them to an uninhabited island, one with more than enough resources to sustain all of them above subsistence level. The question that faces them is how to allocate the island's resources equally.

Dworkin answers that question as follows. The islanders distribute among themselves equal shares of an inherently worthless commodity, namely, clamshells, which will constitute the means of purchasing their island's resources. They proceed, using the clamshells as currency, to bid against one another, in a form of auction, for all the resources on the island, under the aegis of a skilled auctioneer, who varies prices and/or reruns the auction until markets for all of the island's resources have cleared. If the auction is properly conducted, then its results will be 'envy-free', which means that no one will prefer anyone else's bundle of resources to her own, since, had she done so, she could have purchased that different bundle instead of the one that she actually purchased: for she was no less endowed with means of purchase than the one who actually purchased it was. That result would, for Dworkin, constitute complete equality, in the specified world, in which, by hypothesis, there is no inequality in people's talents.

Dworkin proceeds to consider conditions that are more complex and indeed more realistic than those that are postulated for the auction described a moment ago. He addresses the normal circumstance in which some people are disadvantaged by handicaps and in which productive capacities vary across the population, and he argues that some form of post-auction redistribution is required to rectify those differences of fortune. For otherwise, the root intuition, that people's life chances should be equal, will not be satisfied. I need not here assess the adequacy of the devices of insurance and taxation on which Dworkin relies to achieve the needed rectification. What matters here is *that* Dworkin would redistribute against the grain of natural and social fortune, and *why* he would do so, not *how* he would do so.

Now, it is my view that the root intuition which leads Dworkin to revise the auction's results to cater for differential fortune in the matter of powers and talents should also have led him to deny the justice of those results for the special case, described above, in which talents are identical and people differ only in their tastes. Dworkin approves of redistributive compensation for handicaps such as physical paralysis and poor earning capacity and disapproves of redistributive compensation for expensive tastes and preferences,[2] such as those for fine wine, rare seafood, mountain climbing and extensive leisure. I believe that the very thing that justifies the first type of compensation also justifies the second, where the tastes in question are appropriately involuntary, that is, items that the individual is saddled with by birth and history, rather than ones she deliberately and avoidably cultivated.[3] Such tastes are, like a poor supply of talent, bad luck, and people are penalized for mere bad luck if their resource endowment is not adjusted in the light of those tastes.[4]

To motivate my counterview, suppose that there are two things to eat on the island, eggs and fish. Fish are abundant and eggs are scarce. Consequently, fish are cheap and eggs are very expensive. Most people love fish, but Harry hates them. Most people mostly eat fish, reserving eggs for special occasions, and finding themselves consequently with plenty of clamshells to pay for other things, such as shelter, clothing, recreation, and so forth. Unlike them, Harry has a tough choice, which is between regularly eating eggs and therefore having little of anything else, and eating lots of fish, at

[2] Save where the bearer of the taste or preference repudiates it, a complication that I lack the space to discuss here. See Dworkin, 'Equality of Resources', *Philosophy and Public Affairs*, vol. 10, 1981, p. 302, and see my 'On the Currency', pp. 925–7, for criticism of Dworkin's repudiation criterion.

[3] There is no space here for full elaboration of the contrast between voluntarily and involuntarily acquired tastes. See 'On the Currency', pp. 920ff., and *From Each According to His Ability*.

[4] I am aware that it will strike (some) readers as bizarre that I plead in *the name of equality* on behalf of expensive tastes, but I ask you to bear with me while I refine that plea across the course of the ensuing pages.

the cost of gagging whenever he nourishes himself. We may suppose that it is because of how his taste-buds work that he gags, although we could equally well suppose that he gags because fish remind him of his mother, whom he rightly could not bear. Although the example is stylized and peculiar, it stands here for the unpeculiar phenomenon of different people finding the same commodities differentially satisfying, and therefore being differentially placed with respect to what they can get out of life with a given income. And, in my view, that phenomenon explodes the pretension of Dworkin's auction to being an engine of distributive justice. It shows that equality of resources should give way to equality of opportunity for welfare, because identical quantities of resources are capable of satisfying people to different degrees, since people are made differently, both naturally and socially, not only (a fact to which Dworkin is sensitive) in their capacities to produce but also (the fact to which he is insensitive) in their capacities to obtain fulfilments.

II

Harry the fish-hater has expensive tastes, which is to say that he *needs* more resources than the average person does to achieve an average level of fulfilment. Let me emphasize that such is what the phrase 'expensive tastes' is to mean here. There are natural resonances of the expression 'expensive taste' which are inappropriate here, and, to the extent that those resonances dominate the kind, the issue of whether expensive tastes warrant redistributive compensation will be misframed.

Often, when we say that someone has expensive tastes, we have foremost in mind the life-style that she actually lives, one characterized by fine-textile clothes, caviar, and so on. But that is loose talk, since a person's *actual* pattern of consumption may show not that her tastes are expensive, but just that her bank balance is large. Nor are we speaking, here, of someone who is not *willing* to *settle* for a lesser satisfaction, for example, for cod roe, instead of caviar. For that is a matter not of her tastes as such, but of her stance, of the policy that she adopts when seeking to satisfy her tastes.

Here a person's tastes are expensive if and only if they are such that it costs more to provide her than to provide others with given levels of satisfaction or fulfilments. A person who insists on expensive cigars and fine wines is not *eo ipso* possessed of expensive tastes, in the required sense. For she may thereby be insisting on a higher level of fulfilment than the norm. In the present acceptation, a person has expensive tastes if, for example, ordinary cigars and plonk wine which give pleasure to the general leave him cold, and he can get something like that pleasure (and *not*, *ex hypothesi*, a greater one) only with Havana cigars and Margaux. His expensive tastes are a matter neither of his behaviour nor of his will but of his constitution. They concern what he is satisfied *by*, not what he is satisfied *with*.

Someone who loves plonk wine may hate ordinary cigars, and someone who is satisfied by ordinary cigars may need Margaux for ordinary level wine pleasure. More generally, each person's satisfaction function will likely be an amalgam of cheap and expensive tastes, and few may have expensive tastes in an aggregate sense, when one considers the vast variety of commodities available to people. But that fact is irrelevant to the philosophical question, which is whether or not expensive tastes warrant compensation, a question that I pursue by treating individual cases of expensive taste (e.g. caviar vs. cod roe) as representative of generally expensive tastes. Dworkin rejects compensation for expensive tastes as a matter of *principle*, not on the grounds that a principle which might dictate their compensation is never *in fact* satisfied (because everyone can find some things which satisfy her as much as other people are by things which she finds unsatisfying). I attack Dworkin's principled stance (and I show, in due course, that Kymlicka's defence of compensation for cultural disadvantage requires the principle, of, roughly, equal opportunity for welfare, that Dworkin rejects when he disparages the claims of expensive tastes).

Now, expensive tastes, in the specified sense, militate against a fulfilling life because they reduce the opportunity for it. For any given income you are worse off in terms of satisfaction or fulfilments if you have expensive tastes, and I regard that as a reason for subsidies, of a type that I shall describe in section III: such subsidies are demanded by consistent adherence to an egalitarianism which sets itself against the ministrations of luck.

So my own answer, to the question 'Equality of What?', runs, in relevant part, as follows. I agree with Dworkin's most basic proposition, that people should not be better and worse off by virtue of the sheer luck of where they are born, into what class, with what natural and social endowments and so forth. But, while I agree with Dworkin at that basic level, I disagree one level up, where the task of specifying what the basic proposition implies, begins. For I believe, against Dworkin, that people should not suffer worse lives because of those expensive tastes for which they cannot be held responsible.

Now, that may seem to be an exquisitely prissy reservation, but recall what is meant, here, by 'expensive tastes', namely, that a person who has them needs more resources than others do for the same fulfilment. And, as I shall now explain, my disagreement with Dworkin has radical consequences for our respective assessments of the justice of market upshots.

III

In explication of my disagreement with Dworkin about the justice of the market, let me introduce the example of a recreation centre, which subsidizes some at the (money) expense of others by charging the same rate of entry regardless of which leisure activity, be it cheap or expensive, given entrants take up. One reason for a uniform entry price would be aversion to the pettiness of keeping detailed accounts. But I think that a distinct good reason is that which leisure activities they find fulfilling is on the whole not up to people themselves. It is, of course, a matter of choice, if anything is, that a member plays expensive billiards when he could have played inexpensive chess. But he normally has little choice as to whether or not chess engages his powers the way billiards does. When all activities are free at the point of play, and no one chooses as she does out of regard for the centre's budget, and some choose chess, then no one chooses chess because it is cheaper: under those (instantiated) assumptions, so I judge, there is a good case for one entry price, and, therefore, for non-market pricing of the particular activities people pursue, the ground for that being unchosen variations in people's tastes. The distributive norm that I favour for such a context contradicts the market norm and is something like: to each according to her needs (to, that is, what she needs for fulfilments in life).

When there are charges for use according to cost, then some are unfairly penalized for expensive tastes that they could not, and cannot, help having: that is the case against market allocation here.

More generally, because of variation in preference, and in how chosen it is, markets do not deliver justice. But that is not to say that any practicable alternative can do so. Thus, the inter-activity subsidy of the sort I favour does not deliver perfect justice (perfect equality of opportunity for fulfilment) either. It does not do so, since, like the market, general subsidies[5] are insensitive to individual variations in levels of fulfilment. But we may sometimes judge that subsidy is less insensitive than the market is to individual need, and such is the judgment that I would defend, for the recreation centre case.

Dworkin does not himself believe in pure *laissez-faire*, since he thinks that, so far as possible, people should be compensated for handicaps and for poor earning capacity before they enter the market. But that tinkering with the assets that people bring *to* the market implies no administrative adjustment of the prices that they face, save where that happens to be the best means of compensating for disability: wheelchairs, medicine, etc., might be priced cheaply for that reason. My own disbelief in the claim that the (unfettered) market produces justice is far deeper. For me, markets can 'produce' justice only in the Pickwickian sense that they do so when they are so comprehensively rigged that they mirror a distribution which qualifies as just for reasons which have nothing to do with how market prices form.

In sum: Dworkin believes that the market constitutes its results as just when pre-trading assets are suitably equalized, where that equalization is blind to differences of taste, but I believe that, while market results may be more or less just, the market never *constitutes* justice.

IV

Now, I do not conclude, on the basis of the foregoing considerations, that the state should adopt a comprehensive policy of compensating people for unchosen expensive tastes: my topic is what egalitarian justice requires, not, immediately, what the state should do. For one thing, it would almost certainly be impossible for the

[5] *General* subsidies reduce the cost of a given good to *all* comers, and not only to those whose taste for the good is in the relevant way expensive. *Special* subsidies are to particular consumers of a given good.

state to determine which tastes reflect choice and which do not. For another, it could not determine whether a person, as he is now constituted, *needs* more resources than others do, for comparable effect or, on the contrary, simply *demands* more satisfaction than they do from life. If, moreover, the state could indeed determine such things, it could do so only through a monstrous invasion of privacy that would not be justified, in my view, by the contemplated particular gain in egalitarian justice. What our tastes are, and how we got them, should, therefore, largely not be the state's business. To that extent, I agree with Dworkin.

Some will baulk at the idea that what is claimed to be a demand of justice is not something that the state, or, indeed, any other agent, can be expected to fulfil. I cannot here defend the methodology which allows such a result. But it merits comment that Dworkin could not (and, as matter of fact, does not) object to my position on this methodological basis. For, as I remarked,[6] he himself believes that egalitarian justice justifies compensation for expensive tastes whose bearer is disposed to repudiate them, and he can no more infer that the state should see to such compensation than I can propose that it compensate for expensive tastes when an appropriate measure of responsibility for them is absent.

Although I agree with Dworkin that the state cannot put particular individual's tastes on its agenda, two significant disagreements remain. First, in my view, it is false that a person's (unrepudiated) tastes are not the state's business *because* it is reasonable to expect her to take responsibility for them, no matter how she came to have them, and no matter what she can do about them now. Instead, she must assume responsibility for them *because* they cannot feasibly be the state's business.

The second disagreement is consequent on the first. While we agree that the state should not intervene in the consumer market by subsidizing those who have expensive tastes, Dworkin believes that that serves justice, whereas, as I have said earlier, I think that we produce injustice whether we leave the market alone or interfere with it in a generally subsidizing way. Thus, consider, again, the smoker who really needs fine cigars and the one who loves cheap ones. Provided that those two categories of smokers exist, and that their opportunities for satisfaction are otherwise equal, there will

[6] See footnote 2.

be injustice whatever we do, whether, that is, we let market prices prevail, or subsidize expensive cigars.

We have to make guesses, and sometimes, as in the case of the recreation centre, I would guess that justice is better served by general subsidy. That example is importantly different from the cigar one, for there we may suppose that everyone prefers expensive to cheap cigars whereas in recreation people differ not only in the degrees of satisfaction that they get from different leisure pursuits but also in their preference orderings over them. Partly for that reason, the case of different pursuits in the leisure centre is the appropriate model for how to treat different, and differentially expensive, cultural needs, which is the topic to which I now turn.

V

Will Kymlicka supports an opportunity-oriented egalitarianism, and, unlike me, he accepts Dworkin's dismissive view of (unrepudiated) expensive tastes and the associated endorsement of the market. But Kymlicka also approves of subsidy for expensive culture. He believes, that is, that the state should support ethnic cultures to which people are attached but which, for situational reasons, are expensive to maintain, expensive either in the direct sense that their institutions require subsidy to flourish, or in the indirect one that they will flourish only under restrictive regulations which impose costs, monetary or otherwise, on members of other cultures.

Kymlicka's major aim, in his book *Liberalism, Community, and Culture*,[7] was to show that Dworkin's liberalism, with its distinction between unchosen circumstance—for which compensation may be in order—and preference, for which it is not, allows and indeed requires support for minority cultures. So Kymlicka has to deny that a person's culture *is* a set of tastes or preferences, a certain conception of the good, and he represents it, instead, as a context or framework in which choice is made, as a set of options within which the person makes a life.

I shall argue that Kymlicka's would-be distinguishing gambit fails to justify cultural support *by contrast with support for expensive taste:* being attached to a culture which requires special support is *relevantly* like having an expensive taste, from the liberal point of

[7] Will Kymlicka, *Liberalism, Community, and Culture*, Oxford, 1989.

view which maintains that justice abjures judgments about what forms of life are good, and what not so good. But that does not mean that I am hostile to Kymlicka's policy stance, which is one of generosity towards the claims of cultures in difficulty. On the contrary, I agree with it, but precisely because I reject Kymlicka's Dworkinian view of expensive taste.

If I am right, Kymlicka must either part with Dworkin on expensive taste, or abandon his own defence of cultural support. I believe that he should do the first, since, so I have argued, Dworkin's treatment of expensive taste is flawed. But whether or not I am right about that, I might yet be right that egalitarian liberals of the Kymlicka kind must *either* be friendlier than they propose to be about expensive tastes, *or* be less friendly than they want to be to the claims of cultures in difficulty.

The problem Kymlicka creates for himself by advocating support for cultures in difficulty exposes a tension in the Dworkinian egalitarian liberalism that he desires to espouse. The liberal element in that position requires neutrality with respect to conceptions of the good, and Dworkin (and Kymlicka) so interpret neutrality that, if my good is harder to achieve than yours is, then the difficulty is down to me, and I can expect no public assistance with my problem. The egalitarian element in egalitarian liberalism enjoins equal chances with respect to achieving one's good. That the first element, under its indicated interpretation, counsels inconsistently with the second element emerges in Kymlicka's treatment of culture.

Different cultures uphold different conceptions of the good. It is virtually definitive of cultural difference that that should be so: truly different cultures do not merely interpret the same goods differently. So the neutrality element in egalitarian liberalism, in the Dworkin/Kymlicka interpretation of it, would appear to declare against state support for expensive culture, since such support promotes some conceptions of the good, and not others.

Yet membership in a secure culture with a secure value system is, so Kymlicka argues, essential to opportunity for a good life, and he infers that the egalitarian side of liberalism dictates support for a culture which is expensive to maintain. I say that he cannot consistently endorse that support without compromising his Dworkinian view of expensive tastes.

In this essay I am asking both whether egalitarian liberals should treat expensive cultures as they do expensive tastes and whether they are right to treat expensive tastes as they do. I argue that expensive cultures *are* like expensive tastes but that egalitarian liberals should be kinder than they have been to the latter: when they turn their back on them, they mistake what their own principles of neutrality (properly interpreted) and equality require. They may, therefore, extend support to expensive culture, but they must revise their attitude to (other) expensive taste. Neither in supporting threatened culture not in helping a person pursue a good that happens to be expensive (see section II above) are they breaching the principle that the state must be neutral with respect to varying judgments of the good.

I have, accordingly, three disagreements with Kymlicka. First, regarding expensive tastes: I say that they cannot as a category be dismissed from egalitarian attention. Second, regarding the contrasting treatment which he metes out to expensive tastes and expensive cultures. And finally, and of greater political import, I disagree about the justice of market results, *even* when differences in people's resources and powers have been compensated for. Paradoxically, then, a left-wing skepticism about market justice is nourished, here, by what looks like a not very left-wing indulgence towards expensive taste.

VI

I shall now argue that, for purposes of distributive justice, expensive culture is relevantly parallel to (other) expensive preference. I begin by claiming that the very premises that Kymlicka employs to defend support for expensive culture also justify support for (unchosen) expensive taste. I then address four objections to that claim of parallel, which turn on four would-be distinctions between expensive taste and expensive culture. The objections say that, by contrast with (other) preference, a person's culture is: (1) not chosen, (2) a context or framework in which preferences form and choices are made, (3) exceptionally difficult to abandon in favour of an alternative, and (4) not part of a domain in which state neutrality is possible.

According to Kymlicka, two premisses suffice to show that minority cultural rights that impose costs on the rest of society are justifiable: first, that cultural membership is an important good; and, second, that the members of minority cultural communities may face special disadvantages with regard to secure provision of that good.[8]

But these premisses do not relevantly distinguish the good of cultural membership. There are other important goods with respect to which people face special disadvantages, such as the special disadvantage faced by those with unchosen expensive tastes for the central things of life (where they live, what they live in, their major pastimes, etc.). Accordingly, more distinctions are needed to justify a policy difference across cultural and other goods.

Let me describe a specific instance of the parallel that exercises me. Sometimes a taste is expensive because few share it and there are therefore diseconomies of small scale in the production of what satisfies it. Its expensiveness is then due to a circumstance comparable to that which affects a small ethnic group which cannot run its newspaper and radio programme without state support, because of high overheads. Why should a claim to subsidy be justified in the one case but not in the other, when the constraint of liberal neutrality is respected? (Notice that cultural facilities can also be particularly expensive because they serve the *majority* culture. If thousands want to visit the mosque, and only hundreds the synagogue, then costly (e.g. traffic) arrangements are needed at the first but not at the second. A parallel in the domain of taste would be the comparative cost of rare A and equally rare B, where many want A and few want B.)

Kymlicka is right that

> the viability of [some minority] societal cultures may be undermined by economic and political decisions made by the majority. They could be outbid or outvoted on resources and policies that are crucial to the survival of their societal cultures.[9]

But that is also true of those who have a minority taste in non- (or less) cultural (in the relevantly ethnic sense) aspects of life, such as taste for old-fashioned local shopping, or television without advertising, or vegetarian food, or landscapes with hedges, or pre-electric typewriters, and so on. The survival of *their* preferred ways may also be subject to threat from majority preference.

[8] Kymlicka, *Liberalism, Community, and Culture*, p. 162.
[9] Kymlicka, *Multicultural Citizenship*, Oxford, 1995, p. 109.

Kymlicka must claim that, beyond the similarities registered above, there lie important differences. I now consider, and reject, four such possible differences.

(1) Choice will not do the needed distinguishing, in the general case. Many tastes and preferences are inherited and/or nurtured, with choice playing a negligible role in their constitution: non-cultural elements in his formation are, typically, as fateful as cultural ones are in the make-up of a person. And in both cases, there remains a choice, to go with or against the exogenously imposed grain, at greater or lesser cost.[10]

(2) Kymlicka would hold that it is a category mistake to proceed as I have done. That I have miscompared culture, which is an unchosen *framework* in which tastes are formed and choices are made, neither of which form a framework. Culture, he says, is

> the context within which we choose our ends, and come to see their value, and this is a precondition of self-respect, of the sense that one's ends are worth pursuing.[11]

Culture is thus represented as a circumstance of choice, and therefore as a candidate for subsidy, from a liberal point of view, in contrast to particular 'shared practices and projects' which, not being circumstances, are not.[12]

Now, we may indeed distinguish between culture, considered as an ethnically determined set of possible choices, and particular preferences. But we may also distinguish, contrariwise, between a particular culturally phrased preference and a set of possible life-styles not all of which are in all pertinent respects coloured by a particular culture. Kymlicka thinks it right to sustain the cultural framework, but not particular practice, be it culturally constructed or not. I shall argue, first, that the cultural framework is not the only relevant one, that there is also a larger one to the detriment of Kymlicka's attempt to represent support for culture as special, and, in particular, as different from support for (other) expensive taste; and, second, that the framework/practice distinction is

[10] John Danley makes this point very well, in his 'Liberalism, Aboriginal Rights and Cultural Minorities', *Philosophy and Public Affairs*, vol. 20, 1991, pp. 176–7.

[11] Kymlicka, *Multicultural Citizenship*, p. 192.

[12] Ibid., p. 239.

relative rather than absolute, and therefore cannot bear the weight that Kymlicka places on it.

Concatenate all the life-styles that are possible in a given society and you get what can be called its *life-style space*. Now 'life-style space', as I have just defined it, and 'culture' *can* be used synonymously, but 'culture' then denotes a wider idea than ethnic or national culture, which is what Kymlicka must mean by the term. The point to note is that life-style space is no less a context of choice than culture is, in the ethnically charged Kymlicka sense of the term. And it might be no more expensive to keep, for example, Canadian Inuit culture going than to sustain threatened lifeways which do not in every relevant way display a cultural character in the narrow sense of 'cultural' which Kymlicka's purposes require. Think of rural English lifeways. The hunt, forests to walk in, country buses, protection against overdevelopment of villages: these are not particularly cheap, and they bear no specific cultural stamp (you can speak French, English, or Swahili, as you tramp through the countryside), but they represent an unchosen and not specially cultural (in the relevant narrow sense) context of choice for those who are reared in their ambit, and who therefore identify with those lifeways and gain a sense of self from them.

Kymlicka says that 'the range of options [from which ways of life are chosen] is determined by our cultural heritage'.[13] But, unless 'cultural heritage' is used to include a person's *total* heritage, the quoted statement is false, or a relevantly incomplete truth. And as long as 'cultural heritage' denotes a distinguishable part of heritage as a whole, so that the quoted statement is indeed defective, we may then say that support for other expensive life-style space is as justifiable as support for expensive culture is.

Traditions of (not specially cultural) taste are a necessary prior context of choice as much as cultural traditions are. You could not expect an individual to prepare food from scratch, with no dependence on culinary traditions. There is, of course, no danger that such traditions will collapse, but *that* is the reason why subsidizing them is inappropriate: it is not because they are traditions of a relevantly non-cultural sort. Kymlicka himself says that 'no one chooses which class or race they are born into...and

[13] Ibid., p. 165.

no one deserves to be disadvantaged by these facts'.[14] I agree, and I think that facts of taste and preference consequent on the facts mentioned by Kymlicka, and on other facts of upbringing and milieu, should therefore not disadvantage people.

The distinction between choice and framework of choice is—and this is my second point against Kymlicka's use of it—variable, in an accordion-like way. For frameworks of choice may themselves be chosen, and particular choices may enfold sub-choices. Thus one may distinguish between different frameworks of consumer choice (e.g. within food, between vegetarian and carnalian; within recreation, between outdoor sports and indoor games; within culture (in the non-ethnic sense), between movies and books) and particular choices within each (asparagus vs. lettuce, and so on). The contrast between frameworks and particular choices is a relative distinction, along a continuum of more and less specific choices. Strongly contrasting distributive conclusions cannot be grounded in so shifting a distinction.

The two points made above, that culture is not the only framework of choice, and that the framework vs. choice distinction is a variable one—these points combine to undermine the significance of Kymlicka's remark that 'we should treat access to one's culture as something that people can be expected to want, whatever their more *particular* conception of the good'.[15] For we should, equally, treat access to some form of leisure, or of food, as something that people can be expected to want, whatever *particular* such forms they regard as good, and whether or not (why should *that* make a difference?) those forms possess a distinctive ethnocultural character.

(3) Kymlicka might say that the required difference between cultural and other preference is with respect to how *hard* it is to give up one's culture. When his critics object that, even if cultural placement is essential to informed choice of life-style, it does not follow that its members need the *particular* minority culture to which they belong, he responds, cogently, that the cost of shifting to *another* culture is more considerable than the objection allows.[16] But I see no difference between that plea on behalf of the

[14] Ibid., p. 186.
[15] Kymlicka, *Multicultural Citizenship*, p. 86, emphasis added.
[16] See Kymlicka's reply to Jeremy Waldron, ibid., p. 86.

participant in an expensive culture and a parallel plea on behalf of a participant in an expensive life-style, such as the rural one sketched above.

It may be easier to understand that a person cannot shift from his native culture without enormous cost to himself than it is to understand that a person cannot cultivate cheaper tastes in other domains. But the point of principle remain intact, whatever may be the right particular judgments to make. If it counts that 'the desire of national minorities to retain their cultural membership remains very strong',[17] then why does it not equally count that the desire of countryfolk to remain rustic remains very strong?

I should add that my endorsement of Kymlicka's response to Waldron does not mean that I accept the defence offered by Kymlicka of state support for ethnocentric education: he says that children need education in their own culture to be capable of coherently choosing a conception of the good. The justification of state support for ethnic education might rest on a sound principle, namely that there is a right to a capacity to choose well among conceptions of the good. But, allowing that such a principle is both sound and liberal, the stated justification of subsidy to ethnic education remains doubtful on factual grounds: that children need *a* culture for the stated reason does not mean that they need their *parents'* culture, even if it is oppressive to require *adults* to shift to another culture.

Kymlicka also speaks not of the needs of children as such but of 'people have[ing] a legitimate interest in ensuring the continuation of their own culture',[18] as a reason for supporting ethnic education, but I agree with Charles Taylor that Kymlicka cannot treat that interest as a right without departing from liberal individualism. A subsidy to embattled cultures which is 'designed to ensure [their] survival through indefinite future generations'[19] is manifestly unnecessary for coherent choice of life-style by the members of any given generation.

Taylor's own justification of ethnocentric education is that parents need such education to be available so that they can be

[17] Ibid., pp. 85–6.

[18] Kymlicka, *Liberalism*, p. 3.

[19] Taylor, 'The Politics of Recognition', in Amy Gutmann (ed.), *Multiculturalism and 'The Politics of Recognition'*, Princeton, 1992, p. 41.

confident that the culture that they prize will be perpetuated. French-Canadian nationalists, for example, want 'policies aimed at survival [which] actively seek to *create* members of the community, for instance, in their assuring that future generations continue to identify as French-speakers'.[20]

Taylor's case is less controversial than Kymlicka's from a factual point of view, but its principle is offensively illiberal: why should the current generation of a given ethnic community decide what cultural development will be into the indefinite future, with the help of public money, or in some different way at the expense of other living people (for example, by curtailing the latter's language rights)? Why should French Canadians have a right not only (as they certainly do) to pursue, but also to receive public support for the aspiration to self-perpetuation that Taylor attributes to them? I regret that Yiddishkeit is dying, but I do not think that Jews therefore have a right that government subsidize programmes to sustain it. I might want classy wine-bibbing or not so classy football to go on and on, but I cannot see why I have a right that the state ensure it does. Why should cultural attachment be different, to the extent (and this is the distinction, pressed by Taylor, that defeats Kymlicka here) that sustaining the culture is *not* necessary to individuals' capacities to construct good lives? Why should Jews and Greeks whose home is Québec be forced by taxation, and through restrictions on their own self-expression, to help keep Québécois culture alive?

There is a third justification for support for ethnic education, which I think is more robust than the two rejected above (so that children can develop a capacity for coherent choice of a life, and so that the minority culture will indefinitely persist). This is that ethnic education is desired, in certain cases, both by parents and by children, so that they are not cut off from one another. But, as I know from my own experience of growing up in a Jewish immigrant part of Montreal, some parents, usually with their children's compliance, want their children to assimilate into the majority culture, and some children want that, against their parents' wishes. Needs and preferences vary here, in such a way as to justify the state in making ethnic education available, yet not because ethnic education *as such* is needed. Once again, urban and rural education

[20] Ibid., pp. 58–9.

might reasonably be styled differently, for the same reason: to avoid damaging alienation between children and their parents.

(4) Kymlicka's considered view is that special cultural support is consistent with liberal neutrality, his reason for saying so being that such support sustains the *power* to choose, rather than the particular choices, of people whose cultures are threatened. But, at one point in *Multicultural Citizenship*, he shifts ground: he suggests that neutrality regarding the claims of culture is 'actually *incoherent*', which means that the liberal precept dictating neutrality with respect to conceptions of the good cannot be maintained in the case of culture:

> Government decisions on languages, internal boundaries, public holidays and state symbols unavoidably involve recognizing, accommodating and supporting the needs and identities of particular ethnic and national groups. The state unavoidably promotes certain cultural identities, and thereby disadvantages others. Once we recognize this, we need to rethink the justice of minority rights claims.[21]

In order to evaluate the thesis that government *cannot* be neutral with respect to cultural differences, we must pay attention to the distinction between *consequential* neutrality, which is a matter of the *effect* of policy, and *justificatory* neutrality, which is a matter of its *grounds*.[22] Government policy is consequentially neutral when it promotes (or frustrates) the pursuit of competing (cultural or other) values to an equal extent (however such extents are to be measured). It is justificatorily neutral when judgments of the worth of different values do not figure among the reasons animating the policy in question.

Consequential neutrality is sometimes difficult to achieve, but justificatory neutrality is always possible. Thus, for example, a government decision to support a failing automobile industry on grounds of economic justice to its threatened employees may mean that cars, and, therefore, the motoring life-style, will be cheaper than they would be otherwise, but that consequential non-neutrality goes here, *ex hypothesi*, with strict justificatory neutrality with respect to whether or not motoring is a good thing.

[21] Kymlicka, *Multicultural Citizenship*, p. 108.

[22] 'Recognizing', in the first sentence of the Kymlicka passage, relates to justification. 'Promotes' and 'disadvantages', in his second sentence, relate to consequences. ('Accommodating' and 'supporting' are more ambiguous.)

Since government cannot always ensure consequential neutrality, it is no mark of the cultural that such neutrality is difficult to achieve in that sphere. 'The state' indeed 'unavoidably promotes certain cultural identities', but it also unavoidably promotes fulfilments of other preferences. And it is a further question whether it cannot be as justificatorily neutral in the cultural domain as liberals require it to be (and as it appears able to be) elsewhere.

To answer that question, let us take Kymlicka's examples of supposedly inevitable non-neutrality, one by one. Internal boundaries, fateful though they may be in their cultural effects, need not be made on cultural grounds. Public holidays need not be designed to track the religion or customs of one ethnic group rather than another. It might even be questioned whether a truly liberal state has any business designating public holidays at all. And there is certainly no call for a liberal state to adopt symbols which express a particular cultural identity.

Decisions on language indeed have to be made, particularly with regard to schooling, but, once again, justificatory neutrality need not be abandoned when they are made. They can be made by reference to such criteria as numbers of children belonging to a particular culture in a territory of designated size, and so on. The consequences will not always be neutral, but there is nothing special about that.

Although judgments of value can be avoided with respect to choice of language of instruction, they are, in my view, unavoidable with respect to curricular structure, that is, what sorts of literature, history, mathematics, etc., are taught. But judgments about which cultures should and should not be promoted need play no role in that discussion. So far as I can see, then, liberal neutrality in education is sustainable with respect to cultural difference but *not* otherwise. The opposite of what Kymlicka requires is true.

So, contrary to the message of the text given above, culture is not beyond the reach of neutrality (and therefore in that way different from other aspects of what is [thought] good in people's lives). But I must add a *caveat*. Kymlicka's opponents, in the paragraph from which the text on exhibit is drawn, are those who recommend 'benign neglect' of cultural difference. I am with Kymlicka against them. Not, however, because, as he falsely claims, the neutrality that they demand is impossible, but because 'benign neglect' unjustly fails to respond to past injustice, sub-culture poverty, and unavoidably expensive cultural preference.

VII

To conclude, a plausible justification of support for minority culture is inconsistent with the justice defence of the market propounded by liberals like Dworkin and Kymlicka, because the stated justification is inconsistent with the attitude to expensive tastes which that defence of the market requires. There exist good arguments for the market, but justice is not one of them.

I grant that subsidy for expensive tastes *sounds* absurd, whereas special cultural support does not. But the supposed absurdity in the asserted parallel falls away, in two stages, when the precise character of my claim is restated. First, 'expensive tastes' denotes, here, not a person's actual life-style, but the misfortune of requiring more resources than the norm to obtain a normal level of fulfilment. Second, I do not call for the impossible, which is to say individualized subsidies, which discriminate between individuals whose tastes are expensive and others whose tastes are not. The required subsidy is not individualized but a general one on commodities where, so one may judge, involuntary expensive taste is likely: the recreation centre example and rural lifeways are cases in point. My claim is the unabsurd one that what justifies special support for minorities whose cultures are expensive to sustain also justifies subsidizing expensive facilities in a recreation centre and expensive rural transport. And that justification exposes the falsehood of a standard liberal defence of the justice of the market, even, that is, of a market to which people come bearing equal endowments of resource.*

* I thank Daniel Attas, Justine Burley, Selena Chen, Susan Hurley, Will Kymlicka, Joseph Raz, Andrew Robinson, Christine Sypnowich, Bernard Williams, and Arnold Zuboff for their criticisms of an earlier draft of this paper.

4

Governance of Multicultural Polities: Limits of the Rule of Law

❧

R. Sudarshan

Statement of the Problem

India as a multicultural polity has adopted the institutional forms of constitutionalism and the Rule of Law, although its society, economy and history are very different from that of the countries where these forms originated. Pathologies pertaining to the functioning of these institutional forms pose serious problems in all countries where primordial cultural and ethnic identities of different groups are being revived and asserted. The important question is whether these institutional forms of governance can continue as they are and serve the needs of polities which are historically diverse and multicultural as India, or even of those which have become more multicultural in recent years with growing immigrant or refugee populations.

'Unity in diversity', an oft-repeated aspiration in India, seeks to accommodate differences within a framework of shared basic values and common interests. Such a framework requires the conviction that unity is best fostered by tolerating diversity, that dissenting views should freely coexist with the dominant values of society, and interaction among diverse peoples, ethnic and religious groups, cultures and sub-cultures is a positive force for creativity, innovation and change.

The belief that it is possible to govern multi-ethnic societies in a proper manner is based on the premise that there are no insurmountable obstacles to different communities and groups being able to understand and respect cognitive and ethical differences that exist among them.

A major issue is how to fix the parameters of the framework of basic values and shared interests. When conflicts inevitably arise on account of ethnic, racial, religious, linguistic, caste, or even gender differences, how is the state to deal with them? Such conflicts are often rooted in differences in cultural identities which are shaped by collective consciousness, which, in turn, may have little to do with historical events as they might have actually occurred.

What should be the limits of tolerance of violence that is typical in such conflicts? Who can set such limits? What forms of public spheres are best suited to articulate differences while at the same time containing their unreasonable forms of expression?

Narrowing down the varied dimensions of governance, the question now is whether constitutionalism and the Rule of Law are capable of fostering diversity while providing a framework of shared basic values and common interests? What are the limits of the Rule of Law?

Constitutionalism and the Rule of Law: Clarifying Concepts

The claim of modern states to monopoly over legitimate use of physical force, and to sovereignty (in the sense that there is no further appeal against its sanctions) generates an uneasiness. There is an element of circularity in the claim of states to have a monopoly over the legitimate use of physical force. By definition, it renders coercion on the part of others illegitimate. All states now claim such legitimacy. But in order to be able to distinguish between states, it is necessary to examine how states actually secure the required obedience. Some do it through repression or undisguised coercion. Most others claim to do it through the Rule of Law. The formal architecture of liberal democratic constitutions which India, and other developing countries have adopted from Western models, uses as its basic organizational principle the Rule of Law.

The Rule of Law is largely a procedural principle, under which all actions of institutions of the state are required to have a form of legality. But often Rule of Law is misused as a slogan to refer to all kinds of ideals its users wish to uphold. One example of such inflation of meaning of the Rule of Law is the 1959 International Congress of Jurists' New Delhi Declaration:

> The functions of the legislature in a free society under the Rule of Law is to create and maintain those conditions which will uphold the dignity of man as an individual. This dignity requires not only the establishment of his civil and political rights but also the establishment of the social, economic, educational, and cultural conditions which are essential to the full development of his personality.

To be precise, the Rule of Law should not be confused with other ideals of justice, human rights, democracy, or equality. It is one of the important virtues of legal systems which seek to establish 'a government of laws and not of men'. As a procedural principle, it can reduce the efficiency for evil if a government happens to be evil. But it cannot eliminate the possibility of evil. Nor can it guarantee the substance of the common good or secure all aspects of the common good. The Rule of Law is not necessarily rule by good law.

Alongside the Rule of Law, the notion of Separation of Powers, despite its conceptual ambiguities and untidiness, has been very influential. It entails a differentiation in the procedures adopted for legislation, administration, and adjudication, such that the political order is subordinated to the legal order, and *vice versa*. Separation of powers and judicial independence are taken to be hallmarks of states which combine respect for the freedom of the individual with fulfilling the requirements of collective security. Actually, the causation often runs not from the separation of powers to the benign state, but the other way round. Benign states respect separation of powers.

The Rule of Law legitimizes the political order by institutionalizing the principle of restraints on the exercise of power through the form of legality. It simultaneously secures the legitimacy of the legal order through a purported separation of law from politics, thereby absolving the judiciary of responsibility for the substantive content of legislation. The realm of law, therefore, is accorded substantive, methodological, institutional, and occupational distinctiveness emphasized by the 'independence' of the judiciary.

This form of legality has been regarded as a protection against the possible tyranny and arbitrariness on the part of the state. The requirements of generality, uniformity, neutrality, and predictability of laws, all formal characteristics of the Rule of Law, recognize the formal equality of citizens, and reflect the impersonal nature of public power.

The laws themselves are devised by the state. In the modern conception of positive law, they need not be underpinned by any transcendental belief in Natural Law. Still it has been thought valuable to have the state bound by positive law. It is a modern belief that governance through law is superior to the rule of men, no matter how extraordinary or special they might be as human beings and as rulers.

However, reliance on the form of legality alone may not take one very far in ensuring that justice is done to all citizens. It is small consolation if unjust laws are applied with impartiality and certainty. It is not difficult to imagine that a state could have laws of its own devising which are safely obeyed, to the detriment of some sections or all of its citizens.

A low level of popular legitimacy is not antithetical to the survival and effectiveness of a state provided it has the support of critical elites. Many of these critical channels of support run within the state apparatus itself—the military, the police, the civil service, and the judiciary—rather than between state and civil society. It is often the disintegration of elite legitimacy that results in *coups* and transformations in the organization of the state. It does seem that the legitimizing ideology of the law is needed rather more to secure the coherence and consent of the dominant elites than for purposes of mystifying the masses.

The real problem is how to ensure rule by good law, and not by any other kind of law. One solution has been sought by compelling the state to be bound by a superior law, *legum legis*, or a constitution prescribing norms, on the touchstone of which bad laws could be declared invalid. Another solution has been to secure the participation of representatives of citizens in the formulation of laws through democratic institutions.

In England, between 1688 and 1767, the authority to make law shifted from the monarch to the King-in-Parliament. Since then the British have trusted the majority in Westminster to make any law it pleases, relying on electoral accountability and conventions of parliamentary good sense to contain possible arbitrariness and tyranny.

The framers of the United States Constitution believed that the possible tyranny of a legislative majority was as undesirable as that of a sovereign monarch. So they opted for a form of government that combines representative democracy with constitutionally prescribed separation of legislative, executive, and judicial powers.

Judicial Review

The United States Constitution did not assign to the Supreme Court a role as guardian of the Constitution with powers of judicial review over legislation. Judicial review of decisions of the legislature was a technique devised by Chief Justice Marshall to avoid a confrontation with President Jefferson. In *Marbury* v. *Madison*, the doctrine that the written constitution would prevail over ordinary legislation, and that the latter would be void to the extent it is found by the Supreme Court to be inconsistent with the Constitution, was enunciated, not to assert the authority of the judiciary vis-à-vis the executive, but rather to escape the embarrassment of having its authority flouted by the executive.

Judicial review of legislation permits divergences to emerge within the state apparatus over interpretations of the Constitution's provisions. Whether the judiciary's conception of the public good will ultimately prevail depends not on the 'bootstrap' support of legal argument but on realities of political power. The exercise of the power of judicial review and its interpretation of constitutional provisions clearly entails political judgment on the part of the judiciary.

But the integration of law and politics, although it is inherent in the power of judicial review, is considered to be a threat to the legitimacy of a form of government based on the Rule of Law. Judges, lawyers, and jurists, therefore, tend to internalize a belief in the separation of law and politics. They are not readily disposed to engage in critical inquiries into the political role of the judiciary because it is supposed to have none. This actually makes the task of judicial review more difficult, even if it serves the purpose of shielding judges from the kind of accountability expected of politicians.

Imposition/Adoption of Constitutionalism and Rule of Law

From the perspective of evolutionary modernization theorists, formal legal rationality, of the kind Max Weber described, is taken to be a higher form of social organization. Legal rationality is believed to transcend other 'legal systems' which seek to achieve substantive ends on a case by case basis, or which resolve disputes and adjudicate by taking into account moral, ethical, and political dimensions of conflict.

In a simplistic way, Weber's analysis of the connections between the rise of legal rationality and the development of capitalism has been taken to provide the theoretical underpinning for the belief that legal development, the replication of Western legality in the Third World, are prerequisites for economic and political development in the image of the West. This belief has witnessed a resurgence in recent years after the collapse of communist states, and the adoption by China of a 'market road to socialism'. In India's recent appeal to international investors much has been made of the availability of a familiar and modern legal system.

Weber's work does not provide a basis for the belief in the causal efficacy of modern rational law in bringing about economic development. Its features are shown to be accommodating to the imperatives of a free market, and even this process developed differently in England, where the Common Law did not share critical features of European Civil Law. The assumption of evolutionism really reflects an ethnocentrism, combining justifications for legal reforms in the Third World based on foreign expert advice with abdication on the part of advisers of responsibility for normative consequences of displacing other forms of law by eliminating forms of legal pluralism.

The Indian Case

In the case of India, it can be argued that while the British were careful not to impose Western forms of law wholesale in the colonial state, the framers of the Indian Constitution adopted, in a much more thoroughgoing manner, the Rule of Law as the organizational principle of the Indian state. The Indian nation-state was fashioned during nationalist struggles against the British Raj.

When the opportunity arrived for framing a new constitution for India, pre-colonial ideas of state appeared anachronistic to Indian leaders who favoured continuity with colonial institutions of governance.

The institutional division of governance into legislation, administration, and adjudication was established during colonial rule. But the dominant posture of the state was inevitably repressive given its need to 'hold down' the country. Colonial legal institutions were always subordinate to political power dictated from London, and lacked a consensual basis in India society. A regime of rule-governed administration introduced the notion of legality, but rules were accommodated to political expediency.

The Drafting Committee of the Constituent Assembly included prominent lawyers, members of India's small middle class. These men could not bring themselves to see political parties, the key to the working of the Westminster model they adopted, as being necessary for the purpose of *establishing* norms for the new state. Their liberal Western education made them conscious of the illegitimacy of colonial rule, but they were not enamoured of the strengths of indigenous democratic traditions and political practices. They admired the ideal of impersonal exercise of rational, disinterested power espoused by the Indian Civil Service. It did not seem to matter that the civil service, primarily trained to maintain law and order, and collect revenue, could not be sufficiently responsive to the challenge of developing an impoverished country.

Unlike the European middle class which formed part of the bourgeoisie with a class base in property, the draftsmen of the Indian Constitution represented an economically insecure middle class whose fortunes depended on the state. Their ideological orientation was primarily a centrist one based on constitutional legality, but unlike the propertied middle class of Europe they were unsympathetic to the traditional wealth of landlords. They preferred to have a constitutional state whose goals were a mix of liberal and socialist aspirations, hoping that political stability, economic development, and some degree of social justice would keep at bay both revolutionary programmes of the left and conservative authoritarianism of the right. They were more inclined to trust the judiciary and the civil service because these institutions were expected to remain aloof from politics and insulate the state from the consequences of partisan pursuit of narrow interests. The Constitution, therefore, conferred on the Supreme Court and the High Courts, one of the widest jurisdictions in the world.

The Chairman of the Drafting Committee, Dr Ambedkar, was strongly in favour of incorporating ideological goals and principles in the constitution. He tried to persuade members of the sub-committee on fundamental rights to accept his detailed draft incorporating principles of state socialism and 'economic democracy'. The Congress majority accepted his argument for expanding the scope of constitutional law, but rejected the principles he had submitted.

The Constituent Assembly eventually adopted a set of ideological norms which all parties were expected to acknowledge as fundamental in the governance of India. The prescription of norms articulated by them to control and guide political decisions was intended to *displace* politics as an activity that would contend over fundamental ideologies and principles, and seek legitimacy for them through periodic elections.

The affirmation of ideological goals itself together with the enormous powers of the judiciary give the Indian Constitution a highly juristic character. Many political issues are given the aspect of constitutional law, with the result that realization of programmatic goals frequently calls for judicial mediation. A programmatic constitution implies that courts, when interpreting constitutional provisions, would emphasize their teleology, attending more to the 'spirit' of the constitution than to the language of particular provisions. It also leads to the possibility of the judiciary 'mandating' legislation to give effect to constitutional goals, although failure to so legislate may carry no legally enforceable sanctions.

The Constituent Assembly could not adequately appreciate what techniques of judicial interpretation could make out of the ideological goals stated in the Preamble, and the chapters on Fundamental Rights and Directive Principles of State Policy. As they were most familiar with Anglo-American styles of constitutional interpretation, they expected judges to mainly follow a strict statutory construction approach to the interpretation of constitutional provisions. But in fact the Supreme Court of India departed from such an approach in the landmark case, *Kesavananda Bharati* vs. *State of Kerala*, when it held that the 'basic structure and framework' of the Constitution could not be amended by Parliament even after fulfilling all the special procedures prescribed for constitutional amendments to be valid. This kind of decision is unlikely to be made by British judges if they were interpreting a written constitution, but it would make sense to judges in countries like Germany where 'stateness' as a political variable is historically and socio-culturally more important.

The Constitution's eclectic combination of elements borrowed from the state tradition of European constitutions and Anglo-American legal traditions presents a challenge to the judiciary. It envisages a state with the requisite 'steering' capacity over society to fulfill its programmatic goals. A heavy burden is placed on constitutional law and the judiciary to supply what is, in fact, a missing tradition of 'stateness' in India.

The inscription over the seat of imperial power in the Central Secretariat in New Delhi reads: 'Honour the State, the Root of Law and Wealth'. Independent India has not thought it necessary to erase this. The statute of the King-Emperor, however, has been removed but the state is ambivalent about replacing the statute of the King-Emperor with that of Mahatma Gandhi.

Critiques of Constitutionalism: A German Perspective

The concepts of constitutionalism and the Rule of Law elucidated above have been criticized as inadequate devices of governance by some of Germany's most prominent intellectuals.

Carl Schmitt combined radical and conservative critiques of the ideology of constitutionalism, while providing one of the most lucid expositions of the ingredients of the liberal *Rechtsstaat*, whose guiding purpose is to protect the freedom of the individual against the power of the state. But by turning reality against ideal, Schmitt favoured absolute state power. His critique is based on the premise that the twentieth-century state had overtaken dualism of state and society that obtained in the nineteenth century.

Schmitt saw the Weimar Republic as a total state, in a quantitative sense (because it had so expanded), but total only because of its weakness and inability to resist organized interests and factions. The state that is total in a qualitative sense is the state which practises pure politics, rid of the fictions and normativity of liberal ideals of constitutionalism. In reality the *Machtstaat* overrides the *Rechsstaat*, according to Schmitt.

For Max Weber, the bureaucratic machinery of the modern state was producing the 'case of bondage of times to come'. The character of the bureaucrat was counterpoised by Weber to that of the politician. Responsibility in the case of the bureaucrat was to his de-personalized office, but for the politician it was an individual and personal responsibility. Weber admired British parliamentarianism because he believed it was the breeding ground of political leaders and the antidote to professional politicians in the bureaucracy and their monopoly of knowledge. Weber favoured direct election of the head of state, a Caesarian method of referendum so that the president could resist parliamentary absolutism.

Weber makes a concession to liberal democracy in the implicit division of powers in his scheme for the establishment of the new German republic after 1918. But he did not share the liberal concern with minimizing dominion (*Herrschaft*), limiting the power of the state. His main concern was the expansion of political power in the face of the stranglehold of the bureaucracy.

In terms of his classic typology of legitimate forms of authority—the traditional, the charismatic, and the legal-rational—Weber ended up by regarding the democratic form of legitimacy as part of charismatic authority based on a belief in a leader's extraordinary personal qualities. This would be the type of legitimacy Mahatma Gandhi would have had if we could imagine him being elected president in an acclamatory referendum in India.

We might even think of the charisma of Mrs Indira Gandhi which prompted the President of the Congress party to proclaim that 'India is Indira and Indira is India', or the present legitimacy claimed by *Puratchi Thalaivi* Dr J. Jayalalitha in Tamilnadu! Weber underestimated the danger of a Caesarian democracy becoming a Caesarian dictatorship. This could be because he wrote before the rise of modern totalitarian regimes. His belief in the need for election and popular acclaim signifies to an extent an anti-authoritarian shift in the classical charismatic form of leadership, where free choice by the people becomes the basis for legitimacy. What is interesting about his position is that he tried to locate himself in the no-man's land between Machiavellian power politics and democracy, between Caesarism and parliamentarianism, between decisive choice left to the charismatic political leader and constitutionalism.

Both Max Weber and Carl Schmitt shared the view that politics is simply the continuation of warfare by other means. Both believed that conflict cannot be eliminated in the affairs of men. In other words, both would have rejected the problem of governance as formulated in the first section of this paper, based as it is on the belief that it is possible to establish 'peace' by finding ways of enabling diverse groups to articulate and affirm their respective identities, and yet overcome mutual conflicts.

Pathologies of the Rule of Law: Diagnoses and Cures

An influential diagnosis of the pathology of the Rule of Law in South Asian countries was given by Gunnar Myrdal in his monumental work, *Asian Drama*. Myrdal characterized these states as 'soft', implying that they are unable, and unwilling, to enforce laws and expect very little from citizens by way of compliance or discipline. Obviously, even the minimal virtue of a legal system based on the Rule of Law is bound to be emaciated if rules and laws are not properly enforced.

Myrdal speculated that this could be a consequence of the forms of protest fashioned by Gandhi against the colonial state, giving rise to a set of anarchic attitudes with an ideological and emotional force to resist all form of authority. Later observers of the Indian legal system, notably Upendra Baxi, have characterized the government itself as being 'lawless'. A dramatic episode of 'governmental lawlessness' was the destruction of the Babri Masjid, and wilful contempt of the Supreme Court's directives regarding its protection.

Colonial civil servants had a paternalistic attitude towards the people, and ruled largely by negative discretionary powers. Their successors, noting the vast unmet development needs of the people, substituted positive discretionary powers of patronage and subsidies, reinforcing the colonial syndrome of dependency on the '*mai-baap*' state, and at the same time enlarged their opportunities for corruption.

The particular pathology of the Indian court system has been well described by Oliver Mendelsohn in the following words:

The proceedings are extraordinarily dilatory and comparatively èxpensive; a single issue is often fragmented into a multitude of court actions; execution of judgements is haphazard; the lawyers frequently seem both incompetent and unethical; false witness is commonplace; and the probity of judges is habitually suspect. Above all, the courts are unable to bring about a settlement of the disputes that give rise to litigation.[1]

What can explain this state of affairs? One explanation offered by the Chicago historian/anthropologist Bernard Cohen is the following:

In attempting to introduce British procedural law into their Indian courts, the British confronted the Indians with a situation in which there was a direct clash of the values of the two societies; and the Indians in response thought only of manipulating the new situation and did not use the courts to settle disputes but only to further them.[2]

Cohen echoes the great scholar of Hindu Law, J. D. M. Derrett, who asserted:

Elements in Indian law which are traditional have in a sense stood the test of time and are likely to work, either as they were intended to, or in some other more or less predictable way. Elements which are not traditional will either be distorted to perform functions for which they were not intended, or will be failures.[3]

Derrett examined Weber's discussion of the Indian case with reference to his famous theory on the Protestant ethic and the notion of an '"inner-worldly" asceticism'. He argued that it was a mistake to regard ancient Indian law as sacred law and to believe that Sanskrit perceptual texts were ever applied literally as if they were statutes. Indian development has been hindered, according to Derrett, simply because of a want of a true belief in the Rule of Law amongst the public, and because the profitability of honesty across groups is still being discovered. India's achievement of peaceful co-existence between groups has been through a balance of forces favoured by Hinduism. This mode of resolving conflicts

[1] *Modern Asian Studies*, 15:4, 1981.

[2] *Development and Change*, 8, 1959, p. 90.

[3] R. H. Moore, ed., *Tradition and Politics in South Asia*, Vikas, New Delhi, 1979, p. 56.

did not require a public spirit because relative status among groups was traditionally determined, and it was the ruler's responsibility to maintain that balance. The price of this Hindu-mediated balance has been immobility, or the 'Hindu rate of growth', as the respected economist Dr Raj Krishna dubbed it.

Justice V. R. Krishna Iyer, among others, has also commented on the irrelevance of British notions of law in Indian society. He observed:

> We have to part company with the precedents of the British-Indian period tying our non-statutory law to vintage English law christening it 'justice, equity, and good conscience'. After all, conscience is the finer texture of norms woven from the ethos and life-style of a community, and since British and Indian styles of life vary so much the validity of an anglo-philic bias in Bharat's justice, equity and good conscience is questionable today.[4]

These diagnoses of the pathology of the Rule of Law in India locate the source of the problem in the dissonance between the legal regime inherited from the colonial state with either traditional, or even modern, requirements of Indian society. But others, again inspired by Weber, have argued that the source of the problem is not in the legal system *per se*, but in the kind of cases that it has to handle during a phase of major transformation in property relations (Mendelsohn).

A new variant of this kind of explanation is that the legal system has been designed to subserve the needs of a capitalist market economy, while the regulatory and administrative regime of India was designed to subserve the needs of state-led industrialization and some form of 'socialism'. Those who wish to resist the will and policies of the state find in the courts a convenient site to litigate the state into immobility. On this reasoning, the cure for the pathology of the Indian court system is to bring its economy more into synchrony with the tenets of a legal system which evolved with capitalism. This would imply the removal of all discretionary controls on economic activity, and allowing markets to function as freely as they do in fully-fledged capitalist states.

It is unlikely that any of the cures for the malady which call for a return to a more pluralist legal system implicit in the critique of alien transplants can actually be implemented in India. However, the forces of globalization are set to ensure that the Western

[4] 'Rattan Lal *v.* Vardesh' (1976) *2 Supreme Court Cases*, 103 at 114–15.

style legal system remains in force, and legal adjustments and reforms take place only to fit India better into the emerging global economy. But such developments are also unlikely to defeat the arguments made for having a legal regime suited to the people rather than trying to change people so that they behave as the legal system would expect them to behave.

Nationalism versus Nativism

A more dangerous solution to India's problems with the Rule of Law has been stridently espoused by the Bharatiya Janata Party. This is Hindu nationalism to replace the lost nationalist force which energized the movement for independence. It is worth recalling that German nationalism was similarly a response to the breakdown of the monarchical order and the emergence of the bureaucratic modern state. Such nationalisms can arise whenever serious problems inherent in the liberal democratic order remain unresolved. Nationalistic regimes are very likely to marginalize the importance of diversity, and accommodate minorities as 'second class citizens', with token offers of ceremonial public offices to their representatives, or even some guarantees of rights to preserve their religions and cultures, provided they do not question the affirmed basis for nationalism. Nationalism is not the answer to the problems and inadequacies of the Rule of Law.

To avoid a possible confusion on account of the positive connotations of the term 'nationalism' in common currency, it is better to distinguish it from associated ideas of patriotism or nativism which are more positive. When Sir Walter Scott wrote, 'Breathes there a man with soul so dead, Who never to himself hath said, "This is my own, my native land"', he was referring to his place of nativity in Scotland, not to the United Kingdom. Commitment to diversity and multiculturalism requires respect for such nativist sentiments.

It should be observed that the nation-states of Europe, by joining the European Union, have traded in some erosion of their sovereignty for economic benefits. They are taking advantage of the fact that the material dimensions of human life have become ascendant over all other dimensions, and the marketplace has the power to impose a degree of homogenization because it is insensitive to diversity and culture. But we cannot be sure whether this is durable, or whether the 'passing of remoteness' can completely transform the collective consciousness of diverse groups of people.

An optimistic note in the transformation of the Indian nation-state might be struck in the constitutional commitment to establish *panchayats* as a new, and potentially more nativist, tier of governance. Perhaps the local *panchayat*, with all its traditional associations in the collective consciousness in India, might be a good place to begin with some elementary lessons in political accountability, and attempts to foster the kind of public spirit needed for the success of constitutionalism and the Rule of Law. Indian intellectuals and professionals will do well to participate in the political life of their communities more self-consciously as public citizens. Without that they are likely to be irrelevant and sink into cynicism, endlessly diagnosing problems without playing any part in solving them. We must appeal to the optimism of will to overcome the pessimism of this analysis of the career of constitutionalism and the Rule of Law in the governance of multicultural polities.

5

French Republicanism and 'Thick' Multiculturalism[1]

Catherine Audard

'Thick' multiculturalism, in contrast with 'thin' multiculturalism, according to Yael Tamir, characterizes a society where liberal and illiberal cultures have to co-exist and to reach an understanding, be it very limited and superficial, in order to avoid major conflicts and fragmentation. The case of France has often been put forward as an illustration of such a situation, mainly because of the recent events surrounding what has been called 'l'affaire du foulard Islamique', the wearing of the Islamic scarf or *hidjab* by young Muslim girls in schools.[2] The political and philosophical issue at stake is that of the neutrality of the state when confronted by what it sees as a threat to national identity and cultural homogeneity.

[1] The concept of 'thick' multiculturalism is used by Yael Tamir to refer to a society containing both liberal and illiberal cultures. See her paper 'Two Concepts of Multiculturalism', *The Journal of Philosophy of Education* 29, no. 2 (1995): 161–72. She gives France as an example of this situation whereas 'thin' multiculturalism would only involve different forms of liberal culture and thus allow in principle for an overlapping consensus as, according to her, in the case of the Canadian federal government and the Province of Québec.

[2] See, among others, A. E. Galeotti, 'Citizenship and Equality: The Place for Toleration', in *Political Theory* 21, no. 4 (1933): 585–605, N. C. Moruzzi 'A Problem with Headscarves', in *Political Theory* 22, no. 4 (1994): 653–72 for detailed accounts of the events and their political significance.

As Tamir notices, one could give at least three readings of the incident: as a conflict between a tolerant state and an illiberal religious minority, seen as 'fundamentalist'; as a conflict between an illiberal state and legitimate Muslim ways of life (this would be the Anglo-American favoured liberal reading); or, thirdly, as a conflict between two illiberal cultures.

My aim, here, is to situate this case within its proper context and, first, to try and explain the main features of the French view on multiculturalism. Second, I claim that, in spite of obvious differences, French republicanism and political liberalism in the Rawlsian sense are two versions of a common political project that is centred on civil rights and the value of citizenship, by contrast with a community united by a single common good, a single religion or a single culture. Third, I shall conclude by briefly suggesting that the French republican ideal of integration with its universalist and egalitarian principles is not a pre-postmodernist illusion nor is it aimed at the destruction of diversity; on the contrary, with some liberal institutional imports it could still provide a satisfactory answer to the problems of multiculturalism.

The Main Features of the French Republican Model: Integration as 'Assimilation'

France, Britain and the United States have been and still are to a certain extent, the results of important and voluntary fluxes of immigration. They are all three nations built out of many different nationalities, languages, religions, ethnicities, even if this factor is hidden behind the dominant concept of nation-states. They are all, in different ways, of course, multicultural societies and have been so for a very long time. In the case of France, this is a country whose borders were still changing at the turn of the century and which, all through the second half of the nineteenth century, had been integrating new populations, each with different languages, Italian dialects in the case of the Duchies of Savoy and Provence, German in the case of Alsace and Lorraine; a country which was integrating Polish and Italian miners before World War I, Jewish Eastern and Central European craftsmen between the wars, over one million of French colonists and their Muslim partisans, the 'harkis', after the war in Algeria and which has roughly three millions immigrants without full citizenship living on its territory at the moment. It is said that one French person in four has one foreign grandparent.

And still France does not see itself as a multicultural, multi-ethnic society in the way in which Britain or the United States and Canada see themselves. A very timid attempt at some measure of recognition of this rich cultural diversity was met in the eighties with intense criticism and had led to the present violent backlash, which has been widely publicized under the label of 'l'affaire du foulard Islamique'. France still cannot allow pluralism and sees itself as a unitary and single republic, as a community of free and equal citizens, irrespective of their different cultural identities.

The Idea of the 'Universal Republic'

France, as a nation, is the result of a political project, the formation of a community based not on 'blood', but on citizenship. The nation as a community of citizens has been articulated most strongly by the French Revolution, but it has deeper roots, which I cannot explore here. What was most hated in the old regime, in the remains of the feudal system, around 1789, were the many particular interpersonal bonds between the people, the particular so-called rights and obligations which, on the one hand, constituted the fabric of the organic society and of solidarity, but on the other hand, were symbols of oppression and injustice. (See, for instance, during the pre-revolutionary period, the impact of Beaumarchais' play 'The Marriage of Figaro' which epitomized the evils of the feudal system through the magnifying glass of the 'droit de cuissage' or right to rape, the right of his Lordship to the use of Susanna's body before her legitimate owner, her husband.)

The twin processes of modernization and universalization during and since the French Revolution have meant that to be or to become French was not simply to enter a particular ethnic group or nation, but to become an actor in a wider drama, that of an emancipatory process which was to lead eventually to a federation of democratic and peaceful nations, to universal reconciliation, to the dissolution of particularities and differentiations as sources of conflicts, to the recognition of a kind of universal brotherhood or world citizenship. The French Revolution had had the privilege of being the prime mover in this process by freeing the people from their particular roots and bonds and by 'recreating' them as the abstract bearers of rights: no more a Breton or an Auvergnat or a Jew or a Pole, but a French citizen with equal rights and dignity. To be French, therefore, implied special responsibilities, very similar to those carried by the American notion of citizenship, those of enlightening the rest of the world as to the benefits of free and equal citizenship, beyond the differences of race, ethnic origins, language and religion. France had invented the notion of the 'civic nation' and, as such, presented one particular instance of the 'universal republic'.

Such is the deep, long-standing *paradox* of a universal political project, whose embodiment in the French state is necessarily particular. (The same paradox was encountered in the communist project, that of an international movement with national embodiments). Even if the very concept of a 'civic nation' is, in principle, the opposite of the concept of nationalism, it is still not completely free from it. Let us consider first, the exact meaning of the civic nation, of the republic as a community of citizens, united and integrated in spite of their different cultural origins. By contrast with the 'ethnic nation', embodied in contemporary united Germany, for instance, the political project of the civic nation does not take political homogeneity to coincide with similar cultural origins: it is not 'given' as a kind of natural phenomenon, a second nature, as it were, but is the result of a voluntary and conscious allegiance. But this does not mean that the political superstructure is superimposed or, so to speak, forced upon a divided, fragmented civil society. The nation is not given as such by the past, by culture or by tradition, but is created at any given time by the tacit adhesion of the citizen to its political institutions: the nation, as Ernest Renan famously said, is *a daily plebiscite*. This is the best definition of the republic as a voluntary political creation. It is neither given nor imposed, but is the result of an endlessly renewed social compact. Consequently, cultural pluralism and the fragmentation of society into distinct communities are threatening for such a project. The many different components would remain untouched by the social contract. They would remain what they were at the beginning: particular communities and individuals without a common political project. This is why if France is effectively as multicultural a society as Britain or the United States, it does not see itself as such, but rather as having the mission to assimilate this diversity into the one and indivisible republic, to transform these individuals into equal and similar citizens, to dissolve the remaining small local communities into the undifferentiated body politic.

We have, then, two possible readings of the myth of a universal republic. Either we can see the French model of integration as nationalist and illiberal in that its real intent, beyond the rhetoric of equality, is to 'Frenchify' its population, to impose on it one single culture, one language, one way of thinking, irrespective of its various distinct identities, and all this in the name of emancipation. More importantly, we can see it as wanting to create the conditions necessary for the exercise of a strong central political domination. From this point of view, it is clearly an instrument of internal and external colonization and imperialism. Or we can see it as an effective way of avoiding nationalism, because of the *political* nature of the nation. The strength of the nation as a united community comes from its political institutions, not from its language or racial purity. This is a very important feature that one should keep in mind before criticizing too strongly the republican ideal, especially when one thinks of the attempt at articulating a similar conception in contemporary Germany, that of Habermas' 'constitutional patriotism' and its recent failure to win widespread acceptance, since the reunification of Germany and the rise of German nationalism in the nineties. Maintaining a balance between universality and particularity is or could be one of the merits of this model as long as ethnocentricity is avoided, and universality is attributed only to the political institutions of the state and not to the cultural traditions within which they have emerged.

Integration through Assimilation: The Road to Modernity

Assimilation which, since the advent of the 'politics of recognition', we tend to see now as involving the loss of precious and irreplaceable identities, of valuable attachments and traditions, has not always been seen in such an unattractive light. On the contrary, depending on the features of the immigrant population, on the balance of powers and mostly, on the extent of the rights and benefits attached to citizenship, it has long been synonymous with a kind of emancipation and modernization that does not so much mean the painful loss of identity as the creation of a new breathing space in which to develop it in a new idiom.

Of this we could find many eloquent examples. One such is that of the Jews and of the French Revolution which granted them, in 1789, the status of equal citizenship for the first time during the history of the Diaspora. This meant a huge gain in security, dignity and basic life-prospects. For instance, the right to buy and acquire full ownership of property which, for centuries, had been denied to non-Christians in Christian countries (and is still denied to Jews and non-Muslims in many Muslim countries) was for the first time granted to the Jewish population. This has been a historical landmark for the Jewish people all over Europe and is still fondly remembered as a significant event, as witnessed by the famous saying: 'Happy as God in France!' Here, we have a case of assimilation without, on the whole, a loss of identity (though this claim obviously needs a careful analysis of the very notion of a Jewish identity), partly because of the special features of the Jewish religion, partly because of the content of the citizens' right. As citizenship included the right to worship, it allowed for the possibility of carrying on being both a Jew and a French citizen. The only restriction that the secular republic imposed on the citizens and their right to worship was that the exercise of religion should be kept private, so that it would not invade the public domain. Because of the non-proselytizing nature of the Jewish religion, this restriction has never really been a source of conflict. Secularism has benefited the Jewish religion because the latter had no ambition to transform the public life of the country,[3] to intervene as such outside the limits of the Jewish community. All that was required was the possibility of leading a Jewish life within the community without any hindrance. The same should have been true of Islam in France, but this, for reasons that we shall see later, has unfortunately recently proved very difficult. By contrast, secularism has caused a burning and still-on-going conflict with the Catholic Church mainly because of one of the latter's most prominent features, its one time and to some extent still avowed aim to transform French society into a Catholic one, to impose its specific values on the whole of the public sphere, irrespective of the basic rights and freedom of conscience of the rest of the population.

[3] This is, of course, not true of militant orthodox communities such as these Ultra-Orthodox Jews in Israel, who would wish to abolish the secular state and create instead a totally religious society.

Another such example of assimilation without loss of identity has been that of the Frenchification of the peasantry through the working of the education system and the teaching of the French language. Why, for instance, did the people of Alsace, at the turn of the century, feel so strongly attached to France even though their culture, ethnic identities and attachments were much more obviously German than French? One reason is that the equal citizenship granted to them by the republic gave them wider possibilities, opened up for them more new worlds of opportunities, of learning, social prospects, etc. than if they had remained as one of the many provinces of the German Empire. The attraction of modern citizenship weighed much more for the majority of the people than the protection of a second-rate identity in an authoritarian Empire. The same could be said to a lesser extent of peasants from Brittany, Central France, etc., for whom assimilation through the acquisition of the French language has meant an enormous gain, if only from the point of view of social mobility. Georges Pompidou was a typical case for the ideology of assimilation, a President of the republic of very modest origins, whose grandparents did not even speak French, as the small hamlet in rural Auvergne that bears him name reminds everybody in France. One should never underestimate the attractions of assimilation when it means a wider range of basic rights and freedoms, including the freedom to cultivate one's identity within the framework and the constraints of citizenship. The politics of assimilation have been resented mostly when the content of citizenship has become thinner, when the value of fundamental rights has been eroded as in the contemporary case of North African immigrants in France. Assimilation can be seen from the outside as a very illiberal process, but for the population the benefits can be enormous as long as the political and social value of citizenship is sustained.

It is when the process of assimilation is forced upon the people without the compensation of full citizenship that things go wrong. The French colonial enterprise in Algeria was characterized by an extraordinary ambiguity: the values of the republic, equal citizenship, etc. were granted only to the colonists, not to the colonized Algerians. Algeria was part of France, but not all French nationals were full citizens: in 1862, the Court in Algiers stated that 'while not being a citizen, the native was nevertheless French'. All through the period of French colonization, the discrepancies between the phraseology of rights and equality and the actual inequalities of status went uncriticized, all in the name of the benefits of 'assimilation'.[4] This treachery is one among many betrayals that explain the intensity of the rift between France and Algeria and the subsequent rejection of the Algerian immigrants in France.

The Instruments of Assimilation: The State, the School and the Church

THE STATE, INSTRUMENT OF THE NATION

The primary and most visible instrument of these politics of assimilation is the powerful and centralized French state. The state should not be confused with the nation nor with the people itself. The state is *par excellence* the instrument of the nation. It has been, first, the instrument of its creation, then of its consolidation. It secures the permanence of the nation as the latter is faced by internal and external dangers. The legitimacy of state power is grounded on the fragility of the civic nation as an abstract ideal. the state has to be powerful because, as the nation is *not* grounded on a 'natural' or ethnic community, by contrast with the 'ethnic' or 'cultural' nation (B. Anderson) the factors of dissolution are numerous. One could easily explain the 'statocracy' in France by giving historical reasons, but also by reference to the importance of the destabilizing factors and to the number of the various regional communities which had to be absorbed and 'Frenchified' through a kind of internal colonization since the Middle Ages. In modern Britain, by contrast, the process of absorption has, on the whole, been smoother and less authoritarian—with the major exception of Ireland.

Thus the civil service, the service of the state, has had a much more important role than that of mere administration. It has had an economic function, creating huge amounts of jobs during the rural exodus, creating allegiances to the republic as an employer among the provincial lower middle and working classes. It has had a cultural influence, gathering support for republican ideas. It is no wonder that the political elite, in contemporary France, comes

[4] D. Schnapper, *La communauté des citoyens*, Paris, 1994, p. 152.

from top-ranking civil servants (the Conseil d'Etat, the Cour des Comptes, the Inspection des Finances, etc.) and is deeply imbued with the republican credo when faced with any talk of decentralization or self-government, be it of the regions, the universities, the schools or whatever.

A direct expression of the state is to be found in the army, which protects the territorial integrity of the nation and its ideological unity. The army of the republic is seen as a 'melting pot' into which young generations are conscripted and where they are assimilated. The archaism of a compulsory military service, lasting twelve to sixteen months, seems to have no other explanation than the overt will to influence the population and to impregnate it with republican ideas, and to educate the lower classes to the rudiments of a civic consciousness. Its cultural mission, that is to be 'the army of the republic', is a mystery for no one. Again, because it acts as an equalizer in some ways, because it is publicly recognized as such, conscription as such is not seen in general as illiberal or as constituting an infringement of basic rights and liberties. It is part of the citizenship package of rights *and* obligations or duties. It is only recently that the coercive nature of conscription has become unpopular and, even then, it is more the growing inequality of conscription and the waste of time that it involves that is resented rather than the loss of liberty. As long as the balance of rights and duties is seen as fair, the action of the state seems acceptable. But as soon as certain inequalities are thought to be threatening, people will go out in the streets and demonstrate.

THE REPUBLIC AND THE SCHOOL

One sees clearly then why the creation by the state of a public, compulsory, secular and completely free educational system between 1880 and 1905 was an absolute necessity for the republic. It was the best way in which to assimilate the diverse populations and to create a solid basis for the civic nation. The role of the school system, in accordance with the function of the state, has undoubtedly been to shape the mentality and the instincts of the ordinary people in order to produce 'good citizens'. One should pause here and reflect on a striking feature of the republican ideal, namely the permanent conflict between the individual and the citizen or in Rousseauist terms, between the particular will and the general will. The meaning of this conflict is more cultural than is conveyed by this Rousseauist vocabulary; it is actually a conflict between the regional particularities, be they linguistic, religious or cultural, and the unity of the nation. But, at a philosophical level, such a distinction can lead either to absurdities or to a totalitarian discourse which, on the whole, would give a wrong idea of the republic. Here is what Jacques Muglioni, Chief Inspector of Secondary Schools, writes in 1994 in a paper entitled 'The Republic and the School': 'A human being, characterized by his allegiances, identifying himself with particular groups, with collective or individual interests, cannot be a good citizen since *a good citizen, first and for all, does not belong to anyone*.'[5] And he goes on,

> But is it the citizen that makes the Republic or the Republic that makes the citizen? The reciprocical link is only made possible by the school, beyond any respect for family, work or community links, even for traditions, however great they may be. The school is at the service neither of the family nor of the employers. Its only function is to shape the mind, without any consideration for interests or beliefs and to bring it to its highest level of freedom. The Republic admits of individual beliefs, but only what is due to any human being, not in the name of pluralism as such which would go in the opposite direction and lead to discrimination with particular religious or racial origins being signalled by the institution, even by the identity card!

There is a lot to comment on here. Beyond the totalitarian tone—'The School has thus an essential link to truth'—one should recognize the will to create a new type of human being, the *citizen*, that is someone who is no longer a particular individual, Alsatian, Breton or Provençal, but first of all French. This is, of course, the most striking and fascinating difference with the British liberal tradition where the emphasis is on the individual and the culture of the self, as Mill so eloquently shows in his *On Liberty*. One learns how to become French through the study of the great writers, of figures of the past, not through Socratic self-discovery. This explains why, in the very syllabus of the schools and in the methods of teaching, the emphasis is on theoretical, abstract knowledge and on competence rather than on personal experience, because that would mean diversity, heterogeneity, anarchy, perhaps, anyway a challenge to the forces of unification. It says a lot about the ideology of emancipation according to the republic that

[5] J. Muglioni, 'La république et l'école', *Philosophie politique*, no. 4, Presses Universitaires de France, Paris, 1993, p. 75n. Emphasis added.

the Founding Fathers of the schooling system, the most famous of whom was Jules Ferry, should be disciples of Auguste Comte, not of John Stuart Mill![6] But once again one should not see the republic as the enemy of personal, negative freedom, but as a political instrument of integration within a civic, not an ethnic nation, where citizenship is the substitute for cultural homogeneity. One is not born French, one becomes French, to paraphrase Simone de Beauvoir. The birth of a democratic community is made possible by a seemingly totalitarian ideology. The question is to what extent it actually is illiberal.

SECULARISM AND 'LAÏCITÉ'

The most sensitive issue, even now, is, of course, still that of religious peace in France. This is a very difficult question as the kind of secularism developed in France has contradictory aspects. There is a pragmatic secularism, which is based on an on-going compromise between the church and the state that attempts to satisfy contradictory basic claims; there is also an aggressive secularism, which wants to 'liberate' the people from their attachment to Catholicism and to the forces of obscurantism. This secularism becomes all too easily the caricature of the civil religion dreamed of, for instance, by Rousseau.[7] Between passions and compromises, the true story of the relations between the state and the Catholic Church is that of the emergence of neutrality with respect to the various beliefs seen as 'personal, free and changing'.[8] Of that long and complex story, I shall only take two very recent examples, those of the toleration of the 'Islamic scarf' and of the Jewish Sabbath in French state schools.

Since 1986 there has been a growing and often bitter polemic, first between parents, teachers and headmasters, then throughout

[6] See Blandine Kriegel, *L'identité francaise*, Editions Tierce, Paris, 1985, p. 84, and the reference book on the question by Claude Nicolet, *L'idée républicaine en France*, Gallimard, Paris, 1982.

[7] Rousseau, *On Social Contract*, Book IV, ch. 8, 'On Civil Religion'.

[8] Jean Bauberot, *Vers un nouveau pacte laïque*, Le Seuil, Paris, 1990. It is illuminating that 'laïcity' in French has two spellings: (1) 'Laïc' (lay) refers to the status of someone religiously active, but within a secular order, by contrast with the regular orders. (2) 'Laïque' (secular) means the status of the institutions like schools or of ideas that are independent of or opposed to the hegemony of the Catholic Church in the civil society. One should notice the religious dimension that remains part of the expression.

the whole of the country, as to whether the correct interpretation of the principle of neutrality should allow or forbid the wearing of the Islamic scarf in school. In the end, in November 1989, the State Council (the court of arbitration for conflicts between the state and the citizens) laid it down that symbols of religious affiliation as such are not incompatible with the neutrality (laïcité) of the school on condition that they do not constitute a flagrant act of 'proselytism' and that they do not threaten the public order. But, in 1994 (when the full extent of the Islamic guerilla conflict in Algeria and its possible extension to France among the immigrant population began to be known), the Minister for Education issued a circular forbidding the wearing of 'ostentatious religious symbols' in school. By contrast, a strong minority of public opinion claims that the right to education is more important than a strict application of the neutrality requirement and that young Muslim girls should not be excluded from school because of their religious identity. A comparison with the possibility for Jewish students to respect the Sabbath when there is school on Saturdays shows the same ambiguity. On the one hand, Jewish students may be allowed to miss school on some Jewish festivals, but, on the other hand, this is not a right as it conflicts with the requirements of school attendance. Thus, the republican ideal can be the source of two conflicting interpretations. This is another argument to show that the republican model is not, as such, necessarily illiberal and intolerant, but that it provides a contradictory programme, as, indeed, it has done from the start.

The Ambiguities of this Politics of Assimilation

In conclusion, we may point out that the source of the problems in many sectors is the lack of democracy in the interpretation of the myth. First, in its political institutions the republic has identified itself with the sovereignty of the 'people', that is, with a full representative regime with no possibility of recourse against unjust majorities. It is only recently, in 1946, that the Declaration of Human Rights has been incorporated into the Preamble to the Constitution. It is even more recently that the Gaullist regime has introduced a constitutional control of the laws, limiting the scope of the legislator and pointing towards some sort of judicial review in the American sense. But this is still seen by many as something 'undemocratic', and the latest reform of the Constitution (July 1995) with its extension of the use of referendum goes against these very limited attempts at a measure of constitutionalism and gives even more power to the President and to majority public opinion.

The discrepancy between the discourse of republican equality and the reality of social inequalities through the educational system is even more difficult to accept than would have been the case if this rhetoric of equality had been dismissed and the reality of competition and the need for equality of opportunities recognized.[9] The issue of Islam in France also shows vividly how little respect there is, in reality, for freedom of conscience. For instance, certain religious congregations remain banned, as they have been since the French Revolution. The value of citizenship and of basic political rights is also deeply unequal and this creates even more frustration than in a class-ridden society as in Britain because of the egalitarian phraseology. Finally, the omnipresence of the state, the powerful bureaucracy, the almost ridiculous centralization and the limits imposed on the creativity of the civil society all seem to point in the direction of an illiberal rejection of pluralism.

Republicanism and Political Liberalism

Beyond the contrasts, however, the similarities between republicanism in the French sense and political liberalism are nevertheless real. Historically, the two conceptions share the same project of creating a civic nation embodying moral ideals and leading to peaceful co-existence, even though the embodiment of the project has taken different forms. Conceptually, they originate in similar sets of ideas dating from the Enlightenment: the idea of a social contract; the concept of procedural justice; the priority of the right over the good; the priority of basic liberties over utility; the definition of autonomy as a source of self-validating claims; the necessary tension between equality and liberty within the liberal tradition of natural rights (which does not mean, as Rawls tends to think, a conflict); the separation between the public and the private spheres. All these ideas are familiar enough. It is more interesting to stress that the problems encountered recently by liberalism are also those of republicanism.

[9] On that question, see Pierre Bourdieu's famous book, *Les Héritiers*, Paris, 1968.

Political Liberalism vs Comprehensive Liberalism: The Neutrality of the State

I take political liberalism to mean what John Rawls has emphasized in his latest book,[10] that is, a political conception of justice that can serve as the basis for an overlapping consensus between deeply divided and conflicting views of the good held by reasonable and co-operating citizens. His aim is to contrast it with comprehensive liberalism. Comprehensive liberalism, such as that of Kant or Mill, is a view not only of the basis of political association, but of the whole of human life. Its affirmation of the priority of freedom has metaphysical foundations in an individualistic conception of rationality and the will. To ground philosophically the institutions of a democratic pluralist society on such a view would, however, be both unjust and inefficient, as people not sharing an individualistic secular doctrine would deeply resent its influence on the major institutions that shape their lives and those of their families. What about a liberal education, if you are a deeply traditional, religious person? To this question Rawls presents political liberalism's answer: 'Political liberalism has a different aim and requires far less. It will ask that children's education include such things as knowledge of their constitutional and civic rights so that, for example, they know that liberty of conscience exists in their society and that apostasy is not a legal crime.'[11] This means that political liberalism concerns itself only with the citizen, with the political domain, not with what happens in the non-public sphere, as long as the first principles of justice are complied with.

Now, this is exactly the view shared by the republican ideal that leads to the necessary neutrality ('laicity') of the state. This is where republicanism and political liberalism prove to be part of a similar project, that of securing a consensus between reasonable, but opposed conceptions of the good. This project is clearly in deep contrast with the vision of the political association as a community ('Gemeinschaft') racially and ideologically united by a common vision of the good.

The difficulty lies in the recognition of that reasonableness which allows for the possibility of a political consensus. Is it a

[10] John Rawls, *Political Liberalism*, Columbia University Press, New York, 1993; see chs IV and VI.

[11] Ibid., pp. 199–200.

capacity of the individual or of the citizen? How do the two relate? Different answers point to two different brands of republicanism. 'In politics as in educational matters, republicans divide themselves into the religious who want to teach a republican catechism, and the moderates who wish to respect the liberty of conscience.'[12] On the one hand, we have the Jacobin tradition and the pervasive influence of Rousseau's suspicion of the individual; it is only the citizen, educated by the state and exhibiting the civic virtues necessary for the general will, by contrast with particular desires, who can be trusted to 'obey reason and not instinct'. On the other hand, we have Condorcet and his followers during the Third Republic with Gambetta and Ferry, the protagonists of an 'open' republic that sees the individual as a progressive and social being, following Auguste Comte's views on the social determination of human nature; rationality is not an expression of virtue, but the result of instruction and sociability. This second version is not, in its essence, illiberal, even if we find in it tendencies to authoritarianism,[13] and it is not at all opposed to the main features of political liberalism.

Reasonable Pluralism

Conceptually, what has been called *reasonable pluralism*[14] is the common basis for the respect for liberty of conscience and the neutrality of the state. This refers to the fact that a plurality of views is supported by people who nevertheless recognize that other people may have different beliefs from their own while remaining reasonable, that is, while recognizing the limits of reasonable disagreement, what Rawls calls the 'burdens of reason'. In other words, 'reason does not mandate a single moral

[12] Nicolas Tenzer, *La Rëpublique*, Presses Universitaires de France, Paris, 1994, pp. 82–3; see Condorcet, *Projet sur l'instruction publique*.

[13] On this contrast, see J. S. Mill, *Auguste Comte and Positivism*, 1869; the *Correspondence* between the two men is also extremely illuminating (*Lévy-Brühl* (ed.)) Alcan, Paris.

[14] Joshua Cohen, 'Moral Pluralism and Political Consensus', in *The Idea of Democracy*, D. Copp, J. Hampton and J. Roemer (eds) Cambridge University Press, Cambridge 1993 see esp pp. 281–2. Rawls, *Political Liberalism*, p. 36.

view'.[15] This attitude is part of what Rawls calls the 'duty of civility'[16] and Scanlon[17] has described as the principle for moral motivation in its relation to rationality: we have a basic desire to be able to justify our actions to others on grounds that they could not reasonably reject. The ability to recognize reasons other than our own as acceptable reasons, even if we cannot share them, is the basis for a moral participation in the political association. The conception of toleration is at the heart of political liberalism. It means that without the existence of a community of justification, there cannot be a political association. But this community does not have to be united by a common vision of the good, as this would impinge on the freedom to choose his or her own ends which each member can rightly claim as his or her due. In the name of justice, the consensus has to be limited to a view of the principles regulating the political association as such and must not go beyond.

This view of the rational basis for a moral consensus is common to the political projects of both liberalism and republicanism. The common enemy of both is a conception that takes political membership to be based on culture and emotional links with the 'Fatherland', rather than on an appeal to the universal dimension of individuality and to the ability to acknowledge otherness and diversity as positive facts, not as a dangerous alienation.

A Common Political Project: The Republic as a Kantian Regulative Ideal

Kant is the common factor between liberalism and republicanism with his view of the republic as a moral ideal of universalization beyond the particularities of existing human communities. He writes in his *Essay on Perpetual Peace*:[18]

[15] Cohen, 'Moral Pluralism', p. 284.

[16] Rawls, *Political Liberalism*, 'This duty involves a willingness to listen to others and a fairmindedness in deciding when accommodations to their views should reasonably be made', p. 217.

[17] T. M. Scanlon, 'Contractualism and Utilitarianism', in *Utilitarianism and Beyond*, A. Sen and B. Williams (eds) Cambridge University Press, 1982. See also Rawls, *Political Liberalism*, pp. 40n, 81–6.

[18] Kant, *Political Writings*. H. Reiss (ed.) Cambridge University Press, 1970, p. 98ff.

> A *republican constitution* is founded upon three principles: firstly, the principle of *freedom* for all members of a society (as men); secondly, the principle of the *dependence* of everyone upon a single common legislation (as subjects); and thirdly, the principle of legal *equality* for everyone (as citizens)....The republican constitution offers a prospect for a perpetual peace...as it is inevitably the case that under this constitution, the consent of the citizens is required to decide whether or not war is to be declared, and they will have great hesitation in embarking in so dangerous an enterprise.

The ideal republic is, therefore, the best protection against nationalism and imperialism, as actual nation-states are communities of citizens, not organic entities. It is liberal in that sense and congruent with the liberal principle of legitimacy.

This becomes even clearer when one is reminded that liberalism and republicianism do not refer to forms of sovereignty or domination, as when one talks of democracy or of totalitarianism, but to organizational principles of political association which can be based either on the welfare of the community, as in Hegel's conception of the illiberal state, or of the individual. The 'republique', where each subject is also a citizen and where duties are counterbalanced by rights, echoes the liberal community and its ideal of self-government and participation. It is no wonder that both claim the ideal of a non-Hobbesian social contract as the source of the legitimacy of the political union.

Differences in the Embodiments of the Project

For the most part it is the historical embodiments of these projects of a civic nation that have been so extremely different that they have tended to hide their common ideological ground. In France, the republic had a traumatic birth and nearly failed o materialize. It is only with the Third Republic (1870–1948), and not without the opposition of a strong anti-republican movement re-emerging regularly up to the Vichy regime, that the republican ideal has been established and widely accepted. To be a republican in France today, therefore, means without ambiguity to be a democrat, a partisan of the Rule of Law and of democratic representation and participation. But the precise meaning is not clear: does that mean unhindered popular sovereignty with the dangers of majority rule? Many questions remain still open to discussion and may give rise to conflicts, as we shall see.

Whereas Britain has experienced a continuous process where the emphasis has been much less on the active role of the state than on the capacity of civil society for self-organization and on the effectiveness of controls and checks on the power of the state, America, theoretically the most successful republic, has created a political consensus around a constitution and its continuous reinterpretation, and the defence of civil rights combined with a recognition of cultural diversity, which contrasts with the centralized French semi-imperial republic.

In spite of all these differences, however, it is obvious that the contrast goes much deeper with the German tradition, not so much that of Fichte or Hegel who still use a Kantian idiom, but with Herder and the Romantic revolution and then Carl Schmitt and certain aspects of Max Weber, as in his use of the distinction made by Ferdinand Tönnies between the concepts of Gemeinschaft and Gesellschaft. The real divide is between the civic and the ethnic nation, not between republicanism and liberalism.

The Democratization of the Republic

Nevertheless, the need for a democratization of the republic is widely recognized in France at the moment and it figured high on the agenda during the recent Presidential elections. We may identify many different areas where the republican ideal could benefit from political liberalism and be more welcoming to diverse cultures: constitutionalism, decentralization, the exercise of public reason and moral individualism. The main idea to be stressed here is that there should be a re-evaluation of the relations between moral and political concepts within the republican view and that such a transformation should generate more democracy, that is, more respect for the needs and development of the moral person and her cultural identity. Let us briefly examine this thesis.

Constitutionalism and the Democratization of the Republic: Cultural Rights

Can the French Constitution work as a moral paradigm for the political association, as it does in America, without ceasing to be a republican constitution, that is, one marked by the sovereignty of the law as an expression of the general will? As C. Nicolet says,

'It is just impossible for a republican to abstract himself from the dogma of the sovereignty of the law, as the law is still thought to be the expression of national (or popular) sovereignty.'[19] This is a very difficult question, but it is clearly a central one, if one looks for some kind of moral control over mere majority rule. The problem is to combine respect for the wills of the individual voters and legislators and respect for the basic principles of justice that majorities may too easily forget. Rousseau was very conscious of the problem when, with the disastrous consequences which we know, he wrote in the *Social Contract* (II, 7), 'the people always wants its good, but it does not always see it', in other words, the people needs a teacher or a guide to correct it. Thus, the republic had both to recognize the pre-eminence of the legislative power *and* to find ways of restricting it (a strong executive or a Presidency) in order to counteract the disasters of majority rule and populism. The liberal solution, by contrast, delegates to a third instance, the constitution, the responsibility of principles and of constraints on majority rule.

One of the weaknesses of the French regime, therefore, has always been a constitutional instability linked with a chronic disbalance of powers between the legislative and the executive. The Gaullist Constitution, for instance, was an amazing combination of democracy and monarchy, as the theory of popular sovereignty was translated into fact by a strong Presidency, representing the will of the people, and by a Parliament weakened to avoid the political instability of the old 'republic of the parties'. The law was, therefore, seen as having at the same time little dignity and absolute sovereignty. This is a dangerous contradiction.

The remedy for these weaknesses and ambiguities has been the creation of something similar to the institution of judicial review in the United States, the Conseil Constitutionnel. In spite of opposition, the law has partly lost its sacred value, being no longer beyond scrutiny by public debate. The 'Conseil Constitutionnel' was created by de Gaulle in 1946, but it had very limited powers in the sense that, until Giscard d'Estaing allowed the opposition parties to have recourse to it in 1974, only the President, the Prime Minister or the Presidents of the Senate and the National Assembly had access to it. A last attempt in 1990 to extend access to all the

[19] C. Nicolet, *L'idée républicaine en France*, Gallimard, Paris, 1982, p. 357.

citizens has failed. As we saw earlier, opposite tendencies are also at work as the most recent reform (1995) shows all too clearly. It has resulted in two *de facto* constitutions. One is of a parliamentary type, where national representation is slightly improved by the lengthening of parliamentary sessions; the other, of a presidential type, establishes a strong and direct link through referendum between the President and the people, and this link is beyond any control. We are faced again with the dangers of pure majority rule. The moralization of majority rule would really mean democratization of the republic. It would mean a much better deal for minorities.

Moral and Cultural Identity

One other main weakness of the republic concerns its conception of the moral and cultural identity of the individual. Charles Taylor, in *Sources of the Self*, has shown the poverty of the Enlightenment notion of the self compared with the rich Romantic vision of the person. Again, the Rousseauist influence makes itself felt on the republican concept. For Rousseau, the individual as such has no moral dignity, only particular interests. Dignity is acquired through citizenship and political participation. But this notion of dignity remains a *social* concept, not a *moral* or *cultural* one.

We saw earlier that one of the main benefits of integration, according to the French conception of the nation, has been education and the social value attached to citizenship. This should make up for the loss of local identities and attachments in the name of access to a new dignity. What is not present in the idea of the republic is the moral value of this new found dignity. The French story has been more one of social mobility, social status acquired through citizenship than one of personal, moral development. The republican model, inspired by Greek and Latin antiquity talks about the civic virtues and the value of political participation as the source for dignity. But what about people unable or unwilling to participate, perhaps because this means in the end to conform? Has citizenship to be necessarily militant? If so, the totalitarian danger is not far.

More importantly, however, cultural membership, as Will Kymlicka[20] has stressed, is an essential part of our moral develop-

[20] W. Kymlicka, *Liberalism, Community and Culture*, OUP, Oxford, 1989. See also his *Multicultural Citizenship*, OUP, Oxford, 1995.

ment. It is not simply the 'acting together' or the dialogue with the community which is formative nor is it the 'context of choice' that cultural membership provides, which is useful for our exercise of individual autonomy. There is a deeper reason, which is present both in republicanism and in political liberalism: the value of self-respect as acquired through cultural membership. Self-respect, based on the recognition by others of the valuable character of our life, of our activities, is the key to political consensus in a multicultural society. Contrary to the French conception of the republic, it does not necessarily stem from acting together, from political participation and positive liberty. But it does need a political expression through citizenship. The richer the content of citizenship, the better the chances of inclusion are; and cultural rights clearly enrich the content of citizenship as they protect the citizens' own personal moral development, their capacity for a sense of justice and a conception of the good. The destruction of cultural diversity can do nothing for the strengthening of self-respect.

The constitution of the self is an extremely complex phenomenon in which the nature of the political environment plays a greater role than has often been suspected. If the liberal tradition and especially Rawls is guilty of giving too simplistic an account of moral identity, they nevertheless provide us with the notion of self-respect as an essential primary good for a democracy. In that sense, they enlarge and enrich the republican concept of the dignity of the citizen. Self-respect is the basic component of our moral and political identity, it transforms mere individuality into a moral concept and cultural identity into a moral requirement.

CONCLUSION

Just as the traditional model of liberal citizenship, which was based not on political participation, but rather on self-development and personal autonomy has had to evolve and to include cultural membership, so too the concept of republican citizenship can be enlarged and enriched without losing its attraction. The major difficulty is to move from a purely individualistic point of view, from what Tamir calls 'autonomy-based liberalism', towards a more tolerant 'rights-based liberalism'[21] and to convince the

[21] Tamir, 'Two Concepts of Multiculturalism', p. 168, 'rights-based liberalism can express not only toleration, but also respect for decent illiberal

legislator that cultural rights have to be added to the basic rights protected by the Rule of Law, because they are an essential part of the moral identity of any citizen. Enriched in two main directions, those of both cultural and moral dignity, citizenship can once again be the main instrument of integration and cohesion that it has been in post-revolutionary France.

---

cultures which do not foster the ideal of personal autonomy, but which respect their members and allow them some means of participation and social influence'. It recognizes that 'even oppressive cultures can give people quite a lot' (Raz, *Ethics in the Public Domain*, Clarendon Press, Oxford, 1994. This respect is derived from the respect for the right of individuals to live according to their values, traditions, etc.

6

Democratic Exclusion (and Its Remedies?)

Charles Taylor

Democracy, particularly liberal democracy is a great philosophy of inclusion. Rule of the people, by the people, for the people; and where 'people' is supposed to mean (unlike in earlier days) everybody—without the unspoken restrictions of yesteryear: peasants, women, slaves, etc.—this offers the prospect of the most inclusive politics of human history.

And yet, there is also something in the dynamic of democracy which pushes to exclusion. This was allowed full rein in earlier forms of this regime, as among the ancient poleis and republics; but today it is a great cause of malaise. I want in this paper first, to explore this dynamic, and then to look at various ways of compensating for it, or minimizing it.

I

What makes the thrust to exclusion? We might put it this way: what makes democracy inclusive is that it is the government of *all* the people; what makes for exclusion is that it is the *government* of all the people. The exclusion is a by-product of something else: the need, in self-governing societies, of a high degree of cohesion. Democratic states need something like a common identity.

We can see why as soon as we ponder what is involved in self-government, what is implied in the basic mode of legitimation of these states, that they are founded on popular sovereignty. Now for the people to be sovereign, it needs to form an entity and have a personality.

The revolutions which ushered in regimes of popular sovereignty transferred the ruling power from a king onto a 'nation', or a 'people'. In the process, they invent a new kind of collective agency. These terms existed before, but the thing they now indicate, this new kind of agency, was something unprecedented, at least in the immediate context of early modern Europe. Thus the notion 'people' could certainly be applied to the ensemble of subjects of the kingdom, or to the non-élite strata of society, but prior to the turn-over it hadn't indicated an entity which could decide and act together, to whom one could attribute a *will*.

Why does this new kind of entity need a strong form of cohesion? Isn't this notion of popular sovereignty simply that of majority will, more or less restrained by the respect of liberty and rights? But this kind of decision rule can be adopted by all sorts of bodies, even those which are the loosest aggregations. Supposing during a public lecture, some people feel the heat oppressive and ask that the windows be opened; others demur. One might easily decide this by a show of hands, and those present would accept this as legitimate. And yet the audience of the lecture might be the most disparate congeries of individuals, unknown to one another, without mutual concern, just brought together by that event.

This example shows by contrast what democratic societies need. It seems at once intuitively clear that they have to be bonded more powerfully than this chance grouping. But how can we understand this necessity?

One way to see it is to push a bit farther the logic of popular sovereignty. It not only recommends a certain class of decision procedures—those which are grounded ultimately on the majority (with restrictions)—but also offers a particular justification. Under a regime of popular sovereignty we are free, in a way we are not under an absolute monarch, or an entrenched aristocracy, for instance.

Now supposing we see this from the standpoint of some individual. Let's say I am outvoted on some important issue. I am forced to abide by a rule I am opposed to. My will is not being done. Why should I consider myself free? Does it matter that I am over-ridden by the majority of my fellow citizens, as against the decisions of a monarch? Why should that be decisive? We can even imagine that a potential monarch, waiting to return to power in a coup, agrees with me on this question, against the majority. Wouldn't I then be freer after the counter-revolution? After all, my will on this matter would then be put into effect.

We can recognize that this kind of question is not a merely theoretical one. It is rarely put on behalf of individuals, but it regularly arises on behalf of sub-groups, for example, national minorities, who see themselves as oppressed. Perhaps no answer can satisfy them. Whatever one says, they cannot see themselves as part of this larger sovereign people. And therefore they see its rule over them as illegitimate, and this according to the logic of popular sovereignty itself.

We see here the inner link between popular sovereignty and the idea of the people as a collective agency, in some stronger sense than our lecture audience above. This agency is something you can be included by without really belonging to, which makes no sense for a member of the audience. We can see the nature of this belonging if we ask what is the answer we can give to those who are outvoted and are tempted by the argument above.

Of course, some extreme philosophical individualists believe that there is no valid answer, that appeals to some greater collective is just so much humbug to get contrary voters to accept voluntary servitude. But without deciding this ultimate philosophical issue, we can ask: what is the feature of our 'imagined communities' by which people very often do readily accept that they are free under a democratic regime, even where their will is over-ridden on important issues?

The answer they accept runs something like this: you, like the rest of us, are free just in virtue of the fact that we are ruling ourselves in common, and not being ruled by some agency which need take no account of us. Your freedom consists in your having a guaranteed voice in the sovereign, that you can be heard, and have some part in making the decision. You enjoy this freedom in virtue of a law which enfranchises all of us, and so we enjoy this together. Your freedom is realized and defended by this law, and this whether or not you win or lose in any particular decision. This law defines a community, of those whose freedom it realizes/defends together. It defines a collective agency, a people, whose acting together by the law preserves their freedom.

Such is the answer, valid or not, that people have come to accept in democratic societies. We can see right away that it involves their accepting a kind of belonging much stronger than the people in the lecture hall. It is an ongoing collective agency, one the membership in which realizes something very important, a kind of freedom. Insofar as this good is crucial to their identity, they thus identify strongly with this agency, and hence also feel a bond with their co-participants in this agency. It is only an appeal to this kind of membership which can answer the challenge of our imagined individual above, who is pondering whether to support the monarch's (or general's) coup in the name of his freedom.

The crucial point here is that, whoever is ultimately right philosophically, it is only insofar as people accept some such answer that the legitimacy principle of popular sovereignty can work to secure their consent. The principle only is effective via this appeal to a strong collective agency. If the identification with this is rejected, the rule of this government seems illegitimate in the eyes of the rejecters, as we see in countless cases with disaffected national minorities. Rule by the people, all right; but we can't accept rule by this lot, because we aren't part of their people. This is the inner link between democracy and strong common agency. It follows the logic of the legitimacy principle which underlies democratic regimes. They fail to generate this identity at their peril.

This last example points to an important modulation of the appeal to popular sovereignty. In the version I just gave above the appeal was to what we might call 'republican freedom'. It is the one inspired by ancient republics, and which was invoked in the American and French Revolutions. But very soon after, the same appeal began to take on a nationalist form. The attempts to spread the principles of the French Revolution through the force of French arms created a reaction in Germany, Italy and elsewhere, the sense of not being part of, represented by that sovereign people in the name of which the Revolution was being made and defended. It came to be accepted in many circles that a sovereign people, in order to have the unity needed for collective agency, had already to have an antecedent unity, or culture, history or (more often in Europe) language. And so behind the political nation, there had to stand a pre-existing cultural (sometimes ethnic) nation.

Nationalism, in this sense, was born out of democracy, as a (benign or malign) growth. In early nineteenth-century Europe, as peoples struggled for emancipation from multi-national despotic empires, joined in the Holy Alliance, there seemed to be no opposition between the two. For a Mazzini, they were perfectly converging goals.[1] Only later on do certain forms of nationalism throw off the allegiance to human rights and democracy, in the name of self-assertion.

But even before this stage, nationalism gives another modulation to popular sovereignty. The answer to the objector above: something essential to your identity is bound up in our common laws, now refers not just to republican freedom, but also to something of the order of cultural identity. What is defended and realized in the national state is not just your freedom as a human being, but this state also guarantees the expression of a common cultural identity.

We can speak therefore of a 'republican' variant and a 'national' variant of the appeal to popular sovereignty, though in practice the two often run together, and often lie undistinguished in the rhetoric and imaginary of democratic societies.

And in fact, even the original 'republican' pre-nationalist revolutions, the American and the French, have seen a kind of nationalism develop in the societies which issued from them. The point of these revolutions was the universal good of freedom, whatever the mental exclusions which the revolutionaries in fact accepted, even cherished. But their patriotic allegiance was to the particular historical project of realizing freedom, in America, in France. The very universalism became the basis of a fierce national pride, in the 'last, best hope for mankind', in the republic which was bearer of 'the rights of man'. That's why freedom, at least in the French case, could become a project of conquest, with the fateful results in reactive nationalism elsewhere that I mentioned above.

And so we have a new kind of collective agency, with which its members identify as the realization/bulwark of their freedom,

[1] And in fact, the drive to democracy took a predominately 'national' form. Logically, it is perfectly possible that the democratic challenge to a multi-national authoritarian regime, e.g. Austria and Turkey, should take the form of a multi-national citizenship in a pan-imperial 'people'. But in fact, attempts at this usually fail, and the peoples take their own road into freedom. So the Czechs declined being part of a democratized Empire in the Paulskirche in 1848; and the Young Turk attempt at an Ottoman citizenship foundered, and made way for a fierce Turkish nationalism.

and/or the locus of their national/cultural expression. Of course, in pre-modern societies, too, people often 'identified' with the regime, with sacred kings, or hierarchical orders. They were often willing subjects. But in the democratic age we identify as free agents. That is why the notion of popular will plays a crucial role in the legitimating idea.[2]

This means that the modern democratic state has generally accepted common purposes, or reference points, the features whereby it can lay claim to being the bulwark of freedom and locus of expression of its citizens. Whether or not these claims are actually founded, the state must be so imagined by its citizens if it is to be legitimate.

So a question can arise for the modern state for which there is no analogue in most pre-modern forms: what/whom is this state for? Whose freedom? Whose expression? The question seems to make no sense applied to, say, the Austrian or Turkish Empires—unless one answered the 'whom for?' question by referring to the Habsburg or Ottoman dynasties; and this would hardly give you their legitimating ideas.

This is the sense in which a modern state has what I want to call a political identity, defined as the generally accepted answer to the 'what/whom for?' question. This is distinct from the identities of its members, that is the reference points, many and varied, which for each of these defines what is important in their lives. There better be some overlap, of course, if these members are to feel strongly identified with the state; but the identities of individuals and constituent groups will generally be richer and more complex, as well as being often quite different from each other.[3]

The recent constitutional struggles in Canada provide a good example of political identity as a source of contention. No one in

[2] Rousseau, who laid bare very early the logic of this idea, saw that a democratic sovereign couldn't just be an 'aggregation', as with our lecture audience above; it has to be an 'association', that is, a strong collective agency, a 'corps moral et collectif' with 'son unité, son moi commun, sa vie et sa volonté'. This last term is the key one, because what gives this body its personality is a 'volonté générale. *Contrat Social*, Book I, ch. 6.

[3] I have discussed this relation in 'Les Sources de l identité moderne', in Mikhaël Elbaz, Andrée Fortin, and Guy Laforest (eds) *Les Frontières de l Identité: Modernité et postmodernisme au Québec*, Sainte-Foy, Presses de 1 Université Laval, 1996, pp. 347–64.

Quebec doubts that its own 'what for?' question must be answered in part by something like: 'to promote and protect Quebec's distinct character', paraphrasing the wording of the Meech Lake amendment. The major point at issue was whether Canada could take this goal as a component of its own answer to this question. The rejection of Meech was widely read in Quebec as a negative answer to this question, and this predictably gave an immense lift to the Independentist movement. Whether this will be enough to carry it over the top is still uncertain at the moment of writing.[4]

The close connection between popular sovereignty, strong cohesion and political identity can also be shown in another way: the people is supposed to rule; this means that the members of this 'people' make up a decision-making unit, a body which takes joint decisions. Moreover, it is supposed to take its decisions through a consensus, or at least a majority, of agents who are deemed equal and autonomous. It is not 'democratic' for some citizens to be under the control of others. It might facilitate decision-making, but it is not democratically legitimate.

In addition, to form a decision-making unit of the type demanded here it is not enough for a vote to record the fully formed opinions of all the members. These units must not only decide together, but deliberate together. A democratic state is constantly facing new questions, and in addition aspires to form a consensus on the questions that it has to decide, and not merely to reflect the outcome of diffuse opinions. However, a joint decision emerging from joint deliberation does not merely require everybody to vote according to his or her opinion. It is also necessary that each person's opinion should have been able to take shape or be reformed in the light of discussion, that is to say by exchange with others.

This necessarily implies a degree of cohesion. To some extent, the members must know one another, listen to one another and understand one another. If they are not acquainted, or if they cannot really understand one another, how can they engage in joint deliberation? This is a matter which concerns the very conditions of legitimacy of democratic states.

[4] I have looked at this issue in Guy Laforest (ed.) *Reconciling the Solitudes*, Montreal, McGill-Queen's University Press 1993. See especially 'Shared and Divergent Values', pp. 155–86.

If, for example, a sub-group of the 'nation' considers that it is not being listened to by the rest, or that they are unable to understand its point of view, it will immediately consider itself excluded from joint deliberation. Popular sovereignty demands that we should live under laws which derive from such deliberation. Anyone who is excluded can have no part in the decisions which emerge and these consequently lose their legitimacy for him. A sub-group which is not listened to, is in some respects excluded from the 'national', but by this same token, it is no longer bound by the will of that nation.

For it to function legitimately, a people must thus be so constituted that its members are capable of listening to one another, and effectively do so; or at least that it should come close enough to that condition to ward off possible challenges to its democratic legitimacy from sub-groups. In practice, more than that is normally required. It is not enough nowadays for us to be able to listen to one another. Our states aim to last, so we want an assurance that we shall continue to be able to listen to one another in the future. This demands a certain reciprocal commitment. In practice a nation can only ensure the stability of its legitimacy if its members are strongly committed to one another by means of their common allegiance to the political community. Moreover, it is the shared consciousness of this commitment which creates confidence in the various sub-groups that they will indeed be heard, despite the possible causes for suspicion that are implicit in the differences between these sub-groups.

In other words, a modern democratic state demands a 'people' with a strong collective identity. Democracy obliges us to show much more solidarity and much more commitment to one another in our joint political project than was demanded by the hierarchical and authoritarian societies of yesteryears. In the good old days of the Austro-Hungarian Empire, the Polish peasant in Galicia could be altogether oblivious of the Hungarian country squire, the bourgeois of Prague or the Viennese worker, without this in the slightest threatening the stability of the state. On the contrary. This condition of things only becomes untenable when ideas about popular government start to circulate. This is the moment when sub-groups which will not, or cannot, be bound together, start to demand their own states. This is the era of nationalism, of the break-up of empires.

I have been discussing the political necessity of a strong common identity for modern democratic states in terms of the requirement of forming a people, a deliberative unit. But this is also evident in a number of other ways. Thinkers in the civic humanist tradition, from Aristotle through to Arendt, have noted that free societies require a higher level of commitment and participation than despotic or authoritarian ones. Citizens have to do for themselves, as it were, what otherwise the rulers do for them. But this will only happen if these citizens feel a strong bond of identification with their political community, and hence with those who share with them in this.

From another angle again, because these societies require strong commitment to do the common work, and because a situation in which some carried the burdens of participation and others just enjoyed the benefits would be intolerable, free societies require a high level of mutual trust. In other words, they are extremely vulnerable to mistrust on the part of some citizens in relation to others, that the latter are not really assuming their commitments—for example, that others are not paying their taxes, or are cheating on welfare, or as employers are benefiting from a good labour market without assuming any of the social costs. This kind of mistrust creates extreme tension, and threatens to unravel the whole skein of the mores of commitment which democratic societies need to operate. A continuing and constantly renewed mutual commitment is an essential basis for taking the measures needed to renew this trust.

The relation between nation and state is often considered from a unilateral point of view, as if it were always the nation which sought to provide itself with a state. But there is also the opposite process. In order to remain viable, states sometimes seek to create a feeling of common belonging. This is an important theme in the history of Canada, for example. To form a state, in the democratic era, a society is forced to undertake the difficult and never-to-be-completed task of defining its collective identity.

II

So there is a need for common identity. How does this generate exclusion? In a host of possible ways, which we can see illustrated in different circumstances.

The most tragic of these circumstances is also the most obvious, where a group which cannot be assimilated to the reigning cohesion is brutally extruded; what we have come today to call 'ethnic cleansing'.

But there are other cases where it doesn't come to such drastic expedients, but where exclusion works all the same against those whose difference threatens the dominant identity. I want to class forced inclusion as a kind of exclusion, which might seem a logical sleight of hand. Thus the Hungarian national movement in the nineteenth century tried forcefully to assimilate Slovaks and Romanians; the Turks are reluctant to concede that there is a Kurdish minority in their eastern borderlands. This may not seem to constitute exclusion to the minority, but in another clear sense, it amounts to this. It is saying in effect: as you are, or consider yourselves to be, you have no place here; that's why we are going to make you over.

Or exclusion may take the form of chicanery, as in the old apartheid South Africa, where millions of Blacks were denied citizenship, on the grounds that they were really citizens of 'homelands', external to the state.

All these modes of exclusion are motivated by the threat that others represent to the dominant political identity. But this threat depends on the fact that popular sovereignty is the regnant legitimacy idea of our time. It is hard to sustain a frankly hierarchical society, in which groups are ranged in tiers, with some overtly marked as inferior or subject, as with the millet system of the Ottoman Empire.

Hence the paradox that earlier conquering people were quite happy to co-exist with vast numbers of subjects which were very different from them. The more the better. The early Muslim conquerors of the Ommeyad empire did not press for conversion of their Christian subjects, even mildly discouraged it. Within the bounds of this unequal disposition, earlier empires very often had a very good record of 'multi-cultural' tolerance and co-existence. Famous cases come down to us, like that of the Mughals under Akbar, which seem strikingly enlightened and humane, compared to much of what goes on today in that part of the world and elsewhere.

It is no accident that the twentieth century is the age of ethnic cleansing, starting with the Balkan Wars, extending in that area through the aftermath of World War I, and then reaching epic proportions in World War II, and still continuing—to speak only of Europe.

The democratic age poses new obstacles to co-existence, because it opens a new set of issues which may deeply divide people, those concerning the political identity of the state. In many parts of the Indian subcontinent, for instance, Hindus and Muslims co-existed in conditions of civility, even with a certain degree of syncretism, where later they would fight bitterly. The explanations often given for what happened include the British attempt to divide and rule, or even the British mania for census figures, which first made an issue of who was a majority where.

These factors may have their importance, but clearly what makes them vital is the surrounding situation, in which political identity becomes an issue. As the movement grows to throw off the alien, multi-national Empire and set up a democratic state, the question arises of its political identity. Will it simply be that of the majority? Are we heading for Hindu Raj? Muslims ask for reassurance. Gandhi's and Nehru's proposals for a pan-Indian identity do not satisfy Jinnah. Suspicion grows, demands are made for guarantees, and ultimately for separation.

Each side is mobilized to see the other as a threat to its political identity. This fear can then sometimes be transposed, through mechanisms we have yet to understand, into a threat to life; to which the response is savagery and counter-savagery, and we descend the spiral which has become terribly familiar. Census figures can then be charged with ominous significance, but only because in the age of democracy, being in the majority has decisive importance.

Secondly, there is the phenomenon we can sometimes see in immigrant societies with a high degree of historic ethnic unity. The sense of common bond, and common commitment has been for so long bound up with the common language, culture, history, ancestry, and so on, that it is difficult to adjust to a situation where the citizen body includes large numbers of people of other origins. People feel a certain discomfort with this situation, and this can be reflected in a number of ways.

In one kind of case, the homogeneous society is reluctant to concede citizenship to the outsiders. Germany is the best known example of this, with its third generation Turkish 'Gastarbeiter', whose only fluent language may be German, whose only familiar home is in Frankfurt, but who are still resident aliens.

But there are subtler, and more ambivalent ways in which this discomfort can play out. Perhaps the outsiders automatically acquire citizenship after a standard period of waiting. There even may be an official policy of integrating them, widely agreed on by the members of the 'old stock' population. But these are still so used to functioning politically among themselves, that they find it difficult to adjust. Perhaps they don't quite know how to adjust yet and new reflexes are difficult to find. For instance, policy questions are discussed among themselves, in their electronic media and newspapers, as though immigrants were not a party to the debate. They discuss, for instance, how to gain the best advantage for their society of the new arrivals, or how to avoid certain possible negative consequences, but the newcomers are spoken of as 'them', as though they weren't potential partners in the debate.

You will have guessed that the example I'm thinking of here is my native Quebec. I don't mean to exaggerate the phenomenon. It is changing, and I have great hopes that it will go on improving. It took time to learn the reflexes of inclusion, but they are being learned. Moreover, the problem is somewhat worse among extreme nationalists; it's not a universal phenomenon. It's worse among them, because nationalists cherish a dream, that of independence, which virtually no one not a 'Québécois de souche' shares, for understandable psychological–historical reasons. It's only natural that this strand of the Quebec ideological spectrum should have more difficulty opening itself to outsiders, as the catastrophic speech of our ex-Premier after the last referendum showed.

This example helps to illustrate just what is at stake here. I don't want to claim that democracy unfailingly leads to exclusion. That would be a counsel of despair, and the situation is far from desperate. I also want to say, as the slogan above indicated, that there is a drive in modern democracy towards inclusion, in the fact that government should be by *all* the people. But my point is, that alongside this, there is a standing temptation to exclusion, which arises from the fact that democracies work well when people know each other, trust each other, and feel a sense of commitment towards each other.

The coming of new kinds of people, into the country, or into active citizenship, poses a challenge. The exact content of the mutual understanding, the bases of the mutual trust, and the shape of the mutual commitment, all have to be redefined, re-invented. This is not easy, and there is an understandable temptation to fall back on the old ways, and deny the problem; either by straight exclusion from citizenship (Germany), or by the perpetuation of 'us and them' ways of talking, thinking, and doing politics.

And the temptation is the stronger, in that for a transition period, the traditional society may have to forgo certain advantages which came from the tighter cohesion of yore. Quebec clearly illustrates this. During the recent agonizing attempts by the government to cut back the galloping budget deficits, the Premier organized 'summits' of decision-makers from business, labour, and other segments of society. Not only the fact that this seemed worth trying, but the atmosphere of consensus, at least the earnest striving towards an agreement reflected the extremely tightly-knit nature of Quebec society as it has come down to us. The decision-makers still are disproportionately drawn from old stock Quebeckers, quite naturally at this stage of development. The operation might not be as easy to repeat twenty years from now.

So much for historically ethnically homogeneous societies. But we have analogous phenomena in mixed societies. Think of the history of the United States, how successive waves of immigrants were perceived by many Americans of longer standing as a threat to democracy and the American way of life. This was first of all the fate of the Irish from the 1840s. Then immigrants from south and eastern Europe were looked askance at in the last decades of the century. And of course, an old-established population, the Blacks, when they were given citizen rights for the first time after the Civil War, were in effect excluded from voting through lots of the Old South, until the civil rights legislation of our time.

Some of this was blind prejudice. But not all. In fact, the early Irish, and later European immigrants, could not integrate at once into American WASP political culture. The new immigrants often formed 'vote banks' for bosses and machines in the cities; and this was strongly resented and opposed by Progressives and others, concerned for what they understood to be citizen democracy.

Here again, a transition was successfully navigated, and a new democracy emerged, in which a fairly high level of mutual understanding, trust and commitment (alas, with the tragic exception, still, of the Black/White divide) was recreated—although arguably at the price of the fading of the early ideals of a citizen republic and the triumph of the 'procedural republic', in Michael Sandel's language.[5] But the temptation to exclusion was very strong for a time; and some of it was motivated by the commitment to democracy itself.

Thirdly, the cases I've been looking at are characterized by the arrival from abroad, or the entry into active citizenship of new people, who have not shared the ethnic-linguistic culture, or else the political culture. But exclusion can also operate along another axis. Just because of the importance of cohesion, and of a common understanding of political culture, democracies have sometimes attempted to force their citizens into a single mould. The 'Jacobin' tradition of the French Republic provides the best-known example of this.

Here the strategy is, from the very beginning, to make people over in a rigorous and uncompromising way. Common understanding is reached, and supposedly forever maintained, by a clear definition of what politics is about, and what citizenship entails, and these together define the primary allegiance of citizens. This complex is then vigorously defended against all comers, ideological enemies, slackers, and, when the case arises, immigrants.

The exclusion operates here, not in the first place against certain people already defined as outsiders, but against other ways of being. This formula forbids other ways of living modern citizenship; it castigates as unpatriotic a way of living which would not subordinate other facets of identity to citizenship. In the particular case of France, for instance, a certain solution to the problem of religion in public life was adopted by radical republicans, one of extrusion; and they have had immense difficulty even imagining that there might be other ways to safeguard the neutrality and comprehensiveness of the French state. Hence the over-reaction to Muslim adolescents wearing the headscarf in school.

But the strength of this formula is that it managed for a long time to avoid or at least minimize the other kind of exclusion, that of new arrivals. It still surprises Frenchmen, and others, when they learn from Gérard Noiriel[6] that one French person in four today has at least one grandparent born outside the country. France in

[5] Michael Sandel, *Democracy's Discontent*, Harvard, Cambridge, Mass., 1996.
[6] *Le Cruset francais*, Le Seuil, Paris, 1989.

this century has been an immigrant country without thinking of itself as such. The policy of assimilation has hit a barrier with recent waves of Maghrébains, but it worked totally with the Italians, Poles, Czechs, who came between the Wars. These people were never offered the choice, and became indistinguishable from 'les Français de souche'.

It has been argued that another dimension of this kind of inner exclusion has operated along gender lines; and this not only in Jacobin societies, but in all liberal democracies, where without exception women received voting rights later than men. The argument is that the style of politics, the modes and tone of public debate, and the like, have been set by a political society which was exclusively male, and that this has still to be modified to include women. If one looks at the behaviour of some of our male-dominated legislatures at question time, resembling as they sometimes do, a boisterous boys' school at recreation, it is clear that there is some truth to this point. The culture of politics could not fully include women without changing somewhat, even though we may be uncertain just how.

III

I hope I have made somewhat clear what I mean by the dynamic of exclusion in democracy. We might describe it as a temptation to exclude, beyond that which people may feel because of narrow sympathies or historic prejudice; a temptation which arises from the requirement of democratic rule itself for a high degree of mutual understanding, trust and commitment. This can make it hard to integrate outsiders, and tempt us to draw a line around the original community. But it can also tempt us to what I have called 'inner exclusion', the creation of a common identity around a rigid formula of politics and citizenship, which refuses to accommodate any alternatives, and imperiously demands the subordination of other aspects of citizens' identities.

It is clear that these two modes are not mutually exclusive. Societies based on inner exclusion may come to turn away outsiders as well, as the strength of the Front National, alas, so well illustrates; while societies whose main historical challenge has been the integration of outsiders may have recourse to inner exclusion in an attempt to create some unity amid all the diversity.

The present drama of English Canada (or Canada outside Quebec) illustrates this only too well. Partly because of a sense of fragmentation which some Canadians feel in face of the rapid diversification of Canada's population, partly because this sense of fragmentation is often intensified rather than diminished by Quebec's affirmation of difference, partly because of age-old Canadian angst about national identity in face of the traditional seeming security on this score of the USA, attitudes have become steadily more rigid in English Canada towards any possible accommodation of Quebec's difference during the last ten years. Canada's tragedy is that, at the moment where it is becoming more and more necessary to do something about Quebec's status in the federation, it is also becoming politically less and less possible to do anything meaningful.

Quite specifically, there is a growing rigidity around the political formula, visible for instance, in the insistence that all Provinces must be treated identically, a subsumption of this uniformity under the principle of citizen equality. This kind of uniformity is, in fact, very foreign to our history. It is very doubtful if the federation could ever have got going if we had tried to operate like this in the past. But it comes forward now, because it seems to many the only way to recreate trust and common understanding between diverse regions, some of whom bear a grudge against others. This rigidity will make it difficult not only to accommodate Quebec, but also to make space for aboriginal groups who are calling for new modes of self-rule.

Now the obvious fact about our era is that first, the challenge of the new arrival is becoming generalized and multiplied in all democratic societies. The scope and rate of international migration is making all societies increasingly 'multicultural'; while second, the response to this challenge of the 'Jacobin' sort, a rigorous assimilation to a formula involving fairly intense inner exclusion, is becoming less and less sustainable.

This last point is not easy to explain, but it seems to me an undeniable fact. There has been a subtle switch in mind-set in our civilization, probably coinciding with the 1960s. The idea that one ought to suppress one's difference for the sake of fitting in to a dominant mould, defined as the established way in one's society, has been considerably eroded. Feminists, cultural minorities, homosexuals, religious groups, all demand that the reigning formula be modified to accommodate them, rather than the other way around.

At the same time, possibly connected to this first change, but certainly with its own roots, has come another. This is an equally subtle change, and hard to pin down. But migrants no longer feel the imperative to assimilate in the same way. One must not misidentify the switch. Most of them want to assimilate substantively to the societies they have entered; and they certainly want to be accepted as full members. But they frequently want now to do it at their own pace, and in their own way, and in the process, they reserve the right to alter the society even as they assimilate to it.

The case of Hispanics in the United States is very telling in this regard. It's not that they don't want to become Anglophone Americans. They see obvious advantages in doing so, and they have no intention of depriving themselves of these. But they frequently demand schools and services in Spanish, because they want to make this process as painless as they can for themselves, and because they welcome such retention of their original culture as may fall out of this process. And something like this is obviously on the cards. They will all eventually learn English, but they will also alter somewhat the going sense of what it means to be an American, even as earlier waves of immigrants had. The difference between the earlier waves and the Hispanics is that the Hispanics seem to be operating now with the sense of their eventual role in co-determining the culture, rather than this arising only retrospectively, as with earlier immigrants.

The difference between the earlier near-total success of France in assimilating East Europeans and others (who ever thought of Yves Montand as Italian?), and the present great difficulty with Maghrébains, while it reflects a whole lot of other factors—e.g. greater cultural-religious difference, and the collapse of full employment—nevertheless must also reflect, I believe, the new attitude among migrants. The earlier sense of unalloyed gratitude towards the new countries of refuge and opportunity, which seemed to make any revendication of difference quite unjustified and out of place, has been replaced by something harder to define. One is almost tempted to say, by something resembling the old doctrine which is central to many religions, that the earth has been given to the human species in common. A given space doesn't just unqualifiedly belong to the people born in it, so it isn't simply theirs to give. In return for entry, one is not morally bound to accept just any condition they impose.

Two new features arise from this shift. First, the notion I attributed to Hispanics in the USA has become widespread, namely, the idea that the culture they are joining is something in continual evolution, and that they have a chance to co-determine its future. This, instead of a simple one-way assimilation, is more and more becoming the (often unspoken) understanding behind the act of migration.

Secondly, we have an intensification of a long-established phenomenon, which now seems fully 'normal', that is, where certain immigrant groups still function morally, culturally and politically as a 'diaspora' in relation to their home country. This has been going on for a long time—think, for instance, of the 'Polonia' in all the countries of exile. But whereas it was frowned on, or looked askance at, by many people in the receiving society, or where toleration for it depended on sympathy for the cause of the home country (the Poles were lucky in this respect), whereas people muttered darkly in the past about 'double allegiance', I believe now that this kind of behaviour is coming to be seen as normal. Of course, there are still extreme variants of it which arouse strong opposition, as when terrorists use the receiving countries as a base for their operations. But that is because these manifestations shock the dominant political ethic, and not because of the intense involvement in the country of origin. It is becoming more and more normal and unchallenged to think of oneself and be thought of as, say, a Canadian in good standing, while being heavily involved in the fate of some country of origin.

IV

The upshot of the above discussion could be expressed this way: democracies are in a standing dilemma. They need strong cohesion around a political identity, and precisely this provides a strong temptation to exclude those who can't or won't fit easily into the identity which the majority feels comfortable with, or believes alone can hold them together. And yet exclusion, besides being profoundly morally objectionable, also goes against the legitimacy idea of popular sovereignty, which is to realize the government of *all* the people. The need to form a people as a collective agent runs against the demand for inclusion of all who have a legitimate claim on citizenship.

This is the source of the malady. The remedies are a lot harder to find. I believe that an important first step is to recognize the dilemma. For this allows us to see that it can very often only be dealt with by struggling towards a creative redefinition of our political identity. The dilemma after all arises because some often historically hallowed definition cannot accommodate all who have a moral claim to citizenship. And yet the reaction to this is all too often to render this original identity even more absolute and unchallengeable, as though it somehow belonged essentially to a certain people with its territory and history that it be organized under this and no other identity.

This appeal to the origins can occur in both 'republican' and 'national' registers. In the first case, the particular features of our republican constitution are made absolute and sacrosanct, in face of all evidence that they may be impeding the search for a new common ground. Thus there is a certain 'Jacobin' fundamentalism which comes to the surface in France, in reaction to certain demands to accommodate the growing Muslim minority. The wearing of headscarves in school by Muslim teenagers is judged to infringe the principles of 'laïcite', as laid down in the French republican tradition. The general principle of state neutrality, indispensable in a modern diverse democracy, is metaphysically fused with a particular historical way of realizing it, and the latter is rendered as non-negotiable as the former.

As a panic reaction, this is understandable even if disastrous. Faced with the unfamiliar and disturbing, one reaches for the age-old sources of common identity. But the reaction is facilitated by the belief that this original constitution was meant to resolve the issue of political identity once and for all, that somehow it precluded in advance any need for illegitimate exclusion.

This amounts to a denial that the potential for the dilemma is built into democracy itself. It cannot be conjured once and for all by the ideal constitutional settlement. Even if this perfectly suits the population at the time of founding (and what constitution ever has?), the shifts in personal identity over time, through migration and moral or cultural change, can bring the established political identity out of true with the people who are supposed to live within it. This kind of fundamentalism attempts to deny history.

We are more familiar with this reaching back to sources in the national register; its destructive consequences are more immediately evident. The claim is that a certain territory belongs as of right to a certain historical ethnic, or cultural, or linguistic, or religious identity, regardless of what other people are living there, even if they've been there for centuries. And so Hungarian nationalists laid claim to the lands of the Crown of St Stephen in the nineteenth century, and the Bharatiya Janata Party feels it can and must impose a 'Hindutva' identity on all the immense diversity of India today. Even more gruesome examples of the working out of this kind of claim have been visible in recent years in the territory of the former Yugoslavia.

The reflex of many people in liberal societies to this kind of thing is to blame 'nationalism' and not democracy. But this is to take too quick a way with it. To start with, 'nationalism' has many senses. The original idea, for instance in its Herderian form, was a liberating one, and highly consonant with democracy. We do not have to force ourselves into an artificial homogeneity in order to live together in peace. We can recognize different 'national' (Volk) identities, even give them political expression, because each in this act of recognition acknowledges that it is not universal, that it has to co-exist with others which are equally legitimate. Herderian nationalism is a universalist idea, all Völker are equally worthy of respect; it can be used (and was so used by Herder) to defend Slavic people against German encroachment, as well as to defend German culture against the hegemonic claims of French. You do not have to accept French as a universal language in order to live in freedom with guaranteed rights. The political identity under which you live can reflect you too. This demand allows of an impeccably democratic justification.

What this pushes us towards is the idea which I believe is the key to facing the dilemma of exclusion creatively, the idea of sharing identity space. Political identities have to be worked out, negotiated, creatively compromised between peoples who have to or want to live together under the same political roof (and this co-existence is always grounded in some mixture of necessity and choice). Moreover, these solutions are never meant to last forever, but have to be discovered/invented anew by succeeding generations.

The idea of nationalism which creates bitter trouble is that defined by Gellner: the 'political principle, which holds that the political and national unit should be congruent'.[7] According to this idea, the problem of how to share identity space can be solved by giving each nation its territory, on which it can erect its sovereign state. The utopian, even absurd nature of the proposal immediately strikes the eye. Quite apart from the thousands of groups which can claim the status of 'nation', even giving each its parcel of land would still leave each pocket handkerchief state with national minorities, so inextricably mixed are the world's peoples. The utopian scheme could only be carried through by massive ethnic cleansing.

It is clear that this idea will only 'work' by making certain nations more equal than others. These are to get their states, and the rest are to live in their shadow as minorities, if they are allowed to live at all. This idea of nationalism can only be applied by negating its own universalist ethical basis.

It is this distorted idea which justifies the claim by historical national identities to monopoly control over 'their' territory. In the worst cases, this ends in a Yugoslav scenario. In the best cases, as with the Parti Québécois, and the more liberal wing of the BJP, minorities are to be guaranteed their rights, but the idea of sharing identity space, actually negotiating some compromise political identity with them, is vigorously rejected.

Just as with 'republican' forms of constitutionalism above, the unreal idea of a definitive solution to the problem of democratic co-existence is blinding people to the effective situation on the ground in almost all democratic states. The hope is once again to arrest history, to fix it in some original moment when our people attached themselves to this territory. And similarly, what offers itself as a solution to the democratic dilemma can only exacerbate it to the point of bitter conflict.

But the belief that the problem here is 'nationalism' sans phrase can accredit another utopian solution, that of a political identity grounded purely in 'republican' elements, without any reference to national or cultural identities.

In face of the prospect of having to bring together so many differences of culture, origin, political experience, and identity, the temptation is natural to define the common understanding more

[7] Ernest Gellner, *Nations and Nationalism*, Cornell University Press, Ithaca, 1983, p. 1.

and more in terms of 'liberalism', rather than by reference to the identities of citizens. The focus should be totally on individual rights and democratic and legal procedures, rather than on the historical-cultural reference points, or the ideas of the good life by which citizens define their own identities. In short, the temptation is to go for what Sandel calls the 'procedural republic'.

Already this has been evident in the Canadian case. I mentioned above that there has been a tendency in English Canada, in face of growing cultural diversity, to make certain aspects of the political culture central to the national identity. The main element which has been chosen for this has, not surprisingly, been the Charter of Rights, introduced into the Constitution by the 1982 Act. The underlying idea is that, whatever other differences distinguish us, as Canadians we can share a certain schedule of rights, and certain procedures for enforcing them.

What does the procedural republic have going for it? A number of things, some of them tendencies in our philosophical tradition. I have discussed this elsewhere,[8] but I think we can both see and understand the drift away from ethics of the good life towards ethics based on something else, allegedly less contentious, and easier to carry general agreement. This partly explains the popularity of both utilitarianism, and Kantian-derived deontological theories. Both manage to abstract from issues of what life is more worthy, more admirable, more human, and to fall back on what seems more solid ground. In one case, we count all the preferences, regardless of the supposed quality of the goals sought. In the other, we can abstract from the preferences, and focus on the rights of the preferring agent.

The act of abstraction here benefits from three important considerations. First, in an age of (at least menacing, if not actual) scepticism about moral views, it retreats from the terrain where the arguments seem the most dependent on our interpretations, the most contentious and incapable of winning universal ascent; whereas we can presumably all agree that, other things being equal, it is better to let people have what they want, or to respect their freedom to choose. Second, this refusal to adopt a particular view of the good life leaves it to the individual to make the choice, and hence it fits with the anti-paternalism of the modern age. It

8 See *Sources of the Self*, Harvard University Press, Cambridge, Mass., 1989, ch. 3.

enshrines a kind of freedom. Third, in face of the tremendous differences of outlook in modern society, utilitarianism and Kantian deontology seem to promise a way of deciding the issues we face in common without having to espouse the views of some against others.

Now the first two considerations are based on philosophical arguments—about what can and cannot be known and proved, and about the nature of freedom, respectively. They have been much discussed, debated, and often refuted by philosophers. But the third is a political argument. Regardless of who is ultimately right in the battle between procedural ethics and those of the good life, we could conceivably be convinced on political grounds that the best political formula for democratic government of a complex society was a kind of neutral liberalism. And this is where the argument has mainly gone today. The shift between Rawls I and Rawls II is a clear example of this. His theory of justice is now presented as 'political, not metaphysical'. This shift perhaps comes in part from the difficulties that the purely philosophical arguments run into. But it also corresponds to the universal perception that diversity is a more important and crucial dimension of contemporary society. This comes, as I argued above, partly from the actual growth in diversity in the population, through say, international migration; and partly from the growing demand that age-old diversities be taken seriously, put forward for instance, by femi-nists.

So the issue now could be: what conception of freedom, of equality, of fairness, and of the basis for social co-existence are—not right in the abstract, but feasible for modern democratic societies? How can people live together in difference, granted that this will be in a democratic regime, under conditions of fairness and equality?

The procedural republic starts right off with a big advantage. If in your understanding of the citizen's roles and rights, you abstract from any view of the good life, then you avoid endorsing the views of some at the expense of others. Moreover, you find an immediate common terrain on which all can gather. Respect me, and accord me rights, just in virtue of my being a citizen, not in virtue of my character, outlook, or the ends I espouse, not to speak of my gender, race, sexual orientation, etc.

Now no one in their right mind today would deny that this is an important dimension of any liberal society. The right to vote, for instance, is indeed accorded unconditionally; or on condition of certain bases of citizenship, put certainly in a way which is blind to differences of the range just quoted. The question we have to ask is whether this can be the *only* basis for living together in a democratic state, whether this is the valid approach in *all* contexts, whether our liberalism approaches perfection the more we can treat people in ways which abstract from what they stand for and others do not.

It may appear that whatever other reasons there might be for treating people this way, at least it facilitates our coming together, and feeling ourselves to be part of a common enterprise. What we do all have in common is that we make choices, opt for some things rather than others, want to be helped and not hindered in pursuing the ends that flow from these options. So an enterprise that promises to further everyone's plan, on some fair basis, seems to be the ideal common ground. Indeed, some people find it hard to imagine what else could be.

But this retreat to the procedural is no solution to the democratic dilemma. On the contrary, it very often itself contributes to activating it. We can readily see this in two ways.

First, the condition of a viable political identity is that people must actually be able to relate to it, to find themselves reflected in it. But in some cases, the preservation of an historical cultural identity is so important to a certain group that suppressing all mention of it in our answer to the 'what for?' question cannot but alienate that group. The protection and promotion of its 'distinct society' cannot but figure in the common identity of Quebec as a political entity, whether in the Canadian federation or outside. Refusing all mention of this in the canonical definitions of the Canadian identity can only increase the feeling of many Quebeckers that they have no place in the federation. This is not a solution to the conundrum of a common Canadian political identity; it is rather the source of the greatest contemporary threat to it.

Second, the procedural route supposes that we can uncontroversially distinguish neutral procedures from substantive goals. But it is in fact very difficult to devise a procedure which is seen as neutral by everyone. The point about procedures, or characters of rights, or distributive principles, is that they are meant not to enter into the knotty terrain of substantive difference in ways of life. But there is not way in practice of ensuring that this will be so.

The case of the Muslim teenagers wearing the headscarf in school in France is eloquent in this regard. 'Laïcite' is supposedly a neutral principle, not favouring one religion or worldview over another. On this basis the headscarves were refused, but other French girls often wear, e.g. a cross around their necks, and this was unchallenged. In a 'secular' society, this is presumably often just a 'decoration'. The presumption is valid enough, but the religious 'indivisibility' of the cross reflects France as a 'post-Christian' society, following centuries of Christian culture. How can one expect to convince Muslims that this combination of rulings is neutral?

The mistake here is to believe that there can be some decision whose neutrality is guaranteed by its emerging from some principle or procedure. This breeds the illusion that there is no need to negotiate the place of these symbols, and hence to confront the actual substantive differences of religious allegiance in the public sphere. But no procedure can dispense with the need to share identity space.

Something similar holds of the American case. What is meant to be a procedural move, neutral between all parties, the separation of church and state, turns out to be open to different interpretations, and some of these are seen as very far from neutral by some of the important actors in the society. The school prayer dispute is a case in point. One could argue that insistence on a procedural solution—in this case a winner-take-all constitutional adjudication—is exactly what will maximally inflame the division; which indeed, it seems to have done.

Moreover, as against a political solution, based on negotiation and compromise between competing demands, this provides no opportunity for people on each side to look into the substance of the other's case. Worse, by having their demand declared unconstitutional, the losers' programme is delegitimated in a way which has deep resonance in American society. Not only can we not give you what you want, but you are primitive and un-American to want it.

In short, I would argue that the current American Kulturkampf has been exacerbated rather than reconciled by the heavy recourse in that polity to judicial resolution on the basis of the constitution.

V

My argument here has been that a full understanding of the dilemma of democratic exclusion shows that there is no alternative to what I have called sharing identity space. This means negotiating a commonly acceptable, even compromise political identity between the different personal or group identities which want to/ have to live in the polity. Some things well, of course, have to be non-negotiable, the basic principles of republican constitutions—democracy itself and human rights, among them. But this firmness has to be accompanied by a recognition that these principles can be realized in a number of different ways, and can never be applied neutrally without some confronting of the substantive religious-ethnic-cultural differences in societies. Historic identities cannot be just abstracted from. But nor can their claims to monopoly status be received. There are no exclusive claims to a given territory by historic right.

What this means in practice is beyond the ambit of this essay. Solutions have to be tailored to particular situations. But some of the political mechanisms of this sharing are already well-known, e.g. various brands of federalism, as well as the design of forms of special status for minority societies, such as we see today in Scotland and Catalonia, for instance. But many other modalities remain to be devised for the still more diverse democratic societies of the twenty-first century.

In the meantime, it will have helped, I believe, if we can perceive more clearly and starkly the nature of our democratic dilemma, since the hold of unreal and ahistorical solutions over our minds and imagination is still crippling our efforts to deal with the growing conflicts which arise from it.

7

Secular Liberalism and the Moral Psychology of Identity

❧

Akeel Bilgrami

I

It is for some time now that the tension between state and community has had political theory in its grip. Theorizing about the liberal state has been particularly constricted by this grip since any effort the theory has made towards the idea of the rights of communities, for instance in the form of minority rights, has necessarily had the consequence that it must concede to illiberalism towards individuals, if such illiberalism is indeed practised by the community towards any of its individual members. This is a familiar paradox of liberalism and it is particularly familiar in India since it surfaces so much in our ongoing debates about Muslim personal laws.

Current and traditional political theory (constricted as it is by the tension between state and community) has the resources to offer two opposed general directions of resolution. One is toward the pole of a secular liberal state, which imposes legal interventions that amount to reform of such illiberal practices. The other is toward the pole of internal reform within the communities against their own illiberal practices. There may be debate and controversy about specific paths followed in each direction. In the statist direction, we may worry about whether a community has the preparedness or not for the imposition by the state of such reforms,[1] we may worry about whether the right to exit is a realistic and powerful enough liberal tool,[2] we may worry about the relative roles of legislature and judiciary in bringing about reforms, and so on. In the internal communitarian direction we may worry about such things as whether or not reform should take place via representative institutions within communities or whether instead they should be allowed to emerge less formally by mobilization on the sites of intra-communitarian civil society. But these are details, some of which may only be relevant contingently in specific contexts. My concern in the first half of the paper is with the larger theoretical picture, and the point I want to begin with is just the observation I have made above, that the conceptual frameworks of liberal political theory hitherto have only one of these two directions of resolution to offer, a sort of Homeric liberal choice, a constricting disjunction. I believe the disjunction is as intolerable as it is uncompulsory. To try to put it right is the central preoccupation of this paper.

Just in case there is unclarity on this point, what I am trying to put right, and in general the entire issue I am addressing in

[1] As is well known, the directive in the Indian Constitution about uniformity in the civil code was delayed in its application due to the sense of its framers that Muslims were not yet in a state of preparedness to embrace it.

[2] It is a natural worry that, in certain contexts, the idea that members of a community (say, traditional Muslim women in India) can simply up and exit their community so as to be free of the oppressiveness of some aspect of personal law, is not a realistic idea. There may be too much by way of internal inhibition as well as external constraint for them to be able to do this easily. In these contexts, the right to exit will not be a powerful enough liberal tool, merely an academic and formal liberal proviso. As I have argued in my paper 'What is a Muslim?' over and above the right to exit, another thing for liberals to strive for is to democratize the community away from its absolutist leadership so that a sense is created in the community that if the secular state requires it to give up on this or that element in a legal code, it would not mean that it has destroyed the Muslim identity of its members. The idea that one sheds one's Muslim identity if one gives up on some laws is an idea based on a highly codified concept of identity, and need be no part of the self-conception of Muslims, so long as they are not dominated by an unrepresentative fundamentalist leadership which dogmatically distorts the psychology of identity by insisting on such a codified conception of it. For this a certain sort of democratization has to take place, on which more toward the end of this paper.

addressing this disjunction, must not be run together with a quite different issue of whether it is a good thing, or even a consistent thing, for liberal doctrine to countenance group or collective rights. On that issue, this paper takes no position, even though its author happens to have roughly worked out opinions on it. So, the reader should not be misled by the fact that the concrete setting of some of my discussion in the paper mentions minority rights and the question of Muslim personal law in India, to think that the issue under philosophical discussion is one about the worthiness (or not) of group or community rights in general. The issue rather is this. Given the *fact* of group or community rights (i.e. minority rights), and in particular given the particular consequence of this in the case of Muslims in India where the fact of such rights has resulted in legal terms to granting Muslims their own unreformed personal laws, which as we know are in many respects illiberal in their treatment of Muslim women, the question is: is the specific disjunction I have just mentioned of the either/or of statist reform versus internal communitarian reform, a well formulated pair of theoretical options for liberalism?

II

To address this issue in liberal political theory and eventually to repudiate this disjunctive formula, I will first dwell at some distance from liberal political theory in the more abstract ground of moral psychology in order to use some of its concepts and conclusions to construct an argument and an alternative framework for theorizing about the secular state.

By moral psychology, I mean the psychology of agents by which their choices and actions are explained, and in particular explained normatively in the sense that the explanation does not merely say why they chose or did what they did, but also sees it as essential to explanation to assess whether what they did was rational by the lights of their own desires and values. And I don't just mean that one explains why they did what they did in some non-normative way *first*, and *then* makes the normative assessment whether what they did is in accord with their desires and values. Rather such an assessment is *built-in* to the very idea of explaining why they did what they did by citing their desires and values. Thus this normative element in the study of human individual and social behaviour is not some *extra* thing tacked on to an otherwise purely descriptive enterprise. No social science despite the pretensions of its second term ('science') can leave out this normative aspect of explanation without changing its own subject beyond recognition.

To begin with, a bit of terminology. For the convenience of abbreviation, I will use a single term '*desires*' to cover all those motivating states of agents which economists and other social scientists, decision theorists, and philosophers (not to mention, literary people) variously refer to as values, commitments, preferences, subjective utilities, interests, inclinations, motives, etc. The term will therefore cover all such states of mind, from the desire to drink tea to the desire to work for social justice. So despite its restricted popular meaning, my use of the term 'desires' is intended to be as wide as to cover all these states of mind, and should not therefore give the impression that my interest in rationality is a narrow interest in a hedonic calculus. 'Desires' in this use of the term, when coupled with our beliefs and other cognitive states, make sense in this normative way of why we do *anything* that we intentionally do.

I should also add by way of preliminary caveat that my insistence on the relevance of moral psychology begs no questions either in favour of methodological individualism in the social sciences or in favour of a voluntarism in the study of historical events. Perhaps I should put the point in the converse. Any methodological holist position or any position that stresses structural and determinist explanations of historical phenomena can leave out the moral psychology of their subjects only at the cost of becoming desperately implausible, to the extent that they are not entirely hazy.[3]

[3] I have written elsewhere on the compatibility of an intelligibly formulated determinism with agency and moral psychology. See the last few pages of 'Two Concepts of Secularism: Reason, Modernity and the Secular Ideal', *Economic and Political Weekly*, July 1994, and also 'Self-Knowledge and Resentment' in *Knowing Our Own Minds*, Crispin Wright and Barry Smith (eds) Oxford University Press, 1997. It gets a more theoretical treatment in my *Self-Knowledge and Intentionality*, forthcoming from Harvard University Press, 1998. As for methodological individualism, I am, for the purposes of this paper, assuming that everything I attribute in moral psychology to a community can be translated without residue into attributions made to individuals under the aspect of their communal identity. Thus the idea that

Let me now introduce *three* ideas I will need in the construction of the argument.

The *first* I will call '*reinforcement*' among our desires.

A way of characterize this is to explore the idea of a relation among our desires that is stronger than mere consistency among them. Consistency among desires merely requires that they are mutually implementable. But two desires may be consistent with one another in this sense and have nothing to do with one another in a psychological economy. My desire for tea happens to have nothing to do with my desire to do philosophy, and they are both mutually implementable. On the other hand my desire to do philosophy and my desire to be respected by my peers are related by more than mere consistency, they are more than merely mutually implementable, they, as I said, reinforce one another.

However, though reinforcement is in this way more than mere consistency it ought not to be confused with another relation between desires, which is the means/end or instrumental relation. Reinforcement is not a means/end relation because if I were asked whether I pursue my desire to do philosophy *in order to* fulfill my desire to be respected by my peers my answer might well be 'no'.

So reinforcement is a relation between desires that is stronger than consistency *without* collapsing into instrumentality. This is a point of some importance, since it has not been obvious to many who study the rationality of our wants and values and actions that there is a relation between desires other than consistency or means/end. It is hard to say much more about it as a relation because it is an irreducible relation. The best we can do is to give examples to make it intuitive, as we already have. So if someone is sceptical about there being such a relation as reinforcement between our desires over and above consistency among them, we can pose the following challenge to her: tell us how you will mark the intuitive difference in the relation between the following two pairs of desires *without* bringing in the relation of reinforcement between desires: (1) My desire to do philosophy and my desire to drink tea, (2) My desire to do philosophy and my desire to be respected by my

---

Muslims desire or value x can, if one wishes, be translated as the idea that many or most individuals, qua Muslims, desire or value x. So, no attributions of desires or values to communities made in this paper have to be seen as non-supervenient on individual attributions, in order to make their point.

llectual friends. There clearly is an intuitive difference between two pairs, and there does not seem to be any way to say what es the relations in these pairs of desires different, except by ıg that the first pair of desires are merely consistent but do (in the 'normal' case) reinforce one another, whereas in the ıd pair the desires do also reinforce one another.[4] At this ., there will be a natural temptation to deny this and say: 'Well yes, there *is* something more than consistency involved in the second pair but that can be captured by saying that while the first pair is merely consistent, the second pair in addition has a means/end relation between the two desires.' This temptation should be resisted because, as I said above, someone holding the second pair of desires may very well answer 'No' to the question: do you desire to do philosophy *in order* to be respected by your intellectual friends? If so, for that agent, means/end will not capture the intuitive difference in the relation between the desires in the second pair. Only reinforcement will.

I am spending some time on this point because it is an important one to make against those who think that any serious and intrinsic conception of rationality is not applicable to such things as desires and values, but is restricted only to beliefs. Despite their well-known antagonism, both Humean and Kantian traditions of thinking about human behaviour and moral psychology (for very different reasons) share such a sceptical attitude about allowing desires to be the subject of a rich notion of rationality. And since so much of current thinking about this subject sees itself as broadly influenced by one or other of these traditions, this sceptical attitude is very widespread. According to this widespread picture, desires may be subject to an instrumental rationality but they do not

[4] I say 'in the normal case' because of course someone can strain and contrive to cook up scenarios in which for some person the desire for tea may be linked with more than consistency to the desire to do philosophy, in which case the contrast between the two pairs will be lost. In that case one will just have to appeal to different examples to raise the point of the challenge. The challenge holds just in case there are *any* cases of relations where there is an intuitive relation between desires which exceeds consistency in this way without collapsing with instrumentality. The fact is that any psychological economy is ridden with such relations between desires, and that is why reinforcement is such an important and central notion for the study of rationality.

possess any *intrinsic* rationality except for the very thin notion of consistency among desires (which, as I said earlier, amounts only to their mutual implementability.) The notion of reinforcement, by contrast, brings with it a thicker conception of rationality and allows us to think of desires (and not just beliefs) in terms of a coherentist conception of rationality, where coherence is something stronger than consistency. That is why the idea of reinforcement allows us to get beyond the narrowing Kantian idea that our moral rationality cannot traffic in anything so contingent and non-universal as desires, at the same time as it surpasses the equally narrowing Humean idea that the only rationality that motivating states (what he called the 'passions') are subject to, is instrumental.

One final word in the exposition of this crucial idea. Obviously, reinforcement has its other side. That is, just as desires can stand in relations of reinforcement to one another, they can also stand in the opposite relation of infirming one another. Such I suspect is the relation between my desire to do *good* philosophy and my desire for an active social life.

With this simple and irreducible relational idea of reinforcement (and infirmity) among desires in place, we can stipulate a definition of values as well as of rationality. A person's *values* are a subset, a special case of, her desires. An agent's values are those among her desires that are most highly reinforced rather than those which are infirm. And an agent is the more *rational* the more her actions are in accord with her values. This is all pretty hasty and crude, of course, and needs many layers of elaboration, qualification and refinement, but I should be forgiven for not doing so here, since I am merely setting up a very rudimentary apparatus for use at some distance from here.

As an aside, I repeat here—but will not keep doing so—that though all my examples have been of individual moral psychology, I see no reason to deny, in fact I don't see how we can fail to assert, that groups and collectivities can have a psychological economy. Thus, for instance, we may talk of the desire of the vanguard of the French revolution to consolidate private property and contrast it with the vanguard of the Russian revolution which had the desire to abolish it. Any idea that one could come to any historical understanding or explanation of these two revolutions and their differences by leaving out states of mind of this kind, borders on the incoherent.[5]

After 'reinforcement', I turn to my *second* key idea, which I will simply steal from Aristotle. He called it 'akrasia', the medievals called it 'incontinence', and we may, following more recent terminology, call it '*weakness of will*'. Informally it is described as: thinking the better but doing the worse. But we may now give a somewhat more formal description of it using the idea of reinforcement as defined above. Weakness of will is that form of irrationality where the most reinforced among our desires point to one sort of action, but what we actually opt for is something less reinforced in our evaluative economy.[6] Weakness of will is the practical or moral counterpart of the cognitive phenomenon that Kuhn described as the frequent irrationality of the 'normal' scientist, which might properly be described as weakness of warrant, or believing what has less than maximal reinforcement among our scientific beliefs.

The third and last moral psychological notion that I will use is that of '*identity*'. Following some of the basic arguments of an earlier paper of mine ('What is a Muslim?: Fundamental Commitment and Cultural Identity'[7]), the notion of identity can be characterized in terms of what I there called an agent's most 'fundamental commitments'. These are desires that she most identifies with. How are these to be characterized? It is not enough to repeat that these are the desires that are highly reinforced because those will be too many to deliver anything so focused as a notion of identity. To the extent that we believe in the notion of identity, we will have to do better and specify desires that have an even greater centrality in our psychological economy. These are

[5] Saying this here does not take a stand on the question of supervenience of these attributions to collectives upon attributions to their constituent individuals. See the closing remark in footnote 3.

[6] I use the word value 'economy' and psychological 'economy' earlier to talk of a corpus of values, and desires more generally, which have internal relations with one another, relations that contribute to their overall rationality. This is a quite specific use of the term and I hope the reader will not be tempted to think that this use of the word has anything to do with recent uses of such expressions as 'moral economy'. It does not.

[7] *Economic and Political Weekly*, 16–23 May 1992.

specified in counterfactual terms. *A desire is a fundamental commitment if one wants it fulfilled even were one not to have the desire.* In case this sounds too abstract, it can be indexed to times. A desire is a fundamental commitment at a given time, if at that time one wants it fulfilled at a future time, even if one believes that at the future time one may not have that desire. This temporal elaboration of the counterfactual will be crucial to my argument against the classical liberal picture. For now an intuitive sense of such a commitment can be given by an example. Many of our desires are not fundamental commitments in this sense, but a few indeed are. Take for example, the fact that certain sections of the Iranian government are explicitly arguing that increasingly modernizing influences around them may well have the effect in the future that they will lose their desire to live by Islamic tenets, nevertheless they now want their future to be one where they are in fact living by Islamic tenets, even if they do not have the desire to do so then. (And they are in fact arguing that they should entrench things so that that can happen).

Commitments which have this looped counterfactual form, stand out even among our most reinforced desires, and have a right to be seen as rigorously reflecting our identity-shaping commitments for they reveal our deepest self-conception in a way that vague existentialist rhetoric about authenticity fails to do. And formulating the idea of identity along these lines has the distinct advantage that it does not amount to thinking of identities in any essentialist or immutable way. These are *not* primordial or permanent identities since what defines them are desires which are not *themselves* permanent or even necessarily extraordinarily abiding, but rather desires which are *for* something that is more permanent than the desire itself may be. Commitments so defined are therefore quite susceptible to change as well as to conflict with one another. What makes them distinctive, and deep or 'fundamental', is not their immunity from these things; rather it is captured entirely by what is revealed in their counterfactual form. (And I hope nobody is confused by my term 'fundamental' to describe these commitments to think that they have anything to do with 'fundamentalism'.)

With these three moral psychological notions in place, I return now to liberal political theory.

III

Liberalism's most honoured slogan says this: 'Individuals must be left unimpeded to pursue their own conceptions of the good life.' Properly qualified and refined, this stands as the most general defining mark of liberal doctrine, subsuming specific instances of it that specifically mention one or other domain of application, such as that of speech and thought, of religion and worship, of ownership of property, and so on.

The slogan divides into two and each half mentions a key notion, that of non-interference ('unimpeded') and that of conceptions of the good life. The idea of 'Conceptions of the good life' is left almost entirely open since it is just the idea of the values and aspirations of agents, which may be various and variously specific. These are none other than a subset of what we have, in our use of the term, called 'desires'. They could include any substantive set of desires, from a religious way of life to a life playing or even watching cricket. The idea of non-interference, of course is also the idea of a value or good. But as such it is also intended in a critical way to stand in contrast with substantive goods and values, whose pursuit it asks to be left unimpeded. What is the intended contrast in liberalism between the *value of non-interference* in the pursuit of substantive values and the *substantive values themselves.*? There are various familiar answers to this question, ranging from the universality, and the relative non-negotiability of the former in comparison to the substantive values, to the fact that it is procedural rather than substantive since it generates entitlements in a way that one does not routinely expect of the substantive values. That is to say, within certain qualifications which I mentioned when I introduced the slogan, the idea of non-interference is one which provides a *constraint* on certain forms of behaviour (those that amount to interference) and in doing so it *entitles* others to pursue other forms of behaviour freely (those which promote their substantive conceptions of the good). These latter, the substantive values, on the other hand do not themselves have this procedural property of providing constraints and therefore generating entitlements. In any case, whichever of these answers we stress, the crucial liberal assumption is that non-interference as a good cannot be a good which is *weighed on the same scale* as the substantive goods whose pursuit it makes freely possible by placing various constraints. This much is essential to *any* version or variant of the doctrine of liberalism. The idiom of 'rights' is the natural idiom in which to describe the idea of such a special good or value, and the idiom is frequently on our lips.

Let me then make a disclosure of personal opinion. Putting aside the domain of private property and of economic behaviour generally as a serious and systematic exception, the idiom of rights and the procedural constraints it imposes on states (and other institutions as well as on individuals) seem to me entirely salutary.[8] And the idea that the value it expresses is not to be weighed on the same scale as substantive goods is necessarily true because it is innocuous. After all it just spells out the claim that these are procedural constraints which those substantive goods are not.

But all these unimpeachable claims are susceptible to an ambiguous reading. And the ambiguity, when properly stated, separates out the standard and classical liberal tradition from other sorts of position that might also aspire to liberal ideals outside that tradition. The rest of this paper will try to give a rigorous basis for this separation and then apply it to a concrete political issue and historical context.

What defines the specifically *classical* liberal understanding of the idea of non-interference is not just that it is a right or constraint but *that what justifies our taking it to be a right or constraint cannot be derived from any of those substantive conceptions themselves* since that would ultimately make the value expressed in the constraint (non-interference) as contestable as the substantive values they are derived from.

Now if we wished to *deny* this defining point of the classical principles of the liberal state, we would necessarily have generated a quite different reading of the idea of rights—one that has not sufficiently been theorized because criticism of liberal doctrine has predominantly been motivated by a communitarian trajectory that sees the classical tradition of thought on the liberal state as lacking the resources to cope with the claims of community and then, *just as surely as that tradition which it is criticizing, this criticism of it sees*

[8] The reason for this exception to an approval of the ordinary conception of rights should be obvious and familiar. The case for rights of individuals against, in particular, a *socialist* state is notoriously weakened by widespread historical contingencies in which the full exercise and protection of these rights predictably leads to measurable deprivations for large sections of the society.

no scope either for another reading of the idea of rights. It is that crucial space, buried by the classical liberal tradition and which remains undiscovered by its communitarian critics, that I want to try and unearth. My diagnostic claim will be that both parties to the dispute are blind to it because they both work with an impoverished conception of the moral psychology involved in the subject of their disagreement.

So, in effect, I have made a second disclosure of personal opinion. I do *not* feel the sentimental glow for the notion of community and of tradition felt by the critics of liberalism, and I think the focus should rather be on the shortcomings of classical liberalism's understanding of the moral psychology relevant to their own cherished themes.

The traditional liberal claim that the idiom of rights expresses claims which cannot be made contestable by deriving their justification from any of the substantive values whose pursuit they make freely possible, has a venerable history but it was most explicitly stated and elaborated for the first time in Mill's careless masterpiece on the subject,[9] and in more recent times it has had its most sophisticated flowering in a contractualist version of Mill's argument in the writings of John Rawls.[10] I will focus on Rawls.

His argument for the claim is to be found in the celebrated method by which he settles on the basic liberties of liberal theory. Since the method is so well-known and well-studied, I will be brief in the exposition. These liberties are part of the content of a principle (the first of his two 'principles of justice') that Rawls says we would choose in any social contract in which we did not have the information which would lead us to choose principles that are biased in our own favour. In particular, we would contract into this principle of non-interference adumbrating these various liberties when we *lacked knowledge of our own substantive conceptions of the good*, as well as lacked knowledge of other things which might give us clues about what our substantive values are (for example, our status in society, our family and other sorts of background, our professions, etc.) If the principle of non-interference is chosen under these circumstances and is rationally chosen, then clearly

[9] John Stuart Mill, ch. II in 'On Liberty', *Three Essays*, Oxford University Press, 1975.

[10] John Rawls, *Theory of Justice* Harvard University Press, 1971 and *Political Liberalism*, Harvard University Press, 1994.

(that is to say, by definition) its justification will make no appeal to substantive conceptions of the good. And, for Rawls, the fact that we have rationally made the choice under these circumstances would be part of the justification for adopting these liberties (and the policies and institutions that administer them) in the actual societies in which we live.

Rawls therefore is fully aware that moral psychology is of central importance to the argument. He cannot fail to be since, as I just said, the question he sets himself is: what would it be *rational* for someone to choose as principles to be governed by if he lacked information of his own substantive values and commitments. So, if while considering the matter of whether to choose a particular principle one contemplated circumstances in the future in which one thought that one would not be rationally motivated to adopt it, and one nevertheless chose the principle, it follows that one has with rational justification judged those circumstances irrelevant. To repeat, the idea is that the most general principles to be governed by in actual societies would be just and unbiased if they were principles which would be chosen in such a state of ignorance about our substantive conceptions of the good (and about our social circumstances). And when these choices are rational, it is because behind this 'veil of ignorance', we have chosen them *no matter what we contemplate ourselves as being when the veil is lifted*, that is, no matter what substantive conception of the good we contemplate ourselves as having.[11]

Let's then turn to the question of what it would or would not be rational for us to commit ourselves to in these circumstances. Here, we may introduce, as an example, the second of our disjuncts, 'community', and since it is so much on our minds in

[11] This is the most interesting way of reading Rawls, since it makes the project intellectually the most ambitious. If we did not demand that the principles should be chosen no matter what we contemplate ourselves as being, then those contracting might gamble that they would not have this or that substantive conception of the good when the veil was lifted, and so might chose principles which are indeed biased in favour of the range of substantive values in favour of which they have gambled. This would not yield principles of justice, or justice as fairness, to use Rawls phrase. And then to rule out such outcomes, some constraints of a sense of fairness would have to be built in to those contracting, which would make the theory much less ambitious, that is, the method would begin to look like one of fairness in-fairness out.

current debates let the example be one of community defined by politico–religious commitments. (Rawls himself has often been exercised by such examples.) Suppose then while we are considering which principles to chose in this state of ignorance, we contemplate that we will find when the veil of ignorance is lifted that we have a highly religious conception of the good, with detailed substantive commitments to a polity ruled by a set of religious laws (say, the *sharia*), to exercise censorship against serious religious dissent (e.g. against a blasphemous book), and that most others in the society and nation share these views (here I run out of an actual example since I don't believe that this is true even of Iran). Could one while contemplating the possibility find motives to commit ourselves to a principle of non-interference such as the one we have been discussing?

Rawls obviously must think one can, since his first principle of justice precisely speaks to these standard liberties carried by the ideal of non-interference, and Rawls believes that we would rationally contract into it behind the veil of ignorance. But at first sight, it is hard to see why, if one contemplated oneself to be the kind of religious communitarian just sketched, one *would* chose, for example the particular form of non-interference and liberty enshrined in the right to free expression. At any rate that has been the general communitarian dissatisfaction with Rawls. Rawls, it is said, cannot deal with the commitments to religious and other communities, and it is said that his theory is narrowly addressed only to a certain sort of detached, modernist contractor who is *anyway* inclined to liberalism. If that were not so, *why* should someone choose such a principle of liberty of expression, if he contemplated that when the veil is lifted he might be someone with the substantive values of a religious doctrine which demands the censorship of blasphemy? It may well be irrational for him to choose it, and if so, then liberalism will not have an argument for one of its central principles.

But Rawls has an answer. The question, as I said, is really a question in moral psychology. And Rawls in more recent writing subsequent to *The Theory of Justice*[12] has fortified his case with a further argument that explicitly appeals to a moral-psychological consideration to show that even if one contemplated that when the

[12] See *Political Liberalism.*

veil was lifted, it would be revealed to one that one had these substantive religious values, it would *still* be rational to choose the principle of liberty of expression. The consideration he appeals to is a psychological counterpart to his starting point of ignorance of one's own substantive commitments, a psychological counterpart which Rawls indexes to the future. He says that even such a religious communitarian will have elementary psychological knowledge that, like anyone else, he is capable or susceptible to changes of mind and viewpoint, and therefore changes in his desires, in his substantive conceptions of the good. So, if behind the veil of ignorance one is contemplating that when it is lifted one might find that one is such a religious communitarian, one will also contemplate that in the future one might change one's mind and cease to be one. Now if one contemplates this too, then one will want to make sure that one will have the chance to fulfil any future desires that one has adopted which are not that of the religious communitarian. But one may well not have the chance to fulfil them if one contracts and binds oneself to principles approved only by the religious communitarian one presently contemplates oneself to be. In fact to ensure that one protects the fulfilability of one's future, possibly changed desires, one better contract into the liberty of expression and other basic liberties since those desires may not be fulfilled in a society which suppressed dissent and other non-religious points of view.

As I said, this argument from the changeability of our desires just puts into the psychological considerations available to agents choosing these principles, a version of ignorance (this time about possible *future* commitments of theirs), and asks them to take out an insurance policy for possibly very different commitments in the future, just as in the initial contractualist thought-experiment in *A Theory of Justice*, he asked them to take out an insurance policy for what our present conception of the good might turn out to be when the veil is lifted and we are informed about ourselves. So to repeat: the idea is that if someone behind the veil of ignorance, contemplating himself to be a religious communitarian, also contemplates the fact that he might have in the future conceptions of the good which are not the ones he presently has, ones which in fact might be quite radically different from the ones he presently has, he will want to insure that in the future he will not be badly off, which he will be if he repudiates the principle of liberal rights of non-interference on the basis of his contemplated present religious communitarian commitments alone.

Such a proposal presupposes that the psychological economy of agents have in them a belief that they might at some future point have a quite different set of substantive commitments than they now are contemplating themselves to have, and a desire that these revised commitments be successfully fulfilled. Rawls regards this as a sort of higher order desire for the successful fulfilment of our revised or changed desires. Armed with this higher order desire, even somebody contemplating that he is a religious communitarian of the sort mentioned above, would *rationally* choose the principle of liberty as non-interference, and commit himself to it and see no rational justification for undermining the commitment when it was revealed to him that he had a religious conception of the good. The moral psychology that Rawls proposes has it, then, that in his psychological economy, the lower order desires of the contemplated religious communitarian will conflict with his higher order desire for revisability of desires and their successful fulfilment, a desire which he shares with all other agents, if he is rational, and in the contest the higher order desire will win out.

That is Rawls' final word on behalf of classical liberal principles and some of you will recognize how it is a sophisticated contractualist analogue to Mill's famous meta-induction from fallibility to argue for the same conclusion.[13] How shall we assess Rawls' argument?

It is here that the earlier excursus in moral psychology impresses with its relevance. Recall that I had introduced and defined three notions, that of reinforcement among our desires, that of weakness of will as a specific form of irrationality, and that of identity as shaped by certain kinds of very specifically defined fundamental commitments.

Let's begin with the direct and sharp relevance of the last of these. Identity was defined as being constituted by fundamental commitments which took a certain looped counterfactual form, indexed to times. It required of an agent that she make a rather

[13] Mill's argument, crudely put, says that we should embrace freedom of expression as a principle even if we are very devoted to our opinions and find dissent from them repugnant, because it has often been the case in the past that people (including ourselves) have held their opinions devoutly and these opinions have turned out to be false.

specific sort of sacrifice for those of her desires which are at present her fundamental commitments. This is because she is prepared *at the present*, to, *in the future*, live *not* according to the conceptions of the good that she has *in the future*, but rather to live *then* according to the conception of the good she *now* has instead. If that is the moral psychology of identity, then the very notion of identity is something that undermines Rawls' fortified argument for his principle stating the liberal rights.

Let me explain by first recalling our dialectic so far. I remind you that the difficulty for Rawls, for which he must invoke the higher order desire about revisability, was one where it did not seem rational that we should behind the veil of ignorance commit ourselves to his liberal principle, if we contemplated that when it was lifted and we were informed about our own substantive conceptions of the good, we would find that we had the conception of the religious communitarian. The appeal to a higher order desire regarding the satisfaction of our revised desires, in the fortified argument, was supposed to make it rational after all to commit ourselves to the principle because that way we would be taking out an insurance policy for possible *future* conceptions of the good which were significantly different from our religious communitarian one. But now, suppose that the contemplated religious communitarian has what I have defined as *fundamental* commitments to his substantive religious values in the sense I sketched earlier, that is, the commitments to those values have the looped counterfactual form indexed to the future. In that case it may not be rational for him to adopt Rawls' principle of liberal rights, *despite* the considerations of revisability of desires. This is because his fundamental commitments are structurally defined in a way that preclude making any sacrifices now (sacrifices that would ensure from adopting the liberal rights, for example, the tolerating of blasphemous publications, etc.) for a different psychological makeup in the future, and on the contrary demand he make the opposite sacrifice in the future (e.g. accepting the possible non-satisfaction of different future conceptions of the good) for his deepest identity-forming commitments of the present.

The situation is simply this. Rawls has given an argument for a liberal principle that requires us to possibly make sacrifices in the present for the fulfilment of our desires in the future, but the most rigorous description we have of the moral psychology of identity asks us to make sacrifices in the future for the fulfilment of our present fundamental commitments that shape our identities. It would appear that things are at a stand-off.

At this point, let me invoke the other two of the three moral psychological notions I had introduced. The first of these is the idea of reinforcement among our desires. Suppose now that our religious communitarian being contemplated has not only a fundamental commitment in the sense defined but also that that commitment is highly *reinforced*, in the sense defined, by the other substantive desires in his value economy. Supposing this immediately resolves the stand-off and puts Rawls' position in an unrecoverable disadvantage. Why? Because Rawls *cannot make any similar appeal* to reinforcement from substantive conceptions of the good for his higher order desire for the satisfaction of future desires since that higher order desire is introduced by him only behind the veil of ignorance *where, ex hypothesi, there are no substantive conceptions of the good*. That is the whole point of his strategy. For it is this strategy which places him in the centre of the classical liberal tradition, a strategy formulated in order to give philosophical support via a sophisticated contract theory, to that classically defining interpretation of the liberal constraints, that is, an interpretation that sees them as not being justified by appeal to substantive values. This is the position I am seeking to oppose by making the notion of constraint ambiguous, by inviting us to conceive a liberalism where the constraint provided by its principles remains a constraint, but nevertheless is also justified by appeal to our own substantive values as they reinforce one another in an internally coherentist framework of moral and political rationality.

That brings me finally to the third moral psychological notion, that of weakness of will, to complete my description of the point of my argument against Rawls' and this version of liberalism. The point can be put straightforwardly. If the contemplated religious communitarian in Rawls' thought-experiment opts for the liberty of expression behind the veil of ignorance, then his moral psychology can be demonstrated to exhibit a specific kind of irrationality, that of weakness of will. For he would be opting for an outcome which is not only in conflict with his fundamental commitments (which in itself is not decisive since it gives rise only to a stand-off) but also choosing something that is much less reinforced by his other desires. To do this last is to be no different, say, from the weak-willed alcoholic who desires to sober up and fulfil all his other desires (say to be a good husband and father, a good professional, etc.) that are better reinforced than his desire for alcohol, but nevertheless opts for his relatively unreinforced desire for alcohol. To sum up in a facetious word, a proper understanding of moral psychology can only deliver the verdict that sometimes (in the face of strong communal identities) the grand liberal tradition may have to secure its liberal principles by asking us to be addicted to liberalism.

That brings to a close the argument against the classical liberal reading of the ideal of non-interference and of liberal rights and constraints generally. The strategy of my argument has been to show how there can be no justification of the notion of liberal rights that can be guaranteed to meet two conditions at once: (1) That it makes no appeal to an agent's or community's substantive values, and (2) that it sees the agent or community as rational, in the specific sense of not being weak-willed. In short there is no guarantee that an adoption of secular liberalism by a society will be rational if it is not justified by appeal to some substantive values of the members of the society. And since presumably one would want liberal principles to be a rational adoption, we had better give a quite different reading to these ideals and rights than is found in the classical liberal tradition.

There is a point worth noting. My argument against classical liberalism, as represented by a tradition from Mill to Rawls, is entirely independent of the truth of communitarianism. It is based entirely on considerations of moral psychology as I defined them and elaborated them in section II. I have, of course, chosen the *example* of (religious) communitarianism to make my moral-psychological case. But that is merely an example and a quite different example could have been chosen. I chose this one because my eventual interest (in the next section) is a specific historical and political context of secularism and communalism in India. But *any* example that involved the moral-psychological considerations of identity in the sense I have defined it, with reinforcement from other desires in the sense that I have defined it, and giving rise to the threat of weakness of will in the sense I have defined it, could have equally made the point against Rawls. Identity (to take just one of the three moral-psychological notions) is a perfectly general notion involving fundamental commitments as I have defined them structurally and generally in counterfactual terms. It by no means necessarily involves *communitarian* fundamental commitments in particular.

There is another related point. Even if one chooses an example of communitarian identity as I have in making my argument against the classical tradition, there is a distinction to be made of some significance which is often neglected in discussions of liberalism and its opponents, and it is a distinction which I crucially intend to apply it to a particular political context later on. This is the distinction between a *normative* angle on communities as opposed to a *descriptive* acknowledgment of them. Communitarians have a normative angle of regard for communities. They think that it is only within communities and a tradition that individuals form their identities and genuinely flower. So they value communities and decry the modernist tendency of individual detachment from community caused by the more abstractly configured post-Enlightenment constructions of the nation and the state and its various liberal principles and agencies. A quite different angle on communities is the descriptive one, an angle that can be taken even by an anti-communitarian. This is where one only acknowledges the fact that many sections of a given population may have fundamental communitarian commitments, without oneself thinking this to be a good thing at all. In fact one can make such a descriptive acknowledgment and take the contrary normative stance of thinking community to be a crippling curb on individual assertion and self-respect. The point for now is that even if one took this last stance one could embrace my argument against Rawls. All that my argument requires is the descriptive acknowledgment that there are groups who have a certain moral psychology involving certain kinds of communitarian commitments. In short, an anti-communitarian could use a communitarian example to criticize the classical liberal tradition, as I have done. In fact, as I will argue in the next section, it may be well for an anti-communitarian to choose such an example because she will be in a better position then to fashion an eventually more stable secular liberalism, if she took into account the *descriptive* fact of communities and communitarian commitments.

I am labouring to stress this distinction between the normative and descriptive attitude towards communities partly so as to prevent the co-opting of my argument against the classical liberal tradition into the currently fashionable anti-liberal communitarian critique of the modernist legacy of the Enlightenment,[14] a critique which repudiates the very idea of rights and of citizenship as being destructive of tradition and community. My argument does not show nor is it intended to show that there is anything wrong with the notion of rights. What it does show, if it is effective, is that there is no justification of liberal rights in the way that a familiar tradition from Mill to Rawls has tried to argue for it, that is without any appeal to the citizens' substantive values and conceptions of the good.

A reader may think that it is very odd that in my view the standard and most sophisticated philosophical arguments for liberal rights may be found deeply wanting, and yet the notion of rights itself is not found wanting. He may think that if rights are dependent on ordinary and highly contestable substantive values for their justification, they must lose their special status as procedural constraints standing separately from substantive values. These thoughts are confused because they run together modes of justification for a conclusion with the conclusion itself. If one kept these two quite different things apart, there is nothing odd whatever in the claims of my argument. It is true that rights now become more contestable since justifying them will mean taking on arguments dependent on substantive values for premises, values that are in contest with other substantive values. But it is a *non-sequitur* to conclude from this outcome that rights themselves are undermined. Rights, on my view, remain rights. That is, we may still feel that there is need for basic constraints of a certain kind on all citizens, and therefore we may still think of certain values of ours (such as non-interference in certain domains) as standing apart from other values in being procedural rather then substantive, as generating entitlements in the way that substantive values do not. All that would be affected by my argument is that rights

[14] I don't actually think that there is a well-formed debate about the rights and wrongs of modernity. I have argued so in my paper 'Two Concepts of Secularism: Reason, Modernity, and the archimedean Ideal', *Economic and Political Weekly*, 9 July 1994. Also in another paper entitled 'Nationalism, Secularism, and Modernity' in Rajeev Bhargava (ed.) *Secularism and Its Critics* Oxford University Press, Delhi, 1998.

so conceived (both by the classical liberal and by me) are the conclusions of justifications of a very different sort. That is what I meant, when I said toward the beginning of this section, that the unimpeachable claims of liberal doctrine can be ambiguously read. Once disambiguated, the situation is simply this. My argument shows that any justification of rights must appeal to the very substantive values with which rights themselves are quite properly contrasted. Whereas the classical liberal position aspires (unsuccessfully if my critique is effective) to justify adopting rights in exactly the same sense (constraints generating entitlements, etc.,) without appeal to substantive values and instead via a purely philosophical argument of the sort I have sketched and criticized in detail in this section.

Let me end this section by *generalizing into a methodological lesson*, my critique of the classical mode of justification of liberal conclusions. To do so, I will introduce two terms, 'internal reasons' and 'external reasons', familiar to moral philosophers. The critique, to the extent that it has been effective, is a specific case of a perfectly general methodological point. If we have properly understood the point of the particular argument I made against Rawls, a much more general way of putting the point would be to say that *all* reasoning about moral and political value is *internal* reasoning, that is, internal to the substantive commitments of those with whom one is reasoning. We cannot get outside of the agents we are reasoning with to give them reasons. Rawls' appeal to a higher order desire for the satisfaction of our revised desires in his contractualist thought-experiment, Mill's appeal to a meta-induction regarding fallibility, and other such arguments in the classical liberal tradition are all efforts to give arguments for non-interference that are based on universal considerations which *are* intended to be quite independent of and *external* to the specific and substantive values that agents might possess. And that is why their mode of justifying their otherwise impeccable conclusion fails. There is no such archimedean point in reasoning, (whether Rawls' or Mill's or any other). In a word, there *are no* external reasons.

The general methodological idea that there are no external reasons, that there are only internal reasons appealing to substantive values of agents, has liberating possibilities for political theory, and I have tried in other recent work to use this idea to refashion two notions in the Marxist tradition, which have been unjustly discarded altogether in recent political theory because it was (to some extent rightly) thought that they are too closely tied to external reasons—these are the notion of 'false consciousness' and the notion of what Isaiah Berlin anxiously described as 'Positive Liberty'.[15] But here I want just to see through its consequences for an issue I raised at the very beginning of this paper, the issue of the seemingly unavoidable disjunction of statist reform versus internal reform, where the adopting of the one can only be understood as being at the cost of the other losing ground. A proper understanding of the notion of internal reasoning should instruct us how to dismount this seesaw.

IV

In my earlier paper 'What is a Muslim?',[16] which I cited above, I had looked to the structure of the moral psychology relevant to the reform of Islam, most particularly the reform of Islamic personal law. In that paper I had *without argument* made an explicit assumption that there were no reasons but internal reasons, and I had said that rather than plonk down basic liberal truths of the classical liberal tradition established on externalist and purely philosophical grounds, one should provide internal arguments appealing to the substantive values of historically situated Muslim populations to convince them to conclude in favour of internal reform. In a subsequent paper on secularism, called 'Two Concepts of Secularism: Reason, Modernity and the archimedean Ideal',[17] I had again, *without argument*, made the same anti-archimedean (anti-externalist) assumption, and sought to sketch a conception of secular liberalism compatible with the assumption. In the present paper so far, I have tried to *actually present an argument* for this assumption that I have constantly been making without argument. That was the argument I just gave against the classical liberal's (for example, Rawls') archimedean efforts at justifying liberal rights.

[15] I have done so in the last part of my article 'Two Concepts of Secularism' and in an unpublished manuscript entitled 'Marx and Self-Deception'.

[16] Gyanendra Pandey (ed.) *What is a Muslim? Fundamental Commitment and Cultural Identity in Hindus and Others*, Viking, Delhi, 1993, pp. 273–95.

[17] See footnote 14.

This overall, accumulated position,[18] however, expressed as it is in the rhetoric of internal versus external reasons is poised for being subject to a spectacular misinterpretation. (I am being a little coy when I say 'poised' since I in fact spent three months recently trying to correct this misinterpretation among some of my closest friends in Delhi.)

Let me explain by briefly considering a certain Foucauldian position which is adapted by Partha Chatterjee in his recent paper on secularism.[19]

Chatterjee argues that in a multi-communal society like India, which has granted minority rights to minority religious communities in its constitution, secular liberalism is powerless to cope with the need for personal law reform. But he thinks this need not be devastating for those who find the personal law of one or other community unacceptably illiberal. And he boldly proposes that the answer to this impasse is that we should extend the notion of democracy and its representative institutions to intra-community sites, opening up thereby the possibility of internal reform of personal law. Now, a careless and skipping reader of my paper, seeing the word 'internal' in my use of the notion of 'internal reasons', and seeing it again in Chatterjee's account of 'internal reform', may conclude that we have convergent views, even though I have made no commitment to or even mention of intra-community democratic institutions, and insisted throughout on the necessity for statist reform. My point here is not just to say that this is a dumbfounding conflation, but to explore quickly how Chatterjee's Foucauldian position and mine differ, for the difference is essential to this paper's promised task of superseding a certain disjunction.

[18] Actually the accumulation has been longer and thicker in the stewing. Apart from the papers just cited, and also the papers cited earlier on redefining certain Marxist notions along internalist lines, there were papers which discussed the Rushdie controversy along these internalist lines, arguing that the best defence of Rushdie was not to plonk down the free speech principle as an archimedean liberal truth but to argue for the principle by appealing to values internal to Muslims. See 'Rushdie and the Reform of Islam', *Economic and Political Weekly*, 24 March 1990, and 'Rushdie, Islam and Post-Colonial Defensiveness' in *Yale Journal of Criticism*, 1992.

[19] 'Secularism and Toleration', in *Economic and Political Weekly*, 9 July 1994.

Chatterjee is driven to his conclusion about intra-community democracy in India as a result of a crucial use he makes of an idea in Foucault, the idea of governmentality.[20] The critique of sovereignty inherent in Foucalt's idea is put to use by Chatterjee to rule out the possibility that there can be any statist reform which is reason-giving and non-coercive. (Even if we disagree with Chatterjee on a number of things, we may grant to him the general connection between reason-giving and non-coerciveness. In other words, one may take for granted for the moment that any statist imposition which is not at least implicitly reason-giving will be coercive, just as if I impose something on you without giving any reason, that is, without at least implicitly intending to appeal to *something* you would find evaluatively in favour of it from within your set of values, it would be coercive, in at least one intuitive sense of the term.) What Foucault and Chatterjee do is to use this general connection between giving reasons and non-coercion to arrive at a specific conclusion about how liberal states must be coercive. Essential to their way of arriving at this conclusion, is the appeal to a relativism about the very notion of resources.

Though he does not say anything explicitly about external reasons, Chatterjee—following Foucault—assumes that the liberal state and its principles are founded on an externalist conception of reason which is indifferent to specific identities, and again, though there is no explicit argument against the shortcomings of external reason of the sort I have tried to present in the last few pages, it is very clear from his paper and a series of his other works, that he is deeply convinced of its shortcomings (on grounds no doubt very different from the ones I present because they depend on a *normative* communitarianism which I shun). And consequently, because he thinks the basis of the state committed to liberal and secular principles is indeed external reason, which is deliberately blind to communitarian identities, his view is that a community cannot intelligibly give reasons for resisting the anti-communitarian homogeneity inherent in the inevitable secularizing motion of so called 'nationalist' and 'progressive' statist ideologies. To enter into the space of reasons at all is to surrender

[20] Michel Foucault, 'Governmentality', in Graham Burchell, Colin Gordon, and Peter Miller (eds) *The Foucault Effect: Studies in Governmentality*, University of Chicago Press, 1991.

to and be overwhelmed by this alien, modern set of tendencies destructive of community. As he puts it: 'To say "We will not give reasons for not being like you" is to resist entering that deliberative or discursive space where the technologies of governmentality operate. But then in a situation like this, the only way to resist submitting to the powers of sovereignty is to literally declare oneself unreasonable.'

The general trajectory of his paper, and that sentence in particular, reveals something extremely startling and interesting. And that is that Chatterjee, for all his manifestly communitarian sympathies, shares an assumption with his most bitter dialectical foe, the classical liberal tradition. I will describe it in the idiom and framework I have been using earlier in the paper. It is the assumption that if, in the face of identity-constituting fundamental commitments, one cannot make coherent the classical liberal picture of reason or justification for the liberal secular state, then reasons must fall out of the picture and the liberal state must necessarily be coercive because incommensurate. That is the crux of his use of Foucault's notion of 'governmentality'. But, remarkably, it is also the crucial assumption (as we have seen in the last section) of the reading of the notion of liberal rights that is found in the classical liberal tradition. Here too it is taken for granted that if there were no archimedean reason given for the justification of these constraints or rights, if their justification were derived from substantive values and commitments, there is nothing to stop the slide into relativist communitarian mayhem. Chatterjee would find the description 'mayhem' tendentious, but he would be in total agreement that there was a correct point there, which he himself would describe more sympathetically than as 'mayhem'. Hence, for both classical liberalism and for Foucault, it is 'external reasons or bust!' Despite their deep differences of attitude toward the liberal state, for both of them there is a *common assumption*, which is that the liberal state is *necessarily* (and not just in specific historical cases) archimedean. And if archimedeanism, (i.e. if the external justifications of secular and liberal principles) is not able to deal with the moral psychology of communitarian identity, then for both of them, the liberal state must necessarily pass into something else, something more coercive against communities, which, in turn, must be protected in various ways against its coercive power. Thus communitarianism. This is the tension between the liberal state and community that I mentioned at the outset. It's just that now we are in a position to understand the philosophical trajectory by which we have been landed with this seemingly unavoidable tension in our conception of the relation between state and community. And (bizarrely) it is a philosophical trajectory in which the classical liberal and his Foucauldian critic are co-propellers.

I find in this assumption that they both share, the assumption that one must chose between an archimedean liberalism and communitarianism, a quite impoverished conception of the theoretical options; I have already addressed this issue by making theoretical space for an alternative reading of liberal principles provided on the basis of a quite different mode of justification for them than is found in classical archimedean liberalism, but a reading which at the same time makes no *normative* commitment to communitarianism either. I now want to concretely occupy this space by going on to argue against a very specific concrete instance of this shared assumption, a very specific consequence of their seeing the options in the restricted way the assumption sees them.

The failure of the traditional liberal and the communitarian to see any other options to their own and to each others' doctrines translates into the following scenario in the context of a specific issue such as that of Muslim Personal Law in India today, a scenario in which the entire debate must be governed by a certain disjunction, a certain either/or: if there is to be change in Muslim Personal Law, it must *either* be statist reform by a secular liberal state imposing its archimedean secularism *or* it must be internal reform via the civil society or some more formal institutions within the communities. This is just a concrete version of the impoverished theoretical options I mentioned a moment ago. And the theoretical framework I have been setting up in which moral psychology is exploited for political-theoretical analysis offers a tentative way out of such an impoverishing and disjunctive option. Perhaps 'impoverished' is the wrong word to describe what I am offering a way out from since it would be quite wrong to think that what is on offer is an enriching of choices with some *third* option. *Rather what is on offer is to question whether the two disjuncts of the disjunctive option are really disjoint.* In other words, the theoretical space created by this paper allows us to refuse to see why it is that theorizing about the secular state should, in this particular and concrete context, have it that *internal* reform cannot take place on a *statist* site.

This may seem initially startling, a contradiction in terms, but the suggestion is that it will seem so *only* within the standard framework, one which, and I said, is *shared* by Chatterjee as well as his dialectical enemy, the classical liberal. My proposal for an alternative seeks a way to refuse to allow that the liberal secular state necessarily be seen as coercive in the Foucauldian way against the values of a community just because one recognizes the limitations of classical liberalism's archimedean aspirations.

Since for Chatterjee internal reform is *ex hypothesi* non-coercive, if it can be shown that a liberal secular *state* provides for '*internal*' reform in one perfectly plausible sense of that term, then even he would have to grant that such a state is non-coercive. To show this one has to show that the relations between state and community are still within the range of reasons. For, as we saw above, it was the denial of this possibility that underlay Chatterjee's Foucauldian anti-statist proposal for exclusively inter-community reform via intra-community democracy. But, as I have been arguing, the rejection of archimedeanism, of external reasons, still leaves it open for the state to be the site for internal reasoning, whereby the substantive values of communitarian commitments can be addressed and substantive internal reasons be given to communities to agree to a secular outcome. (In fact if necessary *different* internal reasons can be given to different communities, depending on the make-up of their internally reinforced values, for a common secular outcome.) Such a common secular outcome—even though one starts with the descriptive acknowledgment of communities to be addressed by internal reasoning by the secular state—is what I had, in my earlier paper, 'Two Concepts of Secularism', called a 'negotiated' secularism.[21] And it provides for a genuinely liberating perspective which is hidden from view only to the extent that one dogmatically reads the sense of constraint expressed by the idiom of rights exclusively in the classical reading of it. The perspective comes into sight as soon as space is made available for the notion of internal reasons. Chatterjee raises the spectre of governmentality

[21] I had also there called it an 'emergent secularism'. Also see Charles Taylor's fine article on secularism along these lines in terms of the notion of an 'overlapping consensus' in Bhargava (ed.) *Secularism and Its Critics.*

only because he sees no scope for internal reasons. Exclusively non-statist intra-communitarian internal reform, therefore, is the last resort of relativists, who can find no role for internal *reasons*. But a proper understanding of the moral psychology in my framework should demonstrate that relativism poses no such drastic threat. Why not?

One answers this question by getting clear on what it is to give an internal reason to another with whom one is in conflict or with whom one is disagreed.

Relativism is the consequence of thinking that if there is no transparent or externally established value with which a liberal can trump those with whom she is disagreed (for example, if the archimedean version of liberal truth is unavailable) then liberalism has nothing to resort to by way of *reasons*, and everything else will seem like the coercions which Foucault described in terms of the phrase 'governmentality'. So, the Foucauldian says, instead of being coercive we must leave it to those one disagreed with to sort out things *for themselves* and hope they will come around to agreeing with us (*intra*-communitarian democracy being a natural proposal to try and achieve this in the concrete case we are discussing). If *we* intervened, for example by invoking the liberal state's backing as the carrier of liberal principles and truth, it would amount to coercion (governmentality) based on no reason (there *being* no other kind of reason but external reasons, which admittedly, as we saw, are powerless as reasons in the face of communitarian identity). So the implication is that *one* cannot give an *internal* reason to an *other*. They must do it themselves with their own representative institutions.

That implication is what I am denying. The possibility of giving internal reasons to *another*, which I am insisting on, is just the suggestion that despite the powerlessness of external reasons, it is still possible to be non-coercive because it is still possible to *not* ignore the point of view with whom one is in conflict. It is still possible to appeal with reason to the other's point of view in order to resolve the disagreement in our own favour. How? The giving of internal reasons to another doesn't consist in just plonking down a reason by claiming for it that any rational person must embrace it (as Rawls does for instance when he appeals to the suasion inherent in his higher order desire to have our future desires protected and fulfilled). Rather the giving of internal reasons to another necessarily seeks to find the other's moral-psychological economy *infirm* in the relations between its substantive desires, in the sense defined in section II. (Or more strongly, if that is possible, to find it inconsistent.) That is, it hopes to find the moral psychology of the other lacking in *internal* reinforcement of some of the desires it espouses, in particular the desires with which we are disagreed.[22] If one can demonstrate to the other that that is so we would be giving them internal reasons, reasons from within their own point of view, from within their own overall corpus of desires, to change their mind on the particular matter of disagreement. Now of course there is no guarantee that there will be such scope for giving internal reasons in all cases of conflict or disagreement with another. That is why there is perhaps no non-trival *a priori* argument against relativism about values and that is why, no doubt, some cases of conflict will be very hard. Any theoretical view that was blind to this would be unrealistic. All the same there is no reason to think that there is any permanent difficulty or impossibility in the providing of internal reasons to another in cases of conflict. In fact it is the *possibility* of such reason-giving to an agent or community with whom we are disagreed, which is a permanent one, since agents and communities, unlike perhaps rational automata, are not monsters of consistency. Nor are they ever likely to be possessed of a maximal psychological and evaluative equilibrium, that is, possessed of maximally reinforced desires in the sense we have defined earlier. Their desires and values are often in internal conflict, and certainly they are permanently in *potential* internal conflict since agents and communities live in an environment that is changing, and such changes will often inject conflict into their values.

This is just what Hegel called History and the dialectic it engenders. If we keep firmly in mind the cautionary remark stated in the footnote attached to this sentence, one very useful way of reading Hegel's primary insight here is precisely to see History as the movement and sway of internal reasoning in society with the state as the moral agent which is the seat and source of such reasoning.[23] What Foucault fails to see, despite some extraordinarily acute

[22] The reader must keep in mind firmly the broad sense of 'desires' with which I began.

[23] Of course in one sense it would be a highly revisionist reading of Hegel, since it would not embrace any of the determinist and historicist trajectories

specific historical diagnoses of various social institutions, is that the success of these historical analyses yield him his heated relativist conclusions in political philosophy only because he is deaf to this Hegelian insight about History. As I said, it is true that there perhaps is no *a priori* argument against relativism once we see that the application of all archimedean strategies in politics such as Rawls and Mill will sometimes render the moral-psychological economies of certain agents and communities weak-willed and irrational. Even so, I am claiming that the right picture of moral psychology with its permanent potential scope for internal reasons should cause a sea of governmentality and relativistic anxiety to subside. Perhaps relativism is a genuine and intractable threat in situations where one is disagreed with another whose values are perfectly consistent, maximally reinforced, and permanently so. But it is safe to say that that is a contingency which is so remote, if it is coherent at all, that relativism can be dismissed as a possibility raised only by moral and political theorists who simply have not paid enough detailed attention to moral psychology and asked under what conditions is the giving of internal reasons to another agent or community impossible. The conditions, as I've just noted them, are so rarely likely to obtain, if they are even so much as conceivable, that it is quite theoretically unsound to formulate a framework for secularism, as Chatterjee does, that elevates them to the normal circumstances which secular doctrine must address. Relativism, even if one cannot show it to be logically mistaken, all the same appears as a real threat only to those who have responded too generally and too carelessly to the (admittedly) archimedean excesses of classical liberalism. Chatterjee, despite the imagination and occasional rigour of his thinking, is one such thinker. Relativism may not be refutable on logical grounds as archimedean conceptions of reason might imply, but equally relativism cannot be thought to describe the normal conditions for which theories and political frameworks and institutions must be constructed. What I am suggesting by contrast is that a clear conception of the scope for internal reasoning in politics captures far better than either archimedean liberalism or communitarian relativism the

---

that surface in his writings. There is no suggestion in what I am saying of the idea that History and the internalist dialectic it engenders leads inevitably to liberal or any other consummations.

normal conditions in which multi-communal societies find themselves.

So, in our concrete case, I am arguing that we can dismount the seesaw of statist versus internal reform by clearing space for the liberating idea that internal reform can happen on a statist site. By this, I mean that the state can bring about reform in a way that appeals to (some of) the value-commitments of communities whom it is seeking to reform, in particular by appealing to values which stand in infirming tension with those values and practices which it seeks to reform. In other words it is the *state* which addresses them internally in a way that *they themselves* might have done on intra-community sites in Chatterjee's conception. The general point is that internal reasons can be given to a community by another, by the secular state, and so the idea of internal reform can be transformed from something which necessarily happens on intra-community sites (as in Chatterjee's picture of things), to one which can happen on a statist site. And if the notion of coercion is contrasted with the notion of reason-giving, a state which arrives at secular outcomes in this way need not be seen as any more coercive than the procedures by which these outcomes are delivered on intra-community sites. To see things this way is to see the liberal state as being able to provide a field of force of internal reasons addressing different communitarian perspectives from within their own internal substantive commitments and unsettling them into awareness of their own internal inconsistencies so as to eventually provide for a common secular outcome each on different internal grounds.

Such a theoretical view of the liberal state is of course dramatically different from the way in which the liberal state appears in Rawls and Mill. In a moment I will say more historically specific things about such an alternative to their conception of the liberal state. But first I want to stress that it is not merely different from Mills and Rawls and other such archimedean positions in the liberal tradition, it is also measurably different from the face-saving retreat of recent political theorists in the face of communitarian attack, which take all the content out of liberalism in order to save some of its universalism. Thus take for instance Laclau in a recent paper called the 'The Question of Identity'.[24] After considering in detail

[24] In Wilmsen and McAlister (eds) *The Politics of Difference*, University of Chicago Press, 1996.

the difficulty that ethnic identity raises for the universalities of secular liberalism of the classical picture, he explicitly rejects all 'secular psychologies', as he calls them, and is prepared to see universality in politics retreat to the sparest minimum that makes democracy possible in the first place. Pointing out that even the particularists talk in the idiom of rights when they demand rights for minorities, he finds in this idiom a universalist discourse that enables democracy, even if not the full prestige of secular liberalism. He frankly admits that universality so conceived has no body and content; it is, as he puts it, a whole vocabulary of empty signifiers which surface precisely in such paradoxical phenomena as when communitarians necessarily succumb to the rhetoric of minority rights. But why should we allow the difficulties raised by identity to abandon full secular outcomes for such manifestly skimpy universals in liberal politics? To see the state as a possible field of force for internal reasons is precisely not to adopt the strategy of retreating to thinner and thinner neutral ground that all communities and particular identities must minimally share. It is rather to give up on seeking neutral common agreement—necessarily thin gruel in a multi-communal society—and to demand that the state seek the thicker brew of a fully secular outcome via a signing up to a *common* secular outcome for *different* and therefore *non-neutral reasons* from *within* their own very different substantive value economies. This is exactly what I had in the earlier paper on secularism called an 'emergent' and 'negotiated' secularism.

Let me, then, re-introduce explicitly a theoretical term here for this idea of internal-directed changes sought by the state within the value commitments of communities, and call them 'negotiations'. I call it a theoretical term because it is a term of art, a placeholder for anything which brings to effect a certain kind of value outcome via internal reasoning. A secularism, which is the outcome of changes so achieved, would then be a 'negotiated' secularism, and if the changes were brought about on statist sites, it would be the achievement of a non-archimedean secular state, one to which no doubt both the classical liberal and Foucault would take grave objection—the classical liberal because she allows no ambiguity in its reading of the notion of liberal constraints expressed in liberal principles, and Foucault because his exaggerated anxieties about relativism have generated his peculiarly influential kind of anti-statist neurosis.[25]

I am keen to stress the highly theoretical nature of what is intended here by the term 'negotiation' because I want to warn against an unthinkingly vulgar interpretation of the idea that might result by confusing it with what the term connotes in more common usage. In particular I want to warn against what is intended as either certain limited forms of alliances or certain cynical concessions by the state to communities for manifestly unsecular outcomes.

Thus, for instance, it stands apart from something like the Leninist concept of class alliances, where the agreement concerns only circumstantial matters, but the identity of the most reinforced desires, the values, remain unrevised by the negotiation. It stands distinct from this concept since what negotiation is intended to achieve is a *revision* in communitarian commitments, revision toward secularism via internally directed reasoning.[26]

[25] I use the term 'neurosis', despite its edge, deliberately. And I cannot resist recounting an exchange to justify its use. After giving this paper in Calcutta recently, I was asked a question (with a slight sense of challenge) about whether I did not think that all of the states which I thought progressive were coercive. I responded that I did not think it terminologically useful, for instance, to describe the incipient welfare state in Britain immediately after World War II as 'coercive'. And as a counter challenge intended half in jest, I asked whether the person asking me the question would describe an agency of the state which offered an individual free surgery when he was in dire need of it, as 'coercive'. The reply came quickly: yes, it *would* be properly described as 'coercive' since the individual would very likely not know the rules and principles of the state's bureaucracy by which the free surgery was being made available, and that was proof that the state was an external agency to which one simply submitted without any detailed knowledge of its workings over us. To my mind here 'coercion' has become a ludicrously cognitive notion (a grotesque caricature of the cognitive turn that Foucault brought to the notion of power)—as if one would be 'coerced' by a breeze that one was enjoying just because one did not know the principles by which it blew over one! 'Neurosis' seems to me a quite apt description for what such anti-statism has become.

[26] Of course Lenin was quite right that if one understood the concept of class properly, then class alliances would necessarily be of this kind. It's not that I am saying that he was wrong to say what he said about such alliances,

So also it stands distinct from the sort of thing that Sumit Sarkar attributed to me in a recent paper before criticizing my idea of a negotiated secularism. He says:

> Through a detailed critique of Partha Chatterji [*sic*] and Ashis Nandy, Akeel Bilgrami, I think, rightly rejects as unsustainable any vision of secularism which harked back nostalgically to the idea of a pre-modern India. His alternative, however, is to acknowledge secularism as a value through negotiation.... Partha Chatterji [*sic*], interestingly, comes to a rather similar conclusion.... At the practical or pragmatic level the curious thing about Bilgrami and Chatterji [*sic*] is their lack of originality. This, after all, is what the much-abused Indian secular state policy at its worst has often amounted to: efforts at placating conservative or communal Hindu and Muslim community leaders simultaneously. The classic recent example would be Rajiv Gandhi in 1986. Opening the locks of Ayodhya and surrendering to Muslim fundamentalist pressure on the Shah Bano case....[27]

Well, I have already said something at the beginning of this section about conflating my position with Chatterjee's. And I don't know what to say about originality, since I was not in any case trying to be original, I was only trying to say what I thought was true. It did surprise me though to be told that what I did say was anticipated by Rajiv Gandhi. In fact when I first heard and read Sarkar's charge, it flabbergasted me to learn that Rajiv Gandhi's playing of the Hindu card and then the Muslim card during this period, should be seen as an instance of what *I* had in mind by the use of the term 'negotiation',[28] since it was part of that point, and

---

it is rather that I am saying such alliances are not what I intended by 'negotiation'.

[27] Sumit Sarkar, 'The Anti-Secularist Critique of Hindutva: Problems of a Shared Discursive Space', in *Germinal*, vol. I, 1994.

[28] Even more numbingly crude a confusion lay in another charge that my descriptive acknowledgment of communities amounted to a vision like the *millet* system during the Ottoman period, where for instance Russian and Greek orthodox communities were accepted as living under their own codes of law. (This, despite the fact that I had stated repeatedly in that paper that such an acknowledgment was to be the first step to finding a way to arrive at a *uniform* civil code.) I was in fact amused to hear that this was the reason cited for not reprinting my article 'Two Concepts of Secularism' in the publication of a leftist journal. Of course, it is perfectly natural for a leftist publication to not want to reprint an article which made such a claim. The scarcely credible thing is rather that such a claim could possibly be seen by a clear-headed and honest reader to be even remotely implied by the words I wrote.

in fact it was explicitly part of the point of the entire paper that Sarkar was criticizing, that we need a diagnosis of why an avowedly secular state seemed so often to appeal to the most shrill and communal among the voices in a community, when it did appeal to the community. Far from commending this sort of cynical sops to the reactionary communal elements in communities, the paper was demanding a diagnosis for why 'negotiation' (in the very specifically theoretical sense in which I had introduced the idea) was abandoned for those sops. Why, for instance, in the very example that Sarkar cites, did Rajiv Gandhi take it for granted that he should not listen instead to the voices of the impressive mass to Muslim women who demonstrated outside the Parliament during the episode of the Muslim Women's Bill? Or to put it more generally and diagnostically, how is it that an avowedly secular state finds itself repeatedly failing to be in a position to confidently assume that the moderate voices in a community (which even if less shrill are surely the more numerous) are the more representative of public opinion on such things as the status of a mosque or of personal laws, or in an earlier period, the status of Urdu, and so on.[29] How is it that when it does repeatedly appeal to or address an issue that is necessarily located in community, the state has tended to appeal to the far smaller but more vocal reactionary element? *In short, how is it that the state has over decades failed to democratize the vast mass of ordinary people in a community, so that the reactionary element is seen to be exactly what it is, a small and unrepresentative minority within the community*? And I had suggested that part of the longer diagnosis of this phenomenon might be that even before statehood was acquired, secularism was the archimedean rhetoric of a party which for six decades was nevertheless marked by the making of concessions to the Mahasabhite and then subsequently other Hindu Right leaders within the Congress party and the leaders of the communal Muslim elements outside the party. I had speculated that the pursuit of a less archimedean rhetoric and a greater democratization for which there would have to be more descriptive acknowledgment of

[29] There is no reason to believe that the vast masses of ordinary Muslims and Hindus distant from the élite bargaining at metropolitan political sites, had the sort of deeply felt reactionary communitarian commitments needed to bring about outcomes such as the Bill in question, or (in the case of the Hindus) the destruction of the mosque at Ayodhya and—in earlier days—the suppressing of Urdu in northern India.

communities, would have allowed for the sturdy engagement of contestation by internal reasoning with the communities, and may have pre-empted the need for constantly having to make concessions to the most communal elements to keep them subdued. Sarkar thus came to cite his example of negotiation as a criticism of my view only because he quite failed to see the point of what I had termed 'negotiation', which was a process whose outcome was not intended to be such appeasement, the outcome was supposed rather to be *secularism* via internal reasoning with the communities' other values.

The ideal here is necessarily a delicate one to bring to practice. But as an ideal it strives to do at the site of a state what Chatterjee thinks can only be done at intra-communal sites. Chatterjee's argument is a simple one and it has its logic. Though he doesn't put it this way, it is a way to put it: if you grant rights to minority communities, then there is a danger that a small sub-minority of shrill reactionary voices within it will dominate the communitarian space you will create, so you must introduce intra-communal democratic and representative institutions, to stay their influence. But the logic need not get going in the first place, if the state were to be the site and the instrument where this democratization happens.

What a secular state, trying to cope with communitarian political voices on specific issues of the sort mentioned above, can do to give those voices the confidence to attend to the conflicts within their own thinking and values, and then internally reason them towards progressive and secular commitments is not an easy question. But no Hegelian question is easy. What gives confidence and what overcomes defensiveness in a community is various, and it is impossible to generalize about, independent of the local context. It is for this reason that the conditions that make possible a negotiated secularism should not be pinned down more specifically than the concept in its generality allows. It is for this reason that I have insisted on defining the term in a 'whatever-it-takes' formula, and then tried negatively to say what it definitely is not.

It is possible that a refusal to acknowledge communities and communitarian issues even descriptively and a focusing instead exclusively on the issue of class—a familiar, long-standing, and extremely attractive strategy—would be effective. But it is not at all obvious first of all that ongoing issues such as personal laws of

Muslims will go away simply, and by such an indirect strategy, and in any case it is not obvious that the sort of Left programme that would have to be effective for that to happen is one that we can expect to be implemented in our immediate times. Speaking historically, I think it is not at all obvious that even its most vigorous proponent in the mainstream nationalist movement—Nehru himself—seriously believed that it could be implemented except for about two and a half years in the nineteen thirties.

None of this suggests that the Left programme should be abandoned, only that other secular strategies should *not* be abandoned in the interim. Nor do the other strategies have to be in any antagonism at all with genuinely Left thinking, so long as such thinking does not confuse normative and descriptive attitudes towards community and assume that all descriptive acknowledgment must amount to a normative one, or assume that a mere descriptive acknowledgment of community will thwart the ideals of the Left toward class equality. There is no reason for a Left programme to think any of these things because these are all confusions and *non sequiturs*.

My seemingly paradoxical proposed strategy for a *statist* version of *internal* reform has two ingredients that are essential and which will remove the air of paradox. One is the democratization of the community and the second is the arrival at secular outcomes by internal reasoning with the community (for both of which one has obviously to have what I called a descriptive acknowledgment of community[30]). Without the first ingredient, the second is not likely to occur. And the connection between the two is not hard to see. The two ingredients are connected by a background premise essential to the strategy and framework I am proposing, a premise which I actually take to be true even in a country like Iran today. And that premise is the simple fact that in any religiously characterized community, such as Muslims and Hindus,[31] the large

[30] But equally, descriptive acknowledgment of communities without these two elements is obviously not enough for if it were, it might take the form of cynical appeasements to the most communal and reactionary element of the communities, as in Sarkar's example which I discussed above.

[31] I will repeat here something I have been saying as caveat in all my writing on this subject. The very idea of a religious community is a problematic one since 'Muslims' and 'Hindus', as categories which we invoke, are meant to describe a collection of people who are in many senses neither religious nor

majority of its members are not extremist or absolutist or fundamentalist (all these expressions apply to slightly different things, but for the moment I will not be sensitive to the discriminations). The large majority of the members of such communities whether in Teheran, Bradford, Bosnia, Ahmedabad, Mumbai, or Ayodhya, are either indifferent to the enthusiasms of the extremists, absolutists, and fundamentalists, and busy with their own various occupations and preoccupations, or they are positively against the disruptions that those enthusiasms bring into their lives and the distortions that they bring into their understanding of quotidian religious practice and doctrine.[32] It is a distinct minority within the community which has fundamentalist enthusiasms, even though because it makes the loudest noise this may not seem so and it certainly does not seem to have been taken to be so by successive recent occupants of the Indian state.

Beginning with this empirical premise, the strategy's appeal to its first ingredient, democratization, is just the following. Given that the majority in a community are not in any case actively or deliberatively opposed to secularism, how is it that this distinct majority can be put in a position to be seen as exactly that,

---

a community. Like all such categories they homogenize diversified social phenomena. But this anti-homogenization point can also be made into a banality, and it does not follow from it that we shouldn't invoke these categories at all. In describing the politics, say of the Hizbullah in Lebanon or a prominent strain in the Algerian opposition, it is perfectly natural to describe the ideologies as consisting of a highly politicized vision of a religious community. Does it mean that all Muslims share this ideology? Does it mean that Muslims everywhere do not have other identities than their Muslimness? Of course not. But the existence of multiple identities does not cancel the idea that in certain historical and political contexts, religious identities might dominate many of the other identities, in some populations in some parts of the world. And much of the broader application of categories like 'Muslim', as I have said in earlier papers, comes from the fact that many others who may not share any of these ideologies or even these contextually dominant identities in their personal lives, do *not* (out of defensiveness against external alien forces) *reject* the ideologies and contextually dominant identities of the absolutists. See the next few paragraphs in the text for more on this defensiveness. See also 'What is a Muslim?'

[32] In my earlier papers on Rushdie and in 'What is a Muslim?' I had referred to this majority within a community as 'moderates'. I am not happy with that term, but do not have another to put in its place.

the majority, the voice more representative of the community's position on such matters as secularism and reform than the fundamentalists. 'Democratization', in my picture, is a label for the process by which the state sees to it that they come to have this position and can confidently assume them to truly have this position when issues such as reform of personal law come up. For once they can be seen to be the more representative voice, internal reasons can be given much more easily to the overall community to embrace the reform of various things that the state wishes to impose.[33]

Democratization is a necessary condition for successful internal reasoning with the community because until it is achieved even this majority which has no deep shared value commitments with the minority of absolutists, is not likely to oppose the latter. Often there is a seemingly understandable reason why the majority within the community fails to stand up to the absolutist minority. Often it is due to a certain defensiveness against *outside* pressures on the whole community (whether it is the pressures on Muslims of India created by the forces of Hindutva or the pressures created on Muslims in West Asia by the neo-colonial presence of the West and its client states such as Israel, not to mention Saudi Arabia and Kuwait). There is a feeling among the majority within the community, even though they have no sympathy for absolutist tendencies and enthusiasms of the minority, that in the presence of these external pressures on the community as a whole, they would be letting down the community as a whole by opposing the minority of absolutists with it. I have written about such defensiveness in detail in my paper 'What is a Muslim?' I won't rehearse that discussion here. Enough to say here that it is the task of the state in such a situation to help overcome this defensiveness precisely by democratizing the community so that its most

[33] I intend this point to be general and not one just about Muslims and internal reform. That is why I mentioned Mumbai, Ahmedabad, etc. above. I believe that if democratization had occurred of Hindus too, then the state could have confidently assumed that the majority of Hindus felt nothing very strongly about opening of the locks at Ayodhya and left things well alone. It's only because a minority of Hindus had lobbied in the public domain in a frenzy while the majority had remained silent (a failure of democratization) that Rajiv Gandhi could play what he himself called the 'Hindu card'. Failure of democratization is reflected in the fact that Hindu opinion was thought to be represented by this shrill minority.

representative sections can have the confidence to resist both the external pressures *and* the internal pressures of the minority whom they oppose—a good and necessarily dual struggle since it is succumbing to the latter pressures which gives propaganda strength to mount external pressures in the first place (witness the Hindutva propaganda on the Muslim refusal to accept any criticism of their personal laws). Until the democratization takes place and the majority within the community is filled with a certain confidence of its place in the community as the representative voice, they will never allow those of their values that reinforce the need for reform in the community's practices to trump those other values which are engendered by the defensiveness, and so internal reasoning is not likely to have the effect of promoting internal reform.

That explains a little the role of democratization as a necessary condition for the success of internal reasons toward secular outcomes. (I will give below two historical examples of efforts at democratization which can lead to a progressive secular outcome by internal reasoning.) It is not as if Chatterjee does not see this point. But Chatterjee thinks this democratization should happen via intra-communitarian democratic institutions because his relativism makes him start with the assumption that internal reasons cannot be given to a community by any other than the community itself, that is, it cannot be given or provided by the state. Since I think the relativism is not a threat, I think his starting point is wrong; and I also think that his positive proposal for intra-community democratic institutions to effect the democratization has its perils. It is rather the secular state's obligation to produce such a democratization.

The perils in Chatterjee's proposal are obvious. An institutional setting of formal democratic representation within the community would have the effect of entrenching the community in a way that goes well beyond the descriptive acknowledgment of community into a normative promotion of it. Being a communitarian, Chatterjee may not find this perilous, but others who also want internal reform but who do not share that normative commitment to community may find this a case of keeping the bath-water. At any rate, a case of taking several steps back in order to take one forward.[34] If one wants to avoid these backward steps, how else may one think of democratizing communities?

[34] Given his general anti-statism, there is in any case a somewhat inconsistent disregard on Chatterjee's part for the coercive possibilities of

There is no alternative but this: *for the state to actively bypass the élite or reactionary leadership of a community, that is, bypass this small but vocal minority* (found, for example, among Muslims in India, in such leaders and spokesmen as Bukhari) *and intervene in the creation of a broad-based or mass politics directed toward a community in order to democratize them.*

If my dialectic, which begins with a certain empirical premise, is right, this is a necessary precondition for the state's capacity to create a field of force for internal reasoning that might yield a negotiated secularism, as I envision it. Until such democratization occurs, it is premature to ask the question, what are the institutional sites where the state can provide for such a field. On legal matters such as personal law, the eventual sites are bound to be sites such as the constitution, the legislature and the judiciary. But there is no canonical format for the effecting of internal reasoning with communities, that is, no canonical format for what I have called 'negotiation'. Recall that 'negotiation' is not intended by any

---

intra-communitarian statism that would be created by his own proposal. After all if individuals within the community dissent from majoritarian outcomes in the deliberations of a community's representative institutions, why should this not amount to those individuals being coerced just as much as communities claim to be coerced by secular majoritarianism at the extra-community or national level. There are two (related) reasons I can think of for why Chatterjee should be blind to this possibility: (1) his communitarianism conceives communities as the ultimate repository of social good, so statism within the community cannot be objectionable, and (2) statism is acceptable within the community and not at the level of the nation because individuals have *primordial allegiances* only to communities, and not to more *abstract* things like a nation. Both these reasons would allow him to disregard the worry about the intra-communal statism being coercive of individuals within the community since, given the first reason, coercion cannot occur where one is constituted by what is supposed to be coercive, and, given the second reason, one could not be coerced by the agencies of something to which one has a primordial allegiance, only by the agencies of something to which one lacks such an allegiance. I find both these rationales very suspect. In the first, *such* a strong conception of the social constitution of the individual by the community amounts to a rather dangerous theoretical consolidation of traditionalism and social conservatism. In the second, I don't believe that there are any primordial allegiances, that is to say allegiances which could not be overturned as a result of lacking reinforcement in the sense defined above—and when they *are* so overturned, the agencies of the intra-communitarian state should seem no less coercive to Chatterjee than the nation-state.

means to be an élite settlement by discussions around a table. The notion of 'negotiation' does not necessarily even imply—as I hope is clear by now—that communities must sit and talk together.[35] No more so than 'co-ordination' in coordination-theory implies necessarily that the groups or agents that co-ordinate must convene and talk themselves into a co-ordination equilibrium. The state can be the moral agent which effects co-ordination without in any way spoiling the ideals and ideas of coordination-theory. Exactly so for my notion of negotiation. This is why in my earlier paper I had also interchangeably called it an 'emergent' secularism. So it is not possible to say that secularism 'emerges' or the state 'negotiates' things to arrive at a secularism via some particular canonical format, and it is not in general within the scope of this paper to

[35] Not that it need always be a bad thing if they did so. It's just that that is not the point of the notion of 'negotiation' any more than it is (as I say below in the text) of the notion of 'co-ordination' in coordination-theory. Even Sarkar in the preposterous example he cited does not seem to think it is a case of leaders getting together and negotiating. But I can see how the word 'negotiation' might lead a reader to think that it is, if he does not pay attention to what else is being said, and to that extent I should perhaps have chosen another word. I *had*, in fact, in the earlier paper also used the term 'emergent' secularism as a synonym of 'negotiated' secularism and as an antonym of 'archimedean' secularism. Even so Gyan Prakash seems to have been misled by the word 'negotiation' to miss the point when in a comment on a paper of mine given at Columbia University, he suggested that my view of how secularism was to be achieved sounded too much like a debating society ideal. The examples of negotiating moments which I give below in the text, and which I had cited in the paper he was commenting on, that is, Bengal in the period of the Das Pact and the Muslim Mass Contact Programme, do not seem much like debating society events. But, in any case, I don't even think that the *ordinary* use of the word 'negotiate' (quite apart from my theoretical introduction of it as a term of art) always requires anything like people getting together and talking. We often say 'She negotiated that difficulty very well' or even 'She negotiated that crowded intersection very well' without there being any suggestion of getting together and talking with others. It just means that she *came out* of these situations very well by acknowledging a certain problem and deploying the means she had at hand. In my usage; the state similarly negotiates an *outcome* (a secular outcome, in this case) by acknowledging the descriptive fact of communities, and deploying the means (democratization and internal reasoning) which it has at hand, and this need not in any way involve the communities getting together and talking. (The historical examples I give below certainly do not involve it.)

articulate detailed institutional blueprints for what is to be done by a secular state such as India to implement the framework the paper has developed, especially prior to any effort by the state to democratize the communities. It would be pretending to more predictive power about the exact and detailed consequences of specific democratizations to do so. This is because diverse contexts in which different methods of democratization are attempted would yield diverse institutional settings. But all the same there are very interesting (if not sustained) historical antecedents to the idea I am pursuing, and all that this paper can do now after having sketched the beginnings of an alternative theoretical framework, is to cite them so as to give a very rough sense of what in concrete terms its framework envisions. Let me close, then, by citing two.

One is the Muslim Mass Contact programme launched briefly by the Congress party in the late nineteen thirties, which was a very revealing moment in the nationalist movement. What the programme revealed was a somewhat panicky acknowledgment on the part of the Congress party that their archimedean rhetoric (and their rhetoric of 'compositeness'[36]) was quite ineffective and had done nothing very much to democratize the Muslim voices in the country so that the progressive among them could emerge as the representative voice. The archimedean stance of Congress secular rhetoric had all along been something like this: 'Being secular we stand for everyone and don't distinguish between communities!' How did the mass contact programme I am invoking reflect a repudiation (albeit a brief one) of this archimedean rhetoric? The very fact that it was a *Muslim* Mass Contact programme betrayed that the party's archimedean secular stance had been quite blind to the need for descriptively acknowledging Muslims and then democratizing them so that they did not get hijacked into the narrow and élitist communal direction that Jinnah's politics was aiming to direct them. It is not at all surprising therefore that the programme angered Jinnah and filled him with a sense of danger, for it hit him where he was most vulnerable, his élitism and his capacity to manipulate a visible, vocal, and well-placed minority

[36] Congress talk of 'compositeness' was their occasional effort at stepping down from the high horse of archimedeanism to acknowledging the problem raised by the descriptive fact of communities. In 'Two Concepts of Secularism' I had criticized the disingenuous talk of 'compositeness' by the Congress party as a specific way of avoiding the tasks of democratization.

among Muslims capable of sounding communal anxieties to the colonial state.[37] It is only such a democratization of a community at the level of its masses that could have the effect of giving its non-communal leadership a position of centrestage as representing the community, a necessary step for an eventual secular outcome. It would not be idle, in fact it would be most interesting, to speculate whether the Muslim Mass Contact programme, had it not been prematurely and abruptly arrested by the Congress party's own leadership, would have had the sort of democratizing effect within a community whose name the movement took, and therefore had the confidence-inducing effect within the community, which I am claiming is a necessary condition to achieve the eventually negotiated alternative to archimedean secularism on the one hand and to intra-community internal reform on the other. Admittedly in this case the democratization would not exactly have been done on a secular *statist* site since an independent state had not been achieved, but it would have been a genuine proxy for it since after all it would have been at the site of a secular party gearing itself to acquire statehood. That is enough for me to make the point I want to make against Chatterjee's anti-statism and his insistence on intra-communitarian sites for democratization and reform.

Another historical moment (also very quickly aborted) which is not quite so clear a case of an effort at democratization by *mass* contact, is still interestingly revealing of how a broader section of a community can be given confidence by a state and then induced by internal reasoning towards a secular outcome. I have in mind Bengal at the time of the C. R. Das Pact. Consider the following very specific case. A close look at the details which surrounded the woman suffrage Bill which was passed in 1925 in the provincial legislative council, after having been defeated four years earlier, suggests very strongly that it was the Pact (adopted in 1923) which was central to this progressive and secular legislative reversal. Muslim members of the legislative assembly had voted predominantly against the Bill in 1921, but by 1925 it was the Muslim members, specially the Swarajist Muslims behind C. R. Das, who had been emboldened to vote for it in large enough numbers to

[37] There has been a tendency to think that the Mass Contact programme was restricted to a very small area. For a good corrective to this, see Mushirul Hasan's essay 'The Muslim Mass Contact Campaigns', in Mushirul Hasan (ed.) *India's Partition*, Oxford University Press, Delhi, 1993.

make the difference and get the Bill passed.[38] And they did so despite the fact that the party exercised no whip and in fact made an explicit decision not to put pressure on them to do so. The pact gave them the confidence to allow the arguments appealing to their own nationalist and secular values (arguments which were pressed upon them by their nationalist colleagues) to internally trump their own other values by which they themselves had argued for the opposite conclusion four years earlier, namely, that stricter observance of pardah among their women would inhibit them from voting and put the community at a disadvantage. I think one can see in the dialectic of this legislative turnaround and in this moment of the Bengal Pact, which was in other ways too a very dynamic period in Bengali history, a sense of what I had in mind by a field of force of internal reasons being carried out on a statist site by which a progressive and secular outcome can be achieved. The pact and its architect bypassed the aristocratic and westernized Muslim leadership and appealed directly to a far larger class of Muslims in the districts. Such a broad-based support for Das's Swarajist politics no doubt came partly as a result of the pact's fairly generous concessions to Muslims on the matter of their representation in the Council and in local bodies and government appointments, which in today's politics would be rightly considered a non-secular arrangement. But despite this perfectly correct contemporary response to such arrangements, it would be quite anachronistic (in a context shaped by the Montagu–Chelmsford reforms which had explicitly articulated a policy of separate electorates for communities) to say that such concessions as the pact made then to a community that formed the majority in the province, was an entirely unworthy method of giving the community the confidence it needed to reason its way to a less insular and more progressive politics. And in any case, it was not just these concessions that lay behind the democratization for, as Chatterjee himself points out in an interesting article,[39] the background of the Non-Cooperation Khilafat movement did much to broaden the base of Muslim politics in Bengal—a background which made a considerable difference to the pact's capacity to convert Muslim

[38] For details, see *Bengal Legislative Council Proceedings*, September 1921 and August 1925.

[39] 'Bengal Politics and the Muslim Masses, 1920–1947', in Hasan (ed.) *India's Partition*.

leaders to the less insular and more progressive way of thinking. Hence even though the pact was not endorsed by the National Congress party, and its good effects in Bengal were all quickly reversed after Das's death when communal politics returned to Calcutta and Bengal, the fact is that for a very dynamic and revealing period of three years or so, this pact, which was unlike all previous Hindu–Muslim pacts in intention and effect, went beyond élite settlements on seats and offices to the democratization of the Muslim community. And the general point I want to stress in raising this example of the pact is that it was the provincial *state* under Das that was responsible for this democratization which in turn allowed, as in the specific legislative example I gave, for the community's leaders to be internally persuaded out of their communally defensive resistance to a progressive piece of legislation.

These are all details, details about how the state needs to intervene and democratize in a way that the state can then on all matters regarding the secularization and reform of a community's practices assume that the (moderate) majority within a community (which has no absolutist objection to secularism) is the voice which gets heard, thereby allowing for an internal basis for the state's liberal and secular reforms. All of this requires a descriptive acknowledgment of community by the state, which archimedean secularism refused, but it requires no normative commitment to community, which communitarianism pursues.

Getting back then to the overall theoretical framework, I hope these details convey something at a concrete level of the theoretical space I have been trying to clear in these pages. That space was the space which lay under a thoroughly misleading and conceptually impoverishing disjunction that I began with. It is a space sensitive to the moral psychology of identity which is missing in the classical liberal formulations of secular liberal doctrine such as Mill's and Rawls', at the same time as it is a space that does not permit any scope for this sensitivity to degenerate into a relativistic and anti-statist communitarianism. Chatterjee, and Foucault's disciples generally, have their right to be despairing of the state in the face of its many failures, though one wishes they would remember its many successes as well. But despair is one thing to which anyone has a right depending on how they perceive and interpret the facts around them. It is quite another thing to erect their despair into a philosophical doctrine that entails an a *priori* pessimism about the state. This space, which Chatterjee fails to find, is one that gives one an equal right to take a different attitude than despair in the face of the state's failures, since it allows us a question which for him is necessarily bogus, the question: 'Why can't we struggle to improve the state?' This paper has tried to give a very abstract and perhaps needlessly complicated argument to make that space and that simple question possible. Political theory generally, and liberal doctrine in particular, desperately need rigorous formulations to fill such a space.[40]

[40] In writing (and then in revising) this paper, I have been much helped by conversations with Sumit Sarkar, Tanika Sarkar, Aijaz Ahmad, Partha Chatterjee, Alan Montefiore, Sugata Bose, Isaac Levi, Carol Rovane, David Bromwich, Stephen White, Gyan Prakash, Ravinder Kumar, Kumkum Sangari, Rajeev Bhargava, Javeed Alam, Garrett Deckel, and Zoya Hasan. Comments from members of audiences at Bombay University, the Nehru Library at Teen Murti in Delhi, Centre for Studies in Social Sciences in Calcutta, Institute of Advance Studies in Simla, and the conference on 'Multiculturalism and Governance' at Kasauli have also been helpful. A number of the themes of this paper are discussed in much greater detail in my forthcoming book *Politics and the Moral Psychology of Identity*, Harvard University Press, and Oxford University Press, Delhi.

8

The Moral Psychology of Identity by Akeel Bilgrami: A Commentary

Alan Montefiore

In what follows limitations of space must prevent me from taking up any of the many points in Akeel's very stimulating paper with which I completely agree, and even some of those less important ones with which I think that I probably disagree. I shall simply concentrate on two major points of what, at this stage anyhow, do seem to be clear disagreement. These concern (i) the conditions of rationality in the face of certain types of obstacle, (ii) a certain aspect of Akeel's criticism of the Rawlsian version of liberalism; and finally, (iii) I shall add a note of doubt of my own concerning that version.

(i) In the context of his discussion of what it would be rational for a religious communitarian to commit himself to, Akeel says that someone 'who was a compulsive alcoholic despite his best resolve to be sober' would be completely irrational. He adds that he would 'in Augustine's sense be incontinent or weak-willed', and I have no quarrel with the idea that the compulsive alcoholic who wishes to unhook himself from the drink is in some important sense weak-willed. The question is rather whether we have to regard such weakness of will as irrational.

This question is, of course, neither trivial nor uncontroversial. It may seem clear enough that someone who was unable to follow that course of action which 'rationally' he judged to be most appropriate, or quite simply the best, must *ipso facto* be unable (in that context) to act rationally; and that not to be able to act rationally is to be irrational. On the other hand, it would seem equally clear that someone who judged, for example, that the right or best course of action for him to follow would be to remove some huge boulder from blocking his path, but was unable to shift it, would not for that reason be held to be irrational. If one thinks of the alcoholic's inability to keep off the drink as being an inability to shift some internal blockage, functioning internally in ways analogous to the external boulder, there would seem to be no reason to judge him incapable of reasoning about what to do. Indeed, if one finds it really and truly impossible to shift the boulder, it would surely be irrational to go on 'trying' nevertheless. Is there any good reason why the analogy should not hold in the case of the alcoholic?

I judge it to be really important to unblock my path, but, try as I may, I am unable to shift the boulder. How, rationally, should I react? Broadly speaking, the answer would seem to be to seek help, if I can find it; and if not, or if the help should turn out to be ineffective, to readjust to the situation by, for example, seeking a way round the blockage or, if none seems to exist, by abandoning this particular journey and finding some other worthwhile thing to do. If I do none of these things, if in particular I refuse to look at the possibility of seeking help, or reject it when offered, then I may indeed be treated as irrational—or, more probably, as being less than genuine in my protestations of the importance of removing the boulder. Why should not very much the same things be true of the compulsive alcoholic? If he is genuine in his alleged best resolve to be sober, we should expect him to seek or to welcome help, to join Alcoholics Anonymous, for instance. But suppose that, for the time being at any rate, none of this worked? In what way would it be irrational for him to go on drinking, if really he could not help it? Of course, someone who has never experienced the tensions of the addict, who would wish to be cured of his addiction but cannot endure the strain of his immediate situation of deprivation, may be unable to accept that 'he really could not help it'. But that seems to me at least to be as psychologically unreasonable as to suppose that one must always be able to resist the need to relieve the tension of an itch by scratching, however badly and however persistently it is itching;

if the only available concepts seem to impel one in that direction, then there is, to my understanding, something wrong with those concepts. (By which I do not mean that such may nòt in fact be the nature of the concepts available to someone; in that case they would indeed so limit his understanding).

In fact, there is something *prima facie* odd about Akeel's taking the alcoholic's inability to break his habit as analogous to the situation of his religious communitarian at all. After all, he himself characterizes his moral psychology of identity as being concerned with 'the normative aspects that underlie [human behaviour], first in that the most salient motivating states of interest are the *values and commitments* of agents...' But the 'weak-willed' alcoholic's need or desire for another drink does not typically present itself to him so much as a value or commitment as, rather, an urge that he finds it impossible to control. So perhaps we should simply let the analogy go.

Still, it may be worth exploring the alcoholic's case just a little further. Suppose that I am not at present an alcoholic, but am afraid of becoming one. I am perhaps from a family of alcoholics; not only, therefore, do I know the temptations and risks as well as the degradations, I know too how alcoholics may come to lose not only all strength of will, but even all desire to return to a state of sobreity. As things stand, however, I strongly wish not to fall into such a state. If ever I did fall into it, I should wish my friends to do whatever they could to bring me out of it, to effect my cure—*and, if necessary, to do so even in the face of my temporary and deranged efforts (as I now foresee them) to prevent them.* There is presumably nothing irrational about this, any more than there is anything irrational about the man who knows himself to suffer from bouts of psychotic illness, but, while still in a phase of normality, instructs his doctor to prevent him from following out his strongest efforts to harm himself or others when next his illness strikes. More generally, one's knowledge of human frailty and of one's own share in it must surely make it rational to hope and even demand of one's friends that they should try to prevent one from acting on what one would now regard as unacceptably aberrant desires should one ever come to posses them—as one can foresee as a possibility that one might. Indeed, this seems to be precisely the situation of the Islamic fundamentalists that Akeel talks about. Of course, it might equally well be the situation of a convinced Rawlsian liberal, who can nevertheless envisage it as a presently highly undesirable but nevertheless real possibility that he (or, say, his children) might be converted to a fundamentalist Islamic way of life.

(ii) I come now to the relevance of this last consideration to Akeel's criticism of Rawls. He says, quite rightly, that we should not expect those with a fundamental commitment to a certain vision of what constitutes an Islamic way of life to see it as in any way rational to accept the Rawlsian principles, including that of revisability. But equally, if my previous argument is correct, it would not be irrational for me now to ask of my friends and family, to do all that they could to frustrate me in any attempt to act on what we should, in our present states of mind, agree to be unacceptable principles should I be converted to, say, 'fundamentalist Islam' or, to take another example, the doctrines of Dr Moon. Of course, there is always going to be a problem in cases where someone requests that no notice be taken of any change of mind that he himself may have in the future. On the one hand, there is a perhaps natural tendency to treat people as if they were sovereign in respect of their own decisions and hence incapable of binding themselves in this way; on the other hand, where I can foresee the possibility of my own future irrationality, it would seem equally natural that I should be able (in the present) to take rational precations to forestall it. All must depend on how one understands the distinction between the rational and the pathological, and how, too, one thinks of the self-integration of a human agent through time; and such understanding will in turn, no doubt, depend on the prevailing cultural context—in the widest sense of that term—in which one may be immersed. But in any case *these* considerations have no easy or direct application to those which might or should sway Rawlsian subjects in the original position.

In that position, we may recall, subjects have no knowledge of anything whatsoever concerning their own particular state in the 'real' world, and this ignorance includes most notably anything concerning their own particular values or desires. On the other hand, general knowledge concerning the whole range of values and desires that they might have is open to them. Thus they must be perfectly well aware of the possibility that they have the outlook and values of an Islamic fundamentalist such as Akeel describes them. But this is not, and *ex hypothesi* cannot, be to say that they actually have these values in the original position, any more than in that position they can already be full-blown Rawlsian liberals. They may know, of course, that a real life fundamentalist is most likely to find it rational to reject the principle of revisability; but in real life, as we have already noted, even a committed liberal is almost bound to place some restrictions on it. But that does not, and cannot, mean that it would be rational for them to do so in their position behind the veil of ignorance; for there they must be prudentially sensitive to the possibility that, having ceased to hold whatever views they start out with, be they fundamentalist or liberal, they may subsequently come to have a whole set of countervailing values and desires. That this is a possibility is, of course, something of which the real life fundamentalist is himself aware; that, indeed, is precisely why he rejects the principle of revisability. But within the perspective of the original position the desire for revisability is not just an isolated desire, an unreinforced residue in an otherwise solidly fundamentalist make-up. That back in real life it should exist in this solitary way is indeed one possibility to be contemplated. But this possibility has to be balanced against all those other possibilities in which such a desire might exist in a strongly reinforcing environment. Moreover, in the original position one is ignorant not only of which out of all possible states of value and desire is in fact going to be one's own; one is equally ignorant of whether in the on-going particularity of one's own real life situation one is going to experience any (one or more) conversions from one state to another, and if so in what order. And it is a basic condition of this thought experiment that in choosing from behind the veil of ignorance the governing principles of the society in which one is to live one has to give due weight to *all* these possibilities.

So yes, of course, Akeel is right in saying that his real life Islamic fundamentalist would be bound to reject the principle of revisability and with it any form of Rawlsian liberalism. But this is something of which in the original position one must already be aware. In that position itself there can be neither Islamic fundamentalists nor, in principle, liberals, nor indeed anyone with any particular substantive set of values. The whole point of the argument, if it works, is surely that if one can be persuaded to abstract altogether from whatever one's actual substantive values may be and to rely, within the limits of that abstraction, on purely prudential reason alone, then it turns out that one will be led to choose principles of justice that do in fact meet the central requirements of a substantively liberal conception of moral and political values. Not, however, for that reason, but for reasons of strictly universal prudence alone.

It seems to me, therefore, that Akeel's anti-Rawlsian argument does not really work in the terms in which he presents it. I am inclined to think, however, that my own doubt concerning the Rawlsian version of liberalism may provide him with one that would do in effect the same job for him. (I am also inclined to think that at bottom the distinction between the right and the good is by no means sharp enough to justify all the disputes as to which has priority over the other; or not at any rate in those terms. The increasing stress on the importance of a 'sense of justice' that is to be found in the later developments of Rawlsian theory—together with the loss of emphasis on the metaphor of the original position, with its apparent claims for the universal import of a form of games-theoretic prodential reasoning—would also seem to indicate a certain blurring of that distinction.)

(iii) Normal prudence would surely seem to demand that one should always be ready to update one's assessment of one's situation, and of the attitude to be taken towards it, in the light of whatever further information one may have acquired about that situation (including whatever new understanding one may have come to of one's own needs and desires), since the time of one's last assessment. Indeed, this apparently pretty basic requirement of all sensibly prudential reasoning would not seem to be too far removed from that which led Rawls to adopt the principle of revisability itself. But general Rawlsian reasoning would seem to have to rely on any such updating being ruled out of order, when it is a matter of reacquiring all that particularizing knowledge of oneself and one's own situation that one had to surrender before being allowed behind the veil of ignorance. A Rawlsian might reply, no doubt, that from behind that veil everyone would have a prudential interest in establishing rules against future cheating. But that cannot provide historically real individuals with a prudential reason not to try and get away with it all the same once they know what their real situation is. One may very well protest, of course, that cheating is simply unjust. But that is not at all to say that it is necessarily always prudentially unwise. Behind the veil of ignorance every as yet unindividuated individual will have good prudential reason to endorse rules designed to see that, once he and everyone else has been reindividuated, no one else will be able to opt for a free ride and get away with cheating. But, it would seem, only a substantial moral disapproval of cheating as being intrinsically wrong could stand as a reason against the prudentially rational imperative to act always on the basis of the best possible revised assessment of one's most recently updated information when back in the particularity of one's real life situation.

What, in fact, is at stake here is the whole question of what continuity may or may not be established between parties in the original position, on the one hand, and real life, historically situated individuals, on the other; or, even more generally, between that in man which may be said to be universal (his rational or conceptualizing capacities) and that which is particular (that which, through the spatio-temporal particularity of his body, distinguishes him or her from all other individuals). This is also the question of whether in the end it can make any sense (and if so, what?), to speak of prudential reasoning at all in a context where all reliance on the knowledge that particular individuals may have of the particularities of their own situations is in effect disallowed. To face these questions one needs, or so it would seem to me, to take some view on the question of what it is to be a human being, to form at least the outline of a theory of the human subject. But this, as one knows, is something that Rawls is not only deeply reluctant to do, but something that he thinks that his theory of justice can do better without. On that point, I take it, both Akeel and I would be in agreement against him.

9

Multiculturalism, Governance and the Indian Bourgeoisie*

Amiya Kumar Bagchi

Dense, Regimented and Democratic Multiculturalism and Slippage into Intolerant Identity Politics

Human beings have been migrants for most of their history. They have struck roots, assumed new identities—either constructed by themselves or constructed for them by others—and moved on and assumed yet other identities. In the process they have often invented origins, whole histories and believed them, until some upheaval has destroyed or radically altered all these carefully constructed myths, histories and identities. In many different geographical locations, groups with different identities have mingled, jostled with one another, engaged sometimes in armed conflicts, but have often worked out codes for co-existence, in tolerance, if not always in friendship.[1]

The Indian subcontinent has seen almost as much intermingling of different migrant streams and settled populations, with their

* Non-incriminating thanks are due to Javeed Alam and Jasodhara Bagchi for trenchant comments on an earlier version of the paper.

[1] For a fascinating sketch of the intermingling of the city dweller and steppe pastoralist, of Greeks and Scythians, Khazars and Varangians, Muslims and Byzantine Christians, see N. Ascherson, *Black Sea: The Birth Place of Civilization and Barbarism*, Jonathan Cape, London, 1995.

assumed identities, life-styles and belief-systems as the whole continent of Europe. This intermingling did not take place without a great deal of armed conflict, domination of one group over another, and the subjugation of whole groups for centuries under some code of hierarchical order (mostly the caste systems but also distinctions between the Arya and Dasyu, *ashraf* and *ajlaf*, *bhadralok* and *chasa*, and so on). But for ages together, communities with different assumed identities and belief systems have lived cheek by jowl with one another in what could be called a system of dense multiculturalism, where different communities exchanged rituals, put on some of the outer garments and took over parts of the belief systems of the other communities.

Indian business communities lived in this milieu for hundreds, if not thousands of years. Many members of the business community adopted Jainism or Buddhism when these belief systems came up in protest against the *sanatana dharma* characterized by a Brahman-Kshatriya-centred hierarchical order. Many of them remained faithful to Jainism even when a refurbished Brahmanism triumphed over Buddhism and Jainism. When most of northern India and parts of southern India came to be ruled by Sultans or Padshahs who professed Islam, the major business communities remained Hindu or Jain in their religious beliefs. Despite the urgings and the ideological preaching of some Islamic clerics who wanted to convert all the subjects under a Muslim king to 'the true faith' and treat the infidels harshly, most rulers tolerated and some positively encouraged a diversity of beliefs among their subjects. (For a fascinating account of the contention of approaches to multiculturalism and governance in medieval India, see Alam.[2])

The British practised a more schematized form of secularism, overtly putting the state above the contending faiths. However, in some ways the very attempt to make a watertight distinction between affairs of state, and affairs of society and at the same time exercise absolute dominion over the subject peoples led to the outbreak of conflicts which acquired a communal hue.[3] The Indian business communities, partly under the compulsion of authoritarian foreign rule, partly under a traditional dissociation from the

[2] M. Alam, *Sharia and Language in Medieval Indian Politics*, S. G. Deuskar Lectures, Centre for Studies in Social Seiences, Calcutta, 1996.

[3] G. Pandey, *The Construction of Communalism in Colonial India*, Oxford University Press, Delhi, 1990.

mechanics of the exercise of political power, and partly under the influence of such leaders as Mahatma Gandhi and Jawaharlal Nehru, practised an uninvolved multiculturalism, although a few among them became militantly Hindu or Muslim at critical political junctures.

The newly independent Indian republic enshrined a variety of secularism in the constitution of the country. By and large, in overt conflicts over religion, the state apparatus adopted a neutral stance at least so long as Nehru was alive. The Indian business community acquiesced in this democratic multiculturalism even when privately they might have shared a different view of how the Indian state should behave.

In recent years, however, this pragmatist multiculturalism has often been replaced among a section of the business community by an overt espousal of identity politics, and support for parties and organizations which would convert India into a polity of majoritarian despotism, a majority which claims to represent all Hindus. The present paper seeks to understand the many gradations of multiculturalism among the Indian business communities and the structural and ideological limits of that multiculturalism and advance some hypotheses regarding the fracturing of pale multiculturalism by, say, the horrors of the Bombay riots of 1992–3.

The Indian Bourgeoisie in a Multicultural Setting

Most of the rulers in non-socialist states and most capitalists have believed in some religion or other. But not all religions have had a single organization or a religious head acting as the supreme authority. Nor have all religions been guided by a single text or set of texts. In societies without a church or a book ruling a religious community, the relation between religious organizations and the state has been a rather loose one. Where the rulers have felt secure by virtue of their control of the army and the other visible paraphernalia of rule, the people of different religions have been allowed to practise their worship of God or gods any way they pleased. Where the rulers have felt an urge to convert their subjects to their mode of worship out of either a spiritual need or a conviction that subjects of a different religion pose a threat to their secular authority, the relation between rulers and subjects of a different faith have been fraught with contention in the religious arena. These complexities mean that unlike in most European settings since the sixteenth century, the question of the place of religion in the beliefs and practices of subjects, citizens and rulers in South Asia cannot be posed simply as that of relations between church and state. Once we grasp that, we will also see that posing the problem of making room for multiculturalism in the subcontinent of India cannot be couched entirely in terms of the European debate. In India the problem was not that of a religiously oriented ideological make-up breaking through to the simple duality of religion as the sphere of private faith and the state as the sphere of exercise of public virtue or civic consciousness. Here the problem often has been that the subject who was denied all political rights earlier has, as a citizen, wanted to engross both private and public space in the name of a religious faith.

To point out these differences is not to claim that the place of religion in the history of the Indian state and society during the last two centuries can be discussed without invoking some terms of the debate that has been carried on in Europe over the same, or a longer, span of time. But we must watch out for any unjustified extrapolation of the European terms to the Indian scene and unfounded expectation of modes of resolution of the conflict between private faith and public virtue.

Before we proceed, we would like to introduce yet another set of distinctions into the usual debates on multiculturalism. There are the distinctions between multiculturalism as a belief system, multiculturalism as private and social practice, and multiculturalism as public policy. Very often people who invoke a notion of Hinduism as multiculturalism embodied fail to see that this was often only a recognition of plurality in the realm of beliefs, with no recognition of deviant practices in quotidian social behaviour. In this paper I shall discuss the situation of business communities in India in a multicultural setting in pre-colonial, colonial and post-colonial epochs, and the way these business communities have negotiated the plurality of religious beliefs in different political settings.

India had recognizably distinct business communities long before the European merchants penetrated the Indian market or established their political hegemony in the country. There were Hindu *bania* communities all over India, but there were merchants, shipowners and bankers who professed Islam as their faith, and there were bankers and merchants among Hindus whose ascribed caste was not that of a *bania* or a Vaishya. Most of the merchants and bankers in the immediate pre-British period had a subordinate relation to the state apparatus. They would service the armies and the courts of the Mughals, and their *subahdars* or *fauzdars* or those of the successors to the Mughals, or those of the southern principalities under the sway of other rulers. Some even used their position as courtiers and generals to further their mercantile interests.[4] But there is no record of group of merchants who wanted to control the state apparatus as merchants rather than as surrogate rajas or nawabs.

Under the Mughals, especially since the days of Akbar, the spheres of religion and politics were generally kept separate. Akbar, of course, had a remarkably ecumenical attitude towards all religions (see the citations of Akbar's reported sayings, in Moosvi[5]). Even after the re-imposition of the *jizyah* on Hindus under Aurangzeb, Islam did not become the state religion in the sense in which Anglicanism became a state religion of England under Elizabeth I. Along with other subjects of the Padshah in Delhi, Indian Hindu and Muslim merchants could expect even-handed treatment in the hands of the civil authorities. That treatment could be arbitrary on occasion, but the arbitrariness was not systematically related to the faith of the victim.

The merchants, by and large, especially the Hindus among them, eschewed the use of armed violence and resorted to threats of migration, *hartals*, *dharnas*, fasts and boycotts as instruments of protest or pressure.[6] It is significant that the leading Muslim merchants of Surat who did resort to arms in the 1730s in order to enforce their claims, were utterly routed and became completely marginalized when the British established their hegemony.[7] The British, of course, had even less tolerance for armed Indian

[4] S. Subrahmanyam, *The Political Economy of Commerce: Southern India, 1500–1650*, Cambridge University Press, Cambridge, 1990.

[5] S. Moosvi (ed.) *Episodes in the Life of Akbar: Contemporary Records and Reminiscences*, National Book Trust, New Delhi, 1994, pp. 126–9.

[6] A. K. Bagchi, 'Merchants and Colonialism', in D. N. Panigrahi (ed.) *Economy, Society and Politics in Modern India*, Vikas, New Delhi, 1985.

[7] A. Das Gupta, 'The Merchants of Surat, c. 1700–5', in E. R. Leach and S. N. Mukherjee (eds) *Elites in South Asia*, Cambridge University Press,

merchants than their immediate predecessors. But even peace-loving merchants fared badly when they posed any threat to the European aggrandizement of trans-oceanic trade from the time Vasco Da Gama found the route to India round the Gape of Good Hope. For that reason Indian ship-owning merchants almost everywhere in India, suffered severely after the establishment of British paramountcy, since the British exercised a virtual monopoly on most trans-oceanic routes between India and foreign countries.

In pre-British days, especially since the later stages of the Mughal empire, Indian bankers had a close relationship with the revenue-raising activities and the finances of Indian rulers. When the British overthrew those rulers, these financiers went into a rapid decline. This happened with the Maratha bankers of the Peshwa's court as had happened with the family of Jagatseth Mahatabchand in Bengal.[8] However, many of the bankers continued to service the operations of the surviving and subordinate Indian princes and princelings, and found new avenues of profit as suppliers of credit to the landlords and owner–occupiers who had to pay land taxes to the British.

The British used the Indian merchants and bankers as collaborators at the time when they were still to establish a political presence in the country. But once British rule was established these collaborators were subordinated by them and converted into junior partners or eliminated altogether when the Indians proved to be threatening competitors, or were rendered irrelevant because the new rulers controlled the major resources of the government, including the enormous land revenues of Bengal and of the rest of British India. However, even in British territories, bankers and moneylenders remained important for servicing the revenue extracting mechanism. Not only the poor peasants but many of the substantial landlords (variously known as *zamindars*, *talukdars*, *mirasdars*) also were dependent on loans extended by the *sahukars*

Cambridge, 1970. Das Gupta, *Indian Merchants and the Decline of Surat, c. 1700–50*, Wiesbaden, 1979; Bagchi, 'Merchants and Colonialism'.

[8] R. Jenkins, *Report on the Territories of Rajah of Nagpore*, Calcutta Gazette Government Press, Calcutta, 1827; J. H. Little, *House of Jagatseth*, Calcutta Historical Society, Calcutta, 1967; V. D. Divekar, 'The Emergence of an Indigenous Business Class in Maharashtra in the Eighteenth Century', *Modern Asian Studies*, vol. 16, part 3, pp. 427–43, July 1982.

or *mahajans* for payment of the land taxes to the superior right-holders or the government.

It is necessary to recall these situational characteristics of the majority of Indian merchants and bankers during the colonial period in order to grasp that while religion and the state were kept separate under the colonial dispensation, the latter presided over a social and political order in which capitalist and precapitalist elements, tributary or pure rent receiving and entrepreneurial ingredients were intertwined at all levels of society and in all the mechanisms for the exercise of power. Unlike in Europe, the merchants were not struggling to break the links between religion and a state controlled by feudal lords aided by the bureaucracy of emerging absolutist states.

Gandhi and the *Bania* Practice of Multiculturalism

The analytical separation of the roles of individual or micro-level movements in society and the macro-level movements which are generally more, or less, than the sums of the micro-level changes is tricky and it cannot be theorized as mere summations of the micro-level interactions. This issue crops up also in analysing the social and political changes which brought about the transformation of western European societies that allowed capitalists to become the most important controllers of power in those societies. We can then see that the Weber–Sombart–Tawney problematic of the role of the Protestant (or Jewish or Old Believer) ethic in capitalist transformation is not likely to throw up an easy answer, however massive the evidence accumulated is about the exact nature of that ethic or the power and the character of the capitalist class and changes in those characteristics over time.

In the Indian case, the role of the bourgeoisie in fostering or hindering a democratic, multicultural society has not been even posed, although the role of big and small Indian merchants in financing and sometimes directing the activities of communalist organizations seeking to establish the dominance of a particular brand of say, Sikhism, or much more menacingly, Hinduism, has been observed by all serious students of Indian politics and sectarian violence.

It is necessary to recall the moral values of the Indian merchants and bankers who still constitute the predominant sector of the

Indian bourgeoisie because they indicate how implicated they were with precapitalist and colonial state apparatuses and social formations. At the same time, of course, not only the functions but also the values and social practices of the mercantile communities were in many ways different from those of the traditional rulers and military functionaries, and in some ways closely approximated to many of the values designated as the 'protestant ethnic' by Max Weber.[9]

A provisional beginning for such a discourse may be provided by examining some of the statements of Mahatma Gandhi regarding Hinduism and multiculturalism. Gandhi is important for several reasons. He was, of course, the most important leader of the struggle for independence in India. He often used religious idioms for conveying his social and political messages and these idioms made sense to most Indians for whom a language of modernity remained as foreign as the English tongue. (For a powerful portrayal of how the Gandhian message was conveyed to and interpreted by a community of Tatmas—a depressed community of North Bihar—see the novel *Dhorai Charit Manas* (in Bengali) by Satinath Bhaduri.) Finally, Gandhi was in communication with influential groups of Indian merchants and some of them avowed themselves to be followers of Gandhi. They included, among others, G. D. Birla and Jamnalal Bajaj, whose families are counted among the most important business groups of modern India. It is perhaps not an accident in this context that Gandhi was born into a Hindu *bania* family of Gujarat—which can claim to have been one of the major cradles of Indian capitalism—and went out to South Africa as a lawyer employed by another Gujarati *bania*—though the latter was a Muslim rather than a Hindu in his professed faith.

In Gandhi's writings we can find plenty of statements of the 'protestant ethnic' which was claimed by Max Weber to have been one of the impulsive forces of western capitalism:

> Action is my domain, and what I understand, according to my lights, to be my duty, and what comes my way, I do. All my action is actuated by the

[9] Max Weber, 'Die protestantische Ethik un der Geist des Kapitalismus', *Archiv fur Sozialwissenschaft and Sozialpolitik Statistik*, vols 20–1, 1905; concluding part translated by E. Mathews and published as 'Protestant Asceticism and the Spirit of Capitalism' in Runciman, 1978, pp. 138–73.

spirit of service. Let anyone who can systematize *ahimsa* into a science do so, if indeed it lends itself to such treatment...

God alone is omniscient. Man in the flesh is essentially imperfect. He may be described as being made in the image of God, but he is far from being God. God is invisible, beyond the reach of the human eye. All that we can do, therefore, is to try to understand the words and actions of those whom we regard as men of God. Let them soak into our being and let us endeavour to translate them into action, but only so far as they appeal to the heart.[10]

Again, in response to some questions put by Sarvepalli Radhakrishnan, Gandhi answered in 1935:

My religion is Hinduism, which for me, is the religion of humanity and includes the best of all the religions known to me...

Denial of God we have known. Denial of Truth we have not known. The most ignorant among mankind have some truth in them. We are all sparks of Truth. The sum total of these sparks is indescribable, as-yet-unknown Truth, which is God...

The bearing of this religion of social life is, or has to be, seen in one's daily contact. To be true to such religion one has to lose oneself in continuous and continuing service of all life.... Hence for me, there is no escape from social service...'[11]

Similar passages on an inner vision of truth, the necessity of non-violence, or abstinence, especially *brahmacharya* (or abstinence from sexual intercourse) could be culled from innumerable passages in Gandhi's writings.[12] Gandhi's idioms were imbricated with Hindu traditions, and especially the Vaishnavite tradition which he explicitly acknowledged.[13] A poem by Narasimha Mehta (1414–79), Vaishnavite saint-poet of Gujarat, formed part of the daily

[10] M. K. Gandhi, 'Action is My Domain', *Harijan*, 3 March 1946; reprinted in Raghavan Iyer (ed.) *The Essential Writings of Mahatma Gandhi*, Oxford University Press, Delhi, 1991.

[11] M. K. Gandhi, 'Religion and Social Service', reprinted from S. Radhakrishnan (ed.) *Contemporary Indian Philosophy*; also in Iyer, *The Essential Writings*, pp. 158–9.

[12] R. K. Prabhu, and U. R. Rao (eds) *The Mind of Mahatma Gandhi*, second edn, Oxford University Press, Madras, 1946; Raghavan Iyer (ed.) 'The Moral and Political Writings of Mahatma Gandhi', vol. 3, *Non-Violent Resistance and Social Transformation*, Clarendon Press, Oxford, 1987; Iyer, *The Essential Writings.*

[13] M. K. Gandhi, 'The Vaishnava Ideal', *Navajivan*, 5 December 1920; translated from the Gujarati in Iyer, *The Essential Writings.*

prayers of Sabarmati Ashram.[14] Most of the Hindu *banias* of Gujarat in the nineteenth century were followers of Vallabhcharya of the Vaishnava sect; the rest were Jains or Shravaks.[15] They all believed in *ahimsa*, and were vegetarians, and within their own communities or in dealings with other businessmen, they mostly dealt by trust and word of honour, often without any written documents. In addition the thriftiness or miserliness of the merchant was part of the *bania* stereotype virtually all over India. Hence, practically all the virtues extolled by Gandhi (except perhaps social service) were part of the value system of a well-brought-up Hindu *bania*.

Even in the middle of the nineteenth century, in many parts of India, following earlier traditions, when land was either not transferable property or transferable under rather strict conditions, moneylenders and bankers kept aloof from direct landownership.[16] However, with the British bringing in legislation which made rights to the produce of the land and the right to pay taxes on it transferable and heritable property, moneylenders and bankers also became landowners.

Whether the bankers and merchants were or were not distanced from the ownership of land, they could not insulate themselves from the social practices of the landlords who were the dominant strata in most parts of colonial India. For example, the immigrant Marwari community in the Central Provinces (today's Madhya Pradesh) which dominated the trade and banking of that province, might be thrifty but would go on a splurge when a marriage or some other social event was celebrated.[17] The marriage of the thirteen-year old Jamunalal Bajaj, a Marwari *bania* and the adopted grandson of Seth Bachhraj of Wardha to Jankidevi, the daughter

[14] Iyer, *The Essential Writings*, p. 65.

[15] GBP, *Gazetteer of the Bombay Presidency, vol. 9, Part I, Gujarat Population: Hindus*, Government Central Press, Bombay, 1901, p. 69.

[16] D. H. A. Kolff, 'A Study of Land Transfers in Max Tehsil, District Jhansi', K. N. Chaudhuri and C. J. Dewey (eds) *Economy and Society: Essays in Indian Economic and Social History,* Oxford University Press, Delhi, pp. 53–85.

[17] R. V. Russell and Hira Lal, *The Tribes and Castes of the Central Provinces of India*, vol. 2, originally published under the authority of the Government of Central Provinces, 1915, reprinted, Delhi, Cosmo, 1975; see also GBP, *Gazetteer*, pp. 90–3 for a description of the elaborate marriage ceremony of the Meshri or Vaishnava Vanias.

of Girdharilal Jajodia, another Marwari Vaishnava *bania* of Rajasthan, in 1902, was celebrated with 'great pomp'. 'The festivities continued for several days, with dinners, *nautch* performances (dance) and fireworks'.[18] In conformity with the status ranking of the time, G. D. Birla, possibly the most powerful businessmen of his age, and R. K. Dalmia were regularly described as zamindars and not just as businessmen and industrialists.

The self-definition of Indian businessmen as belonging to particular communities characterized by the same caste, originating in the same region and speaking the same language was reinforced by British business practices in India. The Banks of Bengal, Bombay and Madras would often treat, especially in periods of crisis, whole communities, such as Chettiars, Marwaris, or Mutani *banias* with the same degree favour or disfavour, without scrutinizing their credentials as individuals or even as separate joint families. Interestingly enough, one aspect of Mahatma Gandhi's espousal of *varnashrama dharma* would be the retention of the separate identities of particular business communities. Thus the pre-independence plurality and co-existence of separate business communities can be seen both as a device for preserving internal cohesion and as a way of confronting a generally haughty, if not hostile, alien ruling class and dominant business community. The separate existence of business communities as identifiable groups was also facilitated by the existence of a powerful group of landlords and 'native princes' who generally regarded the profession of businessmen with condescension if not disdain. A 'semi-feudal' and colonial structure of society facilitated the separation of the profit-earners as identifiable groups.

Gandhi and Tagore as Exponents of Hinduism as Multiculturalism and the Ambivalence of the Hindu Merchant Community Towards Secularism

Independence was followed by the abolition of legally recognized intermediaries between the government and the legal occupant or owner of the land. But it did not see, except, in a few states, such, as West Bengal, Kerala, and Jammu and Kashmir, the

[18] B. R. Nanda, *In Gandhi's Footsteps: The Life and Times of Mahatma Gandhi*, Oxford University Press, Delhi, 1990, p. 9.

abolition of landlord power in the countryside and its extension into most of the small towns and even state capitals of northern and to a lesser extent, southern India. The abject poverty of the vast majority of small peasants, artisans, casual workers in the formal or informal sectors and agricultural labourers continued to provide the base for a social, economic and political nexus between the power of the landlord, the trader and the money-lender—sometimes augmented by the power of the bureaucrat or politician, and often embodied within the confines of the same family. The law relating to ownership and inheritance within the Hindu undivided family—a law which is applicable to practically all property owning Hindus except Bengali Hindus—also allowed *bania* and landlord families to erect various kinds of barriers against challenges of outsiders, including the state, the creditors in business relations and competitors in business. Many of the initiatives of the post-colonial government seeking to promote business augmented the non-competitive, non-entrepreneurial characteristics of the Indian business community and allowed them to enjoy both profits and luxury. Especially since lavish subsidies were given for construction of hotels and most of the real incomes of businessmen went untaxed (through tax forgiveness, allowances for expenditure, exemption of trust properties, etc.), the life-styles of the erstwhile Maharajas have been emulatmed by the businessmen of India. Many of the trading communities in northern, eastern and western India claim a Rajput or Kshatriya descent and are not happy if they are described as Vaishyas.

The Indian Hindu bourgeoisie, with perhaps a few exceptions, have been intensely religious. This religiosity has been expressed in their strict obedience to the rituals of religion, but also in the endowments they have made to temples, and in the foundation of new temples: the Birlas have dotted the landscape of big Indian cities with temples founded by them. These temples or their appurtenances have been means of earning incomes or avoiding taxes, and have often obtruded into public space. While G. D. Birla and Jamunalal Bajaj were followers of Gandhi, the simplicity of the latter's religious beliefs has obviously not satisfied them or their families. In a period of spiritual crisis during the last days of his life, Bajaj found his 'guru' in Anandamayi Ma (she had also been the 'guru' of Kamala Nehru).

In many parts of Gujarat, the Meshri and Shravak *banias* enjoyed a higher social status than the Brahmans.[19] Yet they were bound by the Brahmanical code for sustaining a patriarchal, hierarchal and ritualistic social order. In medieval and modern Rajasthan, the top crust of society is constituted by the Rajputs, the ruling group, the *banias*, their financiers and revenue farmers and the Brahmans, who provided the rationale for the rank-ordering of access to private and public goods on the part of the different castes and subcastes. Rajputs may be displaced by *bania Sarpanches* as the effective voice of secular authority. But the Brahman provides the (often invented) justification for the burning of widows (such as the case of Om Kanwar in the Jhardli village of the Shekhawati region in 1980 and of Roop Kanwar in the Deorala village of the same region in 1987) and *banias* mime the traditions of Rajputs.[20]

We have already seen how the religiosity of the Indian *banias* could go along with occasional splurges in life-styles. This belies Mahatma Gandhi's stress on correct practice (embodied in the phrase 'experiments with truth') as the true expression of a belief system. How did the apparent catholicity of Hinduism as a congeries of belief systems rather than as a set of rigid precepts guiding the thoughts and practices of believers fare among the *banias* or among the upper-class and upper-caste Hindus in general?

The answer to this question is not easy. Attempts were made in colonial India to convert Hindus into a sect swearing by a set of agreed texts and following them in their daily lives. This can be seen in the emergence of the Arya Samaj movement initiated by Swami Dayanand Saraswati.[21] Dayanand also was born in Gujarat but in a Brahman family and he attacked the Vallabhcharya sect, with a large following among Gujarati *banias*. It is also

[19] GBP, *Gazetteer*, Section III.

[20] See, in this connection, S. Vaid and K. Sangari, 'Institutions, Beliefs, Ideologies: Widow Immolation in Contemporary Rajasthan', *Economic and Political Weekly*, 26(17), 27 April 1991, especially pp. WS-7 to WS-13.

[21] For his career and beliefs, see R. S. Sharma, 'Dayanand (Swami) (1825–1883)', in S. P. Sen (ed.) *Dictionary of National Biography*, vol. 1, Calcutta Institute of Historical Studies, Calcutta, 1972, pp. 406–9. Dayanand, *Autobiography of Dayanand Saraswati*, K. C. Yadav (ed.) second revised edn, Manohar, Delhi, 1978.

interesting that Gandhi should have specifically distanced himself from Arya Samaj and called himself a follower of *Sanatana* (that is, traditional) *dharma*, even while applauding some of the work in the field of education done by the followers of Dayanand.[22] One reason given by Gandhi for differing from Arya Samaj is worth quoting:

> For me Hinduism is all-sufficing. Every variety of belief finds protection under its ample fold. And though the Arya Samajists and the Sikhs and the Brahmo Samajists may choose to be classed differently from the Hindus, I have no doubt that at no distant future they will all be merged in Hinduism and find in it their fullness. Hinduism, like every other human institution has its drawbacks and its defects. Here is ample scope for any worker to strive for reform but there is little room for secession.[23]

Rabindranath Tagore, another major influence on the ideology of nationalism in India, had in many ways a very different outlook on politics from Gandhi. Despite occasionally contradictory statements Tagore was almost entirely free from religious sectarianism. But he expressed his beliefs in very similar terms to those of Gandhi on a number of occasions. In an essay which was originally published around April–May 1912 (Baishakh 1319 of the Bengali era), with the title 'Self-identification'[24] Tagore, who had been born into a Brahmo family, identified himself as a *Hindu Brahmo*.

Tagore was here consciously or unconsciously echoing his contemporary, Brahmabandhab Upadhyay, who edited the nationalist paper, *Sandhya*, during the Swadeshi movement in Bengal. Upadhyay had, a few years back, called himself a Hindu Catholic or a Catholic Hindu, after his conversion to Roman Catholicism (Upadhyay renounced Christianity later).

In a controversy which arose because of critical comments on Tagore's essay by an orthodox Brahmo, Tagore further defended his position.[25] Tagore's arguments are quite detailed and in parts

[22] M. K. Gandhi, 'Swadeshi as an Active Force' in *Speeches and Writings of Mahatma Gandhi*, 4th edn, 1916, pp. 329–35; reprinted in Iyer, 1987, pp. 333–8.

[23] Ibid., p. 333.

[24] Rabindranath Tagore, 'Atmaparichay' (Bengali), *Tatvabodhini Patrika*, Baishakh; reprinted, Tagore 1361 B. S., pp. 452–87.

[25] Tagore, 'Hindu Brahmo' (Bengali), *Tatvabodhini Patrika*, Jaistha; reprinted, Tagore, 1361 B. S., pp. 580–8.

subtle, involving criteria for identification in terms of the self and the other, the nature of religious belief, and the evolution of Hinduism as a complex of belief systems. He claimed that it was possible to remain a Hindu even if somebody embraced Islam or Christianity.[26] If somebody calls himself a Brahmo and not also a Hindu simply because he (she) has abjured superstition and adopted a code of conduct which was superior to that of the average practising Hindu, he (she) denies his (her) identification as a brother (sister) of those Hindus who were steeped in superstition and misery. Believers in monotheistic faiths such as Christianity, Islam or Sikhism might resent what appeared to be the imperialistic tendency of the syncretic religious belief systems proclaimed by Gandhi and Tagore, but the religious reformers who wanted to convert Hinduism into a religion of a single creed and single set of practices would resent them even more. Tagore's novel *Gora* portrays the conflicting ways in which Brahmoism and orthodox Hinduism were expounded by the dogmatists and the liberal humanists for whom secularism and tolerance of other belief systems became the only acceptable norm.[27]

Gandhi's (and Tagore's) difference from militant brands of Hinduism also stemmed from their opposition to any use of force or state power for purposes of religious propaganda or the enshrining of religious orthodoxy. Neither of them could have any truck with the use of the state apparatus, or any force other than that of moral persuasion and inner conviction, for empowering one set of religious beliefs at the cost of the other. Hence the support of sectarian or, in the Indian parlance, communalist organizations such as the Rashtriya Swayamsevak Sangh, the Vishwa Hindu Parishad or Jamaat-e-Islami by anybody, and most of all, in Gandhi's case, the capitalist 'trustees' of property on behalf of the labouring poor would have been anathema.

The discourse of Gandhi and Tagore on multiculturalism is important because their writings show the way in which deep genuine religious beliefs could be combined with genuine belief in multicultural democracy. The idiom of the Indian bourgeoisie has remained religious in its phraseology with but a few exceptions.

[26] Tagore, 'Atmaparichay', p. 464.

[27] J. Bagchi, 'Secularism as Identity: The Case of Tagore's Gora' in M. Dutta, F. Agnes and N. Adarkar (eds) *The Nation, the State and Indian Identity*, Samya, Calcutta, 1996, pp. 47–67.

But they have not shown themselves responsive to the kind of openness that permeates Gandhi's and Tagore's discourse.

Before we leave this section, it would be interesting to note that the lukewarmness Gandhi has been criticized for by later analysts with regard to affirmative action in relation to the Dalits and the Muslims, sprang at least partly from his distrust of state action especially under colonial auspices for addressing social wrongs.[28] But it is probable that he had genuinely underestimated the influence of an initially extremely inequitable distribution assets on the attainability of Swaraj (that is, the acquisition of the ability to control one's destiny). If Gandhi had not convinced the majority of the Indian bourgeoisie of the virtue of multiculturalism, still less could he convince them of such affirmative action as might threaten their entrenched positions which they had tried to defend through two centuries of colonial rule.

Gandhi was regarded as a godhead by many Indians, including many Indian businessmen. This was quite consistent with the infringement of most of the canons of the Gandhian philosophy of praxis. The bestowal of many Hindu spiritual leaders (godmen or more rarely, goddess women) with attributes of a godhead has been quite usual among the Indian bourgeoisie. Of course, in some cases, the circles of the godmen such as Dhirendra Brahmachari, who was at one time close to Indira Gandhi, or Chandraswamy, who is close to numerous politicians, from the ex-Prime Minister Narasimha Rao to Subramanian Swamy, also serve as networks of

[28] cf. B. R. Ambedkar, 'A Note on the Indian Depressed Classes', in *Report of the Indian Franchise Committee*, vol. I, 1932, reprinted in *Fight for the Right of the Depressed Classes*, vol. I, K. I. Chanchreek, S. Prasad and R. Kumar (eds) H. K. Publishers, Delhi, 1991, pp. 249–61; Gandhi, 'Gandhiji's Correspondence and Poona Pact' in Ambedkar, *Fight for the Right*, pp. 265–81; U. Baxi, 'Emancipation as Justice: Babasaheb Ambedkar's Legacy' in U. Baxi and B. Parekh (eds) *Crisis and Change in Contemporary India*, Sage, New Delhi, 1995, pp. 122–49. Of course, those nationalists who were far more fervently Hindu, in an orthodox or militant sense, would have no truck with any affirmative action for the Muslims, which they generally branded as 'appeasement'. For example, Lala Lajpat Rai broke with C. R. Das in 1923 because the latter wanted to work out a Hindu–Muslim pact embodying some bold measures of affirmative action favouring the Muslims (P. Nayar, *Lala Lajpat Rai: The Man and His Ideas*, with a foreword by T. N. Chaturvedi, Manohar, Delhi, 1977, p. 123). On the other hand, unlike Gandhi and Tagore, and following the tenets of the militant Arya Samaj, he wanted Hinduism to be a proselytizing religion (Ibid., ch. 10).

power: in India's political and business milieu they are probably more puissant than Rotary Clubs or Lions Clubs. G. D. Birla was unusual in ordering statues of Marx and Lenin as incarnations of Saraswati, the goddess of learning, to be erected at the university founded by him at Pilani (the village to which the Birlas traced their origin). One of his spiritual mentors, Swami Chinmayananda, who was invited to unveil G. D. Birla's statue in the garden of the Golders Green crematorium, later became a major figure in the Vishwa Hindu Parishad, an organization that gained special notoriety through its involvement in the illegal demolition of the Babri Masjid at Ayodhya in 1992.[29]

If we except the community of Parsis, it was the temple-erecting, conservative, and socially and politically conformist group of Hindu traders and bankers who were responsible for most of the modern industrial firms erected or acquired by Indians before independence.[30] After independence also, in the private sector, it is the same group which has dominated Indian industry. If anything, their predominance and their publicly displayed religiousity have increased. The laying down of foundation stones of factories of business premises by politicians and the performance of a religious ceremony on such occasions have become almost compulsory rituals.[31]

Before we turn to the final tier of *my* argument, it should be emphasized again that Indian bourgeoisie as bourgeoisie had only a minor share in the running of the state apparatus before independence. They did not have to agitate to separate the state from the church or, rather, the organizational apparatus of a religious denomination, because the British had already done so. The first real opportunity for exercising a determinate influence on state policies came with independence. In the initial period, during the Prime Ministership of Jawaharlal Nehru, the Indian bourgeoisie went along with the largely secular policies followed by the government. However, fissures in the coalition of ruling

[29] T. Basu, P. Datta, S. Sarkar, T. Sarkar, and S. Sen, *Khaki Shorts and Saffron Flags*, Orient Longman, New Delhi, 1993, p. 65.

[30] A. K. Bagchi, *Private Investment in India: 1900–1939*, Cambridge University Press, Cambridge, 1972, ch. 6.

[31] cf. the photograph of Arvind Mafatal and his wife at the premises of the National Organic Chemical Industries Ltd. in M. Herdeck, and G. Piramal, *India's Industrialists*, vol. 1, Three Continents, Washington D. C.

classes led to a section of the coalition using religion as a political weapon, and a section of the big bourgeoisie—and a very large section of the smaller businessmen—financed and actively supported political parties that used religious idioms and religious slogans as means of consolidating electoral support and exercising undemocratic power over large sections of religious minorities.

The Cosmopolitanism of Bombay's Indian Capitalists and Its Fragility

The roots of the sectarian use of religion by the Indian bourgeoisie and by the Hindu nationalists and loyalists alike for purposes of self-definition go back to the days before independence. In this conflation of nationalism or national identity with a particular view of what true religion is, neither the Hindu bourgeoisie nor the other protagonists in the pre-independence conflicts can claim any uniqueness. Martin Luther's campaign against the papal control over Western Christianity was often conducted in the name of the freedom of the German nation.[32] In the formulation of Sir Lewis Namier, as quoted by Christopher Hill, religion was 'a sixteenth century word for nationalism'. In England, 'after or before 1640, any threat, real or imagined, to Protestantism at once rallied the majority, as Laud, Charles I and James II all found to their cost'.[33] It took three centuries from the time of the first reformation of the English church under Henry VIII for full toleration of all sects of Christianity to be established in England, after all. Even in those enlightened lands of western Europe, the equality of access of all religions or ethnic groups to civil and political rights still remains a matter of periodic contention.

In colonial India, the state often went by expediency, here recognizing the special privileges claimed by a particular religious denomination, and there refusing to grant similar privileges in the name of equality before law, or the preservation of civil peace ('law

[32] R. H. Tawney, *Religion and the Rise of Capitalism*, Penguin Books, Harmondsworth, Middlesex, 1926–38, pp. 89–1100; G. H. Sabine and T. L. Thorson, *A History of Political Thought*, fourth edn, Oxford and IBH Publishing Co., New Delhi, 1973, pp. 336–9.

[33] C. Hill, 'The First Century of the Church of England' in *The Collected Essays of Christopher Hill*, vol. 2, *Religion and Politics in 17th Century England*, Harvester Press, Brighton, Sussex, 1986, pp. 19–20.

and order'). The allowance of cow slaughter was one of those contentious issues. On that issue, many towns and some villages of northern India found rich, Hindu merchants and landlord, ranged against generally poor Muslims—mostly artisans and peasants. If the exploited weaver tried to target the merchant and convert his struggle into a *jihad* against the infidel, the latter tried to have cow-slaughter banned and use the ban as yet another weapon with which to beat down the rebellious artisan.[34]

The Marwari *banias* constitute the most important business community of northern, and eastern India. Among them, social reform or religious reform meant adjustment to changing economic conditions, especially in the big cities and towns, with the minimum disturbance to their habitual ('traditional') mode of life. Modernity or Western education was to be resisted rather than embraced.[35] In the generation of G. D. Birla, R. K. Dalmia or Jamunalal Bajaj, a business career began at the age of ten or eleven with little time for elaborate formal schooling. It is not surprising that such early apprenticeship, combined with the astonishing cohesiveness among the Marwari migrants, should have made them formidable traders and financiers. But it is remarkable that Bajaj or Birla should have also picked up a very broad education through their sheer drive and curiosity. However, such education did not urge them to break the barriers erected by the injunction of a male-dominated, socially conservative religious ethos.[36]

This conservativeness of the Hindu business community in most parts of India contrasts sharply with the social ferment that prevailed among the business communities in late-nineteenth-century Bombay.[37] That ferment may have been due to the fact that Bombay had several Indian business groups, professing different religions, contending in business and politics. But the fact that the British did not dominate the business life of Bombay to the same extent as they did in the other major port cities of Calcutta, Madras, Rangoon or Karachi also contributed to the upsurge of

[34] Pandey, *The Construction of Communalism*, ch. 3, 'The Bigoted Julaha'.

[35] T. A. Timberg, *The Rise of Marwari Merchants as Industrial Entrepreneurs to 1930*, Ph.D. thesis, Harvard University, Cambridge, Mass., 1972.

[36] Ibid., pp. 90–105 and Appendix B, 'Cartoons from the *Maheshwari Bandhu*'.

[37] C. Dobbin, *Urban Leadership in Western India*, Oxford University Press, Oxford, 1992, chs 3 and 4.

social movements among Bombay's indigenous businessmen. Hence the Indian business groups in Bombay did not have to define their own identities in contradistinction to the 'modernity' flaunted by the British as yet another sign of their superiority as the ruling race. Among the Bombay business groups at that time were the Parsis, who through their earlier and closer contact with the British, had adopted Western-style education and so-called 'female emancipation' much more whole-heartedly than the others. Among the Bhatias or Kapol Banias, the major Hindu *shetias* of Bombay, the move towards social reform was much more tentative. Even more tentative was any attempt to reform the religious practices of Muslim business communities such as the Dawoodi Bohras or the Ismaili Khojas. There were also some inter-community tension between the different groups.[38] However, all these communities had some role to play in Bombay's business world and in municipal, and later on, national politics. All of them—and not just the intelligentsia, as in Calcutta—were touched by various social and religious reform movements.

The cosmopolitanism of the Bombay business community was displayed in the way the leading *shetias*—or rather, the men among them—constantly intermingled with one another socially as well as in business.[39] It was also demonstrated in the way in which the three major Indian business communities—the Parsis, the Gujarati Hindus, and the Gujarati Muslims were represented in the direction of the Bank of Bombay (the leading domestic bank) from 1868 to 1920, that is, till the time it was merged into the Imperial Bank of India. Similarly, the Bombay Chamber of Commerce, and the Bombay Millowners' Association were far more cosmopolitan bodies than their counterparts in Calcutta.

However, the cosmopolitarianism of the Bombay élite even in colonial times had very strait limits: they are illustrated by the difficult relations that Mohammad Ali Jinnah had with his Parsi father-in-law, and later on with a daughter who insisted on marrying a Parsi convert to Christianity against her father's wishes. Jinnah had owed his first step up in his career to the patronage of a Scotsman, Sir Frederick Leigh Croft, who recommended the young Mohammad Ali for employment in the London office of his firm, Douglas Graham and Co. There Jinnah developed his liberal political views, qualified as a barrister, made friends with

38 Ibid., ch. 4.

39 Ibid., chs 1 and 4.

the wealthy and powerful, who included Dinshaw Manockjee Petit, the second baronet, and one of the top leaders of the Parsi community and cotton mill-owners in Bomabay. In 1916, fresh from his triumph in forging the Lucknow Pact, between the Congress and the Muslim League, Jinnah offered for the hand of Ruttie, the sixteen-year old daughter of his friend, Sir Dinshaw, and was rudely rejected. After overcoming all social and legal obstacles, Jinnah married Ruttie in 1918. But the marriage ended in divorce in a few years' time, and Sir Dinshaw never recognized his daughter after her marriage. When Dina, the daughter born of the marriage of Jinnah and Ruttie, married Neville Wadia, another Parsi mill-owner, but a convert to Christianity, Jinnah in turn forswore his relationship with his daughter. Although father and daughter wrote to each other occasionally, Dina never set foot in Pakistan while Jinnah lived, and went there only to attend his funeral.[40] The tragedy of the disharmony of the upper classes in the subcontinent and of its partition of lives of ascribed religious community was reflected in the tragedy of the lonely eminence in the life of the man who carved Pakistan out this multicultural subcontinent.

In Calcutta, there was little multicultural sociability among the Indian business community to start with. The dominant business associations in the city were British, and the new associations set up by Indians either started as bodies dominated by one Indian business group belonging to one religious or linguistic group, or became such one-denomination or uni-ethnic bodies through splits or secession. The Bengal National Chamber of Commerce came to represent the Bengali-speaking, mostly Hindu, businessmen, the Oriental Chamber of Commerce, Muslim businessmen, the Marwari and then the Bharat Chamber of Commerce, the Marwari businessmen. Among the Marwaris themselves there were differences between the loyalists and the nationalists[41] (as indeed there were between the smaller and more nationalistically inclined merchants of Bombay and the big mill-owners organized in the Bombay Millowners' Association.[42] But these conflicts were over political tactics rather than about social reform or the

[40] S. Wolpert, *Jinnah of Pakistan*, Oxford University Press, New York, 1984, chs 2–4 and 23.

[41] Herdeck and Piramal, *India's Industrialists*, p. 109.

[42] A. D. D. Gordon, *Businessmen and Politics: Rising Nationalism and a Modernizing Economy in Bombay, 1918–33*, Manohar, Delhi, 1978, chs 4–5.

opening up of the community to welcome outsiders as social equals.[43]

Indian business communities, however socially conservative, had learned how to negotiate with different political parties with different ideologies. This is typified by the statement attributed to Sardar Vallabhbhai Patel regarding the Walchand brothers, who were leading entrepreneurs in the fields of shipping, construction, sugar and automobiles: 'Gulabchand belongs to the Hindu Sabha, Lalchand belongs to the Congress, Ratanchand belongs to no party, and Walchand belongs to every party'.[44] True to this practical political philosophy, Indian businessmen by and large supported the Congress after independence, and did well out of the policies pursued by it, even though individual businessmen might rail against particular government restrictions. However, Nehru's apparent fraternization with the communists during the heyday of the Non-aligned Movement made some erstwhile followers of the Congress rebellious and look for allies among the non-communist opposition parties. Two of the parties in this group operating in western India were the Swatantra Party which was self-consciously for free enterprise and Shiv Sena which wanted Maharashtra to be ruled exclusively by Maharashtrians (by their construction only Hindus could be true Maharashtrians). Kamal Nayan Bajaj and Ramkrishna Bajaj, sons of Jamunalal, hobnobbed with these parties, and supported J. B. Kripalani against V. K. Krishna Menon, the official Congress nominee, as parliamentary candidate for the North Bombay constituency.[45] The Swatantra Party collapsed but the Shiv Sena has remained as a highly chauvinist and sectarian political party; it was one of the major forces behind the Bombay riots of December 1992 and January 1993.

Businessmen and politicians consciously used the Shiv Sena to try and break up communist-dominated trade unions. The Shiv Sena used a Maratha-supremacist ideology, and major Congress leaders such as Y. B. Chavan and his powerful successors such as

[43] One of the cartoons reproduced from the *Maheshwari Bandhu* in Timberg, *The Rise of Marwari Merchants*, Appendix, 1972, Appendix B, caricatures interdining with people from outside the caste of Maheshwaris—such as Muslims, Europeans and Parsis, and another caricatures a rabble-rousing social reformer speaking against the caste system.

[44] Herdeck and Piramal, *India's Industrialists*, p. 404.

[45] M. V. Kamath, *Gandhi's Coolie: Life and Times of Ramkrishna Bajaj*, Allied Publishers, Ahmedabad, 1988, pp. 166–88.

Sharad Pawar used the same idioms of Maratha prowess and the need to recover lost glory. The Shiv Sena found its financial backers among capitalists and the middle classes in Bombay, and its constituency in an enlarged non-Brahmin, non-Dalit conglomerate of castes led by the Marathas and *kunbis* and its storm-troopers among the disaffected, casually employed or unemployed and often criminalized slun-dwellers. The parallel economy of Bombay generated a parallel politics, which likewise thrived on blatant breaches of the law generally with the connivance and, often as in the case of the Bombay riots of 1992–3, with the active assistance of the custodians of the law. The scapegoats or the other of the Shiv Sena were not, of course, the moneyed real estate speculators or smugglers or owners of declining textile mills wanting to build housing complexes on the grounds of the mills, but militant trade union leaders, Dalits and Muslims. The 'saffronization' of the Shiv Sena, and the fusion of its Maratha-*kunbi* chauvinism and communalism were natural outcomes. Of course, ironically enough, many Dalits also served as its storm-troopers in the Bombay riots and upwardly mobile Dalits seeking to turn themselves into respectable Hindus may have found a welcome embrace in Shiv Sena or the BJP.[46]

As the hegemony of the Congress party over the apparatus of rule was seriously challenged and occasionally fractured, Congress politicians consciously used slogans appealing to different religious denominations: multiculturalism became an arena of manipulation as well as conflict.[47] The few businessmen who openly sided with the opposition often suffered discrimination in the hands of the Congress government.[48] Tensions in urban India mounted with the

[46] J. Lele, *Elite Pluralism and Class Rule: Political Development in Maharashtra*, India, University of Toronto Press, Toronto, 1981; D. Gupta, *Nativism in a Metropolis: The Shiv Sena in Bombay*, Manohar, Delhi, 1982; Lele, 'Saffronization of the Shiv Sena: The Political Economy of City, State and Nation' in S. Patel and A. Thorner (eds) *Bombay: Metaphor for Modern India*, Oxford University Press, Bombay, 1995, pp. 185–212; T. B. Hansen, *The Saffron Wave: Democratic Revolution and the Growth of Hindu Nationalism in India*, vols 1–3, International Development Studies, Roskilde University, Roskilde (Denmark), 1997, chs 8–10.

[47] Lele, 'Saffronization of the Shiv Sena', Hansen, *The Saffron Wave*, chs 8 and 9.

[48] See the story of the persecution of the Bajaj family by Indira Gandhi's government during the Emergency of 1975–7, in Kamath, *Gandhi's Coolie*, ch. 8.

growth of unemployment, the massing of the lumpen-proletariat, and the scramble for ever-appreciating urban land, including slums that could be converted into office complexes or affluent residential localities. This provided an ideal milieu for politicians to foment communal trouble with a view to mobilizing one community as a captive electoral constituency, and as we have indicated earlier, many businessmen were only too willing to go along with this game.[49]

It came about in this way that not only Uttar Pradesh, which had witnessed a number of riots, some of them deliberately provoked by the provincial police, but also western India, the capital of Indian big bourgeoisie, and the land of Mahatma Gandhi, became a scene of regular riots since the late 1970s. These anti-Muslim riots culminated in the city of Bombay in the wake of the demolition of the Babri Masjid. This riot had two phases. In the first phase, riots were relatively unorganized. In the second phase, Shiv Sena, the BJP and the Bombay police played a major role in instigating riots and burning and damaging the slums and houses of Muslims and killing scores of them.[50] This could be seen as a replay of the riots that occurred in Bombay in August 1893 as a fall-out of the so-called cow protection movement, but on a much larger scale altogether.

We have referred earlier to the remarkable atmosphere of co-operation among the leading businessmen of Bombay in the late nineteenth century. The co-operation generally took the form of choice of representatives from separate business communities in elective bodies or business organizations. This propensity for co-operation (or collusion) at the top did not automatically translate itself into a similar attitude among the poorer people, a very large proportion of whom were immigrants. They were badly housed, had practically no public sanitary facilities, had no security of employment, and some of them were regularly organized into

[49] A. K. Bagchi, 'Predatory Commercialization and Communalism in India', in S. Gopal (ed.) *Anatomy of a Confrontation: The Babri Masjid–Ramjanmabhumi Issue*, Viking, Penguin Books (India), New Delhi, 1991, pp. 193–218.

[50] IPHRC, *The People's Verdict: An Inquiry into the December 1992 and January 1993 Riots in Bombay by the Indian People's Human Rights Tribunal Conducted by Justice S. M. Daud and Justice H. Suresh*, second edn, P. A. Sebastian for Indian People's Human Rights Commission, Bombay, 1994, especially pp. 95–116.

syndicates of musclemen willing to defend the *mohalla* or the community as the occasion arose.[51] The official *Gazetteer of the Bombay City and Island*, while giving accounts of the various kinds of riots or civil disturbances in the city repeatedly cited overcrowding and inhospitable living conditions as contributing factors.[52] In 1851 and 1874, there were riots between Parsis and Muslims, provoked by indiscreet (indeed, in one case, according to Edwards, 'scurrilous') remarks on Islam or Prophet Muhammad by a Parsi journalist or a Parsi publicist.[53] There were also riots between rival factions of Khojas and between Shias and Sunnis.[54] But these were rather minor affairs, in most cases resulting in injuries and damages to property (including temples and mosques) rather than to loss of life. But the riot of 1893 was far more serious, leading to an estimated eighty fatalities and enormous damage to property.[55] This riot demonstrated not only that collaboration among big businessmen did not trickle all the way down, but that some businessmen were quite prepared to succour the rioters. Some *shetias* (mostly belonging to Gujarat) funded the agitation of the cow-protection society, which led to the riots of 1893 and later gave money to the rioting masses.[56]

The Structural Determinants of the Choice of a Stance on Multiculturalism by the Indian Bourgeoisie

It is probably not coincidental that the 1893 riot in Bombay occurred at a time when, because of the monetary and tariff policy

[51] R. Chandavarkar, *The Origins of Industrial Capitalism in India: Business Strategies and the Working Classes in Bombay, 1900–1940*, Cambridge University Press, Cambridge, 1994, especially ch. 5.

[52] S. M. Edwardes, *The Gazetteer of Bombay City and Island*, vol. II, Times Press, Bombay, 1909, pp. 150–96.

[53] Ibid., p. 156 and pp. 179–80.

[54] Ibid., p. 156, p. 179 and p. 195.

[55] Ibid., p. 193.

[56] S. S. Upadhyay, 'Communalism and Working Class: Riot of 1893 in Bombay City', *Economic and Political Weekly*, 24(30), 29 July 1989, pp. PE-69–PE-75; see also J. Masselos, 'The City as Represented in Crowd Action: Bombay, 1893', *Economic and Political Weekly*, 28(5), 30 January 1993, pp. 182–8 for another view of riot.

followed by the government, the major industry of Bombay, the cotton mills, had entered into a period of crisis. The Bombay industry was plagued by slow growth and falling exports for a decade after that date. (Not only economic distress but plague played a role in all this, but the effects of plague were aggravated by the wretched living conditions of mill workers). The 1992–3 riots came almost a decade after the collapse of the great Bombay textile strike of 1982–3 and the quickening of the pace of land speculation within the erstwhile mill areas. The Bombay riots of 1992–3 also damaged the growth of Indian exports.

The 1992–3 riots were, however, distinguished from their century-old counterpart in several major respects. First, they lasted longer and caused much more damage to life and property. Secondly, the forces of so-called law and order were, for a time at least, on the side of the rioters rather than on that of the peace-loving citizens. Thirdly, the Indian big bourgeoisie, led by their doyen, the octogenerian J. R. D. Tata, became almost helpless spectators, pleading vainly with the government to stop the riots.[57]

J. R. D. Tata's career in some ways illustrates the problems of operating as a secularly-minded industrialist in the Indian milieu.[58] Born in 1904 of a Parsi father and a French mother, who was received into the Zoroastrian faith after her marriage, Tata spent the first eleven years of his life in Paris, another four years (from about 1915 to 1919) in India and was then enlisted into the French army when he was back in Europe and was preparing for admission into the University of Cambridge. He trained as a civilian pilot and then came to control the first Indian owned civilian airline. Apart from S. L. Kirloskar, J. R. D. Tata was the only big industrialist of his time who had a technical background. His group was the only one to have trained up a cadre of professional managers within the conglomerate. He followed other Parsis, including the founders of the Tata group, in giving large sums for secular philanthropy, including the promotion of science and the arts.

However, the Indian law of Hindu undivided family, which also applies, with some variation, to Parsis, accords unusual privileges

[57] See also in this connection, K. Sharma, 'Chronicle of a Riot Foretold', in Patel and Thorner (eds) *Bombay: Metaphor*, pp. 268–86.

[58] See R. M. Lala, *Beyond the Last Blue Mountain: A Life of J. R. D. Tata*, Viking, Penguin (India), New Delhi, 1992 for Tata's Career.

to ownership of property within the family. So while Tata could professionalize his top management and recruit people from all communities, the ultimate control of the group was left with a family member—a cousin (since Tata was childless). Moreover, the secularization of Tata's public work did little to change the sectarian orientation of other members of the Indian big bourgeoisie (G. D. Birla's motto was to save, to invest in profit-making enterprises or to build temples—which could also, of course, yield profits). A life of Brajmohan Birla (in Hindi), by D. B. Taknet gives pride of place to his association with glittering gods in temples and such conservative Hindu gurus as a Sankaracharya of one of the four major Saiva maths, and has little room for his worldly concerns.

J. R. D. Tata also tried to keep a distance from individual politicians, though, of course, he had often to collaborate with the government and operate through it. In this also he differed from most other successful big businessmen. Finally, his attempt to create an internal labour market for managers in the group was not emulated by other Indian businessmen. Moreover, the attempt to create cadres of workers and managers with firm-specific or group-specific skills would not yield noticeable dividends if the general environment was suffused with a sea of undifferentiated, unskilled labour or skilled labour with unreliable certification.

The Bombay riots of 1992–3 are a vivid illustration of the contradictions of the social order that the Indian bourgeoisie did so much to create through active manipulation of the state apparatus and passive acquiescence in the consequences of the failure of the post-independence ruling classes to provide security of life and existence to major sections of a fast-growing population. The structural conditions of insecurity of the working people were created by a combination of the decline of Bombay's major manufacturing industry, namely, cotton textiles industry, unplanned growth of the city at the service of rich property developers,[59] and rampant crime and corruption supported by bootleggers in a state with nominal prohibition and smugglers operating along the western coast of India. The ideological ground was prepared by the rise, first of militant Hindutva as espoused

[59] S. Banerjee-Guha, 'Urban Development Process in Bombay: Planning for Whom?' in Patel and Thorner, *Bombay: Metaphor*, pp. 100–20.

by the Rashtriya Swayam Sangha, the cult of Shivaji embraced by virtually all political parties except the communists, the anti-communism of all capitalists eager to ward off militant trade unionism, and finally the growth of militant chauvinism of the Shiv Sena. The latter thrived among the deprived who would wreak injustice on the selected 'others' in quest of justice for themselves.[60] The Bombay riots are both a metaphor and a concrete manifestation of the fracturing of multiculturalism among the Indian bourgeoisie and the masses they manipulate.

The unemployed and unemployable mass of unskilled labour in the slow-developing poor country that India is would always attract speculators in land or politics and would endanger the secularist aspirations of individual businessmen. As it is, most of India's big bourgeoisie are far from embracing a doctrine of strict separation between the public sphere of politics and the private sphere of religion. Those businessmen who tried to operate as individualist professionals venturing into industry before independence found that in the country in which trade rather than manufacturing skill, family or clan loyalty rather than professional excellence, conformity to obscurantist social norms rather than conspicuous display of enlightenment prevailed, they were likely to be soundly beaten by the traders and financiers, and their enterprises were almost invariably taken over by the latter.[61] As the protagonist in H. G. Wells' story found out, in the country of the blind the one-eyed man cannot be king.

The above analysis is not to imply that, even apart from the exception of the Tata group, we are dealing with a homogeneous mass of the big bourgeoisie, and even less with a consensual ideological stand of the smaller bourgeoisie. There are enormous differences in their attitudes to collaboration with foreigners, or

[60] For succinct accounts of the economics, culture and politics of manipulation as revealed in the Bombay riots of 1992–3, see Gupta, *Nativism in a Metropolis* and Banerjee-Guha, 'Urban Development', Lele, 'Saffronization of the Shiv Sena', G. Heuze, 'Cultural Populism: The Appeal of the Shiv Sena', in Patel and Thorner (eds) *Bombay: Metaphor*, 213–47; and Sharma, 'Chronicle'

[61] See in this connection A. K. Bagchi, 'Wealth and Work in Calcutta 1860–1991', in S. Chaudhuri (ed.) *Calcutta, the Living City*, vol. I, *The Past*, Oxford University Press, Calcutta, 1990, pp. 212–23; R. K. Ray, 'Introduction' to R. K. Ray (ed.) *Entrepreneurship in Indian Industry, 1800–1947*, Oxford University Press, Delhi, 1992, pp. 1–69.

the role of the state. Many members of the bourgeoisie are adopting liberal or 'modern' codes with respect to marriage or social behaviour. But the core of control in business matters or social power remains in the family. Adopting or inventing conservative codes for family behaviour in face of challenge remains the strategy of defence and can become a weapon of aggression. Multiculturalism for the big or middle bourgeoisie means constructing fortresses of tradition or invented tradition, rather than breaking down barriers to embrace people of all creeds. Secularism under today's conditions will require a much higher degree of economic and social equality with a better distribution of initial assets and a levelling up of chances of betterment for everybody.

In Europe, the businessman with the Protestant ethics wanting to create a distance between God and Mammon did not opt for a multicultural democracy. He was forced to do so through several centuries of popular struggle and changes in the structure of the economy and society. In India, also if multicultural democracy with equality of rights for everybody is to win through, it will be largely in spite of, rather than because of, the Indian bourgeoisie as they are culturally, socially and politically constituted today.

10

Making a Difference: Hindi, 1880–1930

Alok Rai

Liberal and progressive anti-communalism in India is, in a sense, concerned with devising intellectual strategies for the management of difference—and strategies of great subtlety have been aired in the recent past. The assertions and ascriptions of difference happen along several axes—religion, caste, region, language, gender, class—and serve diverse political purposes. It is hardly surprising that these assertions and ascriptions have a great potential for conflict. That, indeed, is why they are made in the first place, as part of a struggle to collar some illegitimate or demand some legitimate share of the social product. There are other kinds of claims to difference—the right to wear headscarves, or to study a wider mix of authors on school syllabi—that can be accommodated with relatively greater ease within the late-capitalist ideology of 'pluralism'. This might be because, and to the extent that, they do not impinge on questions of social order, and so do not pose urgent problems of 'management' in the way that my kind, necessarily, do. The proposed strategies are procedural and constitutional; some take recourse to the idea of 'negotiation' across thresholds of radical cultural difference while others seek to undermine the appearance of radical cultural difference by shifting attention to the underlying internal rationalities which might, patiently, subtend superficial and apparent difference—somewhat in the way that the land both supports and ignores the flags and boundaries over which men fight.[1] These strategies are, in an obvious sense, products of a moment of acute difficulty. Because the earlier liberal faith in the erosion if not erasure of difference seems to be stuck firmly in the mud, it seems unlikely that the ark of universal reason will float again, even though—and perhaps even because—the flood of universal reason appears all set to engulf the world.

However, my concern here is not primarily with the management of difference, but rather with a particular example of the production of difference—and with such clues as the latter might hold for the former. My sample for this enquiry is the process of the making of modern Hindi in the period 1880–1930—the insertion of a tragic wedge into the common language of north India, and the resultant production—'differentiation'—of two mutilated half-languages each of which is a travesty of that great *lingua franca*. I am aware that what I am describing as the production of difference might well be just the obverse of what is more commonly described as the making of identities. But I would like to leave the matter open for the moment, and entertain the possibility that there might be contexts in which one or the other—difference or identity/similarity—should be accorded analytical primacy.

The phenomenon of (or the bloody politics of) difference often prompts people to think in terms of some sort of conspiracy, generally by or at the behest of cynically manipulative ruling élites. Familiar in this kind of context are references to 'divide and rule', with its implicit assumption of a prior and possible harmony. However, it is well to remember that the principle of 'divide et impera' applies as much to modern democracies as it did to the Roman emperors.

Alternatively, on the rebound from subverted harmony, explanation is sought in the notion of primordial identities and differences. Though as almost everybody knows, these claims of primordiality are in fact fake, jumped-up claims, and the phenomena that are sought to be explained thus—the identities and the differences—are unmistakably modern. In trying to speak about

[1] See, in this context, Rajeev Bhargava, 'Giving Secularism Its Due', Akeel Bilgrami, 'Two Concepts of Secularism' and Partha Chatterjee, 'Secularism and Toleration', all in *Economic and Political Weekly*, 9 July 1994.

the production of difference, I am trying to finesse something between 'subverted harmony' and 'primordial difference'.

Let me confess quickly that it is not my intention to try and develop a general theory of difference. Indeed, I would be disinclined to believe in the possibility of such a general theory. In fact, my emphasis on the production of difference is intended to draw attention to the particularity of the differences that jostle for attention in the political marketplace.

In turning to the process of contention that produced modern Hindi, I am immediately overcome by a great sense of difficulty. At least some of this might be, in a way, a subset of the more general problem that the politicization of the Hindi-Urdu linguistic domain brings out: that is, that the language one uses is, perforce, a language that one shares with other users, that words mean what one wants them to mean and what others want them to mean. Thus, I write out of a conviction that there is but one, common language of north India, which is variously described as Hindi, Urdu, and Hindustani. In the course of history, some of which I seek to address below, particular ends of the linguistic spectrum have been sought to be hived off and infected with, on the one hand, Sanskritic, and on the other, Perso-Arabic influences. These latter processes have led to the emergence of two identifiable styles or registers, which I identify as 'Hindi' and 'Urdu'. The substrate middle language which supports these stylistic variants I wish to identify as Hindi because the implicit suggestion of the fertile plains of Hindi which were the site of the prolonged process of cultural mixing that produced that substrate language is more advocative to me than the narrower military associations of the name Urdu. Furthermore, the name Hindi for this language, used it needs to be said, by Hindus and Muslims alike, is older than the nasty controversies that engulfed this domain towards the end of the last century. To call it Hindi, therefore, is, to my mind, to lay claim to that older cultural legacy. I am aware, however, that this substrate language has been, and is, described as Hindustani and as Urdu—which would also be fine with me, provided that these are always distinguished from what either would become when endowed with scare quotes: thus, Urdu becomes 'Urdu', the barbarous Perso-Arabicized lingo of the mullah. As for 'Hindustani'—that is, with scare quotes, it is the embattled variant that Gandhi suggested could be written in either script and which left the pedants on either side, the pandits and the mullahs, committed to 'Hindi' or to 'Urdu', dissatisfied, each side seeing it as merely a Trojan horse of the other. Or, occasionally, in moments of cultural confidence, greedy to annex it by infecting the middle domain with their kind of extremism. Thus, consider the fate, in this kind of force field, of the formulation 'Hindi ya Hindustani', which was offered as a compromise solution. In the embattled context that I am still nerving myself up to essay, the 'ya' could mean either that Hindi was the same as Hindustani, in which case the mullah was up in arms, because the Hindi could easily become 'Hindi'—or that Hindustani was an alternative to, that is, other than Hindi—in which case, to the pandit, who was quite as suspicious as the mullah, Hindustani—and even Gandhi's 'Hindustani'—became only another name for Urdu, or even 'Urdu'. The terminological difficulty is acute, and it has led one exasperated scholar to propose that the contested middle language be called Hindu—but I have no doubt that the other side would call this a biased compromise, and propose the alternative Urdi! However, factious suggestions apart, there is little consolation in the fact that this terminological slipperiness in some sense imitates the intimate and raking difficulty which the Hindi–Urdu tussle of the early twentieth century created, and still creates all round. The fact that the difference happens in a shared linguistic domain does not render the difference superfluous, or transcendable through some mere terminological compromise. For all I know, such nebulous difference might make the resultant politics even more vicious. Because the language that one uses, and in some sense possesses at the same time as being possessed by it, is at each and every moment also owned by and available and malleable to the interference of often hostile others. Thus, for all the fussy precision that I might endeavour to bring to my use of the terms, carefully distinguishing Hindi from 'Hindi', I suspect that the difficulty will not simply go away. But it just might consent to lying down and being stroked, as it were.

Despite this sense of difficulty, and despite the ingrained intractability of this material, however, I find myself returning to this territory again and again. It is almost as if, amid all this sordidness, there is something valuable that has been mislaid, some cultural secret that we must recover if we are ever to find our way out of the present, ever-deepening abyss.

In stressing the process of the production of this linguistic 'difference' in the late nineteenth century, I do not wish to imply a prior, Arcadian harmony. Thus, I am aware that the history of the two great communities of modern India shows evidence of contention and conflict long before the greater traumas of our time. But, and this much is incontestable, language itself was not a site of communal differentiation. Thus, we have the spectacle of Dr Ballantyne in Banaras in 1847, trying to rouse his students to a communal awareness of language, to take pride in 'the culture of...the only language which your mothers and sisters understand.'[2] His students did not understand what he was on about: 'If the purity of Hindi is to consist in its exclusion of Mussulman words, we shall require to study Persian and Arabic in order to ascertain which of the words we are in the habit of issuing every day is Arabic or Persian, and which is Hindi'.[3] The pedants of Fort William, rendering traditional materials into printable prose, did play around with stylistic variations—deleting foreign expressions, using a preponderantly Sanskritic vocabulary—but there is no evidence to suggest that these literary sports had anything like a 'communal' edge or agenda. The language of *Singhasun Butteesee* cheerfully reflects the glorious confusion of the common tongue of north India, drawing freely not only from the classical founts of Sanskrit and Arabic and Persian, but also from the hybrid descendants of a whole range of Prakrits and other linguistic influences.

There is a great danger of reading this history retrospectively. Then, it seems entirely plausible to take the Dariya-e-Latafat, an eccentric late-eighteenth-century attempt to 'purify' the language of the courtly élite of Delhi—to free it of demotic corruption from the localities adjoining the Red Fort—as a foreshadowing of the Hindu–Muslim tensions of our own time, as a sort of distant cause not only of communalism but even of Partition.[4] Whereas such a move would be clearly absurd, it is not all that different from

[2] Christopher R. King, *One Language, Two Scripts: The Hindi Movement in Nineteenth-Century North India,* Oxford University Press, Bombay, 1994, p. 90.

[3] Ibid.

[4] See David Lelyveld, 'Zaban-e Urdu-e Mu'alla and the Idol of Linguistic Origins', *The Annual of Urdu Studies*, No. 9, 1994.

a retrospective reading of, say, Malaviya's *Court Character* agitation of the late-1890s. Of course Malaviya's agitation is part of a process—one link in the chain whereby a certain disadvantaged proto-élite manoeuvers itself into power—but despite the bloody consequences of this, it is important to try and understand the process of the production of difference prospectively rather than retrospectively. Such a strategy would not only be academically more sound, or fair to the protagonists who lived this history without the advantage of hindsight—it might also hold some clues for the management of difference—something more than elegiac gloom or ritual denunciation in the face of this incomprehensible otherness, this will to tragedy.

Two organizations are central to the making of modern Hindi—the Nagari Pracharini Sabha of Banaras, and the Hindi Sahitya Sammelan situated at Allahabad. Of these, the former, the Nagari Pracharini Sabha was founded in 1893, and as its name indicates, its activities were focused initially on the propagation of the Nagari script, although its later activities expanded to include scholarly and bibliographic activities of a pioneering kind. The second body, the Hindi Sahitya Sammelan, was more overtly political from the start and it is the Hindi Sahitya Sammelan which has to a large extent defined the cultural agenda of Hindi, or certainly of the kind of Hindiwallah who *has* a cultural and political agenda.

The first convention of Hindi Sahitya Sammelan was held in 1910 in Banaras under the chairmanship of Madan Mohan Malaviya. The start of this first annual conference was marked by a controversy that needs to be recalled in a little detail, because retrospect has rendered it deliciously symbolic. As it turned out, the conference was scheduled during Navratri and, as Malaviya declared:

नवरात्र दुर्गादेवी के पूजन का समय है, नवरात्र में सरस्वती शयन करती हैं।[5]

The orthodox Brahmins were incensed that ostensibly cultural work—which belonged in Saraswati's domain—should be initiated during the particular festival dedicated to Durga, the goddess of power. Forced on the defensive, Malaviya drew attention to the

[5] Lakshmi Shankar Vyas (ed.) *Sabhapatiyon ke Bhashan*, vol. 1, Hindi Sahitya Sammelan, Allahabad, 1987, p. 2.

cultural unity which was manifest in the spectacle of nation-wide Durga worship:

आज भी हिन्दुस्तान में हिमालय के ऊँचे शिखर से लंका के छोर तक सहस्त्रों करोड़ों हमारे भाई इस नवरात्र में दुर्गाजी की स्तुति करते हैं।

And now comes the rhetorical master move—

एक ही विद्या है, एक ही भाव है, केवल भाषा इसे पृथक करती है।

Ergo, to work for the linguistic unity what eludes the spiritual unity manifest in Durga worship is to, simultaneously appease both Durga and Saraswati!

It is not recorded whether the orthodox were in fact mollified, but setting the controversy in the context of Malaviya's seminal compilation of Nagari/Hindi materials over a decade back—the famous *Memorandum Regarding Court Character*...—one can notice an interesting shift. Thus, the Memorandum was structured around two main concerns: the first was education, and the benefits in respect of social reform that may be expected from its extension; the other was concerned with the language of the administration, and thus addressed the matter of power. In the intervening decade, it appears, the second part of the agenda has subsumed and consumed the first. Thus, Malaviya reminded his listeners that Navratri culminated in Vijayadashami:

यह विजयदशमी वही विजयदशमी है जिसमें भगवान रामचन्द्र ने राक्षसों का नाश करके देश में फिर से सुख-शान्ति की मन्दाकिनी बहायी थी।

The deep conservatism that had engulfed Hindi's fledgling radical agenda (and perhaps more accurately, possibilities) became painfully evident in the next few sentences:

पुराने समय में भगवान रामचन्द्रजी ने जो किया, अब वही देशी राज्यों में होता है। वही मारू बजता है, वही आर्यों के राजा महाराजाओं के विजय का डंका बजता है। अब विजय नहीं है, उसका शब्द है, उसे तो सुन लीजिए।

To those who can read the rhetoric of the traditional symbols, it is significant indeed that the founding moment of the ideological wing of the Hindi movement is located in a time when the Goddess of Learning is deep in her annual slumber, but the militant Durga, Goddess of Energy and War, is being celebrated!

Hindsight makes it look like conspiracy, but it is far more likely that colonial educational policy in the nineteenth century was simply inconsistent and confused—a not unknown characteristic of policy before and since. Thus, by mid-century, it had produced two distinct educational streams. One of these used the Nagari script, associated with Sanskrit and, with minor variations, various other languages and 'dialects' of north India; whereas the other used the Persian script, not quite the Arabic of the Koran, but near enough for the fact to become potentially combustible. Despite this, it was intended that the two streams would remain committed to the common language, though anxiety about the activities of pedants pulling away from the centre towards the 'purer' margins can be heard from fairly early on.[6] But it cannot also be entirely surprising that in time, there emerged some difference in the cultural content of the two streams: if nothing else, the mere fact that there were two streams at all would have created pressures for internal and reciprocal self-justification in both streams—pressure which was manifested also at the level of language—the Nagari stream pulling towards Sanskrit, the Persian stream towards Arabic and Persian.

Without going into the question of whether one or the other script was really beloved of the gods (or God), or scientific or whatever—questions of obsessive interest to the combatants—the fact is that, in the couple of decades after 1857, the Nagari stream was in full flow. There were, however, significant differences between the kinds of people who belonged to the two streams. Thus, the Persian stream consisted predominantly of urban Muslims, professionals, Kayasthas. The Nagari stream, on the other hand, tended to be relatively more rural, as well as drawing upon a higher proportion of the Hindu upper castes, mainly Brahmins and *banias*, but also some Thakurs. However, the most significant difference was that this stream found itself closed off from the newly opening up world of colonial administration after 1857. Not for the first time in history, an aspiring proto-élite discovered that the world had already been divided up.

There were successive attempts to persuade the government to open it up just a little, but the newly created Nagari challenge merely caused the entrenched élite—exercising dominance through their traditional mastery of the Persian script—to gang up even more forcefully. In testimony before the government, in memorials

[6] See King, *One Language, Two Scripts*, *passim*.

and before commissions, there was a fair amount of name-calling, along predictable lines: thus, while the Nagari lot were accused of being upstarts—'shopkeepers'—and yokels, the Urdu élite were identified as the feckless gentry, their language the language of playboys and prostitutes, of indolence and immorality. In the words of one vociferous Nagari supporter, the existing situation was one in which:

धोती वाले कमाते हैं, और टोपी वाले खाते हैं।[7]

The dangerous situation created by the inconsistency in official policy—creating a class of underprivileged Nagari intelligentsia—was made even worse by the 1979 order which, in the teeth of pro-Nagari agitation, further extended the already resented empire of Persian and Urdu by making a knowledge thereof an essential requirement in all public appointments with a monthly emolument of more than Rs 10.

The subsequent period till 1896 is, at least in respect of putting pressure on the government, deceptively quiet. It is almost as if the nascent élite has been forced on the defensive, forced to regroup. Because we know that the Nagari lot—the धोती वाले—were not, and indeed, could not be, acquiescent.

Malaviya's 1897 Memorandum is, on any reckoning, a masterly document. It is a thorough, professional compilation of materials and arguments in favour of Nagari. The crucial argument which he constructs, with much support from official data, concerns education, particularly primary education. He goes on to dwell on the social benefits of mass primary education—benefits that, one might add, are still awaited today. However, the critical part of the argument runs, the anticipated educational benefits will not materialize if the recipients of that education are going to be closed off from any prospect of employment. He rarely lapses into the acrimony that had characterized earlier controversy—he refers once to the fact of Hindus being forced by the lure of employment into learning the Persian script as 'involuntary conversion'. But, in the main, the voice is calm and authoritative, and speaks not of self-interest but of democratic legitimacy. (Of course, all one needs to do is to recall actual literacy levels, or the genuflecting

[7] See Chandrabali Pandey, *Shasan Mein Nagari*, Hindi Sahitya Sammelan, Allahabad, 1948.

to princelings in the 1910 address,—to realize that the democratic claim was mostly empty rhetoric.)[8]

The fortuitous appointment of a sympathetic Lt. Governor—McDonnell—provided the Nagari camp in 1900 with a victory that was as surprising then as it appears inevitable now. McDonnell's 1900 order allowed the permissive but not exclusive use of the Nagari script in the courts of the province—but this was, by an astounding slip that appears incredible even now, modified by the Governor General in Council: whereas the resolution proposed by the Lt. Governor had used the terms 'Nagari and Persian characters', the Government of India amended this—*without acknowledgement or justification*—to read as 'Hindi and Urdu languages'.

Even so, the victory was largely a symbolic one—the entrenched administrative caste was still in place and the Nagari Pracharini Sabha which tried to arrange for Nagari scribes who would offer free services to plaintiffs soon discovered that material support is harder to come by than rhetoric.[9] The 'Urdu' side reacted with shock and a feeling of betrayal, having been abandoned by a colonial administration to which they had been steadfastly loyal in favour of a bunch of no-account upstarts. But after 1900 the struggle was truly joined.

The Nagari agitation of the late-nineteenth century shows clearly the advent of modern democratic political methods. Almost perforce excluded from the corridors of government, the protagonists of Nagari resort to pressure politics, mobilizing support across the province, bombarding the government with memorials and resolutions, in a remarkable, co-ordinated effort. Thus, the North-Western Provinces and Oudh (NWP&O) Provincial Committee of the Hunter Commission of 1884 was bombarded by seventy-six pro-Hindi memorials, all identical, emanating from several different parts of the province, and containing in all 58,289 signatures.[10]

The story so far is simple enough—a new proto-élite, trained in the Nagari script, seeks a share of power through official recog-

[8] See footnote 5.

[9] King, *One Language, Two Scripts*, p.162.

[10] Report of the NWP&O Provincial Committee with evidence taken before the Commission and Memorials addressed to the Education Commission, Calcutta, 1884. In IOL, London.

nition of the script. The already entrenched élite seeks, arrogantly and strenuously, to protect its privileges. Finally, under the pressure of numbers as well as arguments, the government is forced to relent, and straighten out the inconsistency between the output of its education system and the intake of its administration. What follows, however, is a little less straightforward—and is, in ways both expectable and unexpected, the seed-time of our present and future woes. The *Punjab Observer* of 4 July 1900 warned directly: 'We cannot characterize it as anything short of a grave political blunder, and history written a hundred years hence will have to mourn the mistake made in 1900.' The 'mistake' that the *Punjab Observer* had in mind was 'harm to imperial interests'. However, the generations that are the inheritors of the divided legacy of the subcontinent are well within their rights to 'mourn' something else.

As a first step towards unravelling that confusion, let us consider some aspects of the true vernacular of north India—this is truly a middle language, born out of the necessities of intercourse between different peoples, communities and cultures, who are forced to rub together in the daily business of living their lives, over centuries. This is a genuinely secular creation, not only in the sense of its being poly-communal as well as multi-lingual in its sources, but also in in the sense that it is mundane in its origins and purposes. This is also in some sense, for reasons relating to the necessary heterogeneity of the city, an urban tongue—a fact which might give it a somewhat 'Muslim' colour, since a relatively higher proportion of Muslims are urban rather than country dwellers. But it is as well to remember that Nagari—the script but, in some accounts, a language also—is also, etymologically, 'of the town'. Thus, the linguistic analogue of the script which drives so much of the early and divisive agitation is in fact that same, one, common language. This language was unacceptable to the early opponents of Khari Boli precisely because it was perceived to be, essentially, marked by the Muslim connection—or, to use a slightly later rhetoric, that it was, in fact, Urdu. It was, to my mind, the politics generated by the Nagari demand that helped to create the space within which this Khari Boli could be suitably 'decontaminated', purified, Hinduized—and so become modern 'Hindi'. This becomes clearly evident in the Braj/Khari Boli controversy that is associated with the name of Ayodhya

Prasad Khattri.[11] It is over this body, this one language, that the two sides, soon to mutate into the two warring communities, fight.

And are, perhaps, condemned to fight by the exigencies of the socio-economic situation which forces impoverished societies, *then and now*, to practise and devise strategies for practising innovative and brutal forms of triage. It seems to me, therefore, that one cannot deal adequately with the phenomenon of the production of difference without being forced to turn to the process of production—*material production*—itself. It is important to be able to see both in the manifestations and assertions as well as in the ascriptions of difference, the second-order consequences of distortions and injustices deriving from the process of material production. If an inadequate social product is to be shared out, someone must lose. These 'losers', sometimes resigned but resentful, sometimes combative and resistant, enter the historical process in the shape of hungry, contentious groups and individuals.

The democratic legitimacy of both sides derives from their claim to the common language. The Nagari élite has an advantage here, in that it has genuinely plebeian origins. The 'Persian' élite—mainly but not exclusively Muslim—takes some time overcoming its feudal/aristocratic hang-ups. Then, it asserts its claim to the secular inheritance embodied in the language—and mirrored indeed in the communally mixed character of the class which claims to defend it against the disruptive and exclusivist designs of the protagonists of Nagari and 'Hindi'. For the Nagari side, however, the promise of communal harmony is poisoned by the reality of privilege—or, to put it more precisely, they have a different perception of the manifest danger to communal peace.

In parentheses it can be said that the burden of embarrassment that Indian secularism derives from this association with élite privilege, its historical imbrication with the world of the great Avadh zamindars is, perhaps, not germane to the present story. Of course, that zamindari world did not consist only of the cliched exploiters of popular mythology—this was also the world of composite culture, of *tahzeeb* and *takalluf*, of refinement and of significant cultural achievements. Indeed, in a crucial sense, this world not only comprised but was also, in the last analysis, made

[11] See my 'Ayodhya Prasad Khattri's Khari Boli and Braj', in A. Bhalla and P. Bumke (eds) *Images of Rural India*, Sterling, New Delhi, 1992.

by the Avadh peasantry. Thus one would be well within one's rights in this context to talk not only of élite secularism but also, deriving from the shared world, the existential *modus vivendi* of those self-same peasants, of mass secularism. But the critical question is—can that popular secularism be salvaged today, rescued from the fatal embrace of the zamindari feudal order and its successor nostalgias? Rahi Masoom Raza's *Aadha Gaaon* is the classic exploration of the difficult terrain where the nostalgic memory of social harmony is inextricably bound up with a historical awareness of inequality, and injustice, and exploitation. The task is more than merely academic—it is politically urgent. Because one can hardly fail to notice the wholly undeserved populist energy that the politics of Hindu communalism derives from this history of attacking a world of élite privilege, at least in Uttar Pradesh.

Each side claims—as indeed it must—that the other is different and therefore distant from the language of the common people. But the only practical recourse available to these fractious sharers of the common language is in fact to *make* themselves different—and *forget* that they have done so, and must continue to do so. Thus, the Nagari élite seeks to identify the language of the 'Persian' élite—variously, Urdu or Hindustani—with the Arabo-Persianizing lunatic fringe. The Urdu side, in turn, seeks to identify the language of the Nagari élite with the Hindi of the Sanskritizing lunatic fringe.

However, each side, in order to strengthen and make good on its claim of democratic legitimacy, is also forced not only to gesture towards the possible popular constituency of the future—which, if truly mobilized, might force a kind of politics which neither side, neither the Avadh élite identified by Francis Robinson nor the newly arisen *savarna* Hindu one, is prepared to countenance—but also to generate and crystallize an immediately available constituency.

Each side is, thus, forced to move away from the shared middle ground of the common language, and cobble together a symbology and an imaginary that can sustain the necessary cultural exclusivisim: the Hindu myths about the Muslims, and the Muslim myths about the Hindus. Each side, in seeking to prove that the other is different, is forced to evacuate the middle ground and take recourse to diverse strategies in order to differentiate itself. As a result of this process there is born a purified, Sanskritized version of this middle tongue, called 'Hindi'. And similarly, there is born, or born again, an Arabicized and Persianized version of the same middle tongue, called 'Urdu'.

I suspect, however, that this point-counterpoint mode of narrating these developments tends to underplay if not altogether obscure the internal dynamic of these socio-cultural processes. Thus, the Sanskritization of Hindi and the Persianization of Urdu—producing, respectively, 'Hindi' and 'Urdu' from and upon a shared linguistic base—also enjoy a certain autonomy. Thus the moves to de-Persianize Urdu and bring it closer to the vernacular happen at around the same time as the move to purify Hindi and bring it closer to Sanskrit is gaining ground—approximately, the last quarter of the nineteenth century. In time, however, the enforced intimacy of modern democratic politics forces the two processes to move more closely in tandem—ironically, in both cases, by turning away towards their lunatic, culturally exclusivist peripheries.

This is perhaps not the place to narrate the evolution of these dialectically fated internal dynamics. However, in respect of Hindi (which I know better), it may be said that the differentiation is sought to be established around three axes: firstly, the script. This difference, once it is forced into the public domain, is irreducible, and renders the problem, finally, non-negotiable. Secondly, affiliation: this might sound like linguistics, but the attempt to establish family trees, with Sanskrit as the mother, and Hindi as the eldest daughter, etc., not only creates a pedigree for Hindi, it also places Hindi in a superior relationship—this is an Indian family, and age has precedence!—to the other languages of north India, to Bengali, and Gujarati and Marathi. However, another effect that is surely not inadvertent is that this strenuously asseverated genealogy *excludes* Urdu, which is virtually indistinguishable from Hindi in one of its moods, from the genealogy altogether. That which is, at most, a Siamese sibling, is excluded from kinship altogether. This, to my mind, is the politics of the family trees that Hindiwallahs draw up constantly—kinship rules out the claims of other kinds of contiguity. The linguistic and grammatical base, far from being derived from Sanskrit by some Hindi version of immaculate conception is, in fact, a product of the cultural promiscuity that has been the historical experience of the fertile plains of Hindustan.

There are, not surprisingly, problems with their preferred ancestry: the relationship with Urdu is manifest, and that with Sanskrit is largely mythical. Given the grammatical distance between Hindi and Sanskrit, the pernicious fantasists are forced thus—the third axis—to resort to large-scale lexical borrowing, bending the relaxed, loose-limbed grammar of the achieved middle tongue in order to create a consonantal clutter which might, to a largely semi-literate constituency, sound Sanskritoid. It would be fair to note, however, that in the hands of sensitive and skilled users—Hazari Prasad Dwivedi is the name that comes first to mind—this synthetic language is capable of considerable power, drawing upon the technical and philosophical resources of Sanskrit. But in the hands of lesser mortals, the Sanskritic syncopated consonants of 'Hindi' produce merely a ritual sound, whose purpose is not communication so much as it is to reassure the flock. I imagine that the strangulated gutturals of Arabicized 'Urdu' fulfil a similar function.

The point to note in all this is that each side is forced to deny what both sides know—and need to know—is the truth: that the common people have, over the centuries, evolved a rich and various and shared language. If there were not one language at the heart of the conflict, there would be no problem, no need for strenuous differentiation, in the first place. What is more, unless there is to be more than a single 'common people', the claim of democratic legitimacy of both the differentiating, exclusivist factions requires that, in the teeth of mere logic, *even their own*, they must both lay claim to that same 'common people'. But each side ends up justifying and deserving the accusations of the other. Or, to complete the somewhat confusing picture, with its symmetrical, mirror-like quality, the two sides not only need to know the truth about a common, trans-community language, but are also required, by political imperatives, to seek to deny and forget what they know to be true. Indeed, in so far as the body of the common language is always available to its users, partisans on both sides are condemned to endeavour to violate that body and so falsify what they know to be true, and *need* to know to be true, simultaneously.

By the time we arrive at the 1930s, the process of differentiation is already beginning to yield its bitter, familiar harvest. Old soldiers as well as the newest long-distance media-packaged electronic warfare experts know, the dirtiest fighting is the one that happens at close quarters: hand-to-hand combat is all about blood. (And 'blood' perhaps, to family-realists as distinct from family-sentimentalists, is all about hand-to-hand combat!) In any case, the violence that the Hindi–Urdu conflict was skilfully manipulated to generate was very much violence within the family—and it is, as we know, a trauma that is infinitely renewable. However, I have no intention of going once again over this familiar territory. Instead, I would like to indicate, in conclusion, some of the less obvious effects of the process of differentiation narrated above.

Two kinds of consequences come to mind. One effect of the process of contention and difference whereby modern Hindi comes about is that it cannot afford to know the truth about itself and its origins. Thus, a kind of amnesia and dishonesty is a *sine qua non*. It is instructive, for instance, that despite a hundred years of polemic and propaganda, and projects galore, there isn't a single dictionary in existence in which Hindi can bring to mind the sources of its own word-stock. In seeking to narrate how it comes about, Hindi propagandists resort to complicated genealogies simply because they cannot afford to acknowledge that 'Hindi' has come about by ruthlessly Sanskritizing the linguistic base of the common tongue which, from the perspective of an achieved 'Hindi', is anathematized as Urdu. This fear of knowledge also manifests itself in the way in which authority is vested in some 'experts'—in this case, the pandits. Such a delegation/arrogation of authority over the people's own gloriously hybrid language by a class/caste of persons, mainly U P Brahmins from around Allahabad and Banaras, with a sharply ideological agenda works—mercifully with limited success—to create an artificial and stilted tongue. It is important to understand the nature of this authority. It derives not from scholarly or literary or aesthetic considerations but from a politicized form of traditional religious orthodoxy.

The other kind of effect is much more difficult to describe. It derives, I suspect, from the precise nature of the difference that was produced: at one level, that of the script, this 'difference' is non-negotiable, non-compoundable. But at another and equally significant level, the boundary is porous, infinitely, endlessly negotiable, not only in the public space but in the privacy of one's mind. Here is a wound that can always be kept green, a trauma waiting to be inflamed—an offence that can be renewed without hope of interdiction. Ironically, of course, in such cases the perpetrators of the offence are also, in an unmistakable sense, its victims. Their relationship to their own language must, ineluctably, be marked by a crippling anxiety, because the capacity to cause offence is directly predicated on their own vulnerability.

11

The Contest Over Space and the Formation of Communal Collectivities: Burial of a Fakir, Calcutta, 1924

P. K. Datta

I

The course of communal mobilization in this century has often widened the connotations of local conflicts over sacred space, so that they start acquiring general symbolic and institutional implications. In contemporary India, quarrels over sacred space have been fabricated into political campaigns with nation-wide ramifications. The controversy over the Babri Masjid/Ramjanam Bhumi was a local one for over a century, until it was metamorphosed into a symbol of the 'oppressiveness' of secular co-existence, and made to dramatize the necessity of altering the very constitution of the country. The contention over the burial of a Fakir in Calcutta's New Market in 1924, can be seen to belong to this genus of communal conflicts, although with significant differences. The salient thing about this dispute was not so much the overt communal mobilization as the public debate that preceded it. In this paper I will examine the implications of this debate and its outcome.

The crucial years of this controversy spanned the middle of October 1924 to December 1925. These years formed the interregnum between the Non-cooperation/Khilafat (hereafter N/K) movement on the one hand, and on the other, the outbreak, in Calcutta, of the heaviest and most prolonged riots known till then in the subcontinent during April 1926. The contrast between the riots and the N/K movement could not be greater, for the latter marked the last nationalist movement in which Hindus and Muslims mobilized together. The Fakir burial controversy both expressed and shaped this transition.

The controversy arose when the followers of a Fakir buried his body next to a gate in the New Market, a place where he had sat for fifteen years. Objections were made by European residents, who were the main patrons of this market, and their representatives attempted to pass a resolution for the exhumation of the body. The Swarajists who formed the majority in the Corporation, and whose leader, C. R. Das, was the Mayor, adopted an equivocating stance. They tried to sideline the issue by postponing it. There was, however, vociferous support for exhumation from a growing number of Hindu Swarajist councillors. This demand became a dominant trend among them after the demise of Das. Correspondingly, the issue mutated into one involving a simple antagonism between Hindus and Muslims.

The controversy rested on a link between the sources of popular urban religion which invested much emotional and symbolic investment into its sacred space, and the general question of the governance of public civic space. The issue involved a combination of popular mobilization and a public debate, carried out mainly in the representative institution of the Corporation and in newspapers. Although violence was threatened, none did take place. The absence of physical animosity prevents the overwriting of these issues by the binarization that violence imposes. Consequently, this contention gives us a clearer view of the notion of the Public that came into existence in the twenties of this century, in the city of Calcutta.

The Fakir did not spawn a coherent community around himself in his lifetime. One reason for this was that he did not speak, but communicated through rudimentary gestures. Consequently, he propagated no doctrines and demanded no ritual requirements. Even his Muslimness was a function of his reputation. 'As a majority of people say he was a Mahomedan saint, it may be assumed that he was one,' declared Amjad Hussain, a reader of

The Statesman in his letter to that newspaper written after the death of the Fakir.[1] It would be appropriate to say therefore, that there were various collectivities that made up his followers. Those who surrounded him physically were a group of gamblers. They made bets on horse races and looked up to the Fakir as a magical source of tips on winning horses. The socially and economically powerful groups among his followers consisted of the butchers[2] and Peshawari fruit sellers of the market. They sought the Fakir for his benediction. This involved interpreting the Fakir's arbitrary acts of snatching food from their food stalls, as a sign that their trade would prosper that particular day. The market was thriving, and both groups catered to a steadily increasing European clientele. These two professional groups were among the first to settle in the market, for the New Market (which was its popular appellation; it was actually named after Sir Stuart Hogg, Chairman of the Municipal Body of Justices) had been established in 1874 to supply food in hygienic conditions to Europeans. Nevertheless they belonged to those traders who operated from open stalls, encouraging rough and ready transactions, in contrast to the shopkeepers, who engaged in more elaborate exchanges with their customers in the privacy of shop interiors, giving to them a superior social standing with their customers. The affiliation to the Fakir on the part of these two groups was then, also a marker of their socially distinctive sphere. The fourth group was composed of women, and there is too little evidence to indicate who they were and their motivations in visiting the Fakir.[3]

[1] 26 October 1924.

[2] Interestingly, some of the butchers appear to have kept their distance from the gamblers. One of them, Shaukat Ali, who was in his teens during the controversy told me and a friend, that the Fakir was surrounded by *ganja* smokers in the night. Interview with Shaukat Ali, June 1990.

[3] One probable cause for their adherence could be the medicinal powers attributed to Fakirs. In a city whose census could count a pitiable one thousand medical practitioners in a population which was around ten lakhs (*Census of India, Calcutta, vols 1 and 2*, 1931), this was but natural. The use of fakiri medicine is indicated by an advertisement for it in *The Forward*, which reads: 'A WONDERFUL FAKIREE MEDICINE FOR DIABETES.' There is also the possibility of a link via gambling. A biographer of these times recollects a gambling craze that hit Calcutta in 1912, which involved playing with numbers. What is important for our present purposes is that it affected women

Not all followers of the Fakir were necessarily a part of a collective identity, and certainly, there was no single collective identity that bound them. But what can be deduced are facets of a socially common experience, that did not however yield a socially consolidated group. This was the experience of migrancy, that was common to most of the natives who populated Fenwick Bazar, the Corporation ward in which the market was located.[4] At the most elementary level, the presence of gamblers together with the lottery-like way the Fakir's *baraka* worked for the shopkeepers, points to the significance of money for migrants. After all, the poor migrant's life was itself a gamble, for it involved a trade-off between the certitude of a home and the unknown vicissitudes of new life in which the main feature was to make money. And sometimes, access to quick money could shorten one's exile. Stories of Fakirs who defrauded gullible migrant workers of large sums in exchange for the prospect of quick returns, were not uncommon.[5] For the more prosperous trader migrants, especially the Peshawaris whose economy rested on migrancy as a social system, gambling could be attractive for it not only offered an opportunity to extend their

---

in particular. He relates a story in which his neighbour's wife claimed to have received a visitation from Ma Chandi who tipped her off about a lucky number. She won an amount that was more than what her husband earned in a month. This started a movement to the Kalighat temple where devotees did *manat* (a pledge to the gods as exchange for intercession in a problem—a practice that is incidentally a feature of pirism as well), hoping to receive similar inspiration. Atul Sur, *Shatabdir Prattidhwani*, Calcutta, 1986, pp. 29–31. Obviously divinity was not perceived to be, in popular imagination, antagonistic towards these less reputable methods of acquiring money—a moral that has a direct bearing on our Fakir's story.

[4] This ward had a total of 15,114 immigrants (of a total of 30,975 persons). 491 out of every 1000 were born in Bengal, and 509 per 1000, outside Bengal. It should be observed that the first category included those who had been permanently settled due to previous migration from other provinces. *Census of India*, 1931, p. 15.

[5] A Muslim mendicant called Khoda Bax showed a passing lascar that he could squeeze milk out of his hair. He then asked for money from him, promising to multiply it a hundred fold. The lascar was instructed to walk a certain distance and shut his eyes—which he did without acquiring the gift. When the lascar demanded his money back, the Fakir denied all knowledge of the transaction. Later, the magic was traced by the police to a small 'lota' (receptacle) concealed in his matted locks! The Fakir 'was held in high esteem by the local Mohammedans...' *The Forward*, 13 November 1924.

wealth, but also allowed them to play with the tumultuous and uncontrollable force of money, the logic of which they had to obey rigorously in the sphere of their livelihood. Gambling was thus an integrative institution that was posited on the need to emotionally master the vicissitudes of a money economy. And this, needless to add, would be even more unknowable in a market that was linked, through the European clientele, more closely to international price fluctuations.[6]

The practice of converting a person into a Pir, in order to tap the sources of his attributed *keramat*, was not unknown. For instance, Mohammed Waliullah, a contemporary observer, recollected how Fazlul Huq's grave in Dhaka became for some time, a *dargah* for gamblers on the races.[7] What set the New Market Fakir apart from such instances was the fact that he also possessed a popular hagiography, which, even if rudimentary, was remarkable in its implications. The most significant element concerns a couple of stories, which tell of the supernatural powers of the Fakir, the conventional testament of *baraka* (divine grace/powers). The energy involved in creating a cult of the Fakir can be judged by the fact that these stories were widely circulated in print—both in a pamphlet called *Fakirer Keramat* (hereafter FK) that was written to mobilize support for his burial,[8] as well as in newspapers, while it is still retold by butchers and Peshawari fruit sellers in the market today.

The first tale is about the time he used to sit in the southern gate, which was used by the Europeans and their acquaintances. One day, a sergeant came and ordered him out. That same night a huge fire broke out, destroying a corner of the market.[9] After that no one appears to have disturbed him in his new home in the

[6] On the other hand, it should added here, horse racing could be especially significant for the shopkeepers, for it provided one of the few areas where the operations of fortune ensured a certain equality with their customers.

[7] Apparently the reverence that was given to Huq during his lifetime for his extraordinary generosity, transmuted into a faith that his grave could grant tips for race course gamblers. Mohammed Waliullah, *Jugo Bichitra*, Dhaka, 1967, p. 46.

[8] S. Rahman, *Fakirer Keramat: Darbesher Ascharya Jibon Katha*, 1924 (pub. details absent). This was sold for a paltry sum of 3 paise, and ran well enough to go into a second print run.

[9] According to the FK, the loss to the Corporation amounted to the massive sum of 3 lakh rupees, ibid., p. 4. Shaukat Ali, our interviewee, claimed that

eastern gate, a place used mainly by the natives. The second story concerns the Fakir's pet dogs, who created a nuisance for passers-by. They were poisoned anonymously and would have died, had not the Fakir come and resuscitated them. Although this story is not directly connected to any action by the authorities, it belongs to the same species of action as the first, in that the motif of civic propriety plays a key role. Both stories have to do with the civic question of the 'right of way', an issue that was to be repeatedly raised by the Europeans while objecting to the establishment of a *mazaar* (a Pir's grave which is worshipped) being built over the Fakir's body.[10] It is thus not surprising that two butchers I interviewed in the market, telescoped the incidents. They claimed that the authorities first poisoned the dogs, and then evicted the Fakir.[11]

Clearly the Fakir enabled his followers to appeal to a law that was superior to that of the administration which controlled their working space. However, the need for such an appeal in the first place gestures at a set of surrounding tensions. These need to be unravelled, in order to understand the possible extensions of the meaning of these stories.

At this point I will look at the matter from the European point of view. In addition to being better documented, it provides a clearer index of the burden of anxieties that the migrants raised among the people who mattered most in the city; and hence, by implication, suggests the extent of pressure the former had to face. What was becoming painfully clear to the Europeans in this period, was that their spacious enclaves in Calcutta—which stood out from the rest of the city by the luxurious presence of open spaces—were becoming increasingly vulnerable due to the inflow of migrant workers into the city. Between 1921–31, the population of Fenwick

---

the sergeant went to the lake located near Esplanade, and pleaded with the Fakir to come back.

[10] The prospect of a shrine created the apprehension that, 'The passage in question will . . . eventually develop into a sacred spot, and crowds are bound to assemble, interfering with the right of way'. Letter from Dorothea D., *The Statesman*, 22 October 1994.

[11] While Shaukat Ali claimed that the Market Superintendent had done it, Mohammed Maksud Ali, who was one of the owners of the shop under which the body of the Fakir now lies, stated that the sergeant had poisoned them. Interview with S. Ali and M. M. Ali, June 1990.

Bazar increased by twenty per cent, which amounted to over 5000 persons; and while the Europeans increased by over fifty per cent in the whole city, their absolute increase compared unfavourably with the sheer volume of native migrancy.[12] Correspondingly the geography of their prized enclaves was also changing. European Calcutta was acquiring the look that was to inspire that peculiar combination of affliction and warmth which marks it today. It was beginning to look like the old, Indian Calcutta, which presented a spatial continuum between shops, houses, crowds and traffic. The two places of European pride, Park Street and Chowringhee, were falling victim to this pattern. Innumerable letters and articles expressed concern, pointing to the march of unstoppable causes: in addition to migrants, land prices were going up and houses were renting out rooms at the ground level to shopkeepers.

A consequence of these anxieties was several campaigns carried out to evict the recalcitrant poor. A letter to *The Statesman* from a resident of the posh Bishop Lefroy Road proudly related a successful campaign to evict a Fakir, with the help of the Chief Executive Officer of the Corporation.[13] This uncertainty of settlement was not confined to the utterly destitute alone. Much the same experience could be had as a consequence of peremptory bureaucratic decisions. For instance, in the months preceding the Fakir's burial, there had been a large-scale eviction of butchers from their homes in Karaya, a locality that was not far from the New Market.[14] Many of the butchers of the market had lost their homes in this drive. Despite their relative prosperity, the butchers

[12] Fenwick Bazar had on an average 161 persons per acre (which would increase if the market area was taken into account). The Europeans increased there by eleven per cent, although the increase in real terms meant that their numbers only went up from 1498 persons to 1670. *Census of India*.

[13] A letter from one W. St John Church, congratulated the Chief Executive Officer for taking prompt action against a fakir who sat in Lower Circular Road and aroused the pique of his wife and other ladies: 'because they do not give him bukshish or charity that he abuses them not so much in objectionable language, as in innuendos to their presumed financial inability to give him what he demands.' *The Statesman*, 27 October 1925.

[14] According to Q. Ahmed's letter to *The Statesman*, the butchers of the market had been very discontented 'on account of the wholesale acquisition of their hearth and home at Karaya [a neighbourhood locality] by the Calcutta Improvement Trust'. 18 October 1924.

had to undergo the same sort of experience of powerlessness over their home in the city, as poor migrants. Their living condition was equally vulnerable to the dictates of municipality decisions. Vagrancy provided the frightening, alternative life that never disappeared from the horizons of even relatively prosperous migrant groups.

It should be said here that much of the life of the Fakir deals with an incessant pattern of evictions.[15] He was a coolie from Madras (although this could well refer to the popular euphemism for the whole of south India). He got involved in a murder charge and was deported to the Andamans. Fortunately for him, George V's accession intervened. As part of the celebrations, the government ordered amnesty for all the imprisoned. Thereafter he found his way into Calcutta where he was remembered as one who had settled in front of a 'Madrassi' Church in Market Street, a spot from where he was eventually evicted.[16] The vagrant left and settled in front of the main gate of the market, collecting alms but not talking to anyone. He was evicted again. This time he removed himself to the eastern gate, which was not used as frequently by the Europeans and the Indian upper class. He was adopted here by the shopkeepers, and it was here that he found his final niche.

This small story, which would probably have been even more representative if it had been completely unknown, is one in which identity is so completely lost that it almost becomes a blank sheet.

[15] As often happens in such cases, peoples' lives get to be known from hearsay, mostly when they are dead. In this case I shall draw a great deal on Q. Ahmed's first letter to *The Statesman*, which as I have said, was substantially borne out by the investigations of a special Committee formed later by the corporations. Of course this does not mean that the report itself was completely accurate, and it is a fact that its findings were contested by A. Razzak, a Corporation Councillor. He claimed that the evidence was based on the testimony of a Christian, who had reported from hearsay. *The Forward*, 15 August 1925. Nevertheless it was accepted by most, and if nothing else it does reveal in this fact that its story was seen to happen within the range of possibilities the city offered to such a man. Moreover it should be mentioned here that Ahmed says that he acquired his information from the shopkeepers of the market. Obviously, there was general consensus on the details of his story.

[16] *The Forward*, 17 October 1924.

It is not a tale that simply invites empathy, but invests that emotion with a reverence born of fear. The prospect that such a life story held for other migrants was too intimate to repress; like Sitaladebi, the smallpox goddess, it could only be appeased. At the same time it should be emphasized that what restores his identity is his ability to retaliate. And this prowess, it should be emphasized, is something he acquires only in the New Market. What this indicates is a definition of the Fakir's powers as the result, not simply of a personal attribute alone, but of a symbiotic relationship between that and the New Market. In this connection, it may be recalled that it was the active intervention of the shopkeepers that gave the Fakir security of settlement in his new abode near the eastern gate. As such, the Fakir's story gestures at a sub-text of pride in the followers' consciousness of being active contributors to his powers. And if we remember the story of the Fakir's eviction by the sergeant, then the possibility of its extension into an articulation of an anti-colonial sentiment can be visualized. I suggest that there were enough indications in the state of the New Market to warrant the conclusion, that it was on the grounds of anti-colonialism that the followers of the Fakir could behold their own contribution to his powers.

It is significant that the FK prefaced its stories about the Fakir, by relating a tale of the '*pir bhai*' (literally Pir brother) of his alleged mentor. Apparently Tajuddin Baba of Nagpur, the '*pir bhai*', was locked up by the government for insanity. But this did not trouble him, for he magically appeared in the streets one night.[17] Obviously the story derives its ironic significance from the double meaning of madness.[18] More importantly, the representation of the British as jailers who try to confine the sources of the power of the Fakir which they, unlike the followers, cannot comprehend, signals a compete withdrawal of consent given to colonial hegemony. It was in fact an apt story for the prevailing mood of the market. The New Market, along with other markets of the city, played an active political role, especially in conducting *hartals* (total

[17] FK, p. 5.

[18] *Pagal* or *Khepa* signified divine inspiration that was an ontological condition. It was popularly used by popular cults such as the Bauls, often serving as suffixes to some of the names of their singers. The other meaning denoted human madness, as is commonly used.

closure), held in the city.[19] A possible reason was the domination of Muslim politics in Calcutta by merchants. For instance, of the ten Muslim councillors elected with the help of the Swarajists in 1924, five were merchants.[20] Their business ensured intimate links with shopkeepers, while the domination of the Swarajists meant that the New Market amongst others, would play an important role in demonstrating the mobilizing power of nationalists.

Such a self-conscious anti-colonialism was bound to manifest itself within the everyday sphere of market transactions. And this can be seen in the fact that the joys of shopping no longer seemed available to Europeans there. In earlier and happier times, travel writers like H. E. A. Cotton and Col. Newell had indulgently referred to bargaining as the 'norm' in the market.[21] But now letters to newspapers poured in after the burial, complaining of rude behaviour by shopkeepers. Moreover, previously, the covered area of the New Market had allowed a spectacle of crowds, one which blended oriental colour with continental glamour. This human spectacle featured among the charms of the market listed by European travel writers. However, by the 1920s instead of being the people who gazed at the passers-by, the Europeans found themselves in the uncomfortable position of being the object of the latter's gaze. Letters talked of the way the market was getting crowded by people who seemed to have no work, except to look at Europeans.[22]

[19] The nationalist passion of the markets was evident when Gandhi announced his fast on the occasion of the All Party Unity Conference at Delhi, held in the same month that the burial took place. As a gesture of solidarity, Calcutta and its suburbs observed, what *The Mussalman* termed, 'an absolutely voluntary "hartal"', along with 'fast and prayer'; shops along the whole stretch from Shyambazar in the North to Hogg Market were closed or half-open, 3 October 1924.

[20] There were three lawyers, one was a clerk, another a former secretary of the Calcutta Khilafat Committee. Kenneth Mcpherson, *The Muslim Microcosm: Calcutta, 1918–35*, Weisbaden (1974), p. 80.

[21] 'Fixed prices are the exception. Bargaining is the rule.' Col. H. A. Newell, *Calcutta The First Capital of British India: An Illustrated Guide to Places of Interest with a Map* (pub. details absent), p. 7.

[22] A tail editorial item in *The Statesman*, wrote against 'the crowds of undesirable people who haunt the New Market for no ostensible purpose, except to stare at respectable buyers and make remarks about them'. 25 October 1924.

In many ways the decisive story of the Fakir's *keramat* is one that concerns his burial.[23] According to what can be culled from the depositions of the Deputy Mayor, the Market Superintendent and the Chief Executive Officer, given before the Committee appointed by the Corporation, the crowd initially approached Mr Baker, the Market Superintendent, for permission to bury the body where it lay. Baker refused, and they went away to look for an alternate spot. One was found and purchased. Meanwhile however, while they were gathered around the body, someone claimed that the Fakir could not be moved from the ground. In all probability this notion spread like wildfire. Interpreting it as the wish of the Fakir to be buried where he lay, the followers now decided to go ahead with their earlier resolve, regardless of the consequences. By now news had travelled to disturb Corporation bigwigs, and both the CEO, the Deputy Mayor and Shamsul Huq, a Councillor, reached the place. In the parleys that followed, Subhash Bose, the CEO, approached Fazlul Huq who okayed the burial as constituting a part of orthodox Islamic practice. The next day the whole action was given public sanction by the newspapers including *The Statesman*, which reported that the Corporation had given its approval.

The narrative of the burial indicates an extension of the Fakir's *keramat* that transforms the institutions which surround and express it. The process of burial demonstrates the joining of the traditional powers of the Fakir—which in this case drew its powers from the inverted relationship with the migrants' lack of control

[23] Till now I have used Fakir and Pir interchangeably; as a matter of fact, this very elasticity of usage is a result of the way the Fakir's followers wrought his meaning. His pre-eastern gate life can be said to resemble that of a Fakir's, in the sense that a Fakir is distinguished, above all, by his ceaseless travel. A Pir, on the other hand, is a charismatic figure who is settled in a particular locality, with an institutional structure that could outlive him. Clearly, in the fact that the market Fakir was given a settled place, and above all by the attempts described in the following paragraph, he could be said to have attained the status of a Pir. I may add here that the regular rituals that are associated with his shrine, which is still worshipped today (although furtively), has all the trappings of a devotion to a Pir, with incense sticks, flowers, money and finally, according to some present-day followers, an *urs*. I have normally used the designation of Fakir to refer to him, in order to avoid coining a new, awkward appellation.

over urban space and corresponding problems with the ungovernable power of money—with a new positive belief in popular movements and its manifestation of a collective will prepared to assert itself against the wishes of European administrative personnel. It must be observed here that the N/K movement had seen the involvement of renowned Pirs such as Abu Bakr of Hooghly and Badshah Mian of Faridpur.[24] But their involvement had simply meant the incorporation of divine personages to provide legitimacy and confidence to the movement. There was also a more informal sort of pirism, which was a consequence of the importance given to the leaders of the N/K. Thus, for instance, Mansur Ahmad recalls how his speeches were so compelling that he started being regarded as a Pir.[25] The New Market Fakir was however different from both sets of cases. He derived not only his pirship, but also the whole range of its meanings, from his followers. The most important of these significations was produced by the attempts of the followers to legitimize their beliefs through public institutions.

As is well known, a *mazaar* is normally looked after by the heirs of the Pir, with powers being concentrated in the hands of the *sajjada nashin* (the guardian of the shrine). There were, however, local instances in Barasat and Hooghly, of *mazaars* being maintained by the followers of the Pir.[26] The New Market offered a new phenomena. In the course of the negotiations with Corporation officials, a Mazaar Committee was established. Now, the institution of a Committee with its notion of accountability to its constituency was already familiar to the Islamic world in Bengal:

[24] It is said that when Pir Badshah Mian was arrested, he was accompanied by thousands of his followers to Calcutta all the way from Faridpur. A. Y. S. Alam, 'Khilafat Movement and the Muslims of Bengal', unpublished M.Phil thesis, Jawaharlal Nehru University, 1978, p. 178.

[25] Ahmad found himself distributing *Tabiz* (blessed amulets), and had even started receiving donations when he went to Calcutta. He attributes this faith to his socially unclassifiable status: he was from an orthodox Faraizi family, yet he knew English and had even stopped doing *namaz*. A. M. Ahmed, *Atmakatha*, Dhaka, 1978, pp. 195–9. Of course the crucial fact is that all this was being conducted in the course of the N/K movement.

[26] For instance, the *dargahs* of Nirghin Shah in Barasat, and that of Gorachand Pir in Basirhat were looked after by their lay followers. Dr Girindra Nath Das, *Bangla Pir-Sahityer Katha*, Barasat, 24 Parganas, 1383 [1976], pp. 112, 201.

both the Anjumane Ulema-i-Bangla and its Jamaite counterpart had operated with such institutions, in order to both justify their use of public subscriptions as well as demonstrate the accountability of those institutions to all strands of Islamic thought, since their avowed aim was to unite all schools of Ulemas without creating an order of domination for any. To a heterogeneous lot such as the followers of the Fakir, both the imperative of accountability of different persuasions as well as financial responsibility (Rs 3000 was collected on the first day after the burial) were important. But, given the public character of the space in which the Fakir was buried, it was also imperative to acquire authoritative public legitimation. And this additional need could be fulfilled by the idea of a Committee, for it allowed the incorporation of persons who were vested with public authority. The Mazaar Committee included three important members of the new Corporation.[27]

Of course, the whole venture rested on the confidence of the shopkeepers to accomplish what they interpreted as the Fakir's last wish. In turn, this depended a great deal and was in fact determined by, the change wrought by the N/K on the character of the Corporation. After the N/K, the popular significance of the Corporation was seen to lie in providing a hopeful microcosm, or rather, a local test case, for self-governance. Consequently, the Corporation exceeded its constitutional brief, which made it accountable only to its rate payers.[28] In the reception given to him and Lajpat Rai by the Corporation in 1925, Madan Mohan Malaviya proclaimed that, 'The work of Self-Government of the Empire will be judged by the work of the Self-Government in this city, in the most important city of the Indian Empire and the measure of unity and harmony that prevails in the administration of the Corporation of Calcutta...'[29] Since Swaraj was promised as a future state of governance by the people of the country, it followed that the Corporation could become a site of lobbying for

[27] Suhrawardy was made President, while out of the three Vice Presidents, two, Shamsul Huq and Abdur Rauff were well-known Councillors. FK p. 15.

[28] In the March 1924 elections, held under the new Act, there were a mere 70,523 eligible voters. The total number of votes cast, amounted to 49.6 per cent of the electorate. *Report on the Administration of Bengal, 1925–1928*, Calcutta, 1927, p. 50.

[29] *Amrita Bazar Patrika*, 17 April 1925.

those not otherwise enfranchised to vote for it. As a matter of fact, when the Corporation met for the first time to debate the issue, the number of Councillors was heavily outnumbered by the followers of the Fakir who crowded the halls and passages of the building.[30] It was as a consequence of this mass pressure that the attendance of Councillors suddenly went up.

What we have here, in the conjoining of sacred and public authorities and spaces, is an extension of the notion of the public itself. It is true, of course, that the idea of a religious public, whether Hindu or Muslim, was already extant in the nineteenth century, but it had then pertained to the sphere of personal laws alone. And these were premised on a segregation of religious communities. 'Public' in these cases did not operate as a general notion, applicable to all collective identities. The New Market burial posed a different case. For what was involved here was a common space governed by general Municipal laws and procedures, and underwrit by a popular representation that expressed the heritage of a joint struggle. In other words, there was a real opportunity here for the notion of a common public to be consolidated, or conversely, imploded at the point of its realization.

At the moment of its conception in the Fakir's burial, the particularism of the 'Islamic' component did not create a problem. The Swarajya Party was premised on a federation of Hindu and Muslim collectivities, which rested on the Bengal Pact. Passed in December 1923, the main feature of this agreement was the promise of a majority share of jobs to Muslims after the attainment of Swaraj.[31] Consequently, the nature of the legitimation the Swarajists extended in this case, ensured that 'Islam' did not invoke an exclusivist identity. On the contrary, there was a celebration of a joint effort. The very process of negotiations became emblematic of governance by communal unity, for the final consent came from none other than the new darling of the bhadralok, Subhash Bose, who, further, proceeded on the advice of Fazlul Huq, the chief Muslim antagonist of the Swarajists. Further, the sense of

[30] *The Forward*, 24 October 1924.

[31] Its other provisions included the a promise of a larger share of appointments of Muslims to the Corporation, as well as the voluntary banning of the playing of music before mosques and the freedom to perform *korbani*.

unity was consolidated by the newspapers which initially dwelt on the syncretic implications of the Fakir. *The Forward*, which was the Swarajist newspaper, proclaimed explicitly: 'All—whatever it was, men respected him, and claimed by Moslem, Hindu and Christian, he becomes a symbol of unity, which his grave in the market will emphasise.'[32] The *Dainik Basumati*, a leading vernacular newspaper that was also in the forefront of the Hindu communal challenge, approvingly dwelt on the notion of renunciation as embodied in the Fakir, no doubt to appeal to the proclivities of its Hindu readers.[33] Even the initial report in *The Statesman*, written possibly by a junior reporter, referred to the huge numbers of Hindu women who came to visit the shrine.[34]

It was at this moment however, that the apparent city-wide consensus was broken. And this resulted in a sharply communalized notion of a common public space.

II

On 16 October 1924, together with the largely favourable report in *The Statesman*, appeared another item which reported the objections to the Fakir's burial by Col. Crawford, Secretary of the European Association. He seems to have represented powerful interests, since the very next day the lead editorial in the same newspaper criticized the burial. A week later the campaign was joined in the Corporation by the European councillors spearheaded by D. J. Cohen.[35] The main grounds for their objections revolved on the question of hygiene. It was argued that the burial

[32] 17 October 1924.

[33] 31 Ashwin, 1331 [1924]. Cited in FK, p. 4.

[34] 16 October 1924. The deep sympathy with which the reporter witnessed the proceedings is palpable in his following description: 'For over fifteen years Data Sabib sat in the passage, a lonely figure speaking to no one and begging from none', his 'few wants' being supplied by Muslim tradesmen. The report concluded: 'All day yesterday there was a never ceasing flow of visitors to the scene, the crowd completely blocking the lane [which bordered the market, called Kora Bardar Lane] as well as the passage.'

[35] *The Forward*, 24 October 1924, reported that D. J. Cohen had moved a resolution in the Council, wanting the body to be exhumed. He was supported by Campbell Forrester, who demanded an immediate discussion on the Cohen resolution.

of the Fakir near food stalls would pose a health hazard.[36] Their appeal was well-grounded, since the New Market had been founded on that basis. It was established as the first municipal market in the city, on the recommendations of a Fever Hospital Committee which had been perturbed by the dangers of epidemics posed by existing, privately owned, markets, which were considered too dirty and unsafe.[37]

The European campaign stood out as an exemplary intervention in the public sphere, being carried out in newspapers and consolidated in the appropriate public body. Further, the grounds of their appeal, that is of sanitation and hygiene, were themselves of fundamental public importance. It has been shown in other contexts, that these notions were ideologically loaded. But what ought to be stressed here is that they belonged to an order of ideological forms, which were generalized by demonstrating striking practical effects: for instance, it was no coincidence that the European monopoly over sanitation had some relationship with the fact that an immensely larger number of persons died from cholera in the overcrowded and badly serviced, native quarters.[38] Consequently the debate over sanitation normally took the form of unequal access to it, which obviously reinforced its position as

[36] According to Cotton, there was 'an old bazar called Fenwick's Bazar, with... filthy lanes and bustee surroundings' which the New Market was made to replace. H. E. A. Cotton, *Calcutta Old and New*, Calcutta, 1907, p. 948. Two other important markets, both privately owned, were the Tiretta Bazar and the Dharamtolla Bazar. The latter which was located at the corner of Dharamtolla and Chowringhee, offered stiff competition, and the new market did not prosper till the latter was bought up and dismantled. Ibid.

[37] S. Sammadar, *Calcutta Is*, Calcutta, 1978, p. 43. The market consisted of an enclosed space with shops and stalls located in regular intervals. Newell writes with the satisfaction of a schoolmaster on holiday: 'The many stalls are well arranged in neat rows and contain everything from a shaving brush to a costly Persian carpet,' *Calcutta*, p. 255. It suggests a design for facilitating attentive inspection by the administration.

[38] Amiya Bagchi provides eloquent testimony from an earlier period. Out of 697 deaths that occurred from cholera during the fourth quarter of 1882, 540 occurred in wards located in the north of the town, where the native concentrations were most evident, as against 157 in the nine southern wards, while only two deaths had occurred in the Park Street and four in the Waterloo wards. 'Wealth and Work in Calcutta, 1860–1920', *Calcutta: The Living City vol. 1, The Past*, Sukanta Chaudhuri (ed.) Delhi, 1990, p. 214.

a public question of general concern. The fact that the shopkeepers asked for permission from the Corporation, indicates that they were cognizant of the general framework in which the market operated.

Yet sanitation failed to provide a common ground for discussion. In retrospect this may not be surprising, for the invocation of sanitation in this context was employed in a transparently *mala fide* and exclusively ideological manner. The sheer facts of the question militated against its acceptance. In its very first editorial on the subject, *The Statesman* declared that the burial did not constitute a danger to hygiene, since the burial spot was located twenty feet from the nearest food stalls. Later it did a complete turnabout on the same issue.[39] On the other hand, what was clear was the racist character of European objections in the Letters to the Editor column—many of which I have already referred to above—that articulated a profound fear of the breakdown of their segregated lives.[40] More than anything else, what became apparent was the political character of the European objections. That the Fakir's burial raised terrible anxieties about governance was explicitly referred to by *The Statesman*, when it criticized the Corporation's consent to the burial on the grounds that it was 'undoubtedly a legacy from the disastrous policy of the Nonco-operation movement'.[41] What was being implied here, was the new responsiveness of the Corporation to the mass constituency of nationalists. By the time it had mutated into a Hindu–Muslim issue. *The Statesman* provided an even more frank articulation of the political implications of the European position, when it stated

[39] By August of the following year its normal stateliness of tone had been replaced by ranting against the Swarajists as 'sham and imposture'. It exclaimed, 'If a popularly elected Corporation was to survive in Calcutta it was bound to meet the challenge at once to *public health*, to common decency and to its own rights given by the burial of the pir in the principal food market of the city' [italics added]. 16 August 1925.

[40] It is not surprising that *The Statesman* was flooded with letters immediately after the event, that were probably so racist that they could not be published. The editorial politely mentions that they were too 'angry' to be published, but makes their import clear, when it carries on to advise the Europeans that it 'would be indecorous to treat the question on racial lines...' 17 October 1924.

[41] Ibid.

that the controversy had demonstrated the untenability of Hindu–Muslim unity itself.[42]

As I have stated, it was ultimately the Hindu councillors who attracted the ire of the Fakir's followers. No doubt this was occasioned by a displacement of the resentment of Europeans. But this transference was itself determined by the significance of the support that Hindu councillors extended to their European counterparts. There would, of course, be a sense of betrayal on the procedural level. After all the only European involved in the action had made his position clear at the outset; European opposition could be easily seen as part of their long saga of antagonism to Islam. On the other hand, it was Subhash Bose, the bhadralok Swarajist, who had given his consent. This was the backdrop to the spectacle of collaboration of some Hindu councillors with Europeans, that confronted the crowds assembled to witness the Corporation debate. Cohen's resolution was seconded by B. C. Das on that day, while the other Hindu councillors remained silent. In the following months the same pattern continued, except that the other Hindu councillors joined Das to make their objections public. Unfortunately this group included important Swarajist members, such as Sarat Chandra Bose, the brother of Subhash Bose.

Possibly the most alienating aspect for the Fakir's followers was the humour they occasioned. The tone was set by *The Statesman* in its first editorial on the subject. After patronizingly suggesting that their readers ought to understand the psyche of the 'ignorant' masses, it could not resist ridiculing their beliefs: 'It appears that this remarkable man was really a Madrassi Christian, and acquired a thoroughly deserved reputation for wisdom for not uttering a word for 15 years...'[43] Such *bon mots* flourished publicly, but what was less forgivable was when Hindu Councillors also started guffawing. Thus C. C. Biswas in February 1927 stated that if the CEO did not implement the resolution on exhumation, it would prove the truth of the definition of sainthood which he proceeded to recite: 'One whose breath\ The air doth taint\ Before his death\

[42] Its motivations in this respect was stated with child-like innocence: stating that it was useless for the Swarajists to blame Muslims, it elaborated, 'It [the burial controversy] blows away pretence and lays bare reality. The Hindu–Muslim Pact was an unnatural bond...' 16 August 1925.

[43] Ibid.

A bundle of bones\ That fools adore\ When life is o'er.'[44] There was not only irresponsibility involved in these forays into jocularity but it was also a flaunting of the limits of their representativeness, indicating the fact that they did not see themselves as accountable to the Muslim part of their constituency. In other words, their actions proved their complicity with the philosophy of reserved constituencies which underpinned the Corporation elections, and to which many of those struck with hilarity were bitterly opposed.

It should be recalled that what was at stake was not only the functioning of the Corporation, but the whole heritage of the N/K movement which had given this institution its new symbolic charge. The sense of betrayal would then involve more than a disenchantment with Corporation procedures as such. It would indict a large and intense commitment to the ideal of joint governance. But this took a little time to happen, for till the death of C. R. Das, it was still possible to disaggregate the responses of Hindus and not see them as monolithic. But Hindu communalism was growing in terms of ideas, dispositions and organization, its energies deriving from a growing paranoia in the Hindu middle class about the provisions of the Bengal Pact. It had been Das' personal charisma, skills and non-communal reputation, that had prevented a wholesale attack on the Pact. His death signalled a reversal of the situation. And in this new context, the burial of the Fakir became a way of contributing to the general communal unease that was undermining the fundamental premise of mutual trust that underlay the Bengal Pact. Thus five months after the death of Das, *The Forward* reversed its position dramatically. After the decision to give two months notice for the exhumation was passed in the Corporation, it unashamedly editorialized:

> Having regard to this fact [that the Fakir was Christian] as also to the admission by some of them that the burial of the 'Pir' was an encroachment on the rights of the Corporation, the Mohamedans of Calcutta ought not to raise their voice of dissent against the decision of the Corporation. They have fought and lost. Their defeat ought not to leave any sore behind.[45]

This prepared the way for even more direct communalization of the issue. When the question was raised after the murder of Swami

[44] *The Forward*, 10 February 1927.
[45] 18 August 1925.

Shraddhanand in 1927, it was clear that even the discourse of civic rights was being left behind. During the course of the debate as to whether the Corporation should acknowledge Swami Shraddhand's demise as a national loss, B. K. Bose intervened to insist on the burial issue being taken up as a retaliation against certain remarks made against the dead leader.

The removal of the presence of Das, who, more than anything else symbolized the belief in a communally federated polity, encouraged the intervention of leaders like Pir Abu Bakr, who, after the N/K, had turned to an uncompromising anti-Hindu and loyalist line. His presence marked the turn to a campaign for the burial under the banner of an Islamic identity, which was premised on antagonism to the Hindu. In October 1925, about four months after the death of Das, he issued a letter together with the old Khilafatist Abdur Rauf, in which he stated that without Das' leadership, it was useless to expect anything from the Swarajists; the letter then went on to invoke the 'sentiments of the people', declaring that if they were violated, then 'it is feared that it will no longer be possible to keep under control the already excited mob, and the consequence would be... sure bloodshed amongst the Muslims'.[46]

What helped Bakr in giving a communal turn to the movement was that his predilections were not irrelevant to the needs of Peshawaris and the butchers. For the former, the Islamic identity offered a sanctuary, since they were increasingly becoming targets of rioting. An anti-Sikh riot participated in mainly by Muslims during June 1924, had included Peshawaris amongst their targets[47]—a fact which may not be unconnected to the fearsome reputation they enjoyed as moneylenders among the urban poor and workers.[48] The butchers, on the other hand, faced another kind of isolation. They were steadily targeted by Hindu communalists for their association with the slaughter of cows; a Janmashtami resolution of 1925 circulated by the Hindu Mahasabha for instance,

[46] *Amrita Bazar Patrika*, 3 October 1925.

[47] Commissioner of Police Report to Chief Secretary, Bengal, on rioting against Sikhs. File No. 243/1924 NAI.

[48] Although a major exception ought to be mentioned here, which is the story called 'Kabuliwala', by Rabindranath Tagore. Interestingly, the plot revolves around the friendship between an itinerant pathan trader and a Bengali Hindu child. The importance of this plot as an intervention can be appreciated (despite the fact that it was written in the last decade of the nineteenth century), when we take into account the fact that the 1924 riots

recommended an economic boycott of butchers.[49] This was complemented by producing a stereotype of them as the most dangerous and fanatical elements amongst an already bigoted religious community. The aggressive communalization of the Fakir's followers, quite logically produced threats of counter violence amongst the more communally oriented Hindu newspapers like the *Basumati* and the *Vishwamitra*. Although the only bloodshed on this issue was thankfully confined to words, the stage had been set for the mass riots of April 1926 and the gory battles in public space.

The failure of the new public arena to resolve the controversy or, at least, confine it to a public debate, obviously indicated fundamental vulnerabilities in its constitution. Admittedly, it had to take on many burdens: the attempted consolidation of a common public sphere coincided with its taking on the burden of mass involvement, with its attendant interests, intensities and complications. Unfortunately, this large sphere of activity that the new public sphere was burdened with, had to perforce locate its main source of sustenance in the heritage of a mass movement, which, in its wake, expressed itself in the Swarajist party. In other words, the new mass common, public sphere was founded on a political bloc. This did not mean that it was fated to be doomed. As a matter of fact, there were valuable initiatives and essays in mutual functioning. But too much was left to the contingencies of the political process and the play of social interests, for this new public to come into its own. Unfortunately, the most important consequence of the controversy over the burial of the Fakir, was that it underlined the inability of the new common public sphere to acquire a relatively self-sustaining autonomy.

---

took place because of a rumour that children were being abducted and sacrificed by particular communities. Obviously the Pathans qualified for this violent distinction in popular stereotypes.

[49] The actual resolution read: 'They [the Hindus] should also take a vow on the day to stop all monetary dealings with men who kill cows,' *Amrita Bazar Patrika*, 4 August 1925. An impelling factor behind the order of the Calcutta Corporation asking butchers to put up screens in front of their shops, can be seen to lie in the fact that the riots which took place over *go-korbani*, were sparked off by whether the sacrifice had been *visible* to the Hindus. A meeting of Muslim rate payers held under the auspices of Central Mahomedan Rate Payers Association condemned this order as being 'unnecessarily expensive', *The Mussalman*, 5 December 1924.

12

'Nation' from Its Margins: Notes on E. V. Ramaswamy's 'Impossible' Nation*

M. S. S. Pandian

'...the truths of a nation are in the first place its realities'.[1]

'History teaches us clearly that the battle against colonialism does not run straight away along the lines of nationalism'.[2]

It is now part of the academic common sense that nations are narrativized as 'authentic' and 'legitimate' through specific modes of history writing. These national historical narratives selectively invent, erase and usurp distant pasts as their own. Benedict Anderson, for instance, in claiming nation as an 'imagined community', notes, 'If nation-states are widely conceded to be 'new' and 'historical', the nations to which they give political expression always loom out of an immemorial past...' and 'that image of antiquity' is 'central to the subjective idea of the nation'.[3]

* This is a modified and expanded version of a paper earlier published in *Economic and Political Weekly,* 16 October 1993. I am grateful to Anandhi S., J. Jeyaranjan, Padmini Swaminathan and A. R. Venkatachalapathy for their comments on an earlier draft.

[1] Frantz Fanon, *The Wretched of the Earth*, Middlesex, 1995, p. 181.

[2] Ibid., p. 199.

[3] Benedict Anderson, *Imagined Communities: Reflections on the Origin and Spread of Nationalism*, Verso, London, 1983, pp. 19, 47.

Such narrativization of nation constitutes the national subjects as inheritors of a common past, an inheritance which foregrounds their sameness and inscribes them as homogenous national subjects. This sameness of the national subjects in the narratives of the nation is often marked by privileging a single subject position (in the case of India, the upper-caste Hindu male) as the essence of the national. This character of the national identity implicitly inferiorizes other subject positions within the nation-space; and when these subject positions are enunciated in opposition to what is privileged, they are delegitimized, at varying degrees, as the Other of the nation. For this reason, one needs to engage with the 'ambivalent margins of the nation-space'. As Homi Bhabha puts it, 'To reveal such a margin is, in the first instance, to contest claims to cultural supremacy, whether these are made from the "old" post-imperialist metropolitan nations, or on behalf of the "new" independent nations of the periphery.'[4] What is more, '...the ambivalent, antagonistic perspective of nation as narration will establish the cultural boundaries of the nation so that they may be acknowledged as "containing" thresholds of meaning that must be crossed, erased, and translated in the process of cultural production.'

As part of this concern, the present paper attempts to recover the concept of 'nation' propagated by E. V. Ramaswamy, who occupied, in more than one sense, 'the ambivalent margins of the nation-space' and perennially carried the appellation of an anti-national. Freed from the mainstream nationalist binary of nationalism versus colonialism, anchored in history and rationality as progress, troubled all the time about notions of citizenship, E. V. Ramaswamy's concept of nation denied its origin in an invented 'classical' Indian/Tamil past and envisaged it fully in the anticipatory. More importantly, it constantly violated any certitude about boundaries, identities and political agency; and also presented itself as not constrained by the rigid territoriality of the nation-space.

In tracing the contours of E. V. Ramaswamy's 'nation', my attempt is not only to explore the relationship between the nation and its past(s), but also to recover one of the marginalized discourses on the nation, which has been fossilized in the Indian

[4] Homi K. Bhabha, 'Introduction: Narrating the Nation' in Homi K. Bhabha (ed.) *Nation and Narration,* London and New York, 1990, p. 4.

nationalist historiography as belonging to the Other of the national. Such attempts at 'recovering' and elaborating alternate concepts of nation seem pertinent and urgent as the official 'nation' has become one of the most important source of legitimacy for varied forms of violence in India as elsewhere.

I

E. V. Ramaswamy's sojourn in the Indian National Congress was brief, a mere five years in an active political career spanning over half a century.[5] Joining the organization in 1920, during its non-cooperation phase, he not only spent considerable time, energy and money for such nationalist causes as 'khadder' and temperance, but also engaged himself spiritedly in taking up a series of issues which had a direct bearing on the question of citizenship in the nation-in-the-making: he obdurately staged 'satyagrahas' in front of the Mahadevar temple in Vaikkom, seeking rights for the lower castes to enter the temple streets, which earned him two jail terms and the honorific *Vaikkom Veerar* ('Hero of Vaikkom'); opposed bitterly the practice of having separate dining arrangements for brahmin and non-brahmin students in Shermadevi Gurukulam, a 'national' school funded partly by the Tamil Nadu Congress Committee and run by a former 'revolutionary terrorist' V. V. S. Iyer with the objective of imparting 'high ideals of national education'; and repeatedly argued for 'communal representation' or what has come to be named now 'reservations') for the non-brahmins in public services and representative bodies such as the legislature—a demand which was read by the mainstream nationalists as 'detrimental to national unity' and hence opposed. These moves by E. V. Ramaswamy within the Congress refused the possibility of national subjects being constituted within the delimiting binary of nationalism versus colonialism or through the mere process of Othering the colonizers. Instead, his attempt was to stage a contestatory dialogue among different subject positions (a

[5] For details of E. V. Ramaswamy's role in the Indian National Congress, see Eugene F. Irschick, *Politics and Social Conflict in South India: The Non-Brahmin Movement and Tamil Separatism, 1916–26*, Berkeley and Los Angeles, 1969, pp. 268–74; Nambi Arooran, *Tamil Renaissance and Dravidian Nationalism 1905–44*, Madurai, 1980, pp. 152–9; and E. Sa Visswanathan, *Political Career of E. V. Ramaswamy Naicker*, Madras, 1983, pp. 38–65.

point I shall elaborate later), already inscribed by power and powerlessness, within the nation-space. In other words, for him, the community of national subjects could not be a non-negotiated given from above, but had to be negotiated from below.

Given the totalizing desire of mainstream Indian nationalism, E. V. Ramaswamy's alternate nation-making agenda did not evoke the kind of response he had hoped for from the Tamil Nadu Congress, the leadership of which was dominated by brahmin élite. After a series of experiments within the Congress, which may be termed as experiments on the question of citizenship in the nation, he finally broke ranks with the organization in November 1925, when two of his resolutions favouring 'communal representation' were disallowed in the Kancheepuram conference of the Tamil Nadu Congress. Thereafter he declared his political credo to be 'no god, no religion, no Gandhi, no Congress, and no brahmins'.[6]

E. V. Ramaswamy's doubts about the place of subordinate social groups in the Congressite nation were strengthened by M. K. Gandhi's utterances in Tamil Nadu during 1927. In the highly charged Tamil political environment, Gandhi not only said, 'Varnashrama Dharma is not an unmitigated evil but it is one of the foundations on which Hinduism is built [and] defines man's mission on earth', but also described the brahmins as the 'finest flower of Hinduism and humanity'.[7] He added: 'I will do nothing to wither it. I know that it is well able to take care of itself. It has weathered many a storm before now. Only let it not be said of non-brahmans that they attempted to rob the flower of its fragrance and lustre...'[8] In privileging the brahmin as the national ideal, Gandhi, through a hierarchical placement, constituted the rest and their claim to the nation-space as incomplete and lacking.

E. V. Ramaswamy's political career then onwards was more or less an unwavering journey through the Self Respect Movement (founded in 1926) and the Dravidar Kazhagam (founded in 1944) in search of substantive, as opposed to formal, citizenship for the

[6] *Kudi Arasu*, 2 May 1925; see also *Puratchi*, 24 December 1933.

[7] Irschick, *Politics and Social Conflict*, pp. 337–8.

[8] Saroja Sundararajan, *S. Sathyamurthy: A Political Biography*, New Delhi, 1983, p. 457. See Bhikhu Parekh, *Colonialism, Tradition and Reform: An Analysis of Gandhi's Political Discourse*, New Delhi, 1989 for Gandhi's attempts to solve the question of varna on a moral plane—by idealizing hierarchies as differences—rather than on a political plane.

subordinate groups, a search which increasingly alienated him from the dominant binary of the times, and brought him to position himself at the margins of the nation-space and to interrogate totalizing constructions of nation by mainstream nationalists. Here, one needs to account for his simultaneous critique of the nationalist concept of *swaraj* (or self-rule) and the British raj.

At one level, he viewed the nationalist demand for *swaraj* as a conspiracy by local élites (who, for him, were the brahmins as opposed to the sudras, the Marwaris as opposed to the Tamils, men as opposed to women... depending on differing relational contexts) to hegemonize the subordinate social groups, and as a process which would eventually affirm rather than erase their unequal status within the nation-space. At another level, he viewed it as an impossible political project given the innumerable crisscrossing of hierarchies and relations of authority and subordination. Writing in 1928 about the condition of untouchables and women, he noted:

> [We] have been telling that unless the above two oppressions [i.e. of untouchables and women] are destroyed, asking for freedom to India, or claiming that Indians themselves will take care of India's administration and security, or telling that India does not need even a little association with outsiders... is utterly foolish or dishonesty involving selfish conspiracy...
>
> ... we are keeping sections of our people enslaved, oppressed and degraded—without thinking that they are of our society, our brothers; without any compassion; without giving them the freedom we so desire; without thinking that they are human beings. So handing over the welfare and freedom of these oppressed people to us is nothing other than handing over sheep to a butcher...[9]

In 1948, his dream of a separate Dravida Nadu already in shambles, he queried, 'Is the brahmin's rule swarajya for the Parayan [untouchable]? Is the cat's rule swarajya for the rat? [Is] the landlord's rule [swarajya] for the peasant? Is property owner's rule swarajya for the worker?...'[10] He argued that India was not a nation but a mere museum of castes, religions, languages and gods.[11]

Thus, simultaneously setting at play different subject positions within the nation-space, E. V. Ramaswamy freed the meaning of

[9] E. V. Ramaswamy Periyar, *Penn Yean Adimaiyaanaal*, (in Tamil), Madras, 1984, p. 71

[10] *Viduthalai*, 19 January 1948, in V. Aanaimuthu, *Periyar Ee Ve Ra Sinthanaikal*, vol. II, (in Tamil), Tiruchirapalli, p. 673.

[11] *Kudi Arasu*, 1 June 1930, in Aanaimuthu, *Periyar*, vol. II, p. 649.

swaraj from its disabling nationalist connotation and reconstituted it as a site of multiple contestations. In other words, the end of colonial rule in itself was emptied of its ability to signify the arrival of the nation—if at all nation could have a moment of arrival, it would be an embattled process of many fronts. For instance, referring to the position of Indian women—an issue which engaged him all through his political career[12]—he interpreted their freedom and equality as real *swaraj:*

> The concept of husband-wife relationship has been one of master-slave relationship. The essential philosophy of marriage has been to insist on women's slavery... Until women are liberated from such marriages and from men, our nation cannot attain freedom.[13]

He treated this lack of equality for women within the nation-space as a proof of Indians not having the 'spirit of freedom' and they being 'children of slaves'.[14] Thus, 1947 did not signal the nation for him and he declared August 15 as a day of mourning.

Let us now turn to how E. V. Ramaswamy made sense of the British raj. He, as a Congressman 'fanatically' committed to Gandhi, condemned the raj unequivocally: 'The Britishers love to repeat that we Indians are brutes. May be you are and I am too. And it is up to us to demonstrate to them that we are brutish enough to drive them out to wrest our national freedom'.[15] Following his disenchantment with the Congress, he re-evaluated

[12] An obituary of E. V. Ramaswamy published in the *Economic and Political Weekly* (12 January 1974) summed up his involvement with women's issues thus: 'He championed the cause of widow remarriage, of marriage based on consent, and of women's right to divorce and abortion. Pointing out that there was no Tamil word for the counterpart of an adulteress, he fumed, "...the word adulteress implies man's conception of woman as a slave, a commodity to be sold and hired"'. Periyar's demand at a conference two years ago that no odium should be attached to a women who desired a man other than her husband (which the press so avidly vulgarized), as well as Periyar's advocacy of the abolition of marriage as the only way of freeing woman from enslavement, were about as radical as the views of any women liberationist.' For a detailed account of E. V. Ramaswamy's position on gender inequality, see S. Anandhi, 'Women's Question in the Dravidian Movement,1925–48', *Social Scientist*, May–June 1991.

[13] *Viduthalai*, 11 October 1948.

[14] Periyar, *Penn Yean*, p. 73.

[15] Visswanathan, *Naicker*, p.38.

his stance on the raj and found several things of the raj worthy of critical appropriation. He argued, 'The "Hindu India" which believed that people should abide by the authority of the king and the king is the god was taught only by the "English India", that the king should abide by the people and the king is the servant of the people.'[16] According to him,

> *Though we have lost much from being the slaves of the British*, we have profited at least a little and understood ourselves as human beings. If we had remained the slaves of north Indians, we would have remained 'sudran', 'rakshashan', 'chandalan', 'asuran', 'kundakan', 'kolakan', 'pratilokan', 'narakan'...[17]

He, time and again, claimed that substituting the British rule with *swaraj* of mainstream nationalist would be equivalent to the 'suicide of the common people'—unless one could be sure of a new rule based not on *Manu Dharma*, *Varnashrama Dharma* and brahmin hegemony, that is, institutions which, according to him, legitimized inequality across castes, gender and forms of labour, and thus invalidated the possibility of a nation-community.[18]

However, E. V. Ramaswamy's approval of the raj was not unqualified and was often only a grudging approval. He claimed that the British, unlike in their own nation, did not attempt sufficiently to establish a full-fledged rule of *Manithda* (Human) *Dharma* in India, but also followed *Manu Dharma* in large measure. He offered two sets of reasons for such differential politics practised by the British, one in their own nation and the other in the colony.

According to him, the first set of reasons which disabled the British raj from going all the way in affirming *Manitha Dharma* in the colony could be located in the resistance to such *dharma* by the Indian national élites themselves. He repeatedly cited instances of sustained Indian opposition to such initiatives as the Devadasi Abolition Act, the Child Marriage Restraint Act and the Hindu Religious Endowment Act, which were represented by the nationalists as the excesses of the British rule. We may bear in mind here that such nationalist opposition to 'social legislations' was

[16] Speech in Kollampalayam on 19 September 1937, in Aanaimuthu, *Periyar*, vol. II, p. 682.

[17] *Kudi Arasu*, 25 November 1944, in Aanaimuthu, *Periyar*, vol. II, p. 703. (Emphasis mine).

[18] *Kudi Arasu*, 17 May 1931, in Aanaimuthy, *Periyar*, vol. II, p. 777.

rather intense in the Tamil speaking areas. For instance, the Congress leader S. Sathyamurthy threatened 'to perform his little daughter's marriage in defiance of the Sarada Act'; condemned the Hindu Religious Endowment Act as British interference in religious affairs; portrayed devadasis as retainers of national art and culture and said that each of them should dedicate at least one girl to be a future devadasi; and opposed temple entry by the Adi-Dravidas/untouchables.[19] E. V. Ramaswamy reminded the nationalists that it was due to the efforts of '*sarkar dasas*' and 'traitors of the nation' and 'the [British] government' that these acts were passed.[20] The other event which he used as an illustration of native élites' opposition to the efforts of the raj to establish a rule of equality was that of 1857. He argued that '...there [was] no scope to treat the events of 1857 as the first event of national freedom struggle. [It was] an attempt to protect Vedic ideas, obscurantism and religion',[21] and congratulated the British for suppressing it.[22] He viewed the sepoys who participated in the events of 1857 as being used by conservative Indian élites to regain power.

While the first set of reasons offered by E. V. Ramaswamy for the British reluctance to establish *Manitha Dharma* in India placed the responsibility squarely on the indigenous élites, his other set of reasons implicated both the British and the local élite. Here, he claimed that the British reluctance was a result of their need to have local collaborators so as 'to carry on their rule in this country [India] for ever and to generously loot and transfer the wealth of this country to their own.'[23] In identifying such collaborators as the indigenous élites, he implicated both colonialism and the indigenous élites as upholders of *Manu Dharma* instead of full-fledged *Manitha Dharma*.

For E. V. Ramaswamy, both these sets of reasons were enmeshed and in reality articulating together. Discussing the opposition to the Devadasi Abolition Act, he characterized the symbiotic relationship between the indigenous élite and the British thus:

[19] R. Parthasarathy, *S. Satyamurthy*, Delhi, p. 116; Sundararajan, *S. Sathyamurthy*, pp. 54–5, 136; Anandhi, 'Women's Question', pp. 37–8.

[20] *Kudi Arasu*, 17 May 1931, Aanaimuthu, *Periyar*, vol. II, p. 777.

[21] *Viduthalai*, 15 August 1957, in Aanaimuthu, *Periyar*, vol. II, p. 691.

[22] Ibid., 16 October 1966, p. 846.

[23] *Kudi Arasu*, 17 May 1931, in Aanaimuthu, *Periyar*, vol. II, p. 777.

As the selfish brahmins were helpful and acted as spies [in facilitating] the British rule to arrive and establish itself in our India and in turn it became necessary for the British to follow whatever the brahmin said so as to get their [own] things done.[24]

II

Such foregrounding of different subject positions of the subordinate social groups as the key constitutive process of the nation-community placed E. V. Ramaswamy outside the mainstream Indian nationalism as well as the incomplete modernity of the British in the colonial context. In other words, he was free from the need to set the nation in opposition to the colonizer. From this relatively 'unencumbered' political location, he could view the 'national' past as unmitigated narratives of victimization which prefigured and resulted in current hierarchies of power and powerlessness within the nation-space. Through such a narrative of victimization, at one level, he marked out his discourse on the nation as distinct from the discourse of mainstream nationalism which searched for the 'authentic' national self in a classical Indian past. At another level, his narrative refused to be a mere appropriation of the colonialist construction of the Indian past as uncivilized since he implicated the British as unwilling modernists. In this context, his engagement with the past(s) may be characterized as a project of 'denationalizing' the past in the very name of the nation.

In analysing how E. V. Ramaswamy 'denationalized' the past, we shall first take a look at his construction of the pan-Indian past(s) and then move on to his engagement with the Tamil past(s). The need to analyse his engagement with the Tamil past(s) acquires certain urgency given the widespread academic and popular belief that he uncritically privileged a Tamil past and placed it in opposition to an Indian past.[25]

[24] Ibid., 23 March 1930, in Aanaimuthu, *Periyar*, vol. I, p. 173.

[25] Visswanathan, *Naicker*, p. 75; and C. S. Lakshmi, 'Mother, Mother Community, Mother-Politics in Tamil Nadu', *Economic and Political Weekly*, 20–7 October 1990. For a critique of Lakshmi, see M. S. S. Pandian, S. Anandhi and A. R. Venkatachalapathy, 'Of Moltova Mothers and Other Stories', *Economic and Political Weekly*, 20 April 1991.

E. V. Ramaswamy was critically aware of the mainstream nationalists' use of the so-called classical Indian past in their public discourse as a signifier of the nation.[26] For him, this classical Indian past, which was privileged by the mainstream nationalists, was a continuous and contested story of the hegemony exercised by the inequitous brahminical Hinduism and Varnashrama Dharma. As a recent study sums up, though reductively:

> According to [Ramaswamy] Naicker the brahmans were the descendants of the Aryans who were the first to introduce the status-based caste system. This gave them high ritual status and the power to monopolise all secular and religious knowledge, thereby degrading the native Dravidians to an inferior position. The study of the Vedas, the observance of Vedic rites and the practice of Vedic rituals were the prerogatives of brahmans. Naicker pointed out to the non-brahmans that Manu, the chief brahman law-giver, degraded the bulk of the population to a position of sudras, prevented them from accumulating wealth and advocated that their vocation should be to serve the brahmans. In addition to such prejudicial codes, new rules and regulations were incorporated as and when brahmans found it necessary to prevent other caste groups from challenging their status and privileges. As a result of such sectarian laws, a large segment of non-brahman society was degraded to an inferior position....[27]

Through such reading of the Indian past as a narrative of victimization, he came to treat religious texts such as *Manusmriti*,

[26] For instance, see *Kudi Arasu*, 19 March 1933, in Aanaimuthu, *Periyar*, vol. I, p. 376.

[27] Visswanathan, *Naicker*, p. 75. He characterizes E. V. Ramaswamy's reading of the Indian past as based on 'race theory'. But E. V. Ramaswamy used the words 'Aryan' and 'Dravidian' as denoting differing cultural complexes, the relationship between them being mediated by power and powerlessness. In the words of Ramaswamy himself, 'The Dravidians have a distinct origin in society, their languages are independent and belong to separate classes. The terms 'Aryan' and 'Dravidian' are not my inventions. They are historical realities. They can be found in any schoolboy's textbook. That the Ramayana is an allegoric representation of the invading Aryans and the domiciled Dravidians has been accepted by all historians including Pandit Nehru and all reformers including Swami Vivekananda. My desire is not to perpetuate this difference, but to unite the two opposing elements in society. I am not a believer in the race theory propounded by the late Nazi leader of Germany. None can divide the south Indian people into two races by means of any blood test. It is not only suicidal but most reactionary. But the fundamental difference between two different cultures, Aryan and Dravidian,

Puranas, *Mahabharata* and *Ramayana* as fantastic and crafty instruments invented by the upper castes to perpetuate their hegemony.

If such a history of oppression and inequity could have an uninterrupted career for over thousands of years, it was because the superordinate social groups violently put down any challenge to their hegemony, and when violence failed, they co-opted their opponents. He illustrated his claim with the example of Buddhism and argued that the Buddhists, because of their opposition to the hierarchies legitimized by Hinduism, were 'beaten up, kicked and tortured on stakes' by upper-caste Hindu zealots; and when such violence failed to erase the influence and fame of the Buddha, they incorporated Buddha within Hinduism as the 'tenth incarnation of Maha Vishnu' and Buddhism as a sect, similar to Saivism and Vaishnavism.[28] Likewise, he pointed out, the brahminical Hinduism co-opted those lower-caste opponents who used violence by conferring kshatriya status on them.[29]

These counter-narratives by E. V. Ramaswamy ruptured and rewrote the nationalist construction of the past as a nation-space freed from contestations from within. In other words, past could no longer just resonate with the monological voice of the nation, but had to come to terms with a range of other voices which constantly interrupted the nation's desire to monopolize the past.

Equally significant is the fact that E. V. Ramaswamy did not immobilize these pasts as history, but continually established their connections with the oppressive present. Tracing the link between his readings of the past and the current devaluation of physical labour, for instance, he argued '... you should realise that if all of you are workers, it is because you were all made into sudras according to Varnashrama Dharma of Hindu religion. Let that pass. If workers are thought of as lowly people, it is because they [sudras] were thought of as lowly people in Hindu religious

cannot be refuted by anyone who has closely studied the daily life, habits and customs and literature of these two distinct elements in south India' (*The Hindu*, 26 January 1950). The tendency to attribute 'race theory' to E. V. Ramaswamy lies at least partly in translating the Tamil word 'inam' into English as race. 'Inam' is a dexterous Tamil word which can signify different forms of community.

28 Speech in 1954, in Aanaimuthu, *Periyar*, vol. I, p. 312.

29 *Kudi Arasu*, 15 August 1926, in Aanaimuthu, *Periyar*, vol. I, p. 11.

dharma.'[30] Similarly, referring to the current status of women, he noted:

> What Hindu religion tells about women is that god created women at birth itself as prostitutes; so they should not be allowed to be free at any time; they should be controlled by the father at childhood [and] by their sons during old age...
>
> There is more such evidence in religious shastras. Their intention is nothing other than making women slaves of men.[31]

Thus the past was not at a remove: it was here and now, feeding into the present, legitimizing hierarchies and denying free and equal status to all.

Let us now turn to E. V. Ramaswamy's engagement with the Tamil past. During the course of the anti-Hindi agitation, which opposed the compulsory introduction of Hindi in schools by the Congress government in 1937, E. V. Ramaswamy began airing his demand for a separate Tamil Nadu, which evolved over time into a demand for a separate Dravida Nadu. Till the end of his life, he, more or less steadfastly, denied legitimacy to India as one nation and kept his demand alive.

In this context, he did differentiate the Tamil past as more equitous compared to the pan-Indian past. Basing his arguments on ancient Tamil literary texts, he claimed that both the caste system which degraded the non-brahmins and the current marriage customs which emphasized women's subordination were alien to the Tamil past. What is important here is that he used this difference primarily as a heuristic device to deny legitimacy to the Hindu north India to exercise hegemony over other regions and people who had a better record on matters relating to equality. Beyond that, his position on the Tamil past was not different from that on the Indian past, that is, he 'denationalized' the Tamil past too. Interestingly, even in contexts where he favourably referred to the equitous Tamil past, he simultaneously discounted it and claimed that one would not benefit by harping back to that past.[32]

In 1943, when separate Dravida Nadu was very much on the agenda of E. V. Ramaswamy, he wrote: 'The unnecessary ancient principles of the Tamils...have become useful [only] for deceiving outsiders and plunging [oneself] into foolishness.

[30] *Viduthalai*, 20 January 1948, in Aanaimuthu, *Periyar*, vol. II, 786.

[31] Periyar, *Penn Yean*, pp. 84–5.

[32] For instance, see Aanaimuthu, *Periyar*, vol. I, pp. 23, 215.

It has become a duty of the rationalist that such talk [about ancient Tamil ideas] should not be evoked for any reform from now on.'[33] He proceeded further:

If several of our 'Pundits' do not have rational thinking, it is because of the obscurantism of the ancient Tamil principles. There is nothing at present to be achieved by the talk of ancient Tamils. Therefore it is an important duty of the people not to give any place for [such] fraudulent speech...

A striking illustration of E. V. Ramaswamy's contempt for the Tamil past could be his reaction to the glorification of ancient Tamil women by the women leaders of the anti-Hindi agitation. He intervened to tell them: 'It will be worthwhile if you discuss the present status of women and what can be done about achieving women's liberation, instead of glorifying our grandmothers like Allirani, Kannagi and Madhavi.'[34]

His overarching denouncement of the Tamil past spared neither the classical Tamil literature nor the ancient Tamil rulers: the Cheras, the Cholas and the Pandyas. *Thirukural* and *Silapathikaram*, which along with *Purananuru* constitute the three so-called glorious texts of the Tamils, came in for barbed criticism in the hands of E. V. Ramaswamy—for they, in his opinion, degraded women and denied them equality with men. He characterized *Silapathikaram* as a text 'which began in prostitution, grew in "chastity" and ended up in foolishness and superstition'.[35] We may note here that chastity, for him, signified women's unfreedom. He wrote:

The manner in which women are oppressed in Kovalan Kathai [*Silapathikaram*] is extremely bad...

On the marriage dais itself Kovalan desired a dasi and goes with her. Till Kovalan returns, Kannagi...didn't eat any good food, ate only food without salt and remained worried. Why should one do all these? Imagine a man in the place [of Kannagi]. What would happen? If the wife had left with another man, would the husband eat food without salt? Would he remain worried without any physical comfort till god brought the wife back? in it [*Silapathinkaram*], a separate moral is given for women and [a separate one] for men...[it was] written so badly as to degrade women.[36]

[33] *Kudi Arasu*, 10 January 1943, in Aanaimuthu, *Periyar*, vol. II, pp. 1251–2.

[34] Ibid., 27 November 1938.

[35] Periyar, *Penn Yean*, p. 28.

[36] Periyar, *Suyamariathai Thirumanam Yean*, (in Tamil), Madras, 1986, pp. 13–14.

Similarly, despite his qualified approval of *Thirukural*, he subjected it to severe criticism for emphasizing the subordination of women by glorifying chastity. Referring to the couplet, which claims that a woman who does not worship god but her husband, can command rain at her will, he wrote: 'Would Thiruvalluvar have written these... if he were a woman instead of a man?'[37] He viewed *Kamba Ramayanam* as a text which degraded the Dravidians, and posed to those who defended it on literary merits: 'They say [*Kamba*] *Ramayanam* is a rare literature. What is the use? However starved one is, would one pick up food from shit... How can anyone who desires self-respect read *Ramayanam*?[38]

As much as the Tamil literature of the past, Tamil historical personages such as the Chera, the Chola and the Pandya kings too were scrutinized from the point of whether they upheld or denied equality to their subjects. According to him, the Tamil kings lacked intelligence and self-respect, and, but for them, the Tamils would not have remained the lowest of the castes and as degraded people for the past 2000 to 3000 years. They were unworthy of emulation as they impaled the Buddhists and the Jains on stakes for trying to inculcate better sense among the people, and kept the common people illiterate. He referred to their rules as 'malevolent and barbaric'.[39]

E. V. Ramaswamy reserved the most scathing of his criticisms for the Tamil pundits who constructed and propagated a glorious version of the Tamil past through their readings of classical Tamil literature. He derisively characterized their skills as the mere ability to 'memorize "literature", give several meanings to one word, confuse the people and collect money...' The Tamil pundits, for him, were liars, obscurantists, and lacked powers of reasoning.[40]

The past, thus, was bereft of anything worth appropriating for the national agenda. The nation could arrive only as a break from it.

III

A politically unusable and 'denationalized' past and an inequitous present did not lead E.V. Ramaswamy into a politics of despair.

[37] Periyar, *Penn Yean*, p. 15; see also, Aanaimuthu, *Periyar*, vol. II, pp. 1039, 1229, 1257, 1259–66.

[38] Ibid., 26 January 1936, Aanaimuthu, *Periyar*, vol. II, p. 977.

[39] *Viduthalai*, 16 March 1967, in Aanaimuthu, *Periyar*, vol. II, p. 692.

[40] Ibid., p. 984.

Instead, he located the notion of equal and free citizenship for the oppressed in the anticipatory mode. What needs to be underscored here is that this future was denied the facility of being a recovered past. He framed the journey to this future by appropriating aspects of modernity:[41] rationality and science, history, and human emancipation and progress through struggle.

Though he thought of the past as a continuous story of inequality and unfreedom, he insisted that 'change is inevitable: nobody can stop it'.

> Aryan-Dravidian conflict is a conflict which had been going on since the Puranic age. Though we do not know enough about the Puranic age, [we know that] the Buddhists had struggled to destroy the Aryan culture. Mughals, who had the Islamic culture which was opposed to the Hindu, i.e. Aryan, culture, also tried to destroy Aryanism. But they didn't succeed.
>
> That is why the brahmins ridicule us, 'when they [the Buddhists and the Mughals] could not succeed, how can the Dravidar Kazhagam succeed!' Let them ridicule [us]! We are not bothered!
>
> I strongly believe that our efforts will succeed...Two hundred years to British Rule and 25 years of our rationalist propaganda have reduced the hegemony of Aryan culture.[42]

[41] As the paper proceeds, we shall see that E. V. Ramaswamy's engagement with modernity was rather opposed to the mainstream nationalists' engagement with the same. While the mainstream nationalists, through a discourse of modernity, turned the state into the sole spokesperson for the nation (Partha Chatterjee, *Nationalist Thought and the Colonial World: A Derivative Discourse?*, Zed Books, London, 1986, ch. 5), Ramaswamy's modernity perennially remained contestatory. One may differentiate his version of modernity as 'modernity from below' as opposed to 'modernity from above'. Such distinction seems important as scholars ranging from Ashis Nandy to Dipesh Chakrabarty to Ramachandra Guha, in the Indian context, represent modernity only as an élite agenda, and arrive at conclusions like 'caste is eco-friendly'. Madhav Gadgil, and Ramachandra Guha, *This Fissured Land: An Ecological History of India*, Oxford University Press, Delhi, 1992. In fact, the need for such distinctions about modernity is repeatedly emphasized in the feminist criticism of the current wave of post-modernism (for instance, see Sabina Lovibond, 'Feminism and Postmodernism', *New Left Review*, November–December, 1989; and Alison M. Jaggar, 'Sexual Difference and Sexual Equality in Deborah L. Rhode (ed.) *Theoretical Perspectives on Sexual Difference*, New Haven and London, 1990.

[42] *Viduthalai*, 27 January 1950, in Aanaimuthu, *Periyar*, vol. II, p. 683. See also, Periyar, *Penn Yean*, p. 73.

Similarly, he, in one of his innumerable public speeches, illustrated his faith in history through the changes witnessed by the institution of kingship in India:

> Our kings were venerated as gods; [they were] thought of as the incarnation of gods; [people] did to the king whatever they did to god. But what has happened to all those kings? They were turned into kings who [now] receive their salary from the government.[43]

But such change through history would not take place on its own; it needed self-conscious human intervention, and therefore the victims of the past should become active subjects in the present. Here, E. V. Ramaswamy elaborated and energetically propagated the concept of *Suyamariathai* or self-respect—the foremost thing an active political subject required was the realization of his/her self-worth. In other words, the self-depreciating victim has to shed his/her internalized inferiority—similar to what Fanon would elaborate in the context of Algeria. Here, he treated the emulation of the oppressors as politically misplaced and asked his followers to break away from the values of the élites. He roundly condemned the claim that the Adi Dravidas (the untouchables) would progress if they gave up beef and liquor, and reasoned that it was those who had been eating beef and drinking liquor who were the ones ruling the world.[44] He repeatedly urged the Sudras, the women and the Adi Dravidas to renounce Hinduism which had invested them with inferiorized identities. E. V. Ramaswamy privileged the concept of *Suyamariathai* over everything else. He claimed: 'If we attain self-respect, *swaraj* will arrive within a bat of the eyelid ...' He similarly asserted: 'Self-respect is the only means to attain true *swaraj* [and] that is man's birth right...'.[45]

Extending this concept of self-worth to the sphere of political intervention, he argued that it was the victims of inequity and unfreedom alone, who, through their active intervention in history, could ensure self-emancipation. In contrast to the mainstream nationalist thought, he believed that no one could speak for and represent the victims of the past, but themselves. For instance, he discounted men's participation in the movement for women's freedom and argued that only women, by appropriating political

[43] Ibid., 23 December 1954, Aanaimuthu, *Periyar*, vol. I, p. 337.

[44] *Kudi Arasu*, 25 April 1926, in Aanaimuthu, *Periyar*, vol. I, p. 55.

[45] Periyar, *Thathai Periyar Arivurai–100* (in Tamil), Madras, 1978, p. 13.

agency to themselves, could attain independence and equality: 'Can rats ever get freedom because of cats? [Can] sheep and fowl ever get freedom because of foxes? [Can] Indians' wealth ever increase because of the white men? [Can] non-brahmins ever get equality because of brahmins? ...'.[46] He repeated the same line of argument to different subordinate social groups such as the women, the Sudras, the Adi Dravidas and the workers, whom he continually addressed throughout his life as a political propagandist. Thus, his discourse on the nation proliferated with innumerable oppressors and oppressed, each changing into the other contextually and relationally: a sudra male was the oppressed in relation to the brahmin, but simultaneously he was an oppressor in relation to women.

His critique of the 'politics of representation' and his invocation of the contingent and the relational, thus, in their elaboration, denied the Self a single subject position, but viewed it as distributed across several subject positions. The following quote from Annapurna, one of the women activists of the movement may capture this well:

> Generally our country is colonized by the British; the north Indians have colonized our economy; the brahmins have hegemonised our society; but the most important of all these, men have colonized and oppressed women.[47]

If Annapurna privileged women's oppression over the rest in her political agenda, it is because of her gender location; and in other relational contexts, other oppressions might have got privileged. In short, the struggle for the nation through history was multiple, with porous boundaries, shifting identities and numerous agents of change. Its resolution lay beyond the simple binary of national versus colonial.

In operationalizing his agenda of *self*-representation by the oppressed, he encouraged a range of socio-political organizations outside the Self Respect Movement and the Dravidar Kazhagam, and participated in their activities. While he endorsed what he found as acceptable in these formations, he simultaneously critiqued what was unacceptable for him.[48] In the context of the Adi

[46] Periyar, *Penn Yean*, pp. 83–4.

[47] Ibid., 29 November 1947.

[48] For details of E. V. Ramaswamy's critical involvement in Islamic reform organizations in Tamil Nadu, see J. B. P. More, 'Tamil Muslims and

Dravidas joining the Depressed Classes Federation, he noted, 'You should benefit from its activities. Whether you join the Dravidian Movement or not, you, the comrades from the depressed classes, have the right to enjoy the gains of our work'.[49] Within his own movement, he took care to create separate spaces so that different social groups could articulate themselves. The case of women is instructive in this regard. Not only did the Self Respect Movement organize separate women's conferences, but E. V. Ramaswamy, breaking the culture of silence, insisted that even the most inarticulate women activist should utter a few words in such conferences.[50] The success of the movement in this regard had been summarized by Singaravelu Chettiar thus:

> Women who have been confined to the kitchen are speaking today from public platforms; they are debating about public issues; they are involved in social work as equals of men: the credit for facilitating all these goes to Periyar [E. V. Ramaswamy].

It is rare to find women in other movements who were so skilled in public oratory. During the last fifty years, the Indian National Congress could produce only one Sarojini Naidu.

> ...What an ability women belonging to the Self Respect Movement have in organising their own conferences—independently and with true equality. In other movements, women figure only as an adjunct to men's activities; but in our movement, they function as an independent group and involve in the movement's activities demonstrating equality with men.[51]

As we have seen above, in E. V. Ramaswamy's discourse on the nation, self-respect or the recovery of self-worth was the only means to arrive at the nation. What was the modality for the subordinate social groups to recover their self-worth? He thought that it was reason/rationality/science alone that could restore their self-worth and in turn their political agency: 'Man today does not have self-confidence. He doesn't think that [it is] he [who] conducts

---

Non-Brahmin Atheists, 1925–40', *Contributions to Indian Sociology*, vol. 27, no. 1, 1993.

[49] Aadalarasan Thanjai, *Thanthai Periyarum Thazhthapattoorum* (in Tamil), Madras, 1992.

[50] Anandhi, 'Women's Question', p. 31.

[51] See *Kudi Arasu*, 20 October 1940, cited in Anandhi, 'Women's Question'.

himself. [He] doesn't believe that he is responsible for what he does. He has made a confusion of god, god's commands, god's philosophy, all of which were invented by man himself.' Explaining further, he noted: 'God and fate are the direct enemies of reason. Because, the person who is enslaved by god and fate has nothing for himself. He is a [mere] piece of wood, floating on water.'[52] If E. V. Ramaswamy displaced god with reason and endorsed the dictum 'I think, therefore I am', his 'I' was not an abstract individuated 'I', but one embedded in social collectivities of powerlessness.

In treating reason as *the* referential system, he applied his positivist rationality to religious mythologies, read them literally to show how they were impossible tales of fantasy and craft meant to degrade the sudras, the Adi Dravidas, and women. In 1924 he described the idol at the Vaikkom temple as 'a mere stone fit only to wash dirty linen with'. Such criticism continued all through his career: 'Had it not been for the rationalist urge of the modern days, the milestones on the highways would have been converted into gods. It does not take much time for a Hindu to stand a mortar stone in the house and convert it into a great god by smearing red and yellow powers on it...'[53] For him self-respect and rationality could only go together: 'I have...broken the idols of Pillayar or Vinayakar and burnt pictures of Rama. If in spite of these words and acts of mine, thousands of people throng to my meetings, it only indicates that self-respect and wisdom have dawned on the people'.[54]

E. V. Ramaswamy's rational critique, repeatedly questioned the cultural certitudes of the nation. The best example is his attitude towards language. In his opinion, for a language to be acceptable to the nation, it has to be accessible to rational thought, and has to enunciate equality and freedom. His attack on Hindi was premised on the argument that it would help people only to read such irrational texts as Tulsi Ramayana and Puranas, and contained nothing rational: 'Hindi can help only in reaching the heaven; but heaven itself will disappear soon.'[55] On the basis of his understanding language as a social construct, he came to the conclusion that

[52] Ibid., 25 May 1935, in Aanaimuthu, *Periyar*, vol. II, p. 1117.
[53] Aanaimuthu, *Periyar*, vol. I, p. xxix. English translation in the original.
[54] Ibid., p. xxviii.
[55] Speech on 19 September 1937, in Aanaimuthu, *Periyar*, vol. II, p. 655.

Tamil was better; yet it was greatly lacking. He criticized it for, among other things, being derogatory to women, not having words for the male counterpart of adulteress and widow. And he invented the neologism 'vidavan' for widower and 'vibacharan' for those men who went to prostitutes.[56] He argued: 'If Tamil has to progress and join the ranks of the world languages, Tamil and religion should be separated.'[57] In public he often stated that English was better than Tamil. If Anderson wrote, 'What the eye is to the lover—that particular, ordinary eye he or she is born with—language—whatever language history has made his or her mother tongue—is to the patriot',[58] it was a different story in the case of E. V. Ramaswamy. In his view the mother tongue was not a language that a person was born with, but a language that was 'rational'. The mother tongue he endorsed was not historically determined.

Equally important is his view that the teleology of rationality is interminable, continuously invalidating the past, and disclosing newer avenues of freedom all through. He told his followers that the march of rationality would invalidate his own legacy.

> What is known as rationality will keep changing. What we think today as fit for reason, may be rejected tomorrow as superstition. We ourselves will reject several things—even the sayings of those who are praised as great men. Similarly, the future generation may at a time say about me, 'There was a [man] of irrational thinking called Ramaswamy.' That is natural; a sign of change; a sign of the times.[59]

Thus the course of rationality, for E. V. Ramaswamy, is such that it does not offer a fixed goal, a fixed utopia—the search for freedom can only be an ever-continuing endless search.

IV

Let us now turn to the implication of E. V. Ramaswamy's concepts of history and rationality for the career of the nation, for these were the concepts which framed the nation's course. The interminable teleology of rationality which constantly invalidated cultural

[56] Anandhi, 'Women's Question', p. 26.

[57] *Kudi Arasu*, 26 January 1936, in Aanaimuthu, *Periyar*, vol. II, p. 976.

[58] Anderson, *Imagined Communities*, p. 140.

[59] Aanaimuthu, *Periyer*, vol. II, p. 1120.

certitudes and progress through struggle as a process with volatile boundaries, identities and agents, rendered his nation one without a 'moment of arrival'. It was ever-fluid, relentlessly struggling for citizenship, informed by ever-changing contours of rationalism, and continuously violating boundaries—both in the sense of physical territory and otherwise. He could thus, while talking about Dravida Nadu, accommodate the whole of the sudras of the north India in his nation: '...[People] who suffer from this [Aryan] degradation are not only those who speak Tamil...[They are] also there in other states, i.e. states like Bengal, Bihar, Bombay, Maharashtra where they speak different languages. The degraded comrades there are calling themselves Dravidians: In fact, they are Dravidians.'[60] If Dravidian was an inclusive trope for the oppressed, Aryan, too, signified different forms of denial of equality. And, similarly, he could denounce Tamil, while opposing the imposition of Hindi in schools: in 1939, when Hindi was a burning issue in Tamil Nadu, he said in the course of a public address:

> I do not have any attachment to the Tamil language for [the reason] that it is my mother tongue or the tongue of the nation. I am not attached to it for [the reason] that it is a separate language, ancient language, language spoken by Shiva [or] language created by Agastiyar. I do not have attachment for anything in itself. That will be foolish attachment, foolish adulation. I may have attachment [for something] for its qualities and the benefits such qualities will result in. I don't praise something because it is my language, my nation, my religion...
>
> If I think my nation is unhelpful for my ideal and cannot [also] be made helpful, I will abandon [it] immediately. Likewise, if I think my language will not benefit my ideals or [will not help] my people to progress [and] live in honour, I will abandon it...[61]

In short, E. V. Ramaswamy's nation, freed from the past, located in the anticipatory and framed by notions of 'modernity from below' was a metaphor, a metaphor which stood for ever-fluid, free and equal citizenship. Its success can never be assessed in terms of its arrival, but perhaps only in terms of its continuing ability to inspire diverse subordinate social groups in the present-

60 *Viduthalai,* 27 January 1950, in Aanaimuthu, *Periyar,* vol. II, p. 683.

61 Sami Chidamparanar, *Tamilar Talaivar: Periyar Ee V Ra Vazhkai Varalaru,* (first published 1939 in Tamil), Madras, 1983.

day Tamil Nadu to question the Indian nation-state for its failings, and to imagine nations of equity and freedom lying in the future. Perhaps, in the passing, we may remember that E. V. Ramaswamy and his followers, as a matter of principle, refused to participate in elections and offices of power. After all, their nation could not afford to translate itself into a totalizing nation-state.

13

Generic Sentences, Social Kinds, and Stereotypes*

Tista Bagchi

Background: Generic Sentences

This paper is part of an effort to understand an area of vagueness in natural language, an Achilles' heel, so to speak, that is prey to manipulative interpretation for the creation and perpetuation of perceptual stereotypes about people that acquire a special, prob-lem-atic significance in multicultural societies. The area of vague-

* This article (along with the larger project on generics, kinds, and contexts, of which it is a part) is, in a sense, an outcome of my efforts (for the past few years) to analyse the relationship of the meaning-structure of sentences and utterances to the lexicon on the one hand, and to discourse contexts on the other. Before and during its presentation at Kasauli several people provided stimulating comments and suggestions, of whom I would like to thank especially Amiya Kumar Bagchi, Jasodhara Bagchi, Sibaji Bandyopadhyay, Rajeev Bhargava, Akeel Bilgrami (who was in addition the formal discussant of the paper at the conference), Indira Chowdhury, G. A. Cohen, Subrata Dasgupta, Peter DeSouza, P. K. Datta, Alan Montefiore, Alok Rai, Kumkum Sangari, Tanika Sarkar, R. Sudarshan, and Charles Taylor. The writings, lectures, and comments of James D. McCawley in a face-to-face discussion at the University of Chicago provided much of the initial inspiration for this enterprise. None of the above, however, are to be held responsible for the opinions expressed in this paper. Nor are they to be held responsible for errors of fact or judgement, which are mine alone.

ness in question lies in what have been called generic sentences, either asserted as statements or presupposed as given. When asserted as statements they typically (though not always) occur in the simple present tense, and contain one or more topically salient noun phrases that are non-specific in nature (signalled grammatically in English, for example, most often by the bare plural, sometimes by the indefinite article with singular number, and very occasionally by the definite article, as in the sentences (1), (2) and (3), respectively):

(1) *Mexicans/Chicanos* are cheats.
(2) When *a woman* says no she means yes.
(3) *The poor* are poor because they are lazy.

Such tiresomely cliched statements as these, I claim, often have more pernicious force than immediately meets the eye—especially when they act as convenient substitutes for a more genuinely informed understanding of the sets of people sweepingly identified by statements such as these. They are a little more pernicious, perhaps, when they are entailed and/or presupposed in discourse than when they are bluntly asserted: when they are subcutaneously injected into the addressee/hearer's consciousness, so to speak, for more subtly manipulative rhetoric to be built on them—but it is when they take the form of asserted sentences that we see them for what they are.

Generic sentences constitute a major headache for linguists who concern themselves with the meaning-structure of sentences.[1] They do not quite coincide in meaning with corresponding sentences about what are called universally quantified topic noun phrases, that is, noun phrases containing *all, every, each,* etc., so that they denote the (bounded or unbounded) totality of entities that the head noun stands for. For instance, the three sentences just

[1] See Östem Dahl (ed.) (1975): 'On Generics', in Edward L. Keenan, *Formal Semantics of Natural Language,* Cambridge University Press, Cambridge, 1975, pp. 99–111; Greg N. Carlson, 'A Unified Analysis of the English Bare Plural', *Linguistics and Philosophy,* vol. 1, 1997, pp. 413–56; Carlson, 'On the Semantic Composition of English Generic Sentences', in Gennaro Chierchia, Barbara H. Partee, and Raymond Turner, *Properties, Types and Meaning,* vol. 2: *Semantic Issues*, Kluwer Academic Publishers, Dordrecht, 1989, pp. 167–92; Lenart Schubert and F. Jeffrey Pelletier, 'Generically Speaking, or Using Discourse Representation Theory to Interpret Generics' in Chierchia et al.

mentioned are not strictly equivalent, logically speaking, to the following three sentences:

(4) *All Mexicans/Chicanos* are cheats.
(5) When *every woman* says no she means yes.
(6) *All* (*the*) *poor people* are poor because they are lazy.

Instead, the first three sentences purport to express what one *might expect* of anyone who might be described as 'a Chicano', as 'a woman', or as 'poor'. They thus express generalizations whose effect is to validate the lumping together of 'Chicanos', of 'women' and of 'the poor' into respective *kinds* that are characterized by the dubious properties of being disposed to cheat, being mendacious in the use of negation, and being poor on account of laziness.[2]

Notice also that generic sentences make stronger claims than their counterparts with the quantifier *some* (on one interpretation, at least, an existential quantifier):

(7) *Some Mexicans/Chicanos* are cheats.
(8) a. When *some women* say no they mean yes.
b. *Sometimes* when a woman says no she means yes.
(9) *Some* (*of the*) *poor people* are poor because they are lazy.

They are also not quite identical to their counterparts with a non-standard quantifier such *as most*:[3]

[2] The only formal semanticist, to my knowledge, who addresses the issue of the kind-identifying and stereotyping role played by generic sentences is ter Meulen (1986), who espouses the view that this may be because of the typically Western way of viewing the world. Given the global power relations that have developed over the past several centuries, this may well be partially true, and it is certainly the case that the identification of non-Western social kinds and the formation of stereotypes about non-Western peoples have had a much more pervasive and lasting effect on the lives of the peoples so typecast than kind-identification and stereotyping of the peoples of the Western world by non-Western cultures have ever been able to achieve. But, as visitors from the West have often experienced in non-Western countries, stereotypes about the West—including ones that are offensive to them—are also quite pervasive amongst non-Western peoples. The problem therefore seems to be rooted, at least partially, in deeper cognitive features of the human organism rather than being endemic to the Western world, though of course its close ties with imbalanced power relations such as the Western world has with most of the non-Western world are of great significance.

[3] James D. McCawley, *Everything that Linguists have Always Wanted to Know about Logic** (**but were ashamed to ask*), 1st and 2nd edns, University of Chicago Press, Chicago, 1981, 1994, p. 443.

(10) *Most Mexicans/Chicanos* are cheats.
(11) a. When *most women* say no they mean yes.
b. *Most of the time* when a woman says no she means yes.
(12) *Most of the poor* are poor because they are lazy.

The interpretation of nonstandard quantifiers (such as *most* and *almost all*) is a problem area in itself. For the present purposes I ignore that question and simply assign an arbitrary proportional value to *most*, perhaps something like '55 ± 4.5%'. Most Mexicans, taken in this literal sense, may not even be in a position to cheat; when most women, again taken literally, say no (regardless of what they are asked, that is), they are likely to mean no; and most of the poor of the earth, taken literally, are simply not able to afford the luxury of laziness. Yet none of these states of affairs fully succeed in invalidating the generic sentences (1), (2) and (3), or in eradicating the hold that they have on people's minds as beliefs. Any counter-examples that the holders of these beliefs might come across (and recognize as counter-examples) are conveniently pigeonholed as exceptions, without abandonment of, or even a rethinking of, the generic beliefs. They refuse to recognize any inconsistency in doing so, and in this they go unquestioned.[4]

Generic Sentences in Use

As I have already mentioned, when such crude generic sentences as are exemplified by (1), (2) and (3) come to be taken for granted in a communicative situation they can serve as presuppositions on

[4] In my use of the third-person plural *they* to denote the holders of generic beliefs, I do not mean to oppose myself to an essentialized set of individuals whom I (somewhat vaguely) label *many people*. I use the pronoun *they* with the recognition that we ourselves (or certainly I myself) may on occasion be guilty of such beliefs. The opposition *we*: *they* is in fact far from being an innocuous one, especially with reference to the kind of distancing that a generic assumption about a social kind creates between the agent and the social kind thus typecast as an Other. Moreover, this role of the opposition *we*: *they* is by no means specific to English: as Sibaji Bandyopadhyay ('*Chowringhee:* Modernity and Popular Fiction', *Journal of Arts and Ideas*, vols 25–6, December 1993, pp. 87–103) shows, the narrator in *Chowringhee*, the Bengali novel by Shankar that he focuses on, uses the pronouns *ora* ('they') and *amra* ('we') from the outset to demarcate the sharp racial and class divide between the British owners of businesses in Calcutta and the middle-class Bengali functionaries serving (or seeking to serve) them.

which much more subtle rhetoric can be built.[5] In the linguistic literature a distinction is drawn between *accidental* and *nomic* generic sentences.[6] Accidental generics supposedly express some accidental property observed in the set indicated by the topic noun phrase, whereas nomic generics—as the name indicates—are interpreted to be expressive of some *law* of behaviour of the set indicated by the topic noun phrase. It is this latter kind of generics (namely, nomic generics) that I am concerned with here.

Within the class of nomic generics, again, a distinction is made between *descriptive* and *normative* nomic generics. I contend, however, that one cannot always draw a clear-cut distinction between descriptive and normative generics. By way of illustration let me take a piece of information that I was given in the United States, a few weeks after I began life as a graduate student there:

(13) People don't talk about grades here.

As a piece of information, (13) was put to me as a descriptive statement—but the person who gave me this piece of information was also warning me not to express openly my anxiety about grades, even amongst friends. In other words, I was being expected to conform to a norm. Regardless of whether the statement in question in descriptive of the situation at hand, therefore, it is a normative statement. Indeed, a philosopher such as Tyler Burge would probably regard *all* generic assertions as being normative in that their contents, like all statements that are taken to be necessarily true, are dubitable and are believed to hold good simply because they originate from a body of 'experts' (in, I suppose, a rather over-charitably wide sense) accepted as such by a society.[7]

I shall now attempt to clarify the position that I adopt on the *analysis* of generics in isolation and as participants in discourse. I need to do this because there is already a considerable tradition of textual analysis within the (by now much-ramified) area of linguis-

[5] In section 3, I examine a piece of text reported from real life, in which one sees the rhetoric in use. As Tanika Sarkar points out (personal communication), the acceptance of the idea(s) of Hindutva on such a large scale has largely been achieved through a triumph of rhetoric.

[6] See, for example, Dahl, 'On Generics'.

[7] See, for example, Tyler Burge, 'Intellectual Norms and Foundations of Mind', *Journal of Philosophy*, vol. I, 1986, pp. 83, 697–720. Burge's opinion is that in fact the meaning (pure and simple) of a given expression is determined non-individualistically by social norm.

tics called *functionalist linguistics*, roughly beginning with the Prague School (whose most celebrated representatives are N. S. Trubetzkoy and Roman Jakobson) and at present perhaps best known in the Anglo-Saxon world through the work of Michael Halliday and his students and followers in Australia and the United Kingdom.[8] The emphasis in functionalist textual analysis is on the identification of the functional/semantic roles of *individual constituent elements* overtly expressed within the sentences of the text and then the establishment of communicative connections between them, intra- or inter-sententially. In my approach I concern myself both with the covert and with the overt, largely propositional, units of discourse and with certain specific relationships that may obtain amongst them. Another respect in which I differ from most functionalists is in the position that I adopt on cognition. The role of cognition and linguistic competence (in the standard-theoretic Chomskyan sense) is for the most part unacknowledged, if not flatly denied, in the functionalist approach to language. In my view linguistic competence (and all that it presupposes about cognition) needs to be given the central role that it rightly deserves. However, my approach shares with the functionalist approach(es) the concern with social dynamics in linguistic communication arising (partially, at least) from the structure of the text itself. Here, I make use of the concepts of *implicature* and *presupposition* made available by work in pragmatics (the area of linguistics that studies the logic of language in use)[9] I do not necessarily confine myself, though, strictly to the logician's definitions of these terms.[10]

[8] For a sampling of work done on sentence and discourse structure and language typology in India and Australia within a functionalist set of approaches see Verma and Prakasam (1993).

[9] For an introduction to the area of pragmatics see, for example, Gerald Gazdar, *Pragmatics*, Academic Press, New York, 1979. For the relationship between linguistics, logic, and certain issues in pragmatics see McCawley, *Everything that Linguists*. Emile Benveniste, 'La philosophie analytique et le langage' in *Problems de Linguistique generale*, vol. 1, Gallimard, Paris, 1966, pp. 267–76, raises the question of the relationship between the (pragmatically) felicitous use of performative language and relative power and authority in society.

[10] Indeed, for one of the two kinds of implicature defined by Grice (see, for example, H. Paul Grice, 'The Logic of Conversation', William James

There are three linguistic features of generic sentences that are of especial interest in an investigation of their cognitive and social dynamics.

As I have already mentioned, generic sentences typically carry the simple present tense. When they do not do so, they occur in the simple or the habitual ('used to') past tense, and, on occasion, the simple future tense (as in predictions).

Second, a generic sentence is as a rule in the indicative mood. The mood (or, perhaps more generally, the modality) of a generic sentence is a very telling (and possibly convenient) linguistic marker: it represents its own propositional content as being valid for some aspect of the *real* world—as something that *is*, as opposed to something that *might* be or *ought* to be. This, coupled with its so-called 'aoristic' tense-form (that is, without any marking of the *aspect*, the status of completion or of progression of the state, process or event(s) expressed by the sentence), makes the generic sentence an eminently desirable candidate in the art of the expression and maintenance of the *status quo*.

A third feature of generic sentences, noted by Carlson, has to do with the semantic *type* (roughly, the level of semantic abstraction) of the topic noun phrase and the semantic type of the 'comment', that is, whatever is predicated of the topic noun phrase. Carlson writes:

> ...we have cause to hold that the meaning of a generic sentence stems fundamentally from a *relation* between intensional elements: any generic operator would have to be dyadic. It does not relate purely extensional elements to one another or to intensional elements, but only intensions to intensions.[11]

The psycho-semantic reality of 'intensions' as distinct entities is a matter of debate in the philosophy of mind.[12] I am not sure,

---

Lectures delivered at Harvard University, 1967; 'Logic and Conversatio' [William James Lecture II], in Peter Cole and Jerry L. Morgan (eds) *Syntax and Semantics*, vol. 3, *Speech Acts*, Academic Press, New York, pp. 45–58.), namely, conversational implicature, and for pragmatic presupposition a foolproof formal definition is yet to be arrived at.

[11] Carlson, 'On the Semantic Composition of English Generic Sentences', in Chierchia et al., p. 189.

[12] For an argument against the distinctness of 'intensions' as objects-of-thought see Akeel Bilgrami, *Belief and Meaning*, Blackwell, Oxford, 1992.

though, that the opposition between 'intensions' as *functions* in formal semantics and 'extensions' as the denotations of such functions in different states-of-affairs does not serve as a useful tool in the effort to understand the meaning-*structure* (as opposed to the content pure and simple) of a syntactic class of sentences (such as that of generic sentences). Assuming this opposition to be a valid one, therefore, the formal semantics of generic sentences relates to a category of beliefs postulated by H. Paul Grice in an interesting manner. Grice calls this category of beliefs *positive persumptions*:[13] these are beliefs about groups (usually of people) that usually do not include the agent, and as beliefs they are unaffected by the agent's coming upon particular counter-examples to the beliefs themselves. This misses the possibility that the topic noun phrase of a generic sentence may in fact be a rather imperfect 'intension', so to speak, whose extensions in actual states-of-affairs do not always satisfy the relation established by the generic sentence.

One might raise the following question at this point. Since a generic sentence is not the only kind of proposition that can function as a presupposition or an implicature, why is it to be maligned as being responsible in the process of stereotype-building? My reply to this would be: as propositions generic sentences are, to the extent that I can determine, atomic; as assertions they look deceptively infallible; and when presupposed or implicated they are often accepted without question as non-derivative, nomic generalizations, and can eventually acquire the status of positive presumptions. In contrast non-generic assumptions are much more directly verifiable and less likely to be accepted as nomic generalizations. By way of illustration I discuss two examples. The first is the statement (14), often heard by me during my student days in Delhi:

(14) Women are biologically constrained.

The power of this statement, I later came to realize, lies in its vagueness: the predicate adjective phrase *biologically constrained* is ominously non-specific. If the possibility of pregnancy is the biological constraint at issue, notice that not all the women in the

[13] Grice's 'positive presumptions', to which Akeel Bilgrami has drawn my attention in a personal communication, find an echo in the analysis of the form of perception of the self and the form underlying the role of a material item as a commodity along lines proposed by Jacques Lacan. This has been brought to my attention by Sibaji Bandyopadhyay (personal communication).

world at any given point of time (indeed, perhaps not even half of them, if one ignores a woman's age) are under this 'constraint'—which, second, is a 'constraint' not so much because it is biological as it is because of the way the world of people works, an issue (or complex of issues) that is entirely sidestepped by making the assertion (14). May I point out that the specific 'biological' constraint that I just mentioned is, paradoxically, more of a constraint in sections of society (on occasion spanning entire countries) where health care is inadequately accessible to the general population. (Thus I continue to hear this assertion in Delhi, regretfully not entirely without justification.) If some other kind of biological constraint is intended by the phrase (however ominously), my suspicion is that it is not peculiar to women alone—but that fact is, again, masked by the implicature carried by the sentence (14) that it is indeed peculiar to women.[14]

The paradox of generic assertions and assumptions predicated of people lies in their apparent embodiment of purportedly *universal* (or epistemically necessary) laws, since, in the process, they end up segmenting the world of people into *different*, and more often than not *differential*, fragments.[15]

Generic Assumptions and Communalist Rhetoric: A Case Study

Having provided some background to the syntax, pragmatics, and social dynamics of generic sentences in use, with a few illustrations

[14] An example that carried a similar generic presupposition was provided to me through a humorous anecdote recounted by a family friend. This friend and her sister were travelling from Kanpur to Delhi in a 'ladies' compartment of the Kalka mail. A group of Army jawans got into their compartment and began forcing the women to yield their seats to them. When this friend and her sister protested, some of them then climbed on to the upper berths and settled down. Soon a boot was dropped down with a thud right in front of the sister, who picked it up and tossed it back up at the jawans on the upper berth. Immediately, a comment was heard from one of the jawans, addressed to the others (in Hindi):

(i) bhaaii-saab, yeh *lady* nahii hai, yeh *selfish* hai.
'Brother(s), this one is not a lady—she is selfish.'

In the interest of preserving the humour I refrain from spelling out the generic presupposition here. (Courtesy: Sunanda Sen)

[15] I owe the suggestion of this point to Jasodhara Bagchi (personal communication).

from my notebook of linguistic examples, I shall now examine a conversation reported in a newspaper between a political leader of the Bharatiya Janata Party and a visiting woman journalist from Bangladesh.[16] This is with a view to examining the underlying generic premises on which the political leader in question builds his rhetoric. The journalist's questioning of some of these premises becomes too much for him, and he ends up losing his temper at her. I include the interview here with my own reading of the presuppositions and implicatures inserted between sentences or paragraphs.

[X is the journalist from Dhaka, Bangladesh. Y is the Bharatiya Janata Party leader.]
X: What is your policy towards Bangladesh?
Y: We would like them to first stop infiltration[17] in our country and be good friends with us. [Presuppositions introduced: (i) 'They'—Bangladeshis—are infiltrating the Indian people; (ii) 'They'—again, Bangladeshis—are the ones who are hostile to 'us', that is, (Hindu) Indians. Hidden pragmatic presupposition of (i) and (ii): (iii) Bangladeshis are Muslims.]
X: Are you sure about infiltration? [Presupposition (i) being questioned.]

[16] Newspaper report, dated 1 December 1992, cited in Forum for the Future of Our Childrens, *What do the Children Say?*, vol. 1, FFFC, Calcutta, 1993, p. 192.

[17] As Tanika Sarkar points out (personal communication), the term *infiltration* (and derivationally related terms, such as (*to*) *infiltrate*) is used of enemy elements entering the army of a nation under cover with a view to sabotage. The 'infiltrators', in this case, are Bangladeshis, who are thus implicitly set up as enemies. But there is also another implicature stemming from the use of the term *infiltration* to describe migration into India, namely, that the entire population of India is a potential army base in the service of the pro-Hindutva forces. This implicature, perhaps because of its very remoteness, is able to subtly co-opt the Hindu masses into the Hindutva movement more effectively than any explicit claim or exhortation.

Akeel Bilgrami (as discussant) has raised the following objection to my taking up an individual word such as *infiltration* and interpreting it without applying the principle of charity: in other words, to my interpreting the term without taking into account whether my interpretation of the word is consistent with the totality of beliefs that the political leader in question might have. Let me present my response to his objection in a somewhat more explicit manner than I did at the conference: Words, even when used only in

Y: I am pretty sure. I have toured the border areas. [Note that no *specific* border areas are mentioned.] I have talked to many people. [Note again the vagueness of this statement.] The best thing for the Bangladesh government to do is to withdraw all Bangladeshis gracefully from this country. They are aliens who are creating problems in our country. [First explicit statement of a generic nature to be made about Bangladeshis in India. Note the vagueness of the phrase *creating problems in our country*, however—no specific problems are ever mentioned.]

X: What about having a mutual discussion on the problem?

Y: We are always willing to discuss provided the Bangladeshi government first accepts that there is infiltration and is willing to discuss the modus operandi to stop further infiltration. [Presuppositions (i) and (ii) invoked again.]

X: Then there will have to be negotiations. It can't just be one-sided. [Presuppositions (i) and (ii)—cleverly—not invoked at all.]

Y: But your Prime Minister says that there is no infiltration. [Implicature: The Prime Minister of Bangladesh is denying presupposition (i), and is thereby taking the position of an adversary. This may even include a conventional implicature generated by the initial *but*.]

X: But first these people have to be identified. You can't just push them back without a mutual agreement. People who have been pushed back were mostly voters here.

Y: There are many fraudulent voters. [Note the conversational implicature generated by this statement, by virtue of its occurring immediately after X's statement 'People who have been pushed back were mostly voters here'—namely, that people who have been pushed back may well have been fraudulent voters.] A person can commit a fraud or a theft. That does not mean that he has a right

approximate senses, do not stand in isolation, but establish both immediate links between adjoining phrases and/or sentences in the pieces of discourse in which they are occurring *and*—in a less obvious but nevertheless discernible manner—more remote intertextual links between their current occurrences and their histories of occurrence in past discourse Surely if it makes sense to speak of the mastery of words by agents (Bilgrami, *Belief and Meaning*, responding to Noam Chomsky's view of linguistic norm) this would need to be—and, given the existence of other users of those words, present or past, usually *is*—verified against instances of previous usage of the words in discourse.

to stay here. [Note the presupposition of this second statement: (iv) A person committing a fraud or a theft is necessarily from outside India.]

Y: (Shouting at her) Are you discussing on behalf of your government or are you a journalist? [The use of *or* to conjoin what are set up as mutually exclusive options is to be noted. Also noteworthy is the deliberate flouting of Grice's Maxim of Relevance in Y's *ad hominem* attack on X's current position as his interlocutor.]

X: I am representing my country.

Y: Define your role correctly. [Presupposition: (v) X has not done so in her reply.]

X: I am a journalist.

Y: Then behave like a journalist.

[Note that Y leaves unspecified what it is to 'behave like a journalist.']

X: There are lots of Indians who are staying abroad for economic viability. This is an international trend.

Y: (Shouting angrily). You are justifying infiltration. [Note the leap of reasoning here.] Why should the Indian government suffer because of the Bangladeshi government [?] If you can't feed your people, is it my responsibility to feed them? [Pragmatic presuppositions: (iv) 'You' are the Bangladeshi government. (vii) 'I' am the Indian government. Note the contradiction between these two presuppositions and the earlier presupposition (v) that X has not defined her role correctly when she says that she is representing her country.] You just take them back and feed them.[18]

[End of Report]

While not everyone may agree with the specifics of the assumptions as I have laid them out to view, I suspect that

[18] In deciding whether an assumption is a presupposition or an implicature, I have adopted the following criteria: If an assumption must be accepted in order for the main (explicit) utterance to be true and/or felicitous, the assumption is to be taken as a presupposition (in the broad sense that includes entailment, semantic presupposition, and pragmatic presupposition). If an assumption follows as a consequence of the use of a particular expression of the utterance (such as the noun *infiltration* or the conjunction *but*) or as a consequence of the utterance being used in conjunction with other utterances in a piece of discourse (typically, a conversation), the assumption is taken as an implicature.

almost everyone would agree that there *are* underlying assumptions that are at least partly founded on generalizations (perceptually motivated or otherwise) that are predicated of all ill-defined social kind, namely, (Muslim) Bangladeshis, without supporting evidence for these generalizations ever being explicitly mentioned.

In contrast, the near-*absence* of generic statements in the recounting of actual experiences in communal riots by victims is a striking fact.[19] This is not to say that riot victims do not try to make generalizations based on their experiences, if only in order to make sense of the violence perpetrated on them. A striking instance of a non-verbal interpretation of an election symbol painted on the wall, rendered by a severely hearing-impaired Sikh boy who saw his father die in the 1984 Delhi riots illustrates this attempt to make sense of events through generalizing at a fairly substract level. The symbol in question was the uplifted hand, the Congress(I)'s election symbol at the time. While passing by (on a bus ride) a picture of the hand painted on the wall, the boy communicated how the hand in its benign role, as the benevolent right hand of Guru Nanak, is superseded, so to speak, by the hand of the Congress(I) in its destructive role, 'killing, dousing people with petrol and burning them alive'.[20]

It need hardly be mentioned, of course, that riot victims are themselves victims of social stereotyping in some of the most violent ways imaginable. Generic assumptions may have only a partial role to play in such stereotyping—but their role cannot altogether afford to be ignored.

Conclusion: Is There a Way Out?

Although I have no straightforward proposal for an alternative to generic sentences as a means of expressing generalizations and

[19] I have drawn upon Veena Das's ('Our Work to Cry: Your Work to Listen' in Veena Das (ed.) *Mirrors of Violence: Communities, Riots and Suvivors in South Asia*, Oxford University Press, Delhi, 1990, pp. 345–98.) account of encounters with victims of the 1984 Delhi riots, without necessarily adopting her analysis of the victims' narrative. For the reactions of children to the events of 6 December 1992, see Forum for the Future of Our Children, *What do the Children Say*? pp. 262–4.

[20] Das, 'Our Work to Cry', pp. 376–7, 378–9.

assumptions about people and social formations, it seems to me that generic sentences only linguistically codify and make explicit beliefs (including prejudices) and other attitudes that are rooted in a great deal of cognitive and social complexity. Obviously, we cannot *stop* making generalizations and building further discourse on them, given the nature of human cognition[21] and the human condition; nor can we stop using language altogether (and even if we did, prejudices would remain and be embodied in stereotypes expressed in some other form, for example, visual or non-verbal auditory). However, we can try to understand the cognitive icebergs that generic sentences are the tips of and the social process(es) of consensus-building that are involved in the formation of social stereotypes through the discourse of generic assertions and assumptions. Often elaborate systems of classification are developed for different aspects of human existence and appearance (as in the case of different systems of humours in Western and Eastern schools of medicine, the nine *rasas* in the ancient Indian performing arts, and facets of human interaction as identified in a recent Western school of psychology such as transactional analysis), and these play hitherto largely unexamined roles in the implicit function of classification that generic sentences about social kinds carry.[22] Additional insights are potentially obtainable, in two very different directions, from the socially normative account of meaning developed by Tyler Burge and from the notion of 'bounded rationality' elaborated by Herbert Simon.[23]

What is also needed is a constant questioning and reexamination of our assumptions, and especially of our generic assumptions about perceptually identified social kinds insofar as their perceived

[21] Although I adopt a somewhat non-specific position here as to the nature of human cognition, and simply intend a contrast with the cognitive capacities, including linguistic capacities (or lack thereof), of other animal species, the aspect(s) of human cognition implicated in the storing of generic sentences as information and their (deliberate or unpremeditated) invocation as positive presumptions about (social or other) kinds are clearly of interest, and merit much more in-depth study.

[22] This was suggested to me by Kumkum Sangari (personal communication).

[23] Peter DeSouza (personal communication) directed me to Herbert Simon's views on bounded rationality. See, for example, Simon (1982).

identities are (in some broad sense) linked to society.[24] Such questioning and reexamination, I suggest, is crucial to the initiation of any kind of meaningful effort towards the opening up of mutual channels of communication in situations of inter-group conflict and in impasses.[25] Even if one accepts the argument put forth by Parfit (1984) that there is nothing particularly necessary or determinate about personal identity, for practical purposes the matter of social identity figures prominently in the calculations of the people and the institutions that are directly involved in matters of governance (e.g. in the allocation of welfare funds of the reservation of positions of employment for certain sections of society). If such considerations demand the recognition of social kinds it will be the collective responsibility of users of language to ensure at least that generic assertions and assumptions are not misused in the interests of the creation and perpetuation of social stereotypes that constrain rather than liberate.

[24] Bilgrami, 'Two Conceptions of Secularism: Reason, Modernity and Archimedean Ideal', *Economic and Political Weekly*, 9 July 1994, p. 1760, n. 1, for instance, points out that the term 'religious community' is in danger of being (over-)interpreted 'as standing for some sort of social and other kind of reification'.

[25] For a defence of two kinds of secularism as viable modes of religious harmony, see Rajeev Bhargava, 'Giving Secularism Its Due', *Economic and Political Weekly*, 9 July 1994, pp. 1784–91.

14

Public Sphere and Democratic Governance in Contemporary India*

Javeed Alam

I

I begin the discussion of the public sphere with respect to Indian society in an unconventional way.

Most of the pre-modern communities in India in their original moorings, are continuous communities in the sense that they spontaneously renew themselves to be what they have been. This is quite unlike the West where communities are self-created. A self-created community is a reflective collective presence. This implies, at the minimum, two things: first, persons retain their autonomy within it and, as rights attach to these autonomous individuals, their freedom. Secondly, the community generates pressures towards larger units. This further implies that the communities are open to critical evaluations both by the individuals within and the larger units. With all the internal variations, differentiations, and

* I would like to thank Dhirubhai Seth, Sunder Rajan, O. P. Grewal and Suresh Sharma for suggestions without which the argument in this paper would have remained far from complete. I alone am responsible for any shortcomings. This was first presented in a seminar at Kasauli of Multiculturalism and Democratic Governance and later a portion of it was read out at the UNESCO seminar on Human Rights in Shimla. I am thankful to the participants in both the seminars from whose comments I gained a great deal.

differences, the various communities do get unified to become coterminus with the entire society; this seems to be the sense of the community in the communitarian argument.[1] Communities in India, on the other hand, demand total absorption of the individuals and seek uncritical affiliation to the community. They speak for the individual and force into silence assertions contrary to the community's way of thinking or acting. These communities act like *collective personalities.* As such they do not allow to individuals what they seek for themselves. There is little *private space* available to individuals within these continuous communities. The absence of private space here is not a case of transparency in life as Gandhi, perhaps, wanted but rather a situation of denial of autonomy. Transparency as a case of negation of the private–public dichotomy is an act of individual choice in conditions where this distinction is socially intrinsic to our life. This clarified, it is pertinent to ask: what, under such conditions, happens to the public sphere as a component of civil society?

To see this let us continue on this theme for a little longer and look at it from another angle.

If you were to tell people in our society: do not interfere with a person as you may do with an object, they do not understand the sense of this. In other words, integrity of the self is something unintelligible to them. Let us look at this absence of respect for the self through the theme of honour. How do people handle questions of *honour* and what is their notion of it? In a modern community honour stands for self-respect whereas here, in communities in India, it is more a case of vanity and self-indulgent pride. Suppose that a person lets you down or violates your pride as a result of which you are hurt. In a modern person the reaction is more likely to be of *suffering*. The normal reaction in the case of most persons belonging to pre-modern, spontaneous communities is one of *revenge*. Now to tell people in such a community not to overstep moral or legal norms is a non-issue, like asking them to put up with humilitation.

[1] For a quick glance at the communitarian position see Charles Taylor, 'Atomism', and Michael Sandel, 'The Procedural Republic', both in Shlomo Avineri and Avner de-Shalit (eds) *Communitarianism and Individualism*, Oxford, Oxford University Press, 1992; see also Charles Taylor, 'Language and Human Nature', in Michael T. Gibbons (ed.) *Interpreting Politics*, Oxford, Basil Blackwell, 1987.

A look at honour and at suffering or revenge when it is breached may give a clue to the value conditions that inhabit the life of people in these communities. When suffering is induced by a sense of being let down, as against caused by calamity, we normally delve deep and draw upon inner resources to stay calm; this being the minimum demand on us, if we are not to harm others (or hit back at whoever we hold responsible). Or else tolerance in face of what is disagreeable is not possible. Tolerating implies granting others the right to pursue their way of life or interest. Now if someone were to choose to take revenge instead of forgiving then this generally implies a refusal of any kind of introspection. It means that we draw instead upon our physical and social resources to retaliate and inflict pain upon others. This condition breeds intolerance.

The reason for going into this is to show that the value conditions that inhere in the two postures are radically different. In one case the private self is in close alignment with the requirements of the public order as it prevails in the modern (bourgeois) world, whereas in the other an incongruence exists between the private self and the public values that are supposed to inhere in the political arrangement that sustains democracy under bourgeois conditions.

In such conditions, a regime of entrenched rights, a law bound society, is difficult to sustain. Claims of individuals which are contrary to a community's sense of personal worth or inherited values or ritual regulations are over-ridden. You cannot have your way or lead a life of choice unless you run away far from where the community is. Now this freedom is central to any argument about the nature of civil society because the public sphere is meant to render a life of choice unhindered by the exercise of power, a possibility in the day-to-day life of every individual.

To see how such a life of choice can become a hazardous venture, let us look at a few local instances from the recent past. In Haryana, the son of a middle ranking official was killed because he fell in love with a girl not considered suitable. The girl was scalded to death. In another instance, a young couple in love were chased and hacked to death in front of villagers who simply watched. Such instances are not unusual but I am reporting these with a purpose. The reactions of community leaders are something worth going into. Chaudhary Suraj Mal, Congress MLA, said

'Marriage of the Nayagaon girl with the boy belonging to the nearby Ballaur village is not possible because marriages between boys and girls of adjoining villages are not allowed by custom.'[2] The famous peasant leader and agitator for peasant rights, and President of Bhartiya Kisan Union, Mahender Singh Tikait supported such exemplary (!) punishment for violators of social norms 'so that others can learn a lesson', but more significantly he added, 'whoever may take such a decision, it is a fact that *nobody can dare to testify before the police*'.[3] Quite so. No police case till date has been registered. Many prominent leaders tacitly support these actions.

The point is that these communities do not allow individuals even the right of exit; and the *right to exit* is of crucial importance under these conditions if a regime of rights is to be secured on a firm foundation. Now an exploration of this issue is vital to the understanding of the public sphere in India because the right to exit will secure for the individuals what is not easily available under prevailing social conditions. The right to exit does not simply mean walking out of the community in the way one walks out of a restaurant. In the history of human struggles there are varied instances from Socrates to Gandhi of how one can exercise this right without turning one's face against the community; there is, in other words, much more nuanced opposition than mere hostility or indifference. I return to this point later.

In talking to the leaders—social notables—within these communities, interesting variations about the modern world are revealed. They are all for the 'modern'—college, university, trousers, jeans and so on. But any talk of choices about different world-views is 'Western'. They recognize only two rights, the one to vote and the other to criticize the government. All other rights, to infer from practice and reactions, are alien, Western. Now with communities becoming mobilized for political power, there is all the greater need within communities to maintain boundaries and internal cohesion. The route to power in the present configuration of forces is in a condition of disalignment with those which require respect for the individual and his rights. These communities acting as collective personalities deny to individuals within their fold what they claim for themselves as collectivities. The pressure to claim the right to a

[2] *Times of India*, 29 March 1994.

[3] *Tribune*, 28 March 1994.

way of life and culture as something inalienable for these collectivities is certainly very strong. The question, 'Can a right to a way of life be claimed on behalf of a community when the exercise of the same is denied to the individual?' is centrally involved here and I hope to be able to take it into consideration in the course of this argument.

These internal features of pre-modern communities have acquired an intensity within the public sphere in the situation created by the way politics has evolved in the last few decades; intensity in the sense that with the extension of democracy, communities are threatened in backlash as more and more people become individuated persons, and with this severity of resistance to the breach and irreverence by the guardians of local orthodox notions of the good life has risen sharply. With the extension of democracy large groups of people as communities or as parts of these have become empowered and assertive in the society. But this has gone hand in hand with the persistence of the social relations and structures which are constraining—in other words, conditions which make people unfree.

It is precisely because of this nature of interaction of politics and inheritance and its subsequent alteration in Indian society, that democracy as something other than electoral competitiveness faces serious hurdles. Underlying my argument here is a basic question. Is there any necessary link between democracy in society and political democracy understood as a regime of civil liberties? One may argue that lack of democracy in the family or the household may well be compatible with political democracy as, let us say, in nineteenth-century England. But can one extend this to large communities which underpin electoral politics as the prime mobilizational force and also oversee quite vigilantly the regulation of social life? In any conception of democracy whether right-based or a goal-based, rights are, to use Dworkin's term, 'political trumps' possessed by individuals.[4] No collective good, of however large a community, can be a justification in withholding these. In fact, to be free, individuals have to have background rights—as distinct from political-legal rights—against decisions of a community as one form of collectivity.

[4] R. Dworkin, *Taking Rights Seriously*, London, Duckworth 1977; see also his 'Liberalism', in Stuart Hampshire (ed.) *Public and Private Morality*, Cambridge, CUP 1978.

In view of the nature of communities, somewhat cryptically indicated above, rights have a very unstable position in Indian society and even politics remains only superficially informed by the exercise of rights. The framework of rights guarantees claims made by an individual against one or another sort of collectivity. But it becomes difficult to invoke the background right when communities act as collective personalities in the political arena even as we continue to use legal rights against the decisions or acts of state institutions. In such situations, individuals frequently find themselves helpless to assert their claims against the communities to which they belong, and because the manner in which the state gets power—among other factors, constituted through the assertion of the communities—the state too is often reluctant to intervene on behalf of the citizens.

Let me elaborate this. Many communities press claims for a right to a way of life, culture, social customs, practices and rituals, etc. as something inalienable for them. But these communities would not allow individuals within their fold to exercise their rights to choose his/her way of life or even to express an opinion which goes against decisions arbitrarily arrived at by the community. For example, Mushir-ul-Hasan (a professor in Jamia Milia university) is battered for saying that the ban on *Satanic Verses* is wrong. *Sahmat* (a cultural organization standing for radical democracy and secular society) invites the wrath of the militant Hindu right-wing for exhibiting plural versions of the Ramayana. The number of such instances can be multiplied if one sits with a daily newspaper. And note that these are not punishments for the transgressions of caste norms by the lower castes in face of challenges to the domination of *savarnas* but concern 'equals' within certain communities. Communities in India do not give to the individuals, as noted above, the right of exit. The right to exit, as I will try to show later, is crucial if we want conditions appropriate to the making of choices by the individuals in situations where pre-modern communities continue to prevail as strong entities. It is equally critical in the building of pressure for internal reforms within communities.[5]

[5] I remain unconvinced of Partha Chatterjee's persuasive argument that only self-reform through internal representative institutions is a legitimate source of developments in the community and all else is coercive, especially if it is the state which is nothing but an instrument for hegemonization. See his 'Secularism', in *Economic and Political Weekly*, 9 July 1994.

II

In the discussion so far hardly anything is said about the varied treatment of these issues in the Marxist traditions. This is so mainly because they cover a very different terrain of intellectual discussions. From Marx to now there are two main lines of thinking on this issue neither of which is going to be of any great help in understanding what is being attempted here.[6] Instead, I look at the public sphere in India only in terms of presuppositions which are generally referred to as bourgeois. In any case, so far in history there has not been a public sphere except within the capitalist social formations. In the erstwhile socialist societies of USSR and Eastern Europe, the public sphere was simply abolished by silencing the voice of the people and not by overcoming the disjunction between the public and the private. In saying all this I am quite conscious that these understandings have to be recovered in any form of struggle for social emancipation.

[6] Marx, taking the concept of civil society in quite the same sense as Hegel, makes use of it mainly to criticize the Hegelian assumptions that the life rendered unstable by the pursuits of the egoistic individual in the competitive world of the market can become one of freedom and social unity in the realm of the state. In using this term Marx was, in his early writings (see note 18 for references), trying to show that the 'political emancipation' of the citizen by the fact of having juristic equality and political rights is incomplete and inadequate. It is only in the overcoming of the breach between the private and the public, the social and the political and the individual and the citizen that 'social emancipation' can come about where true freedom reigns. In other words, the state as the 'universal interest' as thought about by Hegel is simply an abstraction. Gramsci in contradistinction to Marx uses the term 'civil society' not just as private but the entire non-state realm and therefore it is not just the egoistic individual with his whims and caprices but also, and perhaps much more, the place of organizations through which alternate ideologies contend and where the proletarian worldview also has to win its battles. The civil society is therefore also the sphere of struggles for the extraction of consent by the ruling classes and the making of hegemony by the contending ideologies. It is obvious that Gramsci builds from another side of the Hegelian theory where Hegel looks at the estates and corporations as the organizing principles of civil society. Hence these two alternative intellectual ways of looking at civil society in the Marxist tradition.

It should now be clear why I am not going into any discussion of the writings in the Marxist tradition on the questions concerning civil society. For the purpose of what I am seeking to examine here this mere mention should suffice.

So the prefix 'bourgeois' often attached to public sphere, as of now, is quite unnecessary. Habermas first used it[7] and it became a habit with many later writers. Since the translation of his work in English in 1988, Habermas became the most influential writer on this issue but I continue to have a sense of unease with a few of his formulations in spite of the many insights and enormous erudition. Let me point to some for the purposes of this paper. Given the contradictory developments in the twentieth century, what really is 'refeudalization'? The problem in the argument of Habermas lies in its prefiguration of the public sphere in the literary sphere.[8] It gives rise to two problems. First, if the understanding of public sphere is modelled, even minimally, on the literary, then the growth of now powerful forces like the electronic media, controlled and manipulated by corporate interests, complicates the picture by giving credence to the view that public sphere is on the decline. After all, the literary is not conflictual in the same way as relation of workers with the ruling classes is, composed as it is of near equals who contest only discursively. Prefiguring the

[7] Jurgen Habermas, *The Structural Transformation of the Public Sphere: An Inquiry into a Category of Bourgeois Society*, Cambridge, 1991.

[8] Ibid. At the very beginning in his Preface to the book he writes that his treatment of the public sphere 'refers to those features of a historical constellation that attained dominance and leaves aside the *plebeian* public sphere as a variant that in a sense was suppressed in the historical process' (page xviii; emphasis in the original). The choice he makes to do so is not convincing. He notes immediately after that 'in the stage of the French Revolution associated with Robespierre, for just one moment, a public sphere *stripped of its literary garb* began to function—its subject was no longer the "educated strata" but the uneducated "people"' (emphasis added). He goes on to add: 'Yet even this plebeian public sphere, whose *continued but submerged* existence manifested itself in the Chartist Movement and especially in the anarchist traditions of the workers' movement in the continent, remains oriented towards the intentions of the bourgeois public sphere' (emphasis added). It is unclear why the Chartist movement is 'submerged'. It was an extended and protracted movement and in the years following, drastically altered what will count as public. In fact the creation of the regime of entrenched rights and expanding citizenship is due more to these movements than anything else. To hazard a guess it seems to me that bifurcation of the 'plebeian' from the 'public sphere' and then looking at the trajectories of its decline is one with the Frankfurt tradition. Nevertheless as these are all comments to highlight his own method they are revealing of his own orientation.

public sphere in this way, secondly, also directs it, compellingly, towards the moment of origin; inaugural moments are times of celebrations and become valorized in relation to the contrast seen inevitably in later developments. The fight was between the nascent bourgeois and the hidebound feudal classes in which people, as we understand the word today, were not very much in the picture. In the case of the public sphere it is also important to note in passing that in the capitalist world the nascent bourgeoisie was not big and the intelligentsia, though small in size, was highly influential. The contestation then could relatively remain confined to rational discourse. *Absence* of massiveness, monopolies, perfected arts of public relations and manipulations gave to these moments a happy, convincing simplicity.

The second half of the twentieth century saw the rise of workers' movements which successfully wrested rights for the most exploited of humanity and through the second half of twentieth century we are witnessing equally protracted women's movements fighting for gender equality for, globally, the most oppressed part of humanity. But this period also saw the transformation of non-big bourgeoisie into monopolies organized in transnational corporations, of bureaucracies both public and private which have become completely non-transparent, forms of representation which are suspicious of and disapprove popular participation as unwarranted interference with the mandate.

I consider this as a contradictory expansion. The demise of simplicity and the rise of complications is not quite the same thing as 'refuedalization'. The process in which we are all implicated today is both enabling and limiting at the same time. And what is happening in India today is, in a different way and through a complex reconfiguration of the old and new, a process of contradictory developments.

III

India today presents a picture of great complexity. Cross-currents in the situation are of such a nature that to make judgements with any degree of certainty, on issues we are talking about here, is difficult. Yet it seems to me that the needs and conditions of understanding the situation, though more difficult than ever before, are not very different from those which call for taking positions and are part of the struggle. So one cannot avoid speaking as a partisan.

In understanding what this situation means for the public sphere, I first want to draw attention to two main currents, based on coalitions of communities, which confront Indian politics and society. This confrontation is primarily centred around power, particularly state-power. But the social implications of this are pervasive and deeply affect daily life in Indian society. It is precisely this which calls for careful consideration if we are to examine the public sphere in India. Let me start by looking at these currents.

Over the last ten years, the militant Hindu right-wing—the Sangh Parivar—has risen as a menacing force in India society. The other is the conflictual presence of what in India are called the Other Backward Castes (OBCs) and Dalits (also known as Harijans and Scheduled castes). These combinations, often aligning and quite as often falling apart, are backed up, in different places to varying degrees, by Muslims and an assortment of secular groups of a modern kind. I will look at both these briefly after giving a brief sketch of the social-class position of various communities in India.

In very broad social categories the various pre-capitalist or pre-modern (I take the two terms as almost synonymous) communities in India can be divided first into two broad categories: the *privileged* and the *oppressed*. Among the privileged are the landlords and the upper stratum of the rich peasantry, in short the rural gentry. In urban areas the capitalists and a section of the middle class, both professional and in business, would make up the privileged groups. Overwhelmingly, the privileged classes who constitute the ruling strata belong to the upper castes like Brahmins, Rajputs, Kayasthas, Banias and so on. Within the oppressed come first the OBCs like the Yadavs, Kurmis, Keoris, Mahatos, Julahas, Teli, etc.[9] Most of them are *propertied oppressed*. These are ritually not unclean castes, that is, their touch or presence does not pollute. It is also important to note that across the states the same castes enjoy different status; for example, the Yadavs are OBC in UP but not in Haryana; the Kurmis are OBC in UP but not in Bihar. This discrepancy is not illogical because, being peasants, the criterion used has been to see if the peasant groups were *inferior* or *independent* cultivators and

[9] Hundreds of sub-castes are listed in this category in different states. Details in *Reservations for Backward Classes: Mandal Commission Report*, 1980.

therefore the status of the same castes vary across the state boundaries as they happen to be independent peasants in certain states and not in others. All other non-scheduled craftsmen are also included among the OBCs. Now a section of OBCs owning sizable landed property are knocking at the doors of the ruling classes. Among the oppressed, the second group is made up of the Harijans or Dalits. The Dalits are ritually unclean and to avoid pollution, kept at socially defined (locally albeit varying) distance. Preponderantly these are dispossessed people and can be classified as *propertyless oppressed*. Women have an unusual position within this structure of communities. Within any one category they are oppressed and excluded from deliberations but between any two class or caste categories they are oppressors. But their access to the public sphere remains visibly restricted. In this very brief description I have tried to combine class and caste and the social features of the various pre-modern communities in India. The intention here is to avoid the frivolous hobby of many a social scientist to ask if it is class or caste which is the main determinant of social consciousness in India. It may make better sense to look at it in terms of the category of social being. The category of social being helps us to look at the making of the identity of people in terms of caste and class and other social facets of existence. It is these features other than caste which go to create the openings due to which a modern self is taking shape.[10]

To a consideration of the politics hinted at earlier, let us first take the militant Hindu right-wing. It has been there in Indian politics for a very long time in one form or another but it is only recently, beginning with the Ram Janambhoomi–Babri Masjid controversy in 1986 and the demolition of the Babri Masjid in 1992, together with the anti-reservation (a movement against affirmative action in favour of OBCs) campaign in 1990 accompanied with the worst kind of sustained vandalism Indian public life has ever seen, that it has made rapid strides and has become a force to reckon with. And it is in this period that its fascist face has come to the fore. It claims its ideological roots from late nineteenth century, a period of systematic cultural intervention from above, by the

[10] On the question of the making of modern self, see Charles Taylor, *Sources of Self: Making of the Modern Identity*, Cambridge, CUP 1991; see also Robert C. Solomon, *Continental Philosophy since 1750: The Rise and Fall of the Self*, Oxford, 1988.

new élites. Out of the many themes within the debates, Hindutva restrictively seeks to mobilize peoples' imagination on the need to define the Hindu, to sharpen the boundaries from others—Muslims especially but Christians and (sometimes confusedly) Sikhs too, to demarcate who belongs to India. Over time, difference became more and more important and efforts are on in a methodical way to win over people to a monolithic conception of what it means to be a Hindu and an Indian. According to Hindutva philosophy and political practice, a Hindu is one who minimally accepts two things. At one level a Hindu is one who is ready to fight Muslims militantly, particularly in the cultural sphere, as an alien, bestial presence in India, an Other who poses a threat to the self of the Hindus. At the other level a Hindu is one who equates the immemorial nation India with Hindu culture and religion. Forms of worship, modes of interpretation of scriptures, types of ritual observances and so forth are not consequential. In this sense it is not a fundamentalist movement of a conventional kind. Nevertheless it is a hegemonic trend that seeks to impose monolithic conceptions of nation and culture, all derived from restrictive readings of Hindu religion.[11]

Three types of social forces have played a key role in the rapid rise of this brand of politics. Of these, first are the sadhus and sants and pujaris and an assortment of figures with religious clout in the forefront—all of these under the leadership of Vishwa Hindu Parishad. The second is the very sizable section of Brahmins, Rajputs and Banias who have moved over into the Hindutva camp after the anti-reservation vandalism by the privileged youths from 1990 onwards. The third group, the most important as far the cities and towns are concerned, are the elements organized under the Bajrang Dal. All kinds of social dropouts, misfits, criminals and such other elements make up the body called the Bajrang Dal; this in fact is the lumpen arm of Hindutva politics. It is important to realize that with the huge floating numbers of the unemployed, because of the sharp contraction in job opportunities, and large-scale migration from rural areas of people into towns looking for anything to eke out a living, it is easy to create crime at very low cost and with little risk to those who use crime for political

[11] See on this my recent piece, 'Behind the Verdict: What Kind of a Nation Are We,' *Economic and Political Weekly*, 22 June 1996.

advantage. And when the lumpen-criminal elements have a political cover for activity in the name of the sacred and with some degree of conviction then the self-esteem of these elements also rises; they cannot anymore be simply looked down upon as the 'scum' of society. They have now become a front for the creation of terror and fear among people and silencing all opposition.

The success of Hindutva forces in silencing many other forms of politics, has been based on their ability to bypass and overrule the institutions of state and those of 'civil society'. The Sangh Parivar has activated the hitherto politically dormant institutions of the traditional religious order like the Mutts, the Ashrams, the temples and other religious establishments. The sadhus and sants and mahants have been mobilized from these establishments and sent all over India to win new recruits. I do not want to imply that these institutions were of no importance to the people earlier. They were always there for as long as we can think of but they never enjoyed any kind of political significance. Let us look at one consequence of this development for political life in Indian society.

A new basis of legitimacy is being created in the political life of the society. An act of political importance is now being validated in a transcendental manner. The Bhartiya Janata Party (BJP) may go on insisting that it does not want a theocratic state. But one important side of theocratic politics is to seek sanctions from a realm outside of human reasoning. Priority is accorded to institutions and beliefs over which gods or some supernatural force has presiding power. The political platform created by the BJP-VHP-Bajrang Dal has been doing exactly this. In fact Hindutva forces have created a number of new institutions to unify diverse trends, like the *Dharma Sansad* (religious parliament) whose actions are self-validating; none can question their pronouncements. What then becomes of the modern institutions of contemporary society and politics is of some consequence.

Let us look now at the way the notions of democracy and majority are handled by Hindutva forces.[12] It is true that democracy is politics based on majority. But it is also a known fact that democracy means a majority that is constantly made and unmade.

[12] For a good treatment of this problem see Rajeev Bhargava, 'Secularism, Democracy and Rights', in Mehdi Arslan and Janaki Rajan (eds) *Communalism in India: Challenge and Response*, New Delhi, Manohar, 1994.

It has nothing to do with permanent majorities of a given ascriptive kind. In the arguments being advanced by the Hindutva forces, a majority is nothing other than the presumed voice of a denominational collective. If a majority is to be an unalterable given, then there is no question of a contest. If Hindus are eighty per cent plus, they will always remain close to being eighty per cent plus. Where then is the political contest? God has ordained things to be in a certain order and men are simply instruments of his preordained will. A look at the way *secularism* is talked about by the Hindutva forces is still more revealing. Enlightened opponents of secularism have rejected this notion on the ground that it is an alien concept for India[13] and is an imposition on our society through the post-enlightenment grid of power-knowledge forced on people by colonialism. Interestingly the BJP does not reject secularism but puts a qualification of 'pseudo' to the way it has been put to use by those who control the political institutions of the Indian state; this, it contends, has corrupted Indian nationalism and has been eating into the vitals of the Indian 'nation'. Mainstream politics—both Centrist and Leftist—is culpable in this crime against the nation. In passing, it is not unimportant to note that, unlike the earlier versions of nineteenth-century Hindu thought, the Sangh Parivar's idiom and conceptual baggage as far as the questions of politics are concerned is not very different from that of the others who are contesting them. On the face of it, it is quite modern except that it gets prefixed or suffixed by easily intelligible words, words which drastically alter the normal usage of the terms. Instead true secularism lies in being 'fair' to the Hindu majority, a democratic necessity as Hindutva sees it. The secularism talked by the 'secularists' is pseudo, according to Hindutva because it pampers minorities (read Muslims) and follows policies of appeasement towards them, it is inattentive to the internal enemies of nationalism, it neglects sentiments of the majority (read Hindus), it stifles the memories of the Hindu view of the good life and so on; this is just a small sample of conceptual deceptions which is part and parcel of this kind of politics.

Many a commentator has talked of the efforts of Hindutva to disenfranchise the Muslims. I agree that they want to silence the

[13] See for instance Ashis Nandy, 'An Anti-Secularist Manifesto', *Seminar*, no. 394, June 1992 or T. N. Madan, 'Secularism in its Place', *Journal of Asian Studies* 46 (3), October 1987 or Partha Chatterjee's article cited in note 5.

Muslims, make them politically and culturally voiceless. Muslim presence will then become acceptable; Hindutva is not seeking their extermination. The exclusion of Muslims will be a disastrous development from the angle of democratic life but this will not be a new feature in the understanding of the public sphere in India. Harijans and large section of women have remained disenfranchised for far too long. *Exclusion* has been a feature of the public sphere in India for large sections of people. The point I want to emphasize is that this development has led to the intensification of the *sacralization* of the common space of political debate and contestations. Some de-sacralization is needed under the present conditions. Or else the domain of the secular is going to be on the retreat.

Minimally, I agree, that secularism requires the separation of politics from religion. On this I am in sympathy with Rajeev Bhargava.[14] But I remain very sceptical that such a separation would at all be possible, even minimally on terms that Bhargava has been arguing for. It seems to me, as noted above, that a process of de-sacralization,[15] however slow as a trend, is a necessary condition for the separation itself to begin to work.

Unlike Hindutva which has succeeded in ideologically unifying various communities within its fold, the OBCs remain a loose kind of coalition. It is much more political in its nature. There is hardly any ideological unification or organizational binding. There have always been movements among the OBCs, first in south and western India and then later in the Indo-gangetic plains of north India. But their sudden rise to prominence in the recent period has been the result of the offensive launched by the militant Hindu right-wing. What became decisive in the OBCs combining into a common political platform was the widespread vandalism indulged in by the upper-caste groups in the wake of the announcement by the Janata Dal leader and the then Prime Minister V. P. Singh to accept certain of the recommendations of the Mandal Commission. As a result of this twenty-seven per cent of jobs in the public services, excluding defence and research establishments, were to be reserved for the OBCs. The Congress Party in opposition took an

[14] Rajeev Bhargava, 'Giving Secularism Its Due,' *Economic and Political Weekly*, 9 July 1994.

[15] I have borrowed this term from Alam Khundmiri, 'Secularism: Western and Indian', *Secular Democracy*.

ambivalent stand but the BJP—the political arm of the Hindutva took a stand of violent opposition to it, so much so that a few BJP governments in the states, like that of Himachal Pradesh, appealed to the Supreme Court against this order. In fighting the militant Hindu right-wing, the upwardly mobile OBCs have taken the lead and sought alliances with Dalits and Muslims.

The common purpose of this is to empower themselves and to wield political power directly so as to break the monopoly of upper castes over the state and administrative structures. In this politics of *empowerment*, the various communities retain not only their autonomy but also seek to advance a notion of *good*, not a common good but community-based notion of good and very often these notions are at sharp variance with one another. Many of these uncritically inherited notions of good life are neither in conformity with one another nor informed by some conception of common good. Unreflectively available, these cannot be fully articulated but remain important in holding the community together which is of importance in having a decisive political say in the alliance. The consequences are contradictory. Seeking their own empowerment, the various communities in the political alliance are in the forefront of fighting the Hindutva politics and the monolithic definition of what it means to be a good Hindu and a good Indian. Therefore, consequentially, the effect of this politics is to strengthen the secular tendency; in other words, without necessarily being secular in their internal worldviews, this feeds into the secular basis of politics. It also therefore secures democracy from right-wing fascistic assault. This is paradoxical because what is rightly seen as intensely caste based politics at the micro level has been a source of strength for civic-secular democracy at the macro level. It is a defence of democracy within which there are glaring infirmities as we will see below.

IV

All of this does not mean that the communities in India do not have strong links with any other larger entity or that they are self-contained groups. The intent of my argument has been to show that the links with society which were weak to begin with have further eroded since the 1980s. This coincides with the unending pressures of the crisis of economy which brought forth the cumulative effects of the failure of capitalist development in India to solve social problems. While this has gone on, the links of these communities with the economy have been getting deeper; this has also created territorial links with the Indian nation so much so that many of these groups, intriguingly, support stronger versions of nationalism. Deeply implicated in the political economy of the country, these communities are pervasively surrounded by the bourgeois condition. Capitalism has penetrated everywhere in India, if not always by the productive sector establishing its control over every sphere of economy then precariously but certainly through the sphere of accumulation, by the mopping up of the social surplus. It is this that is undermining the inner unity of communities. Capitalist development has been undermining the original communities and quite unlike early cases of development in western Europe, it has not been able to dissolve them. Under the impact of capitalist development and growing bourgeois aspiration, these communities are being broken up into segments of the original, each quite like the other and acting as the collective self fighting in the name of community for more of economic well being, greater material possessions, worldly gains and so on. To alter Macpherson's phrase, what we have in India today is a '*possessive*' *communal orientation* to life.[16]

To understand this more clearly let us look at what has been happening. Let us take as illustration caste groups, various communities in the last hundred years and more specifically in the roughly fifty years of electoral politics under bourgeois conditions. Originally, these spontaneously renewing caste communities or *jatis* were recognized, at one level, for what they are by two things. These have been (i) ritual and status or ritual-status and (ii) occupation. Over this micro-reality has been the overarching macro-ideology of *varna*. At another level each of the jatis or castes conventionally recognized itself as an egalitarian entity; that is, given the same ritual status and occupation there were minimum variations in income and assets and capacities.

Over the period referred to above, the intrinsic link between the two levels got broken. Upper-caste groups made use of the higher ritual status for gaining access to other resources like

[16] C. B. Macpherson, *The Political Theory of Possessive Individualism*, Oxford, OUP, 1962.

education and employment and through these to further resources like land and mobility. Thus the *savarnas* established (neo-) braminical control over society through modern institutions including bureaucracy; in fact the brahminical control over bureaucracy became the prime factor in the perpetuation of their hegemony over society. As an aside, anybody who has been a part of the democratic teachers movement knows how difficult it is to do anything in face of bureaucratic intransigence. This also shows why there is such a powerful urge to put job reservations on the top of the agenda for empowerment so much so that people will leave every other kind of job for any position in bureaucracy.

Here then began a process of rapid internal differentiations within the caste orders. To the extent permitted by the social situation of relative exclusions and constraints, the enterprising elements among the other castes emulated this. To mimic then is not so comic a thing in India. This process sharpened over the years. Land reforms, especially the abolition of certain types of tenancies in many regions of India, and electoral politics have been the key factors in this process. Land reforms created a very large class of independent peasants from among the socially oppressed castes (the present OBCs) and electoral politics opened the doors for their empowerment. The sequence and speed varied widely over the different regions of the country but within this variation the point to note in passing is the delay in the process in north India.

The point of foremost theoretical importance to note here is the non-materialization in the political process of the latent forces inherent in the situation. This ongoing differentiation has been the *material basis for the individuation of persons and interests* and through this individuation, for the development of class consciousness and class-based politics. This may not have happened to the extent predicted or entailed by the process. What happened, far more as time passed by, is that all these micro-communities or jatis started aligning with one another within a varna-like entity. For example, a century ago there would be hundreds of jatis among Kurmis or Yadavs and so on but they are now emerging as and seeking to represent themselves as a single force. Here is a transition to a single aggressive identity from multiple non-assertive social groupings and through this to a political process of empowerment. This created strongly rooted 'subjective' obstructions to class-based mobilization. Here we have an 'objective' basis for the overdetermination of superstructure. And, obviously therefore, for the non-transition to the making of class-in-itself. The result then is politics in which the terrain of activity has been conglomerates of identities instead of classes as the main agents in politics. True, the rise of OBCs and Dalits has widened the base of democracy but without the constraining structures giving way to emancipatory ones.

However, the question is: are there sheer singular identities at the macro-level? Earlier I talked of segments of these communities which have emerged out of the nominal unity of varna-like entities under the many sided impact of capitalist development. Within each of these large varna-like communities, one will always find a few large divisions. Sometimes some of these divisions work like inner contradictions. For example, English education versus non-English education, urban versus rural, the landed versus landless, metropolitan versus small town are some such important divisions. Under each of these divisions a (false but) class-like consciousness is being displayed; false because it remains Yadav versus Yadav in articulated terms. A few points are worth mentioning to round off this part of the discussion. Around these divisions a material basis exists which undermines the possibility of actualization of the asserted unity of the varna-like communities. But behind varna-like entities there is no material basis. It is the long established availability of the varna macro-ideology that provides the ground for efforts to unify these communities for political competition. This is yet another instance of the overdetermination of superstructures.[17]

V

Two things are worth attending to for an understanding of the evolution of the 'civil society' in India. With capitalist development, as the inner unity of communities gets severely undermined, fragments of these communities act within the public sphere as the equivalent of egoistic individuals in the competitive

[17] For the last five paragraphs starting from the reference to Macpherson, I am deeply indebted to D. L. Sheth. Many of the raw ideas came up first in discussions with him and I have developed them in my own ways which may not be in line with his thinking.

world of bourgeois possessiveness; it is this 'possessive' communal orientation which regulates public contestation and political competitiveness. Thus, one component of civil society, that of the egoistic individual in the market is taken care of in an altered way. But precisely because of this, what remains haphazardly unstable is the citizen. Thus the rights bearing autonomous persons acting together for common concerns are continuously thwarted by communities acting as collective personalities. The unpresentable face of civil society, that of the egoistic individuals, is expanding whereas the public sphere of citizens seeking common grounds of existence, that which makes this society a livable one, is not expanding at the same rate.[18] It is therefore easy to understand the behaviour of the state. While it is always reluctant to concede to class demands it has no hesitation in bargaining with these communal groups. The ramifications of this for the public sphere are far reaching. With the declining faith of the people in the ability of the state to do good for them and with the jettisoning of the transformative agenda of the state, it has become possible to deflect this communally based possessiveness into political mobilization of various kinds cutting across the ideological divide of communal and secular.

The other feature of 'civil society' in India is that the public sphere,[19] because of the persistence of traditional communities, is a fragmented one. The message and its receptivity do not have an unhindered flow in society but are obstructed at the shifting boundaries which define the communities. The content of the message can get altered as it crosses the boundaries of the community. Herein lies the calculation of interest, egoistic, no

[18] My views on what constitutes a civil society are based on those of Hegel as set out in his *Philosophy of Right* which became the basis of Marx's critique in the *Jewish Question* and the *Contribution to the Critique of Hegel's Philosophy of Rights: Introduction*. In that sense they differ from those of Gramsci's as fully discussed in 'State and Civil Society' in *Selections from the Prison Notebooks*.

[19] For an illuminating discussion of the public sphere see Charles Taylor, 'Liberal Politics and the Public Sphere', in *Redefining the Good Society*, issued by the Rajiv Gandhi Foundation Trust, New Delhi, 1995. For a fascinating discussion from a different point of view see Nancy Fraser, 'Rethinking the Public Sphere: A Contribution to the Critique of Actually Existing Democracy', in Bruce Robins (ed.) *The Phantom Public Sphere*, Minneapolis, 1993.

doubt, but the egoism is not just attached to the individual as in the civil societies within advanced capitalist social formation. This became evident in the way questions of 'merit', 'efficiency', 'competence', etc. came into the public arena as issues of debate during the anti-Mandal agitation and the meanings became properties of the community. The same is the case with words like secular and democracy, as we have seen earlier.

Such a political context without the underlying social unification characteristic of civil societies introduces an element of radical uncertainty about the directions of change. The conditions are inherently unstable and prone to rapid fluctuations. During the course of India's freedom struggle one could discern a more visibly coherent public sphere. This was so because of common anti-imperialist struggles and common collective slogans. This was so well into the 1950s and 1960s as hopes of betterment and well-being made people strive for the common good. Since then it has seen a reversal together with the retreat of the state as a 'benign' institution for the benefit of the poor and marginalized. This collapse of the transformative agenda, the decline of politics with minimal emancipatory concerns has pushed democratic struggles into community-based channels.

The argument in this paper has put for consideration the view that the conditions which give rise to the emergence of the public sphere in India were paradoxically the ones which led later to contraction of its boundaries. Today when we look at Indian social and political life we can clearly see the existence of a vigorous civil society but on closer look, below the surface, we can also see its eroding frontiers. This contention is not negated by the observation that powerful 'new social movements' have entered the common space of contestations and taken root in society. It is also true that the media—both print and electronic—have seen enormous expansion and so is the case with other conventional modes of articulation in society. There is greater public knowledge of affairs and also perhaps, greater civility. Whence the problem?

Briefly put, it emerges from three directions. First the reach of the 'new social movements' does not go far enough to affect community-based or communally-charged politics. And this politics has, secondly, activated certain elements of traditional polity through which extra legal coercive methods are employed in extracting compliance. Finally, this politics has based itself largely upon, among other things, an unqualified claim for community rights.

VI

Therefore, the crucial question is: can the right to a way of life be claimed on behalf of a community when the exercise of the same is denied to the individual? Not unsurprisingly, in our struggle for civil liberties we have not properly examined these issues. Not surprising because we have not specified which rights can be violated by the state and which rights are under constant threat from communities fighting to hold on to what they think they are. If the rights of the individual are an important aspect of the democratization of society, then it is important to distinguish the political-legal rights which can be invoked against the institutions of the state, and those background rights to restrain powers invested in the communities to deny choices to their own individual members.

So under the present circumstances, we need a different framework of assumptions to build justifications of what is permissible within the claims of the community. The need arises because there is a problem between (a) freedom of choice and (b) criteria for justifying that the choice is right. If a community's right to a way of life cannot be questioned on democratic grounds[20] then

[20] In the way I read the 'discourse of rights' what seems to me important is the manner in which rights of collectives like those of the trade unions became central from about the middle of the nineteenth-century in the wake of the protracted struggle of the working classes. Together with this the right to property, central to the Lockean scheme, was at one level questioned and at another level was getting continuously qualified by such legislations such as the ten-hour working day. All of this was in the name of a self-created community the working class organized in trade unions. This collective right is not an aggregation because the moment one disaggregates it will simply dissolve; for example the right to picket is inconceivable as the right of so many discrete individuals. The nineteenth century also saw the right to self-determination. The question then is who happens here to be a subject of reference and whether that subject can at all be visualized in any other way than a collective subject. If this is so then the right of pre-modern collectivities cannot be denied, as these fulfill the criterial properties set out above, on grounds that it clashes with the right of the individual. The terrain of struggle therefore has to be different than the denial of rights.

perhaps it can be asked to *justify* and *defend* what it enjoins on the individuals as obligatory. This seems to me to be necessary for the following reasons. A community, first of all, does not exist in a vacuum. It lives amidst and surrounded by other communities in society. Its well-being is dependent on mutually beneficial material and symbolic exchanges with others. At issue here is the question of maintaining one's *difference* from others in the society. The difference that it wants to maintain from others ought not therefore be repugnant to others. Mutual acceptability of *different* norms is a necessity, for democratic rights as well. There is, secondly, in Indian society a deep inter-meshing of ultimate concerns of life with legal injunctions and ritual conventions. What is considered fundamental by a community may sometimes be nothing more than a certain way of dressing or a mode of salutation. Consider the order banning a certain dress by the Principal of a Calcutta school or the silly controversy over Shabana Azmi exchanging a kiss with the great Nelson Mandela: we must be cautious when stating that it is mandatory to defend difference. Briefly, we ought here to make a distinction between *difference in principle* and *difference in the practice of treatment*. Let me give an illustration. A community *may* be justified in asserting that it does not approve of 'adultery' but the same justification cannot be granted if it insists on publicly humiliating those it holds to be guilty. We also ought to be critically conscious, thirdly, that in none of the traditions of the communities in Indian society does there exist a place for egalitarianism; statements of equality on behalf of the weak are, to put it mildly, highly suspect. The worst on this score is the abysmal position of women.[21]

My question in relation to concerns of a society seeking to establish a regime of entrenched rights as a basis of democracy is: how much of difference is to be pushed or defended as the votaries of community rights do today? My fear is that if difference is to count for too much then the dominant within the communities who uphold difference become arbiters in the life of the people—Hindutva or the Jat *khap* or the Muslim Law Board.[22]

[21] Having talked of 'egalitarian statements' it is important here to realize that these enjoy a universal agreement outside of hidebound tradition and therefore suggest that not *all statements* in social sciences or everything concerning the knowledge of society is *essentially contested*.

[22] While I will defend the right to be different as essential to a multi-national/cultural society, I will strongly oppose, in contradistinction to the

To round off the discussion let me come back to the *right of exit* that I raised earlier. In conditions that we are in today exit can have many meanings, each of which is specific to the situation in which vulnerable people find themselves. The right of exit in one sense, in its more general meaning, can mean a struggle within a community that is one of *principled distance* from the prevailing views and practices of the community. The foremost historical instances of these that come to my mind are the figures of Socrates and Gandhi. Such principled distance can go to an extreme and then the community may go to the extent of physically removing a person. But then it leaves us with 'exemplars' who then are a source of constant renewal of the urge to greater fairness in society. In the second sense, consider the case of women, where the right of exit can be internationalized; meaning thereby that given the universal structures of patriarchy (despite all their variations) women's movements may not only have fraternal relations but build a common struggle cutting across national frontiers. In the third sense, consider Dalits, for whom the right to exit may be absolute; you can simply walk out in the way that one walks out of a filthy joint. One can explore here many more variations of the right to exit but the instances above serve the purpose of this paper.

The right to exit from the angle of this paper is quite central in accommodating the claims of community and the rights of the individual. It is central too if we were to historicize the problem. It will be myopic and downright silly to expect a replay of European history all over the world as a lot of us on the Left assumed at one time. There seems no way that communities will dissolve under the impact of capitalism and disappear as happened in the West. Retarded, disordered capitalist development is not in

---

position of Partha Chatterjee, that it is absolute in the sense that no one can be asked to defend the difference. Also it does not seem likely that 'internal representative institutions' will take care of the reforms of the (pre-modern) communities in the way they can with self-created communities; I cannot think of a more representative arrangement created through struggle than among the Sikhs as the Shiromani Gurdwara Prabandhak Committee or an inherited one the *Khaps* among the Jats. We all know how terribly intolerant these can be towards dissent and brutal to the individuals who deviate from what they put out as good and proper and therefore as ordained by 'God'.

a position to do that or, alternatively, the communities in our parts of the world are too powerful or resilient than those of western Europe; which of these is the case is a moot point and of secondary concern to this argument and so can be left as it is; there is no historical ground or criterial basis to decide between these two sets of questions. What, however, seems certain is that the right to exit will compel intra-and inter-community dialogues for change towards a movement for a life of choice.

The more important question concerns the possibility of creating conditions through alternative routes whereby properties which inhere in self-created communities can become available in our communities. Right to exit, in the nuanced way hinted above, may become one such route. It may help create one's own authority in the community of believers like the one implicit in democratic behaviour. It may also allow for constant renewal and regeneration of communities and save them from ossification under the control of vested, hide-bound authority. It may, finally, slowly over time, permit some agreements over notions of good, which, while different, also have a growing consensual core. Communities will be forced to sit up and listen and therefore introspect and negotiate. A process of negotiation once begun cannot remain confined to one specific community but has to eventually spill over to other communities. So the right to exit must be central, in our conditions, to the struggle for a common life that is democratic in essence and form.

15

Civil Society and Community: Reflections on the African Experience*

❧

Mahmood Mamdani

I have resisted the temptation to confine this paper to South Africa, for one reason. For many intellectuals, South Africa is not Africa. The 'real' Africa, from this point of view, is equatorial Africa. In contrast to this land mass between the Sahara and the Limpopo which is increasingly portrayed as a flat, one-dimensional picture of gloom, the South African transition is painted as exceptional, precisely because it is seen as the product of an exceptional experience. Over the past few years, the despair about 'real' Africa has gelled into a tendency with a name, Afro-pessimism, while celebration about the South African transition has grown into an uncritical embrace. My first objective today is to question the notion of South African exceptionalism.

Academic writings about politics in Africa reveal two clear tendencies: modernist and communitarian. Modernists take inspiration from the East European uprisings of the late 1980s; communitarians decry liberal Euro-centrism and turn to Africa's 'intrinsic realities' for a solution. For modernists, the problem is that civil society is an embryonic and marginal construct in Africa;

* An earlier version of this paper was given as the First Oliver Tambo Memorial Lecture at Developing Countries Research Centre, University of Delhi, 10 March 1995.

for communitarians, it is that real flesh-and-blood communities which comprise Africa are marginalized from public life as so many 'tribes'. The liberal solution is to locate politics in civil society, the Africanist solution is put Africa's age-old communities at the centre of African politics. The impasse in Africa is not only at the level of practical politics. It is also a paralysis of perspective.

I would like to put forth two propositions for consideration. The first is Africa-specific: that Africa is more than just a geographical expression. It is actually the name of a distinctive historical experience, even if highly differentiated. From this point of view, South Africa is not a historical aberration but very much a part of the experience that has shaped contemporary Africa. My second proposition has a more general relevance. Faced with the theoretical impasse between modernists and communitarians, between Eurocentrists and Africanists, the answer does not lie in choosing a side and defending an entrenched position. Because both sides to the debate highlight different aspects of the same African crisis, I shall suggest that the way forward lies in sublating both, through a double move that simultaneously critiques and affirms. The point is to arrive at a creative synthesis transcending both positions. Let me, then, put before you my modest contribution to this ambitious task.

My starting point is the distinctive character of the African colonial experience, crystallized in the nature of the African state. Bifurcated, Janus-faced, colonial power was organized differently in urban from rural areas. Urban power spoke the language of civil society and civil rights, rural power of community and culture. I shall begin with a consideration of urban-based civil power.

The contemporary discourse on society reminds one of an earlier discourse. Like the discourse on socialism, it is more programmatic than analytical, more ideological than historical. To cut through these claims requires an historical analysis. To borrow a phrase from that earlier context, we need an analysis of 'actually-existing' civil society, so that we may understand civil society analytically, in its actual formation, rather than programmatically, as an agenda for change. The point is to problematize the notion of civil society.

The history of civil society in Africa is laced with racism. For civil society was first and foremost the society of colons. In the main, it was created and defended by the state. Civil society was racialized. The question at independence was: how to deracialize it? Independence deracialized the state, but not civil society. In the ensuing struggle to deracialize civil society, the key agent was none other than the post-colonial state. The policy instrument it used to wage that struggle was affirmative action. We called it 'Africanization', you call it 'reservations'. The effect of affirmative action was contradictory. Its first moment, that of dismantling racial privilege, unified the victims of racism. But its second moment, that of redistribution, fragmented yesterday's victims along lines of the redistribution, whether of tribe, clan, region, religion, or simply family.

The struggle to defend racial privilege was not confined to white colons. It also included those of Indian origin, particularly in East Africa, and Lebanese immigrants in West Africa. With independence, the defence of racial privilege could not be in the language of racism. No wonder, as it receded into civil society, racial privilege was defended in the language of rights, both individual rights and the right to institutional autonomy.

To victims of racism, the language of rights sounded hollow, a lullaby for perpetuating privilege. Their demands were articulated in the language of nationalism and social justice. Characteristic of post-independence Africa was a breach between the language of rights and that of social justice. Ironically, while rights-talk appeared as a fig leaf over privilege, power appeared as the guarantor of social justice and redress. That breach, however, did not last long. Affirmative action created the institutional context for an indigenous civil society, and the political context for its collapse and absorption into political society. It was a time of a marriage between technicism and nationalism, a time for the flowering of nationalism as a state ideology. The claims of the state were both developmentalist and equalizing. Together, they had a powerful social resonance, particularly in the educated middle strata. And yet, there was clearly a problem: deracialization was not linked to democratization. What would democratization have meant in the African context?

Tribalism

Civil society theorists presume a single system of power, one where civil law frames civil rights for citizens in civil society. Critics point out those excluded and marginalized: on the basis of gender as in late nineteenth-century Europe, or on the basis of race as in colonial Africa. But the colonial system in Africa reveals not one but two systems of power, related but distinct. One was a system of civil power whose function was to guarantee rights. The other was a system of customary power that claimed to enforce tradition.

My claim is that there was something distinctive about the African colonial experience. Late colonialism brought to Africa a wealth of experience. By the time the 'Scramble for Africa' took place, the turn from a civilizing mission to a law-and-order administration, from progress to power, was complete. In this quest to hold the line, Britain was the first to marshal authoritarian possibilities in 'native' culture. In the process, it defined a world of the 'customary' from which there was no escape. Key to this was the definition of land as a customary possession. For in non-settled Africa, land could not be a private possession, of either landlords or peasants. It was defined as a 'customary' communal holding, to which every peasant household had a 'customary' access, defined by state-appointed 'customary' authorities. The creation of an all-embracing world of the 'customary' had three notable consequences.

First, more than any other colonial subject, the African was perceived, not as a 'native', but as a 'tribes person'. Every colony had two legal systems: one 'modern', the other 'customary'. 'Customary' law was defined as the law of the 'tribe'. Correspondingly, a 'tribe' was defined as a group with its own 'customary' law. Thus, there was not one 'customary' law for all 'natives', but roughly as many sets of 'customary' laws as there were said to be 'tribes'. Dame Margery Perham, a semi-official historian of British colonialism, claimed that the genius of British rule was in seeking to civilize Africans as communities, not as individuals. More than anywhere else, there was in the African colonial experience a one-sided opposition between the individual and the group, civil society and community, rights and tradition.

Secondly, in the late nineteenth-century African context, there were several traditions, not just one. The tradition that colonial powers privileged as the 'customary' was the one with the least historical depth, that of nineteenth-century conquest states. On the other hand, this monarchical, authoritarian and patriarchal notion of the 'customary' most accurately mirrored colonial practices. In this sense, it was an ideological construct.

The locus of 'customary' power was the local state, the district in British colonies, the circle in French colonies. Unlike civil power which was organized on the principle of differentiation, customary power was organized as fused power. Customary law was administratively driven, since those who enforced custom also defined custom in the first place. Custom, in other words, was state-ordained and state-enforced.

I wish to be understood clearly. I am not arguing for a conspiracy theory whereby custom was always defined 'from above', invented, constructed, by those in power. The 'customary' was more often than not the site of struggle. Custom was the outcome of a contest between various forces, not just those in power or its on-the-scene agents. My point, though, is about the institutional context in which this contest took place: the terms of the contest, its institutional framework, were heavily skewed in favour of state-appointed 'customary' authorities. It was a game in which the dice were loaded.

It should not be surprising that custom came to be the language of force. It masked the uncustomary power of Native Authorities. The *third* notable consequence of an all-embracing 'customary' power was that the African colonial experience was marked by force to an unusual degree. Where land was defined as a 'customary' possession, the market could only be a partial construct. Beyond the market, there was only one way of driving land and labour out of the world of the 'customary'. That was force. The day-to-day violence of the colonial system was embedded in 'customary' Native Authorities in the local state, not in civil power at the centre. And yet, we must not forget that 'customary' local authority was reinforced and backed up by central civil power. Colonial despotism was highly decentralized.

If 'tribalism' was the form of local power organized 'from above', 'tribalism' was also the form of revolt 'from below'. Every peasant struggle I know of in colonial and post-colonial Africa unfolded as a civil war, within a tribal or a religious community. Peasant insurrectionists organized around what they claimed was an untainted, uncompromised, genuine custom, against a state-enforced version of the 'customary'. Colonial power both reinforced tribalism from above and led to its blowing up from below. But this revolt became a source of a profound dilemma because local populations were usually multi-ethnic, and at times multi-religious. Ethnicity or religion was reproduced as a problem inside every peasant movement. This is why it is not enough simply to separate tribal power organized 'from above' from tribal revolt waged 'from below', so we may denounce the former and embrace the latter. The revolt from below needs to be problematized, for it carried the seeds of its own fragmentation and possible self-destruction.

Apartheid

The bifurcated state form that I am describing, civil and customary, first crystallized in equatorial Africa. Only later did it spread to older colonies to the north and the south. In this movement, the last to reorganize the state structure to incorporate the 'native' population in a world of enforced tradition was South Africa. That reorganization was called 'apartheid', separate development. My claim is that apartheid did not make for an exceptional South African experience; instead, it brought South Africa into the fold of the colonial experience. To make that point, and to explore the creative and the problematic aspects of the resistance against apartheid, shall be my objective in the rest of this paper.

The key riddle in every colonial enterprise was the 'native' question: how can an alien minority stabilize rule over an indigenous majority? To put it differently, how can a subject population be organized so as to fragment and dissipitate revolt? In the history of colonialism in South Africa, there were two responses to this question: 'race' and 'tribe'.

The home of the racial solution was the Cape. Cape settler perspectives were marked by a century of sustained 'native' revolt. They called these the ten 'kaffir wars'. They understood tribalism as a form of resistance, to be crushed. For them, the key to stabilizing rule was to break up tribal institutions and undermine tribal identity in the name of civilization from which they were determined to exclude the uncivilized. The home of the tribal solution was Natal. The settlers of Natal were the first to appreciate that, more than exclusion, incorporation would provide the key to stabilizing alien rule. They were the first to appreciate the other side of 'tribalism', that it could also be a form of control.

The debate between the Cape and the Natal standpoints unfolded over nearly a century. The terms of that debate were shaped by changing conditions. These were material and social, summed up in processes of urbanization and proletarianization. But the change was also institutional, signified by the erosion of tribal institutions and the forging of new solidarities relevant to a changed context. And finally, it was political, a fact crystallized rather dramatically in the emergence of a multi-class popular revolt, organized as the ICU, a trade union of the 1920s with urban origins but a rural social base.

The movement inspired a rethinking of the 'native' question in South African ruling circles. The most prominent voice in that reconsideration was that of Jan Smuts, the South African Prime Minister, also the Chancellor of Cambridge University and one of the framers of the League of Nations Charter. Invited to give the Rhodes lecture at Oxford in 1929, Smuts contrasted 'territorial segregation' based on race with 'institutional segregation' based on the recognition of tribal institutions. Smuts' point was that racial discrimination would be difficult to stabilize unless refracted through an official recognition and reinforcement of tribal institutions. But Smuts felt that urbanization had gone too far in South Africa for the solution to work there. He counseled that 'institutional segregation' be implemented in more agrarian British colonies to the north.

But the debate between 'territorial' and 'institutional' segregation, between race and tribe—between the primacy of exclusion or incorporation—as the locus of 'native' control, did not go away. It was rekindled by post-war revolt: the miners' strike, the struggle of squatters around Johannesburg, and the boycott of commuters, particularly in Alexandra and other townships. As the debate was joined, there was a growing recognition that racial segregation on its own tended to show up rulers as a minority, while emphasizing the majority character of the ruled. Institutional segregation, on the other hand, would further divide this majority into a number of ethnic minorities.

In the 1948 election, the two major white political parties in South Africa divided on the 'native' question. The Nationalist party won that election by a slim margin. Its secretly-organized core, the *Broederbond*, disagreed with Smuts that it was too late to implement a mode of 'institutional segregation' in South Africa. It is the Broederbond which inspired a reorganization of the South African state known as apartheid. Let me briefly sum up the main lines of that reorganization.

In South African historiography, the period before 1948 is known as that of 'segregation', the period after 1948 as that of 'apartheid'. Under segregation, a department of the central state known as the Native Affairs Department (NAD) controlled all 'native' affairs in the rural 'reserves'. In contrast, 'native' affairs in urban areas were under the control of decentralized white local authorities. The post-war revolt, particularly that of squatters and commuters, showed that decentralized local authority was not equal to diffusing resistance that transcended local boundaries. With apartheid, there was a reorganization of the state. The NAD was withdrawn from rural areas, where control over 'native' affairs was decentralized under Native Authorities of tribal chiefs. In the urban areas, on the other hand, control over 'native' affairs was centralized. The NAD was moved from rural to urban areas where it controlled all 'native' affairs, other than health.

If we reread the history of the South African state though the lens of the 'native' question, it would be marked by three significant events which took place in 1910, 1927, and 1948. In 1910, all the white Republics came together and agreed on the terms of an alliance, the key to which was a decentralized legislative civil power over white populations, and a centralized executive rule by decree—unchecked by either the legislature or the judiciary—over 'native' populations. The second hallmark is the 1927 Native Administration Act, which brought all 'natives' under the rule of 'customary' law. In the Cape, though, where reservations about restoring tribal institutions were the strongest, this law was to be dispensed by white commissioners. The third and final turning point in that history is 1948, when apartheid finally brought Cape exceptionalism to an end, creating a decentralized despotism mediated through autonomous tribal authorities in rural areas but a centralized despotism over urban 'natives' by its own Native Affairs Department.

Apartheid was what Smuts called 'institutional segregation', the British termed indirect rule and the French association. There was one difference, though. Because of the marked urbanization that

Smuts had noted, the implementation of apartheid literally required the physical expulsion of millions of 'natives' from urban to rural areas. It is forced removals that signified the particularly cruel and violent twist of 'native' policy in South Africa. Whereas in all other African colonies, force was applied by Native Authorities while the central power wore a mask of civility, it came to be otherwise in South Africa where it was the central power which unleashed the force necessary to effect removals from 'white' areas. This is why it was in South Africa, more than in any other African colony, that the mask of civility was ripped off the central power.

Periodizing the Anti-Apartheid Struggle

The bifurcated state enforced a double separation. The first, between the urban and the rural, was described in legal theory as a separation between 'modern' and 'customary' law. The second, between ethnic groups, was captured by the 'tribal' mould in which 'customary' law was formulated and enforced by the Native Authority. This form of the state reproduced corresponding tensions within the ranks of resistance movements. I shall now try and illustrate this in the specific case of the anti-apartheid struggle in South Africa.

The post-war combination of miners' strike, squatter struggles and commuter boycotts had an opposite effect on the nationalist movement from its impact on state strategy. Just as the state prepared to shift the locus of 'native' control from the urban to the rural through the creation of autonomous Native Authorities, the nationalist movement shifted its organizational focus from the rural to the urban. The shift took place as the result of a larger debate. Methods changed from conciliatory to confrontational, and organization from élite to popular. The change from the old to the new was experienced both as a gravitational shift in existing organizations, like in the African National Congress (ANC) to its youth wing, and as the emergence of new organizations, like the Pan Africanist Congress (PAC) which emerged through an initiative from the ranks of the ANC Youth League.

The culmination of this new politics was Sharpeville 1960. The state responded swiftly through repression. Organizations were banned and activists were rounded up in jail or hounded into exile.

From this context was borne a new paradigm of struggle as armed struggle. Soon earlier Maoist notions of the guerrilla being like a fish in water, were displaced by Gueverist notions of the guerrilla as a professional armed revolutionary. Township militants now sought to move into exile, to get military training in a 'front-line state', awaiting return to liberate 'the people'. Looked at differently, both the force of repression and the perspective of resistance combined to flush militants into exile in the wake of every successive act of resistance.

The result was a period of stability, known in South African official history as the 'decade of peace'. That decade lasted from 1960 to 1972. It was a period of secondary industrialization (primary industrialization having taken place in the aftermath of the discovery of minerals at the turn of the century). Rates of industrial growth in the 'decade of peace' were second only to Japan. This industrialization created two social forces that would bring the 'decade' to a close. These were migrant labour and educated youth.

If the first period of anti-apartheid struggle came to a close with Sharpeville in 1960, and the second period was the lull that was the 'decade of peace', the third period began with a spontaneous wave of strikes among migrant workers in Durban in 1972, spreading to the Cape and the Transvaal over the following year. This strike wave was a meeting point between migrant workers and student radicals, leading to an organizational initiative that culminated in the formation of an independent black workers union movement.

We need to bear in mind that the student radicals of what came to be known as Durban 1973 were not black, but white. The backdrop to that fact was a split in the student movement the previous year, as Black Consciousness-inspired students led by Steve Biko split from the white-dominated student movement to set up as a separate body. The split was a crisis for the small minority of white student radicals. Finding themselves hopelessly outnumbered inside a racial white student organization, they formed a Wages Commission that sent its members to help black workers in Durban factories wage a struggle for reforms. The Durban Strikes of 1973 presented these white radicals their first opportunity to organize and shape a mass movement.

The orientation that white radicals gave the independent union movement was influenced by their own perspective. Distrustful of middle-class nationalism which they claimed gave a greater weight to race than to class, and yet emphasized spectacular action at the expense of sustained organization-building, they were not averse to a critical engagement with the state as part of pursuing a reform struggle. Shut out of townships on account of both their colour and strained relations with black student radicals, the white student left concentrated on organization at the workplace.

On the heels of Durban 1973 followed Soweto 1976. Its course was shaped by radical youth in the Black Consciousness movement. They used the opening created by the Soweto uprising to build community-based organizations. We shall see that the division within the radical student movement, between a handful of whites and numerous blacks, between those stressing class and workplace and those focusing on race and community, would resurface a decade later amongst union activists. For the moment, though, it is interesting to take note of the common ground shared by the two wings of the student Left. Both paid homage to armed struggle, but none used more than a stone in actual struggle.

The point is important. Even if its participants did not consciously voice it, there took place a shift in the paradigm of struggle with Durban 1973 and Soweto 1976. It was a shift of emphasis from armed to unarmed but extra-legal struggle, from struggle by professional revolutionaries to a popular struggle. Like the Intifadah in occupied Palestine, it was a shift that preceded that in eastern Europe by at least a decade. This shift explains the thickening web of organizations over the next decade, culminating in a protracted urban uprising by the middle of the 1980s.

The urban uprising of the mid-1980s was not an armed struggle. To be absolutely clear, there was no armed struggle in South Africa. Armed action was limited to a few spectacular propaganda actions. It is the unarmed urban uprising, and not an armed struggle, that brought the South African army into black townships in 1984 and finally got the South African state to contemplate a political solution to its crisis. But before we can have a perspective on that accommodation, we need to consider the urban uprising in its moment of weakness.

The Dialectic between Domination and Resistance

Ironically, the Achilles heel of the resistance turned out to be migrant labour. This spearhead of the 1973 strike wave had in another decade turned into the soft underbelly of urban resistance. By 1986, migrant labour was alienated from that resistance, and by 1991 the tension between the two had exploded into antagonism between hostels and townships in South Africa's industrial heartland, the Reef. The question is: why?

To answer that question, we need to retrace our steps and our focus, from the creative side of the urban uprising to its weaker side. In 1976, the dilemma of the South African state was how to prevent a confluence of the social forces set into motion by Durban 1973 and Soweto 1976. Its strategy was to split the ranks of labour through a carrot-and-stick approach. Resident black workers were given the right to organize alongside white workers, but the same right was withheld from migrant workers. The independent union movement, Federation of South African Trade Unions (FOSATU), fought this attempted division tooth-and-nail. The attempt failed. And yet, that same division, between migrant and resident labour, took place a decade later. Once again, the question is, why?

Part of the answer lies in a changed setting, the dull compulsion of material and social processes. Continued industrialization led to skilled black labour and the entry of educated township-based youth, the Soweto generation, into factories. There was a corresponding shift in the plant-level leadership of unions, from unskilled migrants to skilled resident labour. But another part of the answer lies in limited perspectives of the union leadership, in choices made and opportunities missed.

In the early 1980s, there took place a debate within the independent union movement, between 'workerists' and 'populists', between those who stressed workplace organization and those who championed community-based organization. The names are labels given by each side to the other in the heat of debate. As urban resistance took on the dimensions of an uprising, the division between workplace and community appeared increasingly artificial. On the one hand, workers who demanded rights in factories were often the same residents who fought evictions and resisted official attempts to cut off services in townships. On the other hand, the entry of South African Defence Forces into townships sharply underlined the limits of a fragmentary and decentralized resistance. Not surprisingly, 'populists' won the argument against 'workerists'. That victory was signified by an organizational shift in the locus of the independent trade union movement, from FOSATU to Congress of South African Trade Unions (COSATU).

And yet, this victory masked a critical weakness of the union movement. For both the 'populists' and the 'workerists' shared the same notion of community. Both meant by the community the urban township, not the rural reserves organized through indirect rule, nor the hostels also organized on the basis of indirect rule. When unions left hostels and concentrated on township-based organization, the consequence of an escalating confrontation with officialdom was contradictory for the hostel and the township. When rent boycotts led to a termination of services, alternate services in townships were provided by community-based civic organizations. But in the absence of a similar alternative in hostels, there was simply a strengthening of indirect rule authority.

The point is that the urban uprising left intact the authority of indirect rule in both rural areas and hostels. In that context, hostel residents were far more likely to experience township-engineered consumer boycotts and work stayaways as not only external but also coercive. The result, predictably, was a tension-ridden relationship between the two constituencies.

Reform of Apartheid

Such was the setting in which the South African state took a reform initiative, first in 1986, and then in 1989. It was a context of an internal stalemate between a resistance confined to urban townships and a repression that had run the course of armed suppression. To understand the decisive shift in South African ruling circles in favour of a negotiated reform, we need also to keep in mind the changed external context in the era of glasnost.

The reform was a double manoeuver. In 1986, the state abolished influx control, and thereby the restrictions on the movement of black people from rural to urban areas. With an eye on the urban limitations of the uprising, it was an attempt to play upon the rural–urban divide. It opened the floodgates of urban entry to rural migrants, counting on them simultaneously to dampen the fires of urban revolt and to inflame the tensions within the urban black population. The rural exodus first moved into hostels, and then spilled over into shanties. By 1991, the shanty population of South Africa was estimated at nearly a fifth, roughly 7 out of 38 million.

The second wave of reform came in 1989, with the release of Mandela and other leaders and the unbanning of exiled organizations. It was an attempt to forge an alliance with a force—the ANC—highly credible in the urban uprising, and yet a force not borne of the uprising. Grown into maturity at a safe distance from the discipline of both repression and resistance, the ANC was more of a middle-aged proto-state organization whose strength lay in its diplomatic skills in the international arena. But the prestige of the ANC was not just based on its historical record. Its centralized organization and country-wide claim also contrasted sharply with a second strategic weakness of the urban uprising, that its organization was local and fragmentary. Confronted by the centralized state, the decentralized resistance that was initially a source of strength turned into a source of weakness.

As the ANC returned home, it began a learning experience that—like most learning experiences—was littered with mistakes. It began by calling for an emptying of hostels so they may be turned into reception centres for returning exiles. When it realized that it had made a brazen mistake, it changed calls: the ANC denounced single-sex migrant labour as an inhumane system, and called for an upgrading of hostels into family units. At both points, the ANC was backed by the civic movement and by unions.

The *ad hoc* mistakes of the ANC created an opening for Inkatha. One needs to understand the history of Inkatha to appreciate its ability to take advantage of this opportunity. Inkatha emerged as a cultural organization after Sharpeville. It emerged using ANC colours, and slogans, even considering itself as the ANC-at-home. With Durban 1973 and Soweto 1976, relations between ANC and Inkatha soured. From the point of view of ANC, Inkatha's call for a critical but constitutional engagement with the apartheid state was tantamount to collaboration. And yet, Inkatha enjoyed considerable popularity, particularly amongst Zulu migrant workers, because it was the one homeland authority that refused a Bantustan-style independence and spoke of South Africa as one country.

Post-1976, Inkatha organized Kwazulu into a one-party state. With the unbanning of exiled movements, it looked for opportunities to break out of its Natal confinement. That opportunity was handed to it on a platter as the controversy over hostels and migrant labour—many of whom were Zulus—grew. When the ANC called for upgrading hostels into family units, Inkatha accused it of wanting to urbanize Africans forcibly. Inkatha championed 'customary' rights of migrants to hold land in rural areas and to maintain rural ties. In the face of a resistance whose organization was limited to urban areas, whose perspective excluded any coherently formulated alternative to 'customary' rule in rural areas, an appeal to Zulu tradition had a strong resonance amongst hostel-based Zulu migrants. In this context, Inkatha moved into predominantly Zulu hostels with arms, and the antagonism between hostels and townships exploded into violence.

The end of that violence was prepared for by an ANC-Inkatha truce leading to a coalition government. Without a perspective on how to democratize 'customary' rule, there was little alternative to such coalition-building from above. This is why this paper should not be interpreted as a critique of the truce, but as a perspective on the strategic weakness of the urban uprising which shaped the terms of that truce.

Most critical appraisals of the transition to majority-based rule have highlighted concessions made to white privilege. My focus has been different, because I consider these concessions to have more of a tactical significance. From a strategic point of view, I find the state-enforced split between the urban and the rural, and as a result between one ethnically-based customary power and another—and the absence of a perspective that can problematize this split—to be of a greater significance. It is this weakness that explains the wisdom behind the tactical truce between ANC and Inkatha, behind this peaceful co-existence between nationalism and 'customary' power. It is a truce illustrative of a trajectory followed by the rest of Africa a few decades earlier, summed up in the phrase deracialization without democratization.

Apartheid refracted racial domination through an institutionally-enforced ethnic differentiation. This is what Smuts summed up as 'institutional segregation'. It was a form of the state which institutionally enforced a double separation on subjects, between town and country, and between ethnicities in rural areas. In this sense, apartheid as a state form was not exceptional to South Africa. It was actually the generic form of the colonial state in Africa. Neither is the South African reform that unique in the African context. African independence brought forth two mainstream experiences. The radical experience was born of a rift between nationalism and customary power. The conservative trajectory, in contrast, was shaped by a marriage between the two. If this outcome, a deracialization without a democratization, goes unchallenged in South Africa as it has in several other countries to the north of the Limpopo, it will reproduce the decentralized despotism characteristic of the colonial state in Africa.

16

Cultures, Communities and the History of Politics in Southern Africa

Preben Kaarsholm

'Community' figures as an ambiguous concept, both in the United Nations Development Programme's (UNDP) *Human Development Report 1994*[1] and in one of the more serious documents prepared for the recent Copenhagen World Summit for Social Development, the UNRISD report on *States of Disarray: The Social Effects of Globalisation.*[2]

In the *Human Development Report 1994*, 'community security' is an important ingredient in 'human security'—'people derive security from their membership in a group—a family, a community, an organization, a racial or ethnic group that can provide a cultural identity and a reassuring set of values. Such groups also offer practical support.' At the same time 'community' affiliation may threaten security—'traditional communities can also perpetuate oppressive practices... Traditional communities, particularly ethnic groups, can also come under much more direct attack from each other...Ethnic clashes often have brutal results...Indigenous people also face widening spirals of violence' (p. 31 ff.).

[1] Inge Kaul a.o., *Human Development Report 1994*, New York 1994.

[2] Dharam Ghai, Cynthia Hewitt de Alcantara, Yusuf Bangura, Jessica Vivian a.o., *States of Disarray: The Social Effects of Globalisation,* An UNRISD Report for the World Summit for Social Development, Geneva, March 1995.

Similarly, the UNRISD report on *States of Disarray*, in its chapter on 'Identity Crises: Ethnic Conflict, Religion and Violence', recognizes that 'community' in the form of 'ethnic identity' (which is understood very broadly) can be something which 'provides richness to the human experience' and may 'be a source of national cohesion: when people feel free to practise their own cultural traditions, speak their own languages and pass this heritage on to their children, they are also more likely to develop a sense of civic identity and a feeling that they share common goals with the rest of society' (p. 106). On the other hand, recent years 'have seen an alarming outbreak of conflicts based on race, religion or ethnic identity. The battles raging in Europe, the genocidal carnage in Africa, the violent political struggles in Arab states—all suggest that the world is heading for increasingly turbulent waters. People are worried not just about the level of violence involved, which is horrific enough, but about the possibility that we may be moving towards dark, ultimate and intractable forms of conflict that lie beyond rational solution' (p. 95).

In this paper, I shall explore some of the reasons why 'community' has come to obtain such an ambiguous status in a region of the world, southern Africa, which seems to be faced with particular challenges to its human security and possibilities for developing democratic forms of governance.

Africa in general has tended to be regarded as continent in which community-based organization is especially important. Anthropological investigations have left an impression of Africa as characterized by myriads of tribes, held together individually by forms of traditional custom, and providing only occasional examples of forms of state organization overriding tribe, and—in such cases—mainly assuming the form of tribal hierarchies (as, for example, in the cases of the Asante and Zulu kingdoms). More recent studies of Africa by political scientists have also been inclined towards a holistic view of the continent and have attempted to outline the *differentia specifica* of a particularly African political culture—from Sandbrook's *The Politics of Economic Stagnation in Tropical Africa* (1985) via Jean-François Bayart's *L'état en Afrique: la politique du ventre* (1989) to Goran Hyden and Michael Bratton's *Governance and Politics in Africa* (1992). Such studies give an impression of Africa as a continent in which 'the significance of cultural variables'[3]

[3] Hyden and Bratton, p. 26.

is particularly great, and which therefore require forms of 'regime' that are in accordance with 'primordial', or as Hyden prefers to put it, 'god-given' structures of trust and compliance and do not necessarily involve democratization 'along lines that are familiar to Westerners'. The particular importance of culture in Africa according to such theories is described by John Martinussen in the following manner:

At the formal level, a considerable amount of variation may be observed. Forms of government may vary from military dictatorships to parliamentary democracies and people's republics. But the point [of theories like Sandbrook's and Hyden's] is that regardless of the formal mode of government, political processes and the overall functioning of the state is determined by the dominating social order which both exhibits signs of great variation and, in decisive respects, a remarkable uniformity.

This uniformity includes the fact that the majority of African societies are governed by almost absolutist rulers. Such top leaders do not govern on account of either popular sovereignty or any other legitimating ideology, but because of their control over significant public funds and goods which they can distribute with a view to securing political support. The rule of such absolutist top leaders is further based, to a certain extent, on their control over the military and the public administration, i.e. the most important instruments of force...

It is another major assumption that, in actual practice, forceful oppression is a much weaker means of political power than *systems of patronage* through which a distribution of bigger and smaller rewards can be effected to social networks...[These systems of patronage] are closely linked to informal and more traditional forms of organisation in society, including in particular patron-client relationships...

Patronage functions when the absolutist top leader is able to distribute lavishly from the public funds and goods which he controls. He does so to his own clan members, but also to a selection of clan leaders, whose political support is necessary. At the next step, clan leaders may then use part of their resources to secure political support in a similar way from selected clan leaders at lower level. And this pattern continues until the crumbs which have fallen from the table of the strong may—possibly—reach small peasants and other poor groups of the population.[4]

It seems that, in such generalized theories of the African state, an anthropological understanding of tribal society and rule has been

[4] John Martinussen, *Samfund, stat og marked: En kritisk gennemgang af teorier om udvikling i den 3. verden,* Copenhagen 1994, p. 235 ff. (my translation).

magnified into comprising the political culture of a whole continent. If such ideas of culture and the organization of communities are to form the basis for recommendations of the most suitable forms of governance in particular African societies, then must indeed not only economics, but also political science be regarded a 'dismal science'.

The theories outlined above represent attempts to break away from a 'classical' modernization theory paradigm that would assume modernization to involve a 'break' with tradition. Instead political modernization or development is now taken to imply or necessitate a 'dialectical' interaction with tradition or the culturally given. This tradition or culturally given, however, is not in itself approached dialectically or historically, but is instead petrified into something uniform and static.

To demonstrate the inadequacy of such approaches and to provide pointers towards a different framework for theorizing possibilities of democratic governance and provision of human security in multicultural African societies, I shall draw into the discussion another set of recent attempts, mainly by historians, anthropologists and sociologists, to understand the historical development of notions of community and culture in southern Africa. An important feature of these contributions has been the effort to replace static and uniform notions of community identities and cultural self-understandings with historically dynamic and flexible ones which have grown out of political struggles and contestations over resources and have been influenced importantly by the different colonization and resistance histories of individual southern African societies. On this basis, the development of a different and more complex understanding of the potentialities of political culture in African societies should be possible.

One can perhaps distinguish two strands in the emergence of the effort to deconstruct and historicize the formation of community identities in southern Africa that was initiated with the publication of two important collections—Hobsbawm and Ranger's *The Invention of Tradition* in 1983 and Leroy Vail's *The Creation of Tribalism* in 1989. One strand has focused on the forming and manipulation of boundaries and self-understandings through colonial administrative policies, welfare schemes and ethnographic interventions; the second strand has taken into account also the ways in which colonial inventions interacted with local imaginings and put greater emphasis on the appropriation of administered identities by colonial subjects and forms in which they were turned into vehicles for adaptation and resistance, as well as on the ways in which colonial hegemonies were themselves changed, modified and delimited by such contestations.[5]

An important point made concerned the way in which colonial administrations had fixated and bureaucratically standardized cultures and identities which before colonialism had been much more 'fuzzy' (to use the term employed by Sudipta Kaviraj and Partha Chatterjee in their not unsimilar efforts to conceptualize the modern historical development of community identities in India).[6] An example of this was Ranger's delineation of the effects on self-understanding and political articulation of the transformation of a wide spectre of dialects, whose outer points would have been unable to communicate, into a standard Shona language through the good offices of Rhodesian missionaries and governmental language committees. And, correspondingly, the creation of the idea of a unified Ndebele 'tribe' which had little to do with the elaborate multi-ethnic manoeuverings through which the hegemony of pre-colonial statehood in Matabeleland was held together.[7] Another, Robert Papstein's description of how more or less arbitrary administrative divisions of north-western Zambian peoples into 'tribes' came to provide the basis for new struggles over land rights based on the subsequently formulated histories of these 'tribes'.[8]

The need for colonial administrations in southern Africa to define and delimit communities grew out of the effort to establish

[5] See Terence Ranger, 'The Invention of Tradition Revisited: The Case of Colonial Africa', in P. Kaarsholm and J. Hultin (eds) *Inventions and Boundaries: Historical and Anthropolotical Approaches to the Study of Ethnicity and Nationalism,* Occasional Paper no. 11, IDS, Roskilde, 1994, pp. 5–50.

[6] Sudipta Kaviraj, 'The Imaginary Institution of India', *Subaltern Studies* VII, Delhi 1992, pp. 1–39; Partha Chatterjee, 'The Agenda for Nationalism', in P. Kaarsholm (ed.) *Popular Movements, Political Organization, Democracy and the State*, Occasional Paper no. 4, IDS, Roskilde, 1992, pp. 73–87.

[7] See Terence Ranger, *The Invention of Tribalism in Zimbabwe*, Gweru, 1985.

[8] Robert Papstein, 'From Ethnic Identity to Tribalism: The Upper Zambezi Region of Zambia, 1830–1981', in L. Vail (ed.) *The Creation of Tribalism in Southern Africa*, London, 1989, pp. 372–94.

a system of dual political and judicial rule which—through segregation—would secure white settler control over land and resource allocation and cement the sovereignty of the colonial state. Such a system of rule through segregation was first established in Natal and Zululand from the 1850s through what came to be known as the Shepstone system:

> The official responsible for controlling the African population was Theophilus Shepstone. Brought up in the eastern frontier region of the Cape Colony as the son of a Wesleyan missionary, he spoke the Nguni languages well. A convinced and skillful paternalist, he improvised a method of African control similar to what the British would later apply in colonial tropical Africa and call *indirect rule*. The key was the use of African chiefs as subordinate officials, made responsible, in the last resort, not to their own people but to the colonial government. Shepstone recognized the existing chiefs in communities that had survived the turmoil of the Mfecane; in other cases, he appointed men as chiefs. He also imposed a dual legal system: customary African law, as codified by him, prevailed among Africans; but the colonial Roman Dutch law, taken over from the Cape Colony, applied among whites and in relations between Africans and whites.[9]

The effects of the system was not only the establishment of dual rule, under which a sort of Athenian democracy could be built for

[9] Leonard Thompson, *A History of South Africa*, New Haven, 1990, p. 97 ff. David Welsh, *The Roots of Segregation: Native Policy in Colonial Natal, 1854–1910*, Cape Town, 1971. In Natal, further characteristics of the Shepstone system were 'the allocation of reserved lands for African tribal occupation,... the exemption of Christian Africans from customary law, and the attempt to prevent large-scale African urbanization through the institution of a system of labour registration' as well as the imposition of rent and taxes. Shula Marks, 'The Drunken King and the Nature of the State', *The Ambiguities of Dependence in South Africa: Class, Nationalism, and the State in Twentieth Century Natal*, Baltimore and Johannesburg, 1986, p. 26. In Zululand, however, the system was faced with the difficulty of attempting to manipulate and integrate a 'customary' form of rule whose comprehensiveness and sophistication forcefully opposed being reduced to 'tribalism'. On the Zulu kingdom, see Marks, 'The Drunken King', p. 26ff., and Jeff Guy, *The Destruction of the Zulu Kingdom: The Civil War in Zululand, 1879–84*, London, 1979—the latter has a wealth of detail documenting Shepstone's personal role and the ambiguity of his paternalism. For a more general perspective on dual rule in the context of African colonization and resistance history, see Mahmood Mamdani, 'Indirect Rule, Civil Society and Ethnicity: The African Dilemma' in P. Kaarsholm (ed.) *From Post-Traditional to Post-Modern? Interpreting the*

white citizens, while 'traditional' forms of mastery were provided for non-white subjects, but through this also the creation of separate forms of civil society. While the settler and colonialist population could interact as citizens within the institutional framework of a common public sphere, the representations and forms of association of non-whites would have to be made within the 'traditional' boundaries and customs of their communities.

The understanding of 'community' among different groups of southern African peoples was further influenced by the different histories and outcomes of their struggles to resist colonization. No matter whether societies had to give in to colonial conquest through heroic defeat in military battle or through negotiated settlement, the outcome would have important consequences for internal understandings of and debates around what constituted 'community'. Shula Marks has described how in Zululand, heroic resistance and a proud defence of 'tradition' might play into the hands of the colonial power and accelerate defeat, and how subsequently this would come to influence internal political debates around identity and community leadership.[10] For Mashonaland and Matabeleland, Terence Ranger has attempted to trace lines of continuity between forms of 'primary resistance' to colonization and modern nationalist movements and to point out differences between political strategies and self-understandings in north-eastern and south-western Zimbabwe on the basis of the different outcomes in the two regions of the 1896–7 revolts against conquest.[11]

Resistance and adaptation of colonial rule meant that the definitions of communities which were imposed on society were met with imaginings and reinventions on behalf of the colonized in a pattern that did not follow a straightforward line of modernizing development from 'traditional' cultural self-assertion to nationalism. Rather, issues of community and identity formed a constant field of contestation, not only between Europeans and

---

Meaning of Modernity in Third World Urban Societies, Occasional Paper no. 14, IDS, Roskilde, 1995.

[10] Shula Marks, *Reluctant Rebellion: The 1906–8 Disturbances in Natal*, Oxford, 1970.

[11] Terence Ranger, *The African Voice in Southern Rhodesia, 1898–1930*, London, 1970.

Africans, but also among Africans themselves as they fought to establish influence and rights for themselves within colonial society and eventually for decolonization and national independence. Thus, side by side with the emergence of 'secular' nationalist movements fighting for civic rights, more localized, cultural or 'ethnic' nationalist groupings would work to articulate and organize the aspirations of communities and fight for group rights in ways which might correspond more or less harmoniously to the divisions of colonial administration and collaborate with greater or lesser amounts of friction with nationalist organizations like the South African and Rhodesian congress movements.

Rather than forming a unidirectional lime from 'ethnic' to 'nationalist' organization, the modernizing trend in this development seems to be much more contradictory and to have consisted in changes of both 'ethnic' and 'secularist' nationalist discourses in a way which have made them increasingly difficult to reconcile. Thus the modernization of 'ethnic', communalist discourse and its interaction with the fixations brought about by colonial state administrations involved a 'hardening', narrowing and essentialization of notions of community identity—a movement from 'moral ethnicity' to 'political tribalism'[12] which provided the ground for greater chauvinism and made alliances with broader nationalist movements more insecure. At the same time, the development of 'secularist' nationalism seems to have involved a centralization and 'hardening' of outlook also as nationalist élites moved closer to independence and the grasping of state power and found increasingly little time to cultivate links with local hinterlands, groupings and modes of political expression which at earlier stages had been important bases for power.

In South Africa, for example, the attempts by the Inkatha Freedom Party in the period just before the dismantlement of apartheid and after to monopolize the representation of a Zulu community interest appear to exemplify a modern type of ethnic politics, as—on the other side—the tendencies within the ANC

[12] See John Lonsdale, 'Moral Ethnicity and Political Tribalism', in P. Kaarsholm and J. Hultin (eds) *Inventions and Boundaries*, pp. 131–50. Idem., 'The Moral Economy of Mau Mau: Wealth, Poverty and Civic Virtue in Kikuyu Political Thought' in B. Berman and J. Lonsdale, *Unhappy Valley: Conflict in Kenya and Africa*, vol. II: *Violence and Ethnicity*, London, 1992, pp. 315–504.

wanting to bypass and ignore 'ethnic' discourse altogether as backward and necessarily disruptive seem to express a form of nationalist thinking which was not prevalent before the ANC was forced into exile in the early 1960s.[13] Similar trends of development could be pointed out in Zimbabwean politics, where the earlier expert capability of a politician like Joshua Nkomo, for example, to reconcile and move adroitly between different concentric layers of Kalanga, Ndebele and Zimbabwean nationalist discourse seems to have become less typical and replaced by greater potentials for confrontation between state-centred nationalism and locally-based 'ethnic' or cultural politics.[14]

While such trends of historical development may be important, there are also more constant features about colonial and post-colonial southern African societies which necessarily give prominence to issues of community politics and group rights and make these uneasily reconcilable with a nationalist politics focusing on civic rights and democratic reform. An obvious example is race and the legacies of a racist government and economy which require forms of positive discrimination to move against imbalances, but where such forms of positive discrimination will involve challenges for a democratic constitution and could bring about different varieties of 'hardening' of community attitudes and outlooks, both on behalf of groups disfavoured by discriminatory policies, and of those of who stand to gain. Examples of this have already been manifest in Zimbabwe where white farmers feel threatened by land reform and redistribution, and where prospects of 'indigenization' policies have brought forth new types of political expression among both businessmen and students. Another example might be

[13] See Shula Marks, 'Patriotism, Patriarchy and Purity: Natal and the Politics of Zulu Ethnic Consciousness', in L. Vail (ed.) *The Creation of Tribalism*, pp. 215–40, Idem, 'Black and White Nationalisms in South Africa: A Comparative Perspective', in P. Kaarsholm and J. Hultin (eds) *Inventions and Boundaries*, pp. 103–30, and Preben Kaarsholm, 'The Ethnicization of Politics and the Politicisation of Ethnicity: Culture and Political Development in South Africa', in F. Wilson and B. F. Frederiksen (eds) *Ethnicity, Gender and the Subversion of Nationalism*, London, 1995, pp. 33–44.

[14] See Terence Ranger, 'Language, Law and Nationalism. Ethnicity and Nationalism: The Case of Matabeleland', seminar paper, ICS, London, 1991, and Preben Kaarsholm, 'Si Ye Pambili—Which Way Forward?: Urban Development, Culture and Politics in Bulawayo', Occasional Paper no. 146, CSSS, Calcutta 1994.

the rallying of large number of so-called 'coloured' voters around the white-dominated National Party at the recent South African elections, apparently seeking in this way to support claims to relative privileges that could become endangered by government policies discriminating positively in favour of black Africans.

Another area where community and identity politics and community confrontation have been and continue to be central issues, involves urbanization and migrant labour. Because of the segregationist history of southern African societies, the rights of non-white people to urban residence have been restricted, and the majority of the large number of people moving to and living in town classified and treated as temporary residents whose 'real' identities belonged to the countryside. This has affected not only the legal and civic rights of non-white urbanites, but also their physical livelihoods, accommodation and possibilities for obtaining labour contracts in towns, and though policies may be changed, it would take decades of growth-sustained effort for the new governments of the southern African states to move towards a position where they would be able to accommodate existing wishes and pressures for urbanization.

While ethnic politics and communalism can be represented as 'traditionalist' and conservative, and—in their ideologies and discourse—may incorporate rural themes as central ingredients, they are, in southern Africa, probably of greater importance in towns than in the countryside, and the insecurity of life in urban conditions and the forced interaction between town and country existence seem to form essential parts of their base. Thus, 'tribal' identities have formed markers around which networks and associations for the allocation of resources could be organized—access to labour contracts, to accommodation, to mutual support and welfare groups, to cultural societies or to membership of criminal gangs fighting to come to terms with conditions of illegality. Jeff Guy and Motlatsi Thabane have interpreted the workings of such networks in the history of Sotho migrants going for labour on the Witwatersrand, and, for Rhodesia/Zimbabwe, Tsuneo Yoshikuni has described the almost cosmopolitan life of Salisbury townships in the early part of the century.[15]

[15] Jeff Guy and Motlatsi Th[illegible]ba[illegible] [illegible]he Ma-Rashea: A Participant's Perspective', in B. Bozzoli (e[illegible] [illegible]ss, *Community and Conflict: South African Perspectives*, Johannesburg, [illegible], Idem., 'Basotho Miners, Oral History and

While towns were certainly to some extent 'melting pots' in which new class based solidarities were formed, cross-marriages would take place and rural identities undermined and dissolved, they were also sites of the crystallization and articulation of new and more expressive 'traditional' identities and communities. In this process—apart from colonial and apartheid officials—urban intellectuals, cultural institutions, artists, musicians, poets and politicians have played a formative part and helped to create new notions of identity and community which have eventually also found their way back into the rural world, and thereby broken up any neat dichotomy between 'rural tradition' and 'urban modernity'.[16] At the same time, differing attitudes towards community identity have been brought into play—while some will emphasize the 'authenticity' of ethnic tradition, others assume a more ironic or 'joking' distance, thus removing from community identity any automatic equation with conservatism. Community identity has in itself become a disputed field, in which debates as well as battles may take place, and subversive as well as authoritarian outlooks promoted.[17]

So what makes people take up community politics and identify more closely with the community aspect of their multiple identities rather than pursue other aspects of class, gender or nationality which would cut across community boundaries? What is special about 'community security'? One explanation could be that 'community' as related to 'home' offers a last-resort identification which can be relied on when other solidarities fail or are obstructed from providing effective networks of support. In the case of the history of southern African townships, ethnic communities seem to have provided primary networks of support and access to

---

Workers' Strategies', in P. Kaarsholm (ed.) *Cultural Struggle and Development in Southern Africa*, London, 1991, pp. 239–58; Tsuneo Yoshikuni, 'Black Migrants in a White City: A Social History of African Harare, 1890–1925', PhD dissertation, University of Zimbabwe, 1989.

[16] For examples of this cultural interdependence of town and country, see Veit Erlmann, *African Stars: Studies in Black African Performance*, Chicago, 1991.

[17] On the 'ironization' of ethnicity, see Kaarsholm, 'The Ethnicization of Politics', p. 38. A famous interpretation of 'joking ethnicity' is provided by J. Clyde Mitchell in *The Kalela Dance: Aspects of Social Relationships Among Urban Africans in Northern Rhodesia*, Manchester, 1956.

resources for groups like migrant workers with a fragile hold on their urban livelihoods. Also, the fluctuation of ethnic communities and community politics between providing human security on the one hand and, on the other, posing a threat to security through violent inter-community confrontation seems to have depended to a large extent on the availability of and pressure upon resources like work, accommodation, etc. The poverty of, and competition around resources thus both help to account for people seeking community identification and for their elaboration of 'negative ethnicities' in the form of 'enemy images' of competing communities and of ideologies justifying a hierarchy of rights of access to resources between communities.

Another equally significant reason for violent confrontation related to ethnic groupings, however, appears to involve exactly disputes over what constitutes the defining markers of community identity. Conflicts erupt not only between well defined communities, but also as 'civil wars' within communities, as different programmes of leadership and discourse get promoted, recognizing or rejecting the 'primordiality' of, for example, ethnic community identification. The not uncommon representations of political violence involving the Inkatha Freedom Party in South Africa as 'tribal wars' between Zulus and other 'tribes' seem much better understood as small-scale 'civil wars' between groupings representing different political programmes of 'cultural' or 'centralist' nationalism and incorporating Zulu-speakers on both sides.[18] In such confrontation, partly because of the internal dynamics of the spiralling culture of violence, 'centralist' or 'universalist' nationalist groups do not necessarily present their programme in a less 'hardened' fashion or behave less chauvinistically or violently than 'cultural' or 'ethnic' nationalist ones. In the case of Inkatha, however, elements of muscular masculinity and war-like Zulu-ness seem to have been developed into central elements of the 'tradition' seen as unifying the community.

The unity of communities is made problematic also by disputations over leadership and representation. In Zimbabwe, the competition around community leadership between chiefs and spirit mediums during the liberation war has been described by David Lan and competition between lineages taking advantage of

[18] Marks, 'Black and White Nationalisms in South Africa'.

wartime upheavals by Norma Kriger, while fluctuations in legitimacy and community support of chiefs in post-war Zimbabwe and Mozambique has been investigated by Jocelyn Alexander.[19] Patterns of political history in Zululand, going back to the period of conquest and the early days of colonization, are continued today in the disputes between Inkatha and the Zulu royal family over 'authentic' leadership and the belated effort of the ANC to engage also in the political contestation of 'ethnic' discourse through the Congress of Traditional Leaders of South Africa (CONTRALESA).

Thus communities, within themselves, form dynamic hegemonies in which power is disputed and sought for, and where competing intellectuals will occupy key positions in formulating the claims to 'authenticity' of the respective ideologies and positions. Communities are controlled by those having the power to articulate and define community, and 'community security' does not reside in any automatic unity of community identification. How these dynamics may erupt in conflict and violence have been demonstrated graphically in South Africa since the mid-1980s, as the dismantlement of the controls of apartheid led to increased pressures of urbanization and population movement, of confrontations between 'old' and 'new' residents, between 'authentic' and 'inauthentic' community members, and brought 'war lords' to the fore as the mobilizers of community unification or cleansing.

While there is therefore no reason to accord to community identification and politics any particular primordiality and unity, it would be equally unjustified to classify political organization according to ethnic or religious community *per se* as particularly 'unreasonable' discourses with special potentials for violence. Indeed, the outlawing of community politics could deprive disprivileged groups of a register for possible articulation and

[19] David Lan, *Guns and Rain: Guerrillas and Spirit Mediums and Zimbabwe*, London, 1985; Norma Kriger, 'Popular Struggles in Zimbabwe's War of National Liberation', in P. Kaarsholm (ed.) *Cultural Struggles*; Jocelyn Alexander, 'Things Fall Apart, the Centre *Can* Hold: Processes of Post-War Political Change in Zimbabwe's Rural Areas', in L. S. Lauridsen (ed.) *Bringing Institutions Back In: The Role of Institutions in Civil Society, State and Economy*, Occasional Paper no. 8, IDS, Roskilde, 1993. On the chaos of conflicting layers of legitimacy in post-civil-war Mozambique, see Gregory W. Myers, 'Competitive Rights, Competitive Claims: Land Access in Post-War Mozambique', *Journal of southern African Studies*, vol. 20, no. 4, 1994, pp. 603–32.

organization to resort to when other channels of representation fail.

The challenge is rather to be sought within the field of political culture and institutional frameworks for political competition and conflict mediation. As far as political culture is concerned, the 'cultural' or 'traditional' features of tribalism, patrimonialism and clientelism outlined at the beginning of this paper as considered by political scientists particularly African, could be more adequately regarded as what conservative or fundamentalist politicians in African might want to promote as the parameters of politics.

An alternative with greater potential for furthering 'human security' would be a more ambitions and flexible notion of a democratic political culture which would be able to contain within it, groupings finding identification in a variety of discourses, but accepting a certain basic level of tolerance of each other's right to articulation and also agreeing that—because of social discriminations and economic injustices rooted in the past—group rights will have to protected and furthered alongside individual rights within national constitutions allowing considerable degrees of local autonomy as well as securing an equitable distribution of national resources among regions. For group rights to be situated in a democratic context, to counteract claims of monopoly of representation, and to safeguard a balance between group and individual rights, however, rights of association would also have to be constitutionally guaranteed that allow for differences in the understanding of collective identities to be represented and for exit opticns.[20]

In the southern African context, 'good governance' would seem to involve an increased rather than a diminished level of democracy. The majorization practices and endeavours to undermine opposition pursued by governments based on formally established multi-party systems in societies like Zimbabwe and Mozambique work against the development of such a democratic culture of politics and could promote or reactivate, eventually, the emergence

[20] For a discussion of the relationship between different types of constitutional rights, see Mahmood Mamdani, 'Pluralism and the Rights of Association' in M. Mamdani and J. Oloka-Onyango (eds) *Uganda: Studies in Living Conditions, Popular Movements and Constitutionalism*, Vienna, 1994, pp. 519–63.

of forms of fundamentalist or violence-oriented organization, choosing to turn their backs on any consensus around toleration.

To promote 'human security' and 'good governance' in the above understandings in South Africa, the contemporary 'centralism' and front-like unity of the ANC would have to give way to a more pluralist structure of party representation. Meanwhile the Inkatha Freedom Party, which has so far been extensively accommodated by both constitutional and government arrangements, would have to accept that limits are prescribed for its lability and flirtation with fundamentalism and violence. And that pluralism and tolerance will also have to be hallmarks of the Natal/Zululand political arena, in which no single organization can be allowed a monopoly of representation at either regional or local levels.

Paradoxically, the hopes for a development in such directions might reside with the very reflexivity with which notions of 'community' have been invested through the harshness and brutality of colonization and the management and manipulation of identities effected through apartheid. At least, in the South African context, it would be difficult to assert any straightforward substantiality and depoliticized cultural uniformity as pertaining to communities whose defining characteristics and boundaries have been continuously contested and embattled for the last one-and-a-half centuries. If 'the narrative of community', in the South African situation, is to mobilize a 'rhetoric of love and kinship against the homogenizing sway of the normalized individual', it will have to do so through an appeal to 'elective affinities' rather than to blood affiliations.[21]

Hence, South Africa may continue to constitute a special case, also in a world in which the 'waning of the great cold war ideologies has shifted the goal posts and ethnic and religious movements have emerged in their stead' with 'culture' 'taking on a novel prominence'.[22] In South Africa, it will be more difficult than elsewhere, both for the state to impose 'monocultural control', and for any local culture or community to assert that it is not 'a terrain of power with its own patterns of stratification,

[21] See Partha Chatterjee, *The Nation and Its Fragments: Colonial and Postcolonial Histories*, Princeton, New Jersey, 1993, p. 238 ff.

[22] Jan Nederveen Pieterse, 'The Cultural Turn in Development: Questions of Power', *The European Journal of Development Research*, vol. 7, no. 1, June 1995, p. 176.

uneven distribution of cultural knowledge and boundaries separating insiders and outsiders—hierarchical and exclusionary politics in fine print'.[23]

Because of their central involvement in the confrontations of political history, 'culture' and 'community' have lost in South Africa their innocence as concepts more radically than elsewhere. While the history of colonization and aparthied domination provides a background against which contemporary violence and ethnicization of politics can be understood, its overcoming also presents the foundations for their dissolution. If communities and cultures attained their undemocratic features through the manipulations of a particular form of historical regime, they will also be able to relieve themselves of such features through the effecting of historical change.

Whether this will happen, will be the outcome of political struggle—in the realm of the South African state as well as within the disputed boundaries of individual communities. Until it does, apartheid will continue to rule South Africa through its shadow, and the insecurities on which its 'bad' governance was based will continue to hold sway.

[23] Ibid., pp. 180, 182.

17

Recognizing Whom?: Multiculturalism, Muslim Minority Identity and the Mers*

Shail Mayaram

Multiculturalism is a term that is beginning to come increasingly into currency in writings of Indian intellectuals. The question that arises is how we are going to think of multiculturalism in relation to the identities in the Indian subcontinent? This paper argues that the writing on ethnicity/multiculturalism presupposes a segmented view of society. Societies are seen as comprising several communities which have distinct identities derived from religion, language, race, and so on. The problem arises with respect to a universe of highly complex multiple, plural and cross-cutting identities, of overlapping circles within circles, and ambiguities where boundaries are both fluid and highly permeable.

* This paper is a much revised version of an earlier draft presented to UNDP's International Seminar on Human Security and Problems of Governance in Multicultural Societies, Kasauli, 25–30 March 1995. I am also grateful for comments on some aspects of this paper from participants of the Sixth Subaltern Studies Conference, Colombo, 2–5 June 1995 and the Indo-French Colloquium on Representations and Uses of the Sense of Belonging, Centre for the Study of Developing Societies, Delhi, 1–2 November 1995. Professor Daya Krishna and Dr Mukund Lath have considerably aided my understanding of subcontinental identities.

Let me begin with the theorization on ethnicity which has so far been grounded on certain assumptions. Much writing has emphasized the primordial basis of identity and stressed the 'resurgence' or 'revival' of traditional identities. It is argued that political organization must take cognizance of ethnic diversities.[1] As one of the major sources of difference, religions are seen as largely bounded, demarcated and distinct in terms of their essential characteristics. Moreover, identities are viewed as more or less fixed rather than as the site of constant negotiation. The primordial is taken for granted and primordiali-zation itself is hardly problematized. Denis-Constant Martin seems to share my concern when he comments, 'From the start, it appears that part of the problem lies with the uses to which the word *identity* is put. As a tool for describing political clashes, it connotes homogeneity and permanence. In the process, the polysemy of identity is erased and the complexity of the relationships needed in order to define the concept of identity is diluted.'[2]

Recently a more theoretically sophisticated position called multiculturalism has been proposed to reformulate the liberal response to cultural pluralism. Its major spokesperson, Charles Taylor, argues cogently that the assertion that the self is embedded in culture derives from the eighteenth-century view of the self as a reflexive and moral being deserving of dignity. It arose from the decline of hierarchical society in which position defined identity and conjoined with the notion of authenticity which is that being is defined by a moral voice within the self, that is, that identity is inwardly generated rather than socially derived. Transposed from individual selves to cultures in the work of Herder it develops into the idea that cultures must follow a principle of originality and realize their distinctive ways of being. While the politics of equal dignity calls for civil rights and entitlements, Taylor asserts that the politics of difference must be based on mutual respect of the right to culture of each group: the right of the minority to preserve its cultural integrity and resist its assimilation by a dominant or majority identity. This is the principle of equal recognition between cultures. Instead of rights

[1] Martin Doornbos, 'Linking the Future to the Past: Ethnicity and Pluralism', *Reviews of African Political Economy*, vol. 40, 1991, pp. 53–65.

[2] Denis-Constant Martin, 'The Choices of Identity', *Social Identities*, vol. 7, 1995, pp. 5–20.

liberalism's 'difference-blind' social space, we have one in which distinctiveness is privileged and must be affirmed and sustained by the political order.[3]

While I am empathetic to the moral vision on Taylor and Walzer's advocacy of the multicultural commitment of liberal democratic polities, it certainly raises the question of which communities and which minorities are to be 'recognized' and whose cultural claims are to be affirmed? Indeed, I would argue that the 'politics of recognition' takes for granted an *a priori* notion of fairly well formed ethnic identities. Multiculturalist arguments often assume minorities and a majority to be pre-existing congealed collectivities. While the politics of difference is supposed to 'recognize and even foster particularity', my problem begins when the very constitution of a minority and majority involves transgressing the authenticity and originality of a series of minori-ties.

Multiculturalism, that professes its commitment to the right of several cultural communities to survive, dangerously propounds their very erasure in homogenizing minorities. Possibly the Western multi-ethnic experience is amenable to analysis, given the conflicts of relatively homogenous and well differentiated groups such as Quebecois or French and English Canadians in Canada or African-Americans and whites in the United States and aboriginals and colonizers elsewhere. Ambiguity is seen primarily in terms of hyphenated identities arising from inter-ethnic marriages and diasporas. In the US, criticism of unitary ethnic multiculturalism comes from the vantage point of hybridities.[4] In older cultures the problems are compounded. Multiculturalism is eminently suited to the move from an individualist to a communitarian theoretical position. But it reaches its limits with respect to societies which have for centuries earlier been organized on communitarian principles. By constructing groups into homogenous moulds it fails to apply the same logic within that it fights without of resisting the oppression of the majority. It culminates in negating the very first principles that it upholds, namely the protection of plural identities.

[3] Charles Taylor, 'The Politics of Recognition', in David Theo Goldberg (ed.) *Multiculturalism: A Critical Reader*, Blackwell, Oxford, 1994, pp. 75–106.

[4] Homi K. Bhabha, *The Location of Culture*, Routledge Kegan and Paul, 1994.

In the Indian context contemporary multiculturalist discussion invariably focuses on the Hindu majority and minorities such as Muslims, Christians, Sikhs, and so on. In particular, the primary cleavage of the Hindu–Muslim question, fraught as it has been with conflicts, has preoccupied a good deal of attention if one is to judge from the burgeoning genre of communal riot studies. If one is to visualize public policy on multicultural foundations one could think about many issues where a multicultural understanding would be beneficial, particularly those revolving around secularism. Given the increasing incidence of majoritarian violence in India the multiculturalist position helps conceptualize notions of group security, and the need to safeguard the democratic and human rights of minorities. Multiculturalism provides a moral ground when it comes to critiques of verbal and physical violence. It is useful when it comes to challenging premises of a melting pot model of 'national integration' and the dictum of mainstreaming minority identities that is being forcefully articulated, including by the top echelons of the Indian judiciary today. It is enormously valuable when it comes to contesting a politics based on universalism, exclusivism and segregationism. The politics of equal citizenship and of universal dignity assists in the denunciation of discriminations on the basis of caste, community and gender. The politics of equal recognition would extend cultural rights to all groups. It can also aid in resisting doctrines of legal assimilation and homogeneity which recast laws in terms of majoritarian notions of reform and gender justice.

The rest of this paper is addressed to thinking aloud the limits of present multicultural understanding and possibly about modes of its reformulation in relation to subcontinental historical experience. I draw upon the area of my present fieldwork to examine the specificity of local contexts to evaluate the global normative model of multiculturalism. I will raise four issues: the complex nature of cultural identities; intra-Muslim disputes over curricula; the debate on legal pluralism; and the project of 'reform' in relation to women. Through these four areas I will address some of the major concerns of multiculturalists and ask the following questions: Whose identity are we upholding as minority identity? What version of Islamic theology and curricula is 'correct'? What is the extent of pluralism in the debate on common laws and personal laws? What are women's perceptions with respect to self-proclaimed leaders of minority groups such as clerics and reformers?

The Mer (also spelt Mair) are a group which have inhabited a complex interstitial space in between Hinduism and Islam. They inhabit the rural areas of Ajmer in north-western India that is locally called Magra-Merwara. Contemporary identity politics has cleaved this group into two sections, the Muslim Merat and Hindu Rawat. The suspension of intermarriage between them in this century is the primary sign of ethnicity and community. But even in a state of acute tension arising from the attempts of Hindu and Muslim religio-ideological groups to convert them, their religion and social practice continues to be extremely complex and variegated.

Mer genealogies suggest at some interesting features of pre-modern Indian identities. The group is said to have 'converted' to Islam in the fifteenth century when the brothers called Satal, Duda and Gora received *dīkshā* or initiation from a *pīr*. Satal founded the Satalkhani Chitas, spread across over twelve villages, who are presently Muslim. Quite obviously a father's 'conversion' did not automatically imply that of his descendants, for Mer genealogists state that one of the three sons of Duda called Harraj was again initiated into Islam. As he was given the title of 'Katha' his descendants were called either Kathat or Merat. His brother, Gora, is also said to have become Muslim and from him are descended the Gorat also called 'Rawat'. Later descendants of Gora reverted to their original practice and are presently called Hindu. What I want to stress here is how Mer genealogies suggest the availability of multiple choices with respect to sectarian affiliation as also the possibilities of switching affiliation which were present for a large number of groups in medieval India.

The local terms used for a shift in religious affiliation towards Islam are *dīkshā*, suggesting a process of initiation. Conversion for the Mer meant primarily the practice of circumcision. Being Muslim for the Chita and Merat, was, thus, signified by the practice of the male rite of passage called the *musalmānī* or *sunnat*. Gorat men were circumcised for only three generations after Gora, but this continued among Merat men. The Merat were indistinguishable from the Rawat with the exception of following three Muslim 'rules' of circumcision, burying the dead and eating *halāl* meat.

Although contemporary movements oriented to conversion such as the Vishwa Hindu Parishad are attempting to pummel them into an appropriately Hindu identity, the phrase most frequently used by Merat and Rawat genealogists is '*shākh ek se do bhayo*'. Lineage is imaged by the single trunk of a tree which has branched into two. Individual memories of descent also emphasize a common origin asserting that they are *bhāī* (brothers) in kinship terms, that is, a single *quam* or community. As I have stated, the Merat and Rawat intermarried till very recently. There are few Rawats who do not have memories of a Meratni in their families a couple of generations ago and conversely. This was until the sustained work of religious groups oriented to conversion for over a century helped cleave the group into religious communities. Thus, in the making of ethnic identities, new ascriptives are scripted and primordial identities derived from genealogy, kinship, memory and history are overwritten by new primordialities that stress the norms of unitary religious communities.

Pre-modern Indian identities were both fluid and complex. Taylor argues that in pre-modern times people didn't speak of 'identity' and 'recognition'—not because they didn't have identities but because they were too unproblematic to be thematized as such.[5] Possibly that was the European experience but in India the politics of difference and its recognition was well established. It was incumbent upon the ruler to recognize even the most heterodox of identities—in one case this meant recognition even to a sect called *nīlkambalī* in which couples comprising a single man and woman went about clothed in a blanket. Several such sects advocated very different norms with respect to religious practice and sexuality.

The picture of bounded religious universes much as it seems axiomatically self-evident today needs to be modified enormously. Conversion did not mean a conception of irretrievable entry/exit with respect to a fixed religious universe. Rather there was a constant movement back and forth across sects and also possibilities of multiple affiliation. Individuals had possibilities of affiliating themselves with different gurus, sects and *mathas* which were run by the *sampradāyas*. Identities were thus dynamic, subject to making and unmaking as they were renegotiated, reassembled and drew upon several intersecting ethnic pluralities.

[5] Taylor, 'The Politics of Recognition', p. 80.

Among the Mer even after 'conversion' to Islam a large domain of ritual life continued to be shared. Marriages could be performed with either Hindu or Muslim rites, that is, with either the *nikāh* or the *pherās*. To date most Merat do not eat beef. At childbirth a brahman was called, and on the sixth day, the rite of *chatī* involving the worship of the sun was done with the help of either the brahman or the Bahi Bhat (genealogist). Rural festivities took place in the summer months of Baisakh suggesting sharing of the seasonal agricultural calendar by different communities irrespective of religious denomination.

It was not only that Islam incorporated considerable diversity of belief and practice. Conversely, ethnographers commented on the promiscuity of Hindu practice. For instance, Dixon, colonial administrator in Ajmer, wrote that although the Rawat call themselves Hindu 'their observance of that religion are extremely loose; nor would any one brought up in the tenets of that faith acknowledge them as associates...'. He remarked on the 'extraordinary melange, dignified by the name of religion' that the Mers represented.[6]

At the popular level one needs to also take into account the several cults that cut across religious boundaries. The cult of Ramdeo Pir spread over western India involves a multi-caste following comprising largely untouchable Dalit castes such as the Meghwals and the Bhambis and also Muslims.[7] If one conceives of ritual as manifesting resistance[8] this cult certainly challenged religious difference. Ramdeo is variously perceived as an incarnation of Krishna, as an Ismaili missionary, as the disciple of a saivite guru, and as the exponent of the tantric *kundā panth*. Stories of his life suggest his repeated contests with central Muslim authority, with clerics of the Sunni religious establishment and with brahmanic orthodoxy. This is not to suggest an endless fracturing of communities in terms of postmodern individual subjectivity but merely

[6] C. J. Dixon, *Sketch of Mairwara*, Smith, Elder and Co. 65, Cornhill, 1850, p. 7, 28.

[7] Dominique Sila Khan, 'Ramdeo Pir and the Kamadiya Panth', in N. K. Singhi and Rajendra Joshi (eds) *Folk, Faith and Feudalism*, Rawat, 1995, pp. 295–326; Mira Reym Binford, 'Mixing in the Color of Ram of Ranuja' in Bardwell L. Smith (ed.) *Hinduism: New Essays in the History of Religions*, E. J. Brill, 1976, pp. 120–42.

[8] Taussig, 1980.

to sensitize ourselves to the multiple cultural practices that constitute the category Muslim. The priests of Ramdeo temples are usually non-brahmins and might be from among the Rawat, Merat or the Kamad. Interestingly, till recently Dalit groups have had more in common with Muslims than with upper-caste Hindus, for instance, with respect to the burial of their dead.

Religious identities were not seen in either/or terms. Religious difference could and were absorbed into the family, lineage, clan, tribe, *jātī* or caste and village. This did not mean an absence of religious tension and/or competition which was persistent. But this is important when one thinks of the sources of tolerance at the civilizational level. To reflect on this is not an exercise in the recovery of innocence for conflict, sectarian and other, was endemic in the subcontinent. Moreover, sectarian tolerance co-existed with forms of intolerance along the axes of caste and gender.

Historically in large parts of India religious identities were not conceived as mutually exclusive. A large number of castes consisted of both Hindus and Muslims. Census reports of Rajputana reveal a complex terrain of difference and identity. The *Census of India 1921. Rajputana and Ajmer-Merwara* (vol. 24) refers to a fascinating universe where all castes with the exception of the Baniyas and Khatiks encompass multiple faiths, Hindu, Arya, Muslim and Jain. As in the case of several groups in Punjab religious difference was encompassed within the family, the *jāti*, and the village.[9] The otherness of the religious community was substantially mediated by the fact that the other was also part of the self.

If anything, it is a proliferation of sects and movements that has characterized the history of the Indian subcontinent. A process of fission is suggested by the constant emergence of new beliefs, sects and orders. Not surprisingly, a large number of religious centres in India were multi-religious. Temple towns included Vaishnava, Saiva and Jain, and Muslim places of worship.

[9] S. Arasaratnam ('The Christians of Ceylon and Nationalist Politics'. In *Religion in South Asia: Religious Conversion and Revival Movements in South Asia in Medieval and Modern Times*, G. A. Oddie (ed.) 231–48. Manohar) shows that in Sri Lanka in the early nineteenth century when Christian missionary activity began in both urban and rural Ceylon, families had Buddhist or Hindu and Christian branches. Dutch sources also suggest intermarriage between them. Further, Christian families co-existed with Buddhist, Hindu and Muslim families.

Besides this, several castes also underwent splintering and upward and downward mobility. The processes of fission were intensified by the constant violation of *jāti* rules with regard to endogamy. Marriage across caste and religious boundaries further aided processes of intermingling and fluidity of religions. Konkani Muslims and Portugese Catholics, for instance, married with local women after their arrival in India. Religious traditions filtered downward and practices of popular religion were textualized. Most Hindus were *smārta* or followers of the *smritis*. This made the latter particularly pliable texts as they tended to follow *lok āchār* or popular practice. The *purāṇas* themselves were constantly being written as, for instance, when Brahmans became Sunars or goldsmiths and sought to establish a separate identity.[10] The existence of multiple and layered identities was well established as one could simultaneously be a member of a *śrenī* or guild, a *jāti* and a *sampradāya*. Added to this was the creolization that occurred in languages over the last millenium that facilitated more localized identities grounded in shared speech.

Regional cultures developed collages as groups drew upon the practice of other neighbouring groups and bricolage as new cultural forms came into existence. A large number of groups fell in between religious traditions and often bridged them. Indeed, colonial ethnographers often despaired of the large number of groups who were Hindu and not Hindu, Sikh and Hindu, Catholic along with Hindu, and Muslim but also Hindu.[11] They, however, forced the myriad, unclassifiable little traditions into denominational boxes.

The category syncretic is often used for these groups. This tends to carry connotations of a mindless and mechanical mixing arising out of cultural contact. Great traditions are produced as given entities and syncretic forms are seen as 'deviant'.[12] Comaroff and Comaroff suggest how syntheses become reproduced without

[10] Kantilal Sompura, *The Structural Temples of Gujarat*, Gujarat University, Ahmedabad, 1968.

[11] R. S. Newman, 'Faith is All! Emotion and Devotion in a Goan Sect', *Numen*, vol. 28, 1981, pp. 216–46; Harjot Oberoi, *The Construction of Religious Boundaries: Culture, Identity and Diversity in the Sikh Tradition*, Oxford University Press, 1994.

[12] Droogers, 1989.

discursively available intentionality.[13] I have preferred the term liminality to suggest aspects of resistance to a lens which privileges binary identities. These are not weak identities nor do they suggest an absence of certainties. Neither are they to be seen as arising from confusion. Indeed, these groups preferred ambiguity and doublespeak. They often saw theirs as a privileged position with respect to working out sociability and everyday interaction. On several occasions they even mocked at the functionaries of institutional religion.

In Magra-Merwara the signs of conflict and dispute are apparent as modes of popular religion are now being overwritten by authoritative models of 'Hindu' and 'Muslim'. Nonetheless, cultural modernity has, if anything, also enhanced the intense levels of theological disputation. Even in a state of tremendous ethnic polarization the question of what it means to be a Muslim is being debated and challenged. The Jamiat ulama-i Hind runs *madrasahs* such as at Bithur. Its leader, Maulana Asad Madani, visits the area frequently and has mosques named after him. On questions of both curriculum and language there is no unanimity. The schools of the Jama`at-i Islami stress the need to go beyond teaching *dīnī talīm* in Urdu and Arabic and emphasize the need to teach both Hindi and English. The Jamiat, on the other hand, pursues a more conventional theological curriculam. The Jamiat and the Jama`at-i Islami, it might be noted, had taken totally divergent positions on the partition of India. Whereas the former has stressed Muslim nationalism, collaboration with the Indian National Congress and upheld secularism the latter actively advocates the vision of a Muslim state.[14]

Several Muslim organizations such as the Rajasthan Dini Talim Society of Jaipur and the Majlis Tamir-i Millat of Hyderabad have also been working in the area. The Tablighi Jama`at, however, constitutes one of major competing normative models of Muslim practice. Its enunciation of Islam emphasizes a re-spiritualization of Muslims and strict adherence to the *shari`a*. Unlike the Jama`at-i Islami the establishment of an Islamic order is only a secondary priority and subordinated to the need to spread *din* or religion.

[13] Jean Comaroff and John Comaroff, *Ethnography and the Historical Imagination*, Westview Press, 1985, pp. 28–9.

[14] Christian W. Troll, 'Two Conceptions of Da`wa in India: Jama`āt-i Islām and Tabligh Jamā`at', *Arch. de Sc soc. des Rel.* 87, 1994, pp. 73–98.

Further, Muslim organizations are deeply divided with respect to what constitutes appropriate Islamic faith and ritual. They are at variance even on the details of *sālāt* or the performance of the *namāz* prayer. The intense disputation is apparent from a brief survey of written tracts collected from different persons in Merwara. Maulana Wahiduddin Khan's work stresses the need among Muslims for self-control, the need to actively avoid 'communal' conflict but is conformist when it comes to the advocacy of the *shari`a* with respect to gender rights. A former adherent of the Jama`at-i Islami and Deoband school, he is deeply critical of the Sunni ulama for its failure to prevent the ghettoization of Muslims and champions the cause of education.[15] Tablighi Jama`at texts describe its own agenda as an exclusively spiritual one in terms of its 'call to Islam'. *Jama`ats* or groups comprising Muslims teach Muslim groups both 'correct' belief and ritual. The movement now operates in ninety countries all over the globe. In western India it is well known that in areas of its control the Barelvis, also Sunni Muslims, cannot enter. Tablighis are also critical of the eclectic ritual followed at the *dargah* of Khwaja Muinuddin Chishti of the Sufi *silsilāh* at Ajmer. Several Muslim communities in India are now cleaved and characterized as pro-Tablighis and anti-Tablighis.[16]

When I visited the village of Shamgarh a major dispute was underway between a Mewati maulvi who had organized popular opposition to a Qadiyani maulvi. Among the Mers the purveyors of 'reform' are predominantly the Mewatis. The latter constituted the initial field where the experiment with respect to the Tablighi Jama`at was first tried and then replicated on a global scale. The Mewati maulvi at Shamgarh alleged that the Qadiyani maulvi who had been living in the village for several months was 'corrupting' children's minds. The Qadiyani belief in multiple *paigambars* or prophets (including Krishna and Ahmad who lived in the fifteenth century), according to him, was 'unIslamic'. 'Foreign' funding was alleged as the sect has its headquarters at London. Also that at Ahmadiya *jalsās* or congregations, texts of different religions such as the Ramayana, Gita, Bible were read in addition to the Qur'an.

[15] M. Wahiduddin Khan, *Islam Kya Hai*, Ishaat-e-Islam Trust (1974), 1986.

[16] G. A. Pandor, 'The Tabligh Jamat: An Islamic Revivalist/Reformist Movement: A Case Study of Gujarat', University of Baroda, Department of History Series no. 11.

The Qadiyani maulvi pointed out the intolerant and disruptive presence of the Tablighi Jama`at vide the Mewati maulvi. The Qadiyanis, more popularly known as the Ahmadiyas, have undergone considerable persecution and discrimination in Pakistan. They have borne the brunt of riots against them in Lahore and are an Islamic sect whose Islamism is disputed.

In contrast to the manichean dualism of Hindu–Muslim that is at the centre of identity politics in contemporary India, there is a large volume of anthropological and historical research that stresses the heterogeneity *within* Indian Muslim identity. Community is not defined by religion alone but by a variety of historical, cultural and ecological factors. 'Muslim' has to be seen both as an emergent ethnic identity as well as a denial of several ethnicities that it subsumes. Caste, kinship, language, geographic location, shared history and class are as much determinants of the large number of Muslim communities as is religion. Further, a range of Muslim practices is indicated in the divergence between *shari`a* and *tarīqā*, the Islamic ideal and the actual; the contrast between high culture and myriad forms of folk and popular culture. These are often read as 'remnants' of pre-conversion Islamic belief and practice which have not been affected by conversion. In fact, these also arose in contexts of cultural encounter. To the Ismaili Khojas who are followers of Agha Khan, the Prophet is simultaneously an incarnation of Mahesh, Ali and Vishnu. Their prayers draw from both Hinduism and Islam. For other groups the Ka`aba is spatialized locally.[17] What I want to stress here is the simultaneous existence of competing notions of Muslim belief and practice. What emerges from popular and the local level interpretations of the Qu`ran, *shari`a* and *hadith* is a rich diversity of conceptions of what it means to be a Muslim.

Ambiguity persists among the Mer contrary to optimistic claims. It can be sensed in the Muslim reformists' accusation of local Muslim intransigence. I spoke to the Tablighi Jama'at group from Bombay then on a tour of the rural areas of Ajmer who commented that they found the Merat 'highly backward' Muslims. Another maulvi complained to me how difficult it was to get the villagers to come to the *madrasah:* 'They learn for two days, then disappear for the next four so that all that has been learnt is

[17] A. R. Saiyed, *Religion and Ethnicity among Muslims*, Rawat, 1995, p. 88.

forgotten.' At Suava, a dominantly Merat village, a maulvi from Bihar led the opposition to the building of a Ramdeo temple by the untouchable Bhambis and Merats. After persisting tension he was, however, eventually turned out for creating 'faction *bāzī*' in the village. Eventually the villagers appointed a local man in his place to look after the *madrasah*.

Let me now shift to the need to reopen within multicultural contexts the question of gender. Patriarchy cuts across religion and defines the status of both Rawat and Merat. All married women must maintain the *ghunghat*, that is, be veiled before older men of all castes. For both the Hindu Rawat and the Muslim Merat a woman's labour is important in the subsistence peasant economy and if she elopes her new husband has to pay *jhagrā* or compensation to the older one. New patriarchies seek to overlay the old patriarchy within the group under the name of socio-religious reform.

Tablighi Jama`at's advocacy of *purdāh* is, however, seen as impractical to women who are accustomed to 'going' in the fields and who have to work as industrial and agricultural labour. Among the Meo Muslims I had noticed a very selective appropriation of Islam, the *burqah* being seen as a hindrance given the climate and existing division of labour in which women have to do most of the work in relation to the household, agricultural operations and animal husbandry. The case of the Merat women is not unsimilar. Women's dialogues with local maulvis and imams are particularly revealing in this respect. When I went to visit Dhanni who had herself been part of a women's jama`at she was away from home having taken three cases for sterilization to a family planning camp at Jawaja. She was aware that the *hadith* prohibits tampering with the body; the local maulvi had told her that sterilization is in violation of the wishes of Allah. But the fragmentation of tiny landholdings, as a result of subdivision among all the sons is for her an irreducible, material reality of her lifeworld. In one generation even the three acre landholder will be reduced to a half acre holder, she reprimanded him. The small landholdings are able to yield a small, subsistence single crop in a good year but devastating famine recurs almost regularly.

All over what was formerly called Mairwara are signs of an erstwhile shared cultural space that continues to persist. There are still large numbers of families who obstinately insist that they will follow their traditions rather than be pulled in the direction of exclusivist Hindu/Muslim reform. Shanti devi, a Merat woman who has just been elected a woman Sarpanch from Shamgarh told me:

> We are both Hindu and Musalman. Muslim because we do *khatnā* and do not eat *jhatkā* meat. I have just got my daughter engaged, the marriage will be in Baisakh. I have told the maulvi I will have *pherās* (rounds of the sacrificial fire) done for my daughter.

Shanti devi is representative of a subject position that stresses Merat right to represent their identity and define their own norms of correct belief and ritual.

Weeks before Holi, I noticed in several Merat fields the pile of wood collected to be burnt on the spring festival. Salimi, a Merat woman told me, 'Come during Holi and you will see such dancing like you have never seen.' Salimi has been elected a Member of the Zila Parishad of Ajmer. She has been resisting Tablighi Jama'at's criticism of local forms of festivity and particularly of women's dancing. Tablighi Jama'at ideology emphasizes in addition to the reform of ritual the surfacial aspect of the body. For Merat males the Muslim practice of keeping the beard is stressed and for women the appropriate clothes and jewellery are defined. 'Whereas for men the sign is *khatnā* (circumcision), women must not wear a *bindī*. We wear the *kamīz*, and the younger girls wear the *ghararā* or *salwār*,' Amina told me. Women are thereby constructed as erotic, the *aurat* (which is also in man) as an object to be concealed. The injunctions against dance arise as women's gesture and physical movement are seen as a site that eroticizes. The body thereby becomes a significant site of the display of ethnic identity. As Metcalf puts it, women are made the 'public signs of Islam'.[18] The emphasis of the Muslim ulama-led reform movement on *purdāh* and seclusion is also oriented to greater control over women's sexuality. It suggests at the social origins of the nineteenth-century Muslim reform movement in the male, landed and service gentry of the United Provinces.[19] A member of a Jama'at, thus, expressed the inability of the women of his family to come on a Jama'at

[18] Barbara Daly Metcalf, 'Reading and Writing about Muslim Women in British India', in Zoya Hasan (ed.) *Forging Identities: Gender, Communities and the State*, Kali, p. 4.

[19] Faisal Fateshali Devji, 'Gender and Politics of Space: The Movement for Women's Reform, 1857–1900' in Hasan (ed.) *Forging Identities*.

to Ajmer because of the lack of provision of indoor toilet facilities.

Even as multiculturalism situates conflict *outside* the community, that is, in terms of inter-ethnic polarities, we have seen that *internal* disputation is also central to its very constitution. Mer identities still continue to be characterized by complex processes of dialogue, combination, overlay and overlap. In the fields of the Merat peasantry (despite the marginal landholdings) a tiny space is still set aside for the *jhunjhār* or deified ancestor. Only in the fields around Rupnagar where the Tablighi Jama`at has a greater hold has the practice been given up. In certain other fields it was almost as though a compromise had been affected as a *mazhār* or tomb was built beside the *jhunjhār* or the latter was covered by a green cloth, denoting an Islamist symbol. Although a young boy in Lulva told me 'now we say salām malikum, not rām rām', he pointed out to me the shrine of Ramdevji where the entire village goes for the annual fair. The low-caste Dholi still plays a major role in rituals of marriage and childbirth as he makes the *chauk* design out of wheat flour and conducts the *pūjan* of the newborn child and mother.

Simultaneously there are large-scale processes taking place in national and global contexts involving modernization, the media, shifts in political and religious institutional articulations that are helping to translate, produce and reproduce the categories of Hindu and Muslim. The Indian state is implicated in the production of ethnicity as it affirms the principle of religious community as the criterion for 'minority' identity.[20] It is also complicit in the reproduction of religious community by establishing exclusive dialogue with both Muslim and Hindu orthodoxy whether it is Deoband ideology represented by the Muslim Personal Law Board or Vedanta vide the Shankaracharyas antithetical to heterodox/alternative streams among both. It has systematically supported religious orthodoxy against popular demands for reform within communities such as the Bohras.[21] One might certainly presume that this would be the case under Congress rule. But, interestingly,

[20] According to the Government of India, Ministry of Welfare Notification of 23 October 1994, Muslims, Christians, Parsees, Buddhists and Sikhs are minorities (cited in Dipankar Gupta, 'Secularization and Minoritisation: Limits of Heroic Thought', *Economic and Political Weekly*, vol. 30, p. 2205).

[21] Asghar Ali Engineer of Space 'Udaipur Masjid Case Judgement—A Comment', Ikhwansu Safa Trust and the Central Board of the Dawoodi Bhora Community, Bombay, n.d.

the Bhartiya Janta Party (BJP) that also cries itself hoarse against Islamic fundamentalism has hardly supported protest movements within Muslim communities. As the opposition in Rajasthan it raised questions on behalf of Bohra reformist groups. But after having come to power as one of the longest serving BJP state governments it has maintained a stoic silence on the popular demand for internal democracy and accountability within the Bohra community.[22] The state thereby helps create religious boundaries and sustains ideologies of anti-syncretism.

Religious reformist organization is itself oriented to distinct ethnic differentiation and boundaries that establish explicit distance. One villager told me, 'The Tablighi Jama`at tells us take to one path. If you are Muslims then do the *nikāh*, otherwise do the *pherās* and be fully Hindu. Either celebrate Id or Holi–Diwali.' A Rashtriya Swayam Sewak (RSS) activist similarly echoed, 'People were asked to decide whether they wanted to be Hindu or Muslim.' As for the Jama`at reformers there can be only either Hindus or Muslims. If as Gelner puts it, the state 'monopolizes legitimate culture almost as much as it does legitimate violence, or perhaps more so',[23] so do religious institutional structures monopolize sources of definition and the institutionalization of what constitutes legitimate culture and religion.

Multiculturalism has also been identified with the project of legal pluralism in India. 'Minority rights' and a distinctive Muslim cultural identity are said to validate separate personal laws over a common civil code.[24] One cannot, however, circumscribe the question of legal pluralism in India to statutory, enacted and textual legislation whether Hindu or Muslim, as is happening in the contemporary debate posed along the lines of polarity, Uniform/ Common Civil Code versus Muslim Personal Law. Legal pluralism must be pushed further beyond the Shariat Act to look into the specificity of Mer, Mapilla, Meo, Bohra and Khoja customary legal practice. The enactment of the Shariat Act in 1937 categorized all forms of such practice as corrupt and deviant. But there still remain

22 Asghar Ali Engineer, personal conversation, January, 1996.

23 Ernest Gellner, *Nations and Nationalism*, Basil Blackwell, Oxford, 1983.

24 Lloyd Rudolph, and Susanne Hoeber Rudolph, 'Occidentalism and Orientalism: Perspectives of Legal Pluralism' in Sally Humphreys (ed.) *Cultures of Scholarship*, University of Michigan Press, Comparative Studies in Society and History; Kumkum Sangari, 'Politics of Diversity: Religious

several Muslim communities in India who follow customary law. I will not examine the issue of gender justice here that needs to be done at all three levels of common, personal and customary laws which I propose to deal with elsewhere. But the unilateral progressivism inputed by jural textualists needs to challenged. In certain cases among the Mer, *nātā* (a form of widow and other remarriage) has accommodated women's sexual choices although there are also cases where natal families have forced women into undergoing such relationships. Similarly, reformist legislation with respect to the age of consent has devalued the legal cultures of low-caste, subsistence agriculturalists and landless labourers who have used mass child marriages to cut down expenditures associated with marriage.[25] Statutory law is often presumed to be emanicipatory with respect to existing patriarchies. As has been pointed out, the Shariat Act of 1937 itself violated and departed from the traditional *shari`a* by not mentioning women's share in agricultural property. Women's groups have also raised questions about the masculinist perspectives implicit in the Hindu Code Bill and the Special Marriages Act.

To conclude, the theories of ethnicity and multiculturalism are grounded on notions of cultural segmentation. They are extraordinarily difficult to apply in the Indian context where they presuppose relatively homogenous communities. In contrast, within the subcontinent there has been considerable theoretical reflection within different religious traditions of the need to recognize not only the differentiated identities of cultural clusters, but also to endow them with political and juridical autonomy in order that they may enact their own norms and rules. Ethnicity is corrosive of this far more radical multiculturalism. Indeed, its core image of colliding cultural boundaries bares familial resemblance to forms of nationalism. Even as Hindutva claims to be the inheritor of 'Hindu tolerance' what it threatens to bring to fruition is an attack on communitarian civilizational identities in terms of homogenizing laws, norms, languages and cultures.

Further, even as the new international human rights regime seeks to protect 'cultural identities' and minority rights (and even autonomy) as a solution to global nationalism and ethnic violence

---

Communities and Multiple Patriarchies, Part 1', *Economic and Political Weekly*, 1995, pp. 3287–3310.

[25] Shankar Singh, Nikhil Dey and Aruna Roy, 'Child Marriage, Government and NGOs', *Economic and Political Weekly*, vol. 29, 1994, pp. 1377–9.

it must be recognized that it is addressed only to modern forms of community. Such communities (in the Indian case, Hindu, Muslim, Sikh and so on) then designate codes of correct religio-social practice. Even as 'majority' and 'minority' are constituted in ethnic terms, and by international law, there is an implicit erosion of minorities in the constitution of both, a marginalization of plurality as part of the agenda of social and legal reform. 'Minorities' protest ethnic assimilation of the majority, but in effect, their own members must comply with the cultural standards defined therein. Multiculturalists in India must also ask themselves the question, 'recognizing what and whom?'

Multiculturalism has thus become implicated in a project of anti-syncretism. But it must not stop at the politics of ethnicity which is becoming, following nationalism, a doctrine of progressive monoculturalist biculturalism. It has been pointed that certain forms of multiculturalism in the United States in resisting the cultural colonialism of the melting pot became implicated in the construction of 'authentic' identities and the erasure of signs which signalled the blurring and fluidity of such identities. The presence of the American Yoruba movement in an Afro-Cuban religion called Santeria, thus, tried to erase faces of Spanish and Catholic provenance in order to create a re-Africanized religious practice for its new African-American membership.[26] Dernersesian is similarly troubled as identity politics imputes exclusivist labels leading, for example, to a Mexican-American binary.[27] Multiculturalism virtually seems to work as a principle of totalizing minority identity. Both the nationalist and the multiculturalist position cohere in this respect by marking, stereotyping and segregating the minority/Other.

Ethnic absolutism is hardly less devastating than universal monoculturalism and often degenerates into assimilationalism through doctrine. Both 'Hindu' and 'Muslim' are categories that silence the plurality that derives from different histories, mask the numerous tensions within, and the lines of cross-cutting alliance. If identity is dialogical, as Taylor argues, this is an inherently

[26] Rosalind Shaw and Charles Stewart 'Introduction' in Shaw and Stewart (eds) *Syncretism/Anti-syncretism: The Problems of Religious Synthesis*, Routledge, 1994.

[27] Angie Chabram Dernersesian, '"Chicana! Rican? No, Chicana Riquena!" Refashioning the Transnational Connection' in David Theo Goldberg (ed.) *Multiculturalism*, p. 273.

unequal dialogue since the practices of minorities among both are seen as contaminated. In the forms of identity politics derived from multiculturalism, cultures become naturalized as bounded, complete, internally homogenous. As Turner would put it, they become 'badges of group identity'.[27] Such ethnic closure, however, hardly yields an understanding of alternative notions of aesthetics, self-expression, health, law and medicine.

Binarism is, however, displaced by alternative cultural subjectivities as the case of the Mer suggests. Little religious traditions must also be extended a right to freely practise their cultures, their languages (disparagingly called dialects) including their modes of loving, celebrating, and art. Further, they must have the right of naming and representing themselves. If I may push Charles Taylor's argument to its extreme, their 'originality' must be sustained, that we not only let them survive, but acknowledge their *worth* and see that it does not suffer from *mis*recognition by others.[28]

Questions of curricula then cannot be addressed on lines of Hindu–Muslim identity. They are just as disputed among Muslims as clerics offer competing definitions of what constitute true and authentic identity and authorized theology. Attempts are being made to standardize religious practice, but there is great divergence on questions of norms and values inculcated in *madrasahs*, the books that are taught, the visual material deployed. Allied to these are disagreements over appropriate modes of greetings and salutation, dress codes, worship and what days should be declared holidays.

Thus, even in the context of change, the making of ethnic identities can hardly be seen in terms of sameness. How then are questions of canon, curricula and cultural rights to be seen in terms of the multicultural debate? What version of Hinduism/Islam is to be 'recognized' as legitimate? The advocacy of community rights, further, is hardly conducive to questions of citizenship and issues of gender justice now being demanded by women's groups. This is a terrain that has yet to be addressed by proponents of multiculturalism.

[27] Terence Turner, 'Anthropology and Multiculturalism: What is Anthropology that Multiculturalists should be Mindful of It?' in David Theo Goldberg (ed.) *Multiculturalism,* p. 407.

[28] Taylor, 'The Politics of Recognition'.

In valorizing religious community, multiculturalism upholds the scriptural interpretation of the dominant voice and its version of what constitute appropriate texts, canon, curricula and practice. But we cannot stop by saying Muslim texts in addition to the 'classical' Hindu *śastric* texts as part of the pluralization of canon. We must go beyond this to think about ways in which to decentre the divergent notions within Muslim and Hindu groups of legitimate theology, ritual and cultural practice. The question of legal pluralism cannot halt at personal laws of religious communities but must address a range of practice. Multiculturalism must transcend the binaries on which much of political and academic discourse is presently hinged—of state and community, majority and minority, universalism and culturalism.

18

Politics and History after Sovereignty*

Vivek Dhareshwar

'If men wish to be free, it is precisely sovereignty they must renounce.'
—Hannah Arendt (*Between Past and Future*)

Caught between an unimaginable future and an irredeemable past, it would seem that the postcolonial is left with an unrepresentable present. It may be that once again history has cheated the postcolonial—or he/she has been cheated of history: just when it seemed possible to inaugurate a postcolonial interrogation of modernity—the self-inauguration of the (Western) subject, it turns out that the project has been rendered otiose either because modernity has already realized itself (history, and with it politics, has come to an end) or because its realization itself testifies to its failure (history and politics have lost their intelligibility). The proliferation of 'posts'—postnational, postpolitical, posthistory—attests to a condition for which we may as well accept the term 'postmodern'.

* The conceptualization of this essay owes much to Partha Chatterjee, Tejaswini Niranjana and J. G. A. Pocock. In addition, they have given extensive and stimulating written comments, some of which I have made my own. In preparing this version, I have benefited from the comments of A. K. Bagchi, Rajeev Bhargava, and G. A. Cohen. Dedianne Felman, Mary E. John and M. Madhava Prasad gave perceptive written comments, some of which I have tried to incorporate here. Still, the usual caveats apply.

This paper is designed to raise questions about how we might understand the ways in which the political present is disposed to theorize itself. What happens to some of the central concepts or the key words of our cultural and political self-understanding—such as sovereignty, citizenship, rights, democracy, secularism, the nation—when the conditions that rendered them intelligible no longer obtain? Would it be possible to map the semantic shifts wrought in them by the emergent configuration of institutions and practices? Do they retain their intelligibility today, and can they still mobilize our politico-ethical horizon? If not, what new concepts are replacing them and what are their semantic fields?

Without pretending to answer these questions, I shall attempt to sketch at least the programmatic outline of an approach to them by looking at three concepts: history, sovereignty and the subject. The hypothesis is that none of these concepts can be understood without the other two. Postmodernity is a problem or a challenge for the discourse and history of sovereignty in so far as the history that we are living as well as practising is bound up with the discourse/history/institution of sovereignty. History has always been a discourse of sovereignty and sovereignty has always been structured in a form implying the presence of a subject, whether we take the latter to refer to the citizen subject or to the collectivity named by the nation.[1] These concepts, moreover, have defined the

[1] See Etienne Balibar, 'Citizen Subject', *Who Comes After the Subject?* Eduardo Cadava, Peter Connor, Jean-Luc Nancy (eds) London, 1992; and "Rights of Man", and "Rights of Citizen": The Modern Dialectic of Freedom and Equality', *Masses, Classes and Ideas*, James Swenson (trans.), London, 1994. These two important essays of Balibar show how the antimonies of the modern concept of the subject arise from the problematic of what he calls the citizens' becoming-a-subject (*devenirsujet*). My own discussion of citizen subject and sovereignty is indebted to the insights in these two essays. On the subject-structure of the historicist notion of history itself, see Jean-Luc Nancy, 'Finite History', in *The Birth to Presence*, Brian Holmes et al. (trans.), Stanford, 1993, p. 148. For an illuminating discussion of the links, historical and conceptual, between property, sovereignty and history and between property and citizenship, see J. G. A. Pocock, 'Tangata Whenua and Enlightenment Anthropology', *New Zealand Journal of History* 26: 1, April 1992, 28–53, and 'The Ideals of Citizenship since Classical Times', *Queens's Quarterly* 99: 1, Spring 1992, 33–55.

very intelligibility of 'politics', indeed of political modernity itself.[2] Other political concepts, too, derive their context and force from these three. The link between sovereignty, history and politics has been mutually constitutive because sovereignty has involved creating a political structure capable of defining its own past and determining its own present. Now this history/subject of sovereignty finds itself threatened above all by what one might call the 'sovereignty' of market. The play of market forces is not only indifferent to the history/subject of sovereignty, but it is also capable of reconstituting it at will, thereby denying or negating history and politics. J. G. A. Pocock, the historian of political discourse (as he styles himself), whose formulation of the issue seems to me to capture the theoretical and political perplexities of the issue of sovereignty, has argued that:

> It can be seen for the first time that the interplay of market forces is capable of abolishing whole national cultures if it does not need them any more, and whatever the outcome, the mere realization that this is possible raises problems in human values alarming if stimulating to the critical intelligence. Should this happen? What in fact happens if it does? Among the problems arising is that of historical self-location. In what history is one living if one lives in a world where this can happen? The question is complicated and enriched if the experience begins with the demolition of the national histories which, if they did not encourage the belief that one had a share in determining one's fate, at least located fate and its mastery in an intelligible culture, tradition, and politics.[3]

Historical self-location becomes a problem because of the intimate link between sovereignty, the state and history. The logic of capital seems to force the state to reassert its (crumbling) sovereignty in order only to surrender it. Historiography, which was the product of the liberal state, suddenly seems to lose its focus. The crisis, however, raises even more serious questions for politics, some of which I shall try to briefly indicate. That we find the very notion of the 'political' opaque is because politics as a notion and practice derived its meaning from the unity, as it were, of history, sovereignty and the subject. So when we speak metaphorically of

[2] J. G. A. Pocock, 'History and Sovereignty: Response to Europeanization in Two British Cultures', *Journal of British Studies*, 31 October 1992, 358–89; see also his 'Deconstructing Europe', *London Review of Books*, 19 December 1991, 6–10.

[3] Pocock, 'History and Sovereignty', pp. 361–2.

the sovereignty of the market that is threatening the cultural/political autonomy of the nation, we are obliquely confessing that politics has lost its meaning; and it has lost its meaning, as I just indicated, because, we no longer make sense of the triad history, sovereignty and the subject.[4] This is evident in the Indian state's ambivalence about its own identity—does it derive from the discourse of market or from the discourse of sovereignty? As we shall see later, this ambivalence has precipitated a crisis in the state's primary political task: that of creating the subject of sovereignty.

Although I began by considering the threat posed by the market to the history/subject of sovereignty, our interrogation of political modernity—an interrogation that seems indispensable to ascertain the possibilities of the political present—would have to show when and how the 'play of market forces' detaches itself from the discourse of sovereignty, especially since, in the early modern political debates, the discourse of the market was internal to or part of the discourse of sovereignty.[5] Furthermore, we would need to come to terms with the arguments which, without necessarily welcoming or positively evaluating the effects of globalization,

[4] My discussion so far has, I hope, set the context for understanding Pocock's suggestion (this, I take it, is the 'stimulating' part of what he otherwise regards as an 'alarming' state of affairs) that 'The classic questions of early modern politics [citizen-subject, sovereignty, rights, and so on] may be renewed under postmodern conditions...' 'History and Sovereignty', p. 368. This is then the sense in which 'our' situation has affinities with the early modern situation: fundamentally we too are required to institute or reinstitute the political, or accept its demise and draw the consequences.

[5] As is evident from the work of what used to be called the Cambridge School. See J. G. A. Pocock, *Virtue, Commerce and History*, Cambridge, 1985 and 'A Discourse of Sovereignty: Observations on the Work in Progress', *Political Discourse in Early Modern Britain*, Nicholas Phillipson and Quentin Skinner (eds) Cambridge, 1993; James Tully, *An Approach to Political Philosophy: Locke in Contexts*, Cambridge, 1993; Richard Tuck, *Philosophy and Government: 1572–1651*, Cambridge, 1993; see also, Albert O. Hirschman, *Passions and Interests: Political Arguments for Capitalism Before its Triumph*, Princeton, 1977. There is no work, to my knowledge, that attempts to relate the contemporary relationship between the discourse of market, property, capital to political discourses. In his suggestive essay ('What is a Politics of the Rights of Man', *Masses, Classes and Ideas*), Balibar has underlined the political importance of theorizing the contemporary forms of property for an understanding, in particular, of new forms of inequality and difference.

seem to suggest that the nation-state's—and hence of sovereignty's—decreasing significance opens up other political possibilities which may be able to avoid some of the major problems that the nation-state creates or at least is unable to resolve.[6] We need then to explore, on the one hand, the limits or possibilities of existing political concepts when confronted with new forms or structures and, on the other, whether any new political concepts are being generated in the process. It may be that the discourse of sovereignty is not tied to any given conception of the nation-state and that the debate about the appropriate form of the state is internal to the historical dialogue that constitutes the discourse of sovereignty.

The career of these concepts in non-European contexts creates impasses or aporias that are yet to be resolved. What is the logic of history/sovereignty in India (and in postcolonical places in general)? It is on this site that both their constitutive force and their present crisis can be made perspicuous, and questions asked about the reflexive possibilities of the political present.

The history/subject of Indian sovereignty has been constituted as a 'biography of the nation-state'[7] and this history, in fashioning itself as a history of sovereignty, has had to exclude and delegitimize other idioms and agencies. It would be instructive here to look at the problem of secularism. There is an obvious sense in which it is culturally alien (imposed, like most of our political institutions, by the British and deriving its authority in large measure from that) and it is also what the nationalists—more precisely Nehru and Nehruvians—saw as a rational normative choice which a multi-religious sovereign state would do well to make. But it has been unclear what it means for Indians to share its history as henceforth part of theirs or what history it enjoins Indians to determine. For

[6] This is not the place to discuss the complicated and fascinating arguments for post-national identities or social forms. See Arjun Appadurai, 'Patriotism and its Futures', *Public Culture* 5(3), Spring 1993, 411–40; Manuel Castells, 'European Cities, the Informational Society, and the Global Economy', *New Left Review* 204, March/April 1994, 18–32; Michael J. Shapiro, 'Moral Geographies and the Ethics of Post-sovereignty', *Public Culture* 6(3), Spring 1994, 479–502; Yael Tamir, *Liberal Nationalism*, Princeton, 1993; William E. Connolly, *Identity and Difference: Democratic Negotiations of Political Paradox*, Ithaca, 1991.

[7] Gyanendra Pandey, 'In Defence of the Fragment: Writing about Hindu-Muslim Riots in India', *Representations* 37, Winter 1992, 27–55.

this question could not arise as long as the authority and value of political concepts embodied in the post-colonial state (taken over from the British) legitimized only one history. Only when that authority began to be undermined and challenged by very different processes did questions long suppressed come to the surface.

To put it very schematically, the state's espousal of secularism entailed, paradoxically, an active attempt on its part to secularize what it took to be religious institutions (Hindu/Muslim/Christian). This was far from being a benign process.[8] Secularism, as an ideology of the modernizing state, involved not only the formulation of a frame or mould within which different religious groups could co-exist, but the elaboration of a cultural and political ideal which began to define who constitutes the 'proper' subject of democracy. The constitution of the 'citizen subject' involved, in the Indian context, the devaluation of the communitarian subject—the one tainted either with religion or caste.[9] Thus secularism as a (supposedly neutral) frame or mould sought to justify or legitimize itself through a politics that was trying to articulate a hegemonic conception of the citizen-subject. If the cultural ideal of secularism disavowed caste, the political ideal of secularism sought, through the deployment of juridical and disciplinary power, to place religion outside politics. We are now living through the consequences of this politics—both religion and caste have asserted themselves in politics with something of a vengeance. If secularism as a doctrine or policy as well as a politico-cultural ideal has not only failed but has in fact created a space which the Hindu right is mobilizing to take over in order to marginalize (to put it euphemistically) an already marginalized community, then we seem to need something more, or, at any rate, something other, than mere reiteration of secularism (which most leftists and liberals end up doing). Secularism as a doctrine of toleration is closely linked to the principle of sovereignty (and the juridical power associated with it). It is in this sense an absolutist doctrine: the state must claim a power in order to renounce it, or to grant it to a sub-group. Therefore, rather than argue that the only consistent, viable position for Muslims is to demand, and for the state to grant,

[8] Partha Chatterjee, 'Secularism and Toleration', *Economic and Political Weekly*, 28 July 1994, 1768–83.

[9] See my 'Caste and the Secular Self', *Journal of Arts and Ideas* 25–6, December 1993, 115–27.

sovereignty in 'cultural' matters, I would argue that we must work toward a political space from which we can question the very principle of sovereignty as embodied in the state. This questioning would have to begin with an attempt to redefine citizenship, and in the process explore the limitations of the politics of rights. This questioning may end up deconstructing these notions, not, as some of our nativists would advocate, merely or primarily on grounds of their Eurocentricity, but because they no longer tell us the terms of our practical and passionate relationship to one another.[10] Because they no longer embody a politics. The state functions by naturalizing the classes and groups of civil society.[11] When these groups and classes form or mediate representations of themselves through the state, antagonisms and dislocations of the social emerge in the open. What we have called 'political identity' emerges as the articulation of these antagonisms. Thus the 'Hindu' as a *political identity* is irreducible to the interests of any one group in civil society and to the cultural/religious entity called Hindu. The attempted new equation—Indian citizen-Hindu—is a result of the attempt to compensate for the excess of universality; it is not primarily intended to appropriate the state or to make it religious. In fact, one could argue the radical proposition that religion is not the issue at all. And therefore the focus on 'secularism' is misplaced—yet another instance of left/liberal literalism that negates politics. The citizen's becoming a subject depends on the state—and, as we know, in the post-colonial context the state is the

[10] The phrase is taken from Roberto Unger, *Social Theory: Its Situation and Its Task*, Cambridge, 1987.

[11] It's hard to improve upon Marx's classic statement of the issue: 'The state in its own way abolishes distinctions based on *birth, rank, education and occupation* when it proclaims that every member of the people is an equal participant in popular sovereignty regardless of these distinctions, when it treats all those elements which go to make up the actual life of the people from the standpoint of the state. Nevertheless the state allows private property, education and occupation to *act* and assert their *particular* nature in their way, i.e. as private property, as education and as occupation. Far from abolishing these *factual* distinctions, the state presupposes them in order to exist, it only experiences itself as *political state* and asserts its *universality* in opposition to these elements. Karl Marx, 'On the Jewish Question', *Karl Marx: Early Writings*, Rodney Livinstone and Gregor Benton (trans.), Harmondsworth, 1975, p. 219.

most powerful modernizing agent--in so far as the abstract, universal slot (whose ideality is given as interior to itself) needs the state to guarantee it as such. It would be possible to show, following Foucault, that, governmentality in the colonial/postcolonial context deploys both sovereignty and discipline to institute modernity, including the institutions and practices of political modernity. It also in the same process inscribes or reassigns inequality as difference (usually onto those it constitutes as not-yet-citizens—women, 'minorities', 'scheduled castes/tribes').[12] Can we then invoke sovereignty to defend difference? The problem with secularism—and, more generally, with the liberal approach to the problem of difference—is precisely that it freezes difference in its attempt to locate identities outside of politics.[13]

The Muslim and the Dalit are in a similar position in relation to the state: their identity is too particular and too excessive. In imposing an identity on them, the state seeks in effect to circumvent their agency. Their identities become excessive because they are blocked from the space of citizenship. The political identity 'Hindu', on the other hand, emerges as a reaction to the excess of universality. What the 'Hindu' envies/hates in the Muslim is precisely the predicament of the Muslim, namely, the Muslim's confinement to his/her identity (the excess of it).[14] If we now readily accept that there is violence in the denial of identity, we must begin to understand the conditions in which the affirmation of identity can turn into an imposition of identity (as well as an

[12] Michel Foucault, 'Governmentality', *Foucault Effect: Studies in Governmentality*, Graham Burchell, Colin Gordon and Peter Miller (eds) Chicago, 1992. However plausible, this must for the time being at least remain a hypothesis.

[13] For a stimulating discussion of such an 'agonistic' conception of politics, see William E. Connolly, *Identity and Difference: Democratic Negotiations of Political Paradox,* Ithaca, 1991.

[14] Why this reaction now to the excess of universality? A hypothesis could be that the citizen feels deprived of those factual distinctions or they are threatened. The consumer-citizen, who emerged in the eighties, and those who identified with or aspired to that identity, feels a dislocation that threatens his very identity. In this situation, the Muslim appears as the person most secure in his identity, who is stealing our 'enjoyment'—our nation-thing, as Slavoj Zizek puts it. See his *Tarrying with the Negative: Kant, Hegel, and the Critique of Ideology*, Durham, 1993, ch. 6.

incitement to identity) and thus lead to a kind of violence not dissimilar to that involved in the denial of identity.

Is there a sense of historicity and agency that does not obey the structure of sovereignty? This formulation imposes itself on us; however, one must resist turning it into yet another expression, or an inversion, of the sovereignty principle. Rather, what we should look for is the process of imbrication whereby the principle of sovereignty assimilates—or tries to, at any rate—structures and practices that do not conform to the logic of sovereignty. For example, caste, whatever kind of an entity or a practice we take it to be. A theory of caste-practice would have to converge on the attempt to explore a politics that interrupts the logic of sovereignty. Such a politics would see conflict and strife as constitutive of identities and, therefore, would not attempt to reify difference, whether cultural or religious, by rendering identities sovereign and external to the contestatory process of politics.

When scholars and political commentators look at caste-practices they note the irony of various caste-groups declaring themselves 'backward', and demanding that their caste too be included in the list of castes deserving of reservation. There is nothing at all ironical in this if we reverse our perspective and see them as redefining citizenship and reaffirming the singularity of their identity. Despite the regimentation of caste by the state, it remains a fuzzy concept. The redrawing produces a different kind of thickness. The task for a political theory is not simply to identify or clarify or criticize or justify their statist goals nor describe the state's view of them, but to *reflexively* explore the possibilities opened up by the enormous fluidity of caste-practices and identities. It can also go some way towards resisting and recasting classifications such as 'Scheduled Castes and Tribes' and 'Backward Castes', so that a new vocabulary, which embodies the new possibilities, may come to replace the statist bureaucratic categories; so that identities are open to political agonism, and do not merely remain state-mediated. 'How', Balibar has rightly asked, 'can we inscribe the programme and the very name of equaliberty in singularities?'[15] The present then requires redescription—which

[15] Balibar, '"Rights of Man" and "Rights of Citizen"', p. 59. He coins the neologism 'equaliberty' to argue for their inseparability. The question of singularity marks, for Balibar, the turning point between the modern form of politics based on universality and the post-modern questions that take shape within and against it.

is not to suggest that mere redescription will somehow take care of the problem, but to argue that the attempt at redescription requires rethinking history, subject and sovereignty. The futurity, understood as the reflexive possibilities of the present, depends perhaps on the excessive figures generated by the citizen-becoming-a-subject, rather than on the universalization of the citizen subject, for the latter's impossible sovereignty forever requires a supplement or a doubling.[16]

The larger problem here involves, of course, understanding what modernity has meant in India and how the state as a modernizing agency *par excellence* has functioned and with what consequences. Let me present a highly simplified—but not, I hope, simplistic—spectrum of positions with which we would need to contend.

(1) Modernizers and postmodernizers: The first position would argue that despite all the problems encountered and even created by modernity, carrying through the project of modernity (politically, economically) is still the best choice. It would see the recent attempt by the state to 'liberalize' the economy as a betrayal of the goals of modernity, as a surrender of sovereignty. In its left-liberal version (dominant until recently) it organized its politics around the agency of the state and predicated the identity of the citizen–subject on the rationality (and hence modernity) of that agency and its ideology of sovereignty. Politically, however, this position has lost its persuasive power, and it would be important for us to analyse the loss of hegemony of this position. Where did it derive its authority from and how does it respond to its loss of authority? What changes can one envisage in its idiom? What new 'moves' is it capable of? The postmodernizers, those who wish the state to follow globalization, would argue that politics will take care of itself if economy is freed; their vision is inspired by the International Monetary Fund model of civil society. That is to say, in this neo-liberal vision, only the agency of the market is recognized as rational and, unlike its earlier incarnations, it presents market itself as its own justification. However, as an idiom

[16] For an elaboration of this question, see my 'Caste and the Secular Self'; and Vivek Dhareshwar and R. Srivatsan, 'Rowdysheeters: An Essay on Subalternity and Politics', *Subaltern Studies IX*, Shahid Amin and Dipesh Chakrabarty (eds) Delhi, 1997; see also Susie Tharu and Tejaswini Niranjana, 'Problems for a Contemporary Theory of Gender', *Subaltern Studies IX*.

it is yet to articulate itself fully and in the Indian context at least its constituency, the globalizing middle class seeking access to the cosmopolis of communication (apart of course from the state itself), is yet to establish its dominant motifs politically.

(2) The more radical position, admittedly a minority position held by a section of the intelligentsia, but which may reflect a fairly pervasively, if incoherently, felt experience, would argue for a rejection of modernity itself. Or, at least, it would see modernity itself as the problem; although many are tempted by this position, its articulation as a viable political position faces insurmountable difficulties. The claim that modernity has been an imposition of something alien, that we non-Westerners would do well to evolve our 'own' institutions and practices, runs into difficulties when it tries to narrate and make sense of the history of, say, the last two hundred years. In so far as its critique of modernity seems to involve a rejection of modernity (and, consequently, of the present) this position seems headed towards an untenable nativism. Nonetheless it does open up some very serious questions about what history we are living in and how we characterize our political present.[17]

(3) There might conceivably be another position (opened up to a large extent by Partha Chatterjee) which, taking its bearing from the insights as well as the impasses of the previous positions, would argue that what needs to be rejected is perhaps not modernity but the modernist understanding or interpretation of modernity.[18] This position would start with an acknowledgement that there is

[17] Ashis Nandy would be the most articulate representative of this position. See, among innumerable other works, his 'An Anti-Secular Manifesto', *Seminar* 314, October 1985, 14–24, and 'The Politics of Secularism and the Recovery of Religious Tolerance', in *Mirrors of Violence: Communities, Riots and Survivors in South Asia*, New Delhi, 1990. The historian Dipesh Chakrabarty's position too seems to be leaning in this direction.

[18] I take this insight from Anthony Appiah's elegant, 'The Postcolonial and the Postmodern', *In My Father's House: Africa in the Philosophy of Culture*, New York, 1992, pp. 144–7. My interpretation of what that rejection means, however, differs from his, mainly because my interpretation of what constitutes the modernist interpretation differs from his interpretation of it as quasi-Weberian. See my 'Postcolonial in the Postmodern: Or, the Political after Modernity', *Economic and Political Weekly* (forthcoming), for a discussion of Appiah's position.

something like a 'suspension' of history—the inability of the history that has constituted our present to 'go forward', as it were—in order to begin an interrogation of the different idioms as well as a dialogue between different historicities.[19] The history that is under suspension—for various heterogeneous reasons—is the history that has constituted itself or has been written as the 'biography of the nation-state'. If this history/subject of sovereignty is in crisis now, does it mean that our present is post-historical and post-political, given over entirely to the market and its sovereignty? Or can we speak of other political possibilities contained in different historicities and agencies that have a chance, a future, precisely because of that impasse?

Unlike the position above, this position would not reject political concepts simply on the grounds that they are Western. Instead it tries to ask, conceptually and historically, why those concepts/institutions have turned out to be inadequate, troublesome and even disempowering—not only for minorities but for what the state calls 'scheduled castes and tribes'. And it hopes this questioning will generate a more complex sense of the historicity of our present. But would that help us ascertain the political possibilities of the present? This question forces us to address difficult issues—which are both philosophical and historical—such as how political concepts relate to cultural practice; under what conditions they change; how new political concepts come into being (if they do). If culture is supposed to tell us *who* we are, politics, one imagines, has the task of telling us *what* we are and how we are related and should relate to others. The problem with the sovereignty model in India (as elsewhere) has been that it both sutures and reproduces the split between culture and politics.

Partha Chatterjee has formulated the problem elegantly and forcefully:

> Here lies the root of our postcolonial misery: not in our inability to think new forms of the modern community but in our surrender to the old forms

[19] As Partha Chatterjee puts it, 'Now the task is to trace in their mutually conditioned historicities the specific forms that have appeared, on the one hand, in the domain defined by the hegemonic project of nationalist modernity, and on the other, in the numerous fragmented resistance to that normalizing project.' Partha Chatterjee, *The Nation and Its Fragments: Colonial and Postcolonial Histories*, Princeton, 1993, p. 13.

of the modern state. If the nation is an imagined community and if nations must also take the form of states, then our theoretical language must allow us to talk about community and state at the same time. I do not think our theoretical language allows us to do this.[20]

If Foucault sees sovereignty, and the juridical representation of power associated with it, as superseded by governmentality, and surviving, in conjunction with disciplinary power, as an instrument of governmentality, and if for Pocock modernity is defined by the discourse of sovereignty, which renders possible history as a meaningful structure and politics as an activity that defines and redefines that structure, Chatterjee's work opens up a way of mapping the colonial articulation and post-colonial interrogation of disciplinary power, governmentality and the discourse of sovereignty.[21]

Chatterjee argues that Indian nationalism first established its sovereignty in the cultural domain constituting it as the 'inner' and 'spiritual' (family, education), where it began to carry out the process of 'normalization'. Its political articulation, however, never challenged the ideology or the political form of the colonial state. Subsequently, of course, this state was appropriated and 'domesticated'. Yet the imagining of the nation-state remained within the logic of sovereignty as the latter was deployed as an instrument of governmentality, often in conjunction with disciplinary power. What remains suppressed or denied, both in Western theories and in Indian nationalism, is the possibility of articulating the nation by acknowledging the claims of community

[20] Chatterjee, *The Nation and Its Fragments*, p. 11.

[21] These radically different evaluations of sovereignty issue in different conceptions of what history we are living in and what kind of subjects we are. The difficulties in making these different conceptions address each other are considerable, especially in view of Foucault's brilliant, but often idiosyncratic and inconclusive interpretation of the triad of power, sovereignty/discipline/government. His conception of the relationship between normalizing or disciplinary power and juridical or sovereign form of power as we find them in 'Two Lectures', Colin Gordon (ed.) *Power/Knowledge: Selected Interviews and Other Writings, 1972–7*, New York, 1980, pp. 104–8 and in *The History of Sexuality: Volume 1*, Robert Hurley (trans.), New York, 1980, pp. 143–4, undergoes considerable modification with his formulation of the problematic of governmentality in 'Governmentality', *Foucault Effect: Studies in Governmentality,* see especially pp. 102–3.

itself. The thinking of community remains, and will remain, impoverished because our imaginary and our institutions have so far found no place for it. So, Chatterjee's provocative hypothesis is that:

> an investigation into the idea of the nation, by uncovering a necessary contradiction between capital and community, is likely to lead us to a fundamental critique of modernity from within itself.[22]

The crucial question, then, is how the 'who' (of 'culture') and 'what' (of 'politics') relate to each other. This question lies at the heart of the concept of citizen-subject. What is involved in the *translation* of political idioms?[23] How to characterize the resulting imbrications? Are there any 'prerequisites of citizenship'—economic, cultural, or gender? Are the problems and antagonisms generated in the process of putting citizenship (and other related concepts such as rights) into practice contingent by-products, or are they internal to it? So the post-modern condition has perhaps only precipitated a debate that was long overdue. And that debate would have to address the question: what are the ways in which the concept of 'history' is being, should be and can be formulated with regard to the necessities and reflexive possibilities of the modern Indian state? Are there conceptions of historicity, community and political agency that are not tied to the subject-structure of sovereignty and its conception of history and politics? In other words, what are the possibilities and dilemmas of post-modernity in India?[24]

[22] Chatterjee, *The Nation and Its Fragments*, p. 237.

[23] A theory of translation would be crucially important for an exploration of the modalities of citizenship. In contemporary political theory, only Bruce Ackerman (*Social Justice in a Liberal State*, New Haven, 1980, pp. 73–3) has pointed to the link between a theory of translation and a theory of citizenship. His observation that 'the relationship between the theory of translation and the theory of politics has...been ignored in recent liberal writings' (p. 72) applies to other political and cultural theories as well. For a different way of formulating this link, see Tejaswini Niranjana, *Siting Translation: History, Post-structuralism and the Colonial Context*, Los Angeles, 1992.

[24] The project I have in mind is similar to, say, Foucault's proposal for a critical ontology of ourselves which 'will separate out, from the contingency that has made us what we are, the possibility of no longer being, doing or thinking what we are, do, or think'. ('What is Enlightenment', Paul Rabinow

The problem of 'historical self-location', with which I started, intersects with the problem of inventing a language (or languages) which would help us break out of the shackles of the modern state and the form of politics that it imposes. It is at the intersection of these problems, I have tried to suggest, that the concept of community re-emerges as the great unthought of our political and philosophical theory.[25] If we now combine Chatterjee's hypothesis

---

(ed.) *The Foucault Reader*, New York, 1984, p. 46). Or to Bernard Williams' attempt (*Shame and Necessity*, Berkeley, 1993) to recover a sense of agency and responsibility that was present in antiquity, which persists despite the modern moralized notions of agency, and can perhaps be used to tell 'us not just who we are, but who we are not' (p. 20).

By focusing on *political modernity*, I have tried to point to the conditions necessary for a critique of modernity and for a proper formulation of the impasses of post-modernity. Chatterjee's formulation of the problem of the imbrication of idioms allows us to propose a critique of modernity which renders perspicuous the problem of another historicity and agency at the same time as it (to put it in Hegelese) 'comprehends' our modernity. I say that this project is similar (not identical) to Foucault's or Williams because, for one thing, I want to deemphasize the 'uniqueness' of the project we as postcolonials are burdened with. True, the question of historicity and agency arises focus now because of what has happened to the concepts/practices of modernity (sovereignty, secularism, etc.). Our situation now is such that we cannot escape our modernity; at the same time, however, because of the impasse that we call post-modernity forces us to ask questions about our historicity, our noncontemporaneous present, we can draw upon, learn from projects such as Williams' critique of Liberal/Kantian notion of the self—a notion which, as he puts it so lucidly, 'leaves only a limited positive role to others in one's moral life' (p. 94). That is one vector for exploring how community might be thought or rethought. Foucault's is a much more complicated case—in his case it's not only its analogical or heuristic value; his discussion of sovereignty as form of power opens up historical and conceptual questions about the colonial/post-colonial modernity (institution of legal-juridical apparatus, the subjectivities that it makes possible). At another level, however, his concern has affinities with Williams' in that his examination of antiquity too is geared toward freeing us from the modern conception of the self (he calls it the juridical conception of the self, which is after all another side of the liberal/ Kantian self Williams talks about).

[25] Since 'community' has long been a charged political trope within the political rhetoric of both the left and the right, and since the construct of India as in essence communitarian has a long history, it is just as well to emphasize the novelty of Nancy's concept of community: '*Society* was not built on the

with my suggestion that we need to think the historicity of history itself, there opens up a possibility, but no more than a possibility, of thinking about the nation differently.

To think the history of historicity is to suspend history as the self-presentation of a subject or an Idea. This is not of course the end of history which is much in the news recently; or, rather, it is the end precisely of that history whose end has been announced. For that history was/is the history of historicism—with or without

---

ruins of a *community*. It emerged from the disappearance or the conservation of something—tribes or empires—perhaps just as unrelated to what we call "community" as to what we call "society". So that community, far from being what society has crushed or lost is *what happens to us*—question, waiting, event, imperative—*in the wake of society*. Nothing, therefore, has been lost, and for this reason nothing is lost. We alone are lost, we upon whom the "social bond" (relations, communication), our own invention, now descends heavily like the net of an economic, technical, political and cultural snare. Entangled in its meshes, we have wrung for ourselves the phantasms of the lost community.' *The Inoperative Community*, Peter Connor, Lisa Garbus, Michael Holland, and Simon Sawhney (trans.) Minneapolis, 1991, pp. 11–12.

Community has, of course, figured in various languages of politics; and philosophically, the conceptualization of politics and ethics has involved explicit or implicit use of community (Kant vs Hegel; Rawls vs Sandel). In contemporary debates liberalism and communitarianism have been regarded as embodying contrasting visions of political life. Rawlsian liberalism, for example, explicitly delimits the realm of the political; freedom is essentially freedom from politics (and hence from history), not merely in the sense that the Rawlsian citizen is free not to pursue politics and does not share the civic humanist aspiration to make politics the highest good, but in a more fundamental sense a well-ordered society has no need for politics or renders it superfluous. Communitarians like Sandel, in contrast, regard politics as the highest good and argue that the liberal delimitation, if not denial, of politics would end up creating an all encompassing bureaucratic state which in turn would disempower the community and alienate the citizen. See John Rawls, *Political Liberalism*, New York, 1993, pp. 2056–66); Michael Sandel, *Liberalism and the Limits of Justice*, Cambridge, 1982, and 'The Procedural Republic and the Unencumbered Self', *Political Theory* 12:1, February 1984, 81–96.

The question for us is: how is community conceived of here? What role is it playing? As a term in the political idiom its primary function seems to be to resist the discourse of 'right'. And the discourse of right is seen, and sees itself, as a repudiation of the claims of community, since right is always the right of an individual. In this debate the liberals tend to have the upper hand because communitarians are unable to articulate a politics without teleology. As Nancy puts it, 'historicism in general is the way of thinking that *presupposes* that history has always already begun, and that therefore it always merely continues. Historicism presupposes history, instead of taking it as what shall be thought' (emphasis original).[26] That also means that historicism cannot think the present—our time—as inaugural, as a promise that is not predetermined by an origin or a telos. History, finite history (and, as Nancy says, there is no other kind) is always the history of community, of a being-in-common; the in-common, however, cannot be thought of as substantiality, as substance or subject, despite the fact that the 'in' of in-common is always figured, as fraternity, as nation, as proletariat. Community is not to be thought of as a subject or a supra-individual. Fusion, immanence or oneness is the death of community, for 'Community is, in a sense, resistance itself: namely, resistance to immanence'.[27] Nancy's ontology (for the lack of a better term) of community attempts to describe it as finitude of singularities. But this singularity is not produced or extracted; it takes place in the unworking of being-together. Or as Nancy puts it, 'In myth, community was proclaimed: in the interrupted myth, community turns out to be what Blanchot has named "the unavowable community".'[28]

We need then a critique of modernity which involves neither a denial of the history of political modernity that has made us what we are, nor an acceptance of that history (the end of history) that

---

naturalizing the concept of community, which makes the task of their liberal critics easy. Although communitarians, especially Sandel, have been able to articulate a powerful critique of the 'characterless' self presupposed by liberalism, they are unable to avoid convening of community as subject. Community as value or a substance to be shared leads to an essentially conservative adoration of tradition and history. The discourse of right and the discourse of community confront us with an aporia: they reinvent and reinforce each other, even as they try to negate each other.

The discourse of rights culminates in the ideology of the end of history—there is nothing more to be done once the regime of right is in place. And the communitarian discourse ends up by venerating history and tradition for their own sake. It would not be difficult to show that the sovereignty structure plays an important role in both Rawls and Sandel.

[26] Nancy, 'Finite History', p. 146.

[27] Ibid., p. 35.

[28] Ibid., p. 58.

denies the *eventuality*, the noncontemporaneous historicity of our present. Neither a denial of the hegemonic work of nationalist modernity that has produced 'our' national identity, nor a ratification of that identity as the sovereign embodiment of community. As Nancy argues:

> Community cannot arise from the domain of *work*. One does not produce it, one experiences or one is constituted by it as the experience of finitude. Community understood as a work or through its works would presuppose that the common being, as such, be objectifiable and producible [in sites, persons, buildings, discourse, institutions, symbols: in short, in subjects].[29]

The task is to formulate a conception of historicity that allows us to think the history of community, but community thought without and against the subject-structure of sovereignty, to think our singularity—contingent, without origin or end—rather than our sovereignty—which cannot do without origin or end because it so centrally involves property (real as well as imaginary, legal as well as cultural). So we need to ask, what sort of a community is the nation? What do we understand by community and its relation to politics? Is the idea of the nation exhausted by nationalism—cultural or political—and by the claim of the nation-state to embody it? There is a sense in which nationalism is always cultural nationalism. If one wants to theorize the nation without recourse to nationalism (or to the nation-state), how does one get around the fact that it is always the 'culture' of the people that provides the ground for political claims (sovereignty, autonomy, etc.)? That, ultimately, nationalism—the enjoyment (*jouissance*) of the nation-thing, as Zizek would put it, subtends all claims regarding the nation (including, and especially, the elementary and elemental claim implicit in the 'magical' pronoun 'my' or 'our')?[30] The only way out lies in constantly interrogating the relationship between work (nationalism, nation-state) and unworking (the nation as community).

A culture, as Derrida reminds us, is never identical to itself.[31] It is this self-difference of a culture—unstable, precarious, yet

[29] Ibid., p. 31.

[30] The phrase 'magical' is taken from Alasdair MacIntyre, 'The Magic in the Pronoun "My"', *Ethics* 94: 112–25. See also Yael Tamir, *Liberal Nationalism*, New Jersey, 1993, ch. 5.

[31] '*What is proper to a culture is not to be identical to itself.* Not to not have an identity, but not to be able to say "me" or "we"; to be able to take the

always present—that allows for the possibility of a different signification than a total and remainderless identification with the figures generated by the 'work' of modernity or the nation. The figuration of the community has produced a singularity—a shared identity that we call national identity. But this figuration has tended to deny or disavow its own non-foundation, its finitude. Because nationalism is always an attempt to dissimulate this non-foundation or finitude, it always requires an excess or a *supplement* of nationalism.[32] Nonetheless, can we not think of the nation as the interruption of myth?

> Thus once myth is interrupted, writing recounts our history to us again. But it is no longer a narrative—neither grand nor small—but rather an offering: a history is offered to us. Which is to say that an event—an advent—is proposed to us. What is offered to us is that community is coming about, or rather, that something is happening to us in common, neither an origin nor an end: something *in* common.[33]

Once the myth is interrupted, including the myth of history as sense, direction, telos, the principles, questions and formulations that had organized the myth are prohibited; but this prohibition is 'a decision without justification'.[34] Perhaps no justification can be offered without restoring the myth, without the fiction of another foundation. 'Thus', to put it in the words of Blanchot,

> one will discover that it [the unavowable community] also carries an exacting political meaning and that it does not permit us to lose interest in the present time which, by opening unknown spaces of freedom, makes us responsible for new relationships, always threatened, always hoped for, between what we call work, *oeuvre*, and what we call unworking, *desoeuvrement*.[35]

---

form of a subject only in the non-identity to itself or, if you prefer, only in the difference *with itself* [*avec soil*]. There is no culture or cultural identity without this difference with itself' (emphasis in original). Jacques Derrida, *The Other Heading: Reflections on Today's Europe*, Pascale-Anne Brault and Michael B. Naas (trans.) Bloomington, 1992, pp. 9–10.

[32] Balibar, Classes, Masses and Ideas, p. 203.

[33] Nancy, *The Inoperative Community*, p. 69.

[34] Blanchot argues that 'it is not history that comes to an end with history, but certain principles, questions and formulations that will from now on be prohibited through a decision without justification, and as though with the obstinacy of a value'. *The Infinite Conversation*, Susan Hanson (trans.), Minneapolis, 1993, p. 272.

[35] Blanchot, *The Unavowable Community*, Pierre Jorris (trans.), New York, 1988, p. 56.

When we initiate a critique of nationalist modernity, the basis for it cannot be found in residual practices—the practices that are (as we used to say) left behind by modernity or those that somehow survive into modernity, but to what is engendered by the process of normalization of modernity: namely, the figures of unworking. There is a sense in which those who claim to critique modernity cannot avoid repeating the Tonniesian/Weberian story of increasing thinness of practices, concepts. Bernard Williams, for example, repeated that story in his theory of thick and thin ethical concepts, our ethical modernity being characterized by thin ethical concepts such as ought, good, right and by the disintegration of thick concepts such as shame, treachery, courage. Chatterjee too shows a certain weakness for the myth that the pre-modern was thick and the modern is thin when he implies a contrast between the polysemy of pre-colonial *jati* and its regimentation into caste by colonial modernity.[36] His idea of imbrication of idioms, however, militates against that interpretation, and has the potential for providing a different way of interrogating modernity. Our modernity too has produced thick concepts, produces it all the time; but we will not find it if we look to the self-understanding or self-justification of modernity. That is to say, we will not find it if we look to the 'work' of modernity, but to the figures of its unworking, the forms of community that come into being in the very unworking of modernity. Therefore, unless one is committed to a certain historicism, there is no reason to deny that modernity might also be creating polysemy, around other concepts and practices. Thus, for example, one could look at post-Mandal India, in the thick to thin version, as the result of that thinning process; or one could, without committing oneself to any teleology, look at it as creating or at least making possible the creation of other polysemic concepts/practices.

I have suggested that we must interrogate and reject the modernist interpretation or self-understanding of modernity, but it is an absurd project, historically and conceptually, to reject

[36] Bernard Williams, *Ethics and the Limits of Philosophy*, Cambridge, Mass., 1985, pp 129–45. His recent work (see note 24 above) shows that a critique of modern conception of morality, agency, responsibility, need not have recourse to this myth. The ambivalence of Chatterjee's position stems from his use of Sudipta Kaviraj's distinction, fuzzy and enumerated communities, which, while reworking the *Gemeinschaft* to *Gesellschaft* story, is unable to avoid the teleology and value-coding inherent in that distinction.

modernity itself. 'We' are modern. The state and sovereignty are as much an Indian thing as, say, caste. The issue is really this: given that the post-colonial spaces (India, Ghana or Kenya) are in the state they are—their precarious position in the world-economy, the crisis of the state and of the history/discourse of their sovereignty as nations—how do any of the practices and institutions that derived their legitimacy from modernity interrogate themselves in such a way that the problems created in large part by the very logic of modernity itself can become the focus of a politics?

One conclusion that we could draw from the impasses that we witnessed would be that today it is impossible just to be a nativist post-modernist or a modernist liberal/leftist or a nationalist or a post-colonial humanist. To say this is not to imply either some fragmented subject-position or a liberal 'multiculturalist' position which tolerates all these positions. It is to recognize the non-coherence of our present experience and the deeply conflicting idioms with which we struggle to decipher its reflective possibilities. The coherence of our identities and politics was achieved by the modernist interpretation of modernity: the belief in progress and the confidence that reason could organize and order our cultural and social world, and the belief that true universality would be achieved when all human practices could be brought under the rule of reason. By rejecting that interpretation one is not rejecting reason but, to use a very Kantian formulation, the illusions of reason. The many forms of reasoning underlying our diverse practices cannot always be abstracted from those practices. As Wittgenstein and Heidegger in their different ways showed, reasoning itself is a form of practice, embedded in a form of life, although not identical with it. Once we give up the desire for that kind of coherence—the false coherence, as we might be tempted to put it now—we are faced with the task of constructing a politics no longer derived either from philosophy of history or from the dictates of reason standing outside the practices and claiming to replace them. The task is all the more daunting since among the things this politics will have to make reparation for is the very interpretation of modernity whose own institutional logic is so pervasive and deeply embedded. For the people of the left (to use a deliberately fuzzy expression), then, the task is to rescue the project of communism and its promise of an egalitarian and democratic society from its forcible re-occupation by both modernity and varieties of nativism/nationalism. This would mean not a deliberate pursuit of non-coherence, but the eschewing of forms of coherence that do violence to and delegitimize practices that give us what reasons we have for reflection and action.[37] We need to undertake, therefore, the construction of coherences and idioms that will involve us in an exploration of the reflective possibilities of our practices, which include, it is needless to add or repeat, the cultural and political practices of our modernity. One could, therefore, argue that a critique of modernity that entails its rejection can only be an evasion of the present; it cannot be a critique of the present. Thus the question of community is a

[37] Susan Hurley has formulated this Wittgensteinian insight particularly well: 'The existence of certain shared practices, any of which might not have existed, is all that our having determinate reasons to say or do anything rests on. Still...it is compatible with their existence that other different forms of life also exist.' *Natural Reasons: Person and Polity*, New York, 1989, p. 32. Also see her discussion of theorizing itself as a practice, on pp. 200–2. In a different, but not unrelated, context, Anthony Appiah makes some philosophically subtle suggestions regarding how one might develop the idea of 'noncoherence of practices'. 'I am insisting...that there is much to be said for the noncoherence of our different practices, for the existence of theories that empower and illuminate certain projects in ways that simply say "so what" to the fact that they contradict other theories that belong to other projects. Once motivated, this noncoherence can be seen as both necessary and desirable.' Anthony Appiah, 'Tolerable Falsehoods: Agency and the Interests of Theory', *Consequences of Theory*, Jonathan Arac and Barbara Johnson (eds) Baltimore, 1991, p. 83.

The remarks that I have offered are not be taken as conclusions; they are meant, rather, to indicate what seems to me to be a fruitful direction in which a theory of the Indian modern can be pursued as a problematization of our modernity. There are, I think, clear affinities between what I say here and what I see as the approach underlying Partha Chatterjee's proposal for a critique of modernity. However, the idea of the fragmentary recommended by Chatterjee, following Gyanendra Pandey, remains too metaphoric, its metaphorical charge even obscuring its conceptual reach. Furthermore, Chatterjee seems to think the fragmentary needs no justification. That raises many complex questions which I cannot discuss here. In invoking the rhetoric of the fragment, we should, as Maurice Blanchot advises us, 'heed' Derrida's 'warning': 'There is reason to fear that, like ellipsis, the fragment...makes mastery over all that goes unsaid possible, arranging in advance for all the continuities and supplements to come.' Cited in Maurice Blanchot, *The Writing of Disaster*, Lincoln, 1986, p. 134.

question *par excellence* of modernity. If we take the critique of modernity to imply a rejection of it, then community can only mean a residual, traditional thing, and, consequently, the politics based on that notion would have to be a rescue or recovery act—to recover a language, reclaim a tradition (even a resistance tradition). It would be a redemption project. In contrast, we take community as what 'happens' to us now and politics as the exploration of the new space of freedom opened up by the relationship between 'work' and 'unworking'. One leads to a protective, redemptive politics: how can the sovereign identity of a culture, community, way of life be preserved or protected? In short, the 'multicultural' problem; the other makes possible new experiences of 'our time'.

I have argued, rather schematically and programmatically, that deploying the problematic of community should enable us to delineate the authority as well as the conceptual limits of the political languages of modernity; to show the impasses of post-modernity as well as the reflexive possibilities of the political present. The suggestion has been that a new principle of community might enable us to overcome the impasse created by the discourses of sovereignty and market. To say anything more about this principle we need to generate a political theory for the present whose idiom will derive its layered reflexivity from a reinterpreted conceptual history. And the question for that political theory would be: if political agency has been theorized in the form of a subject (rights of the citizen, sovereignty of the subject), can we now legitimately ask: *who* comes after the subject and *what* replaces the discourse/history of sovereignty? The challenge, in other words, is nothing less than to make theoretical sense of a political language at the moment of its emergence.[38]

[38] This way of putting the matter, I owe to Partha Chatterjee.

Index